Essentials
of
Real Estate
Investment

5th Edition

David Sirota

**Real Estate
Education Company**
a division of Dearborn Financial Publishing, Inc.

While a great deal of care has been taken to provide accurate and current information, the ideas, suggestions, general principles and conclusions presented in this text are subject to local, state and federal laws and regulations, court cases and any revisions of same. The reader is thus urged to consult legal counsel regarding any points of law—this publication should not be used as a substitute for competent legal advice.

Publisher: Carol L. Luitjens
Senior Development Editor: Diana Faulhaber
Project Editor: Debra M. Hall
Cover Design: Salvatore Concialdi

94 95 96   10 9 8 7 6 5 4 3 2 1

ISBN: 0-7931-1108-0

Library of Congress Cataloging-in-Publication Data

Sirota, David.
    Essentials of real estate investment / David Sirota.—5th ed.
        p. cm.
    Includes index.
    ISBN 0-7931-1108-0
    1. Real Estate investment. 2. Real estate management. I. Title
HD1382.5.S52 1994   94-20892
    332.63'24—dc20   CIP

Contents

Preface

Democracy as a political system, when coupled with capitalism as an economic system, is based on *the private ownership* of personal as well as real property. Therefore, in the United States, any individual may own real property under the laws of the country. Such private ownership, known as the allodial system, expands the simple rights of property use during an owner's life to include the powerful right to designate to whom a property passes on the owner's death. As a result, owners may effectively translate their work efforts into tangible real and personal property assets and thus accumulate an estate to enjoy and control into the future.

The desire to accumulate a measurably valuable estate is no doubt one of the major reasons for the tremendous interest in the ownership of real property in this country. It appears that almost everyone gives high priority to the ownership of real estate, from the smallest condominium apartment to the largest shopping center.

In the 1950s, income and potential growth were the primary considerations when analyzing a real estate investment. Then, in an effort to stimulate the nation's economy, Congress devised a number of tax shelters to encourage developers and investors to construct new housing, offices and stores, commercial centers and industrial parks. The idea of using excess *losses* from real estate investment, losses generated largely by accelerated depreciation allowances, to shelter income from other activities led to a restructuring of investment priorities. Taking advantage of tax shelters became the primary motivation for investing in real estate. Income disappeared in the face of negative cash flows, and inflation created huge windfall profits, sheltered in turn by capital gains exemptions.

The 1960s and 1970s were the decades in which investors flocked to the real estate market. Everyone, it seemed, wanted to avoid most, if not all, income tax obligations. And many did! Right through to the mid-1980s, tax shelters were the *buzz* words for real estate investors. The laws allowed investors to write off two to three dollars of their income taxes for every dollar invested. Many large real estate investment syndicates were formed for the purpose of buying large commercial and/or multifamily properties with little or no concern for whether the property would ever have a positive cash flow. However, grumblings were soon heard throughout the land. The tax laws were considered inequitable: apparently they proved that the rich as well as the poor were exempt from taxes. The working middle class was groaning under the entire burden.

In 1986, in a climate ripe for tax changes, Congress forcefully stepped forward and successfully followed President Reagan's directions to change the tax code by enacting one of the most dramatic tax reforms in 30 years. The sweeping revisions of the Tax Reform Act of 1986 (TRA '86) affected every taxpayer in the United States directly or indirectly, both adversely and positively. Essentially, TRA '86 eliminated accelerated depreciation and capital gains exclusions. In addition, it prohibited carrying over any excess losses from real estate investments to shelter wages and other active income. Despite the dampening effects of TRA '86, real estate is still an important investment vehicle for accumulating, enhancing and preserving wealth today.

During the two and a half decades before 1986, investors became ingenious at devising new techniques to create leverage, shelter income taxes and offset the IRS at every level. Large profits were achieved when investors could take cash out through sophisticated land leases and high-leverage financing at the start of a project. They then could shelter all income during the holding years with such intriguing techniques as accelerated component depreciation. By refinancing and selling on the installment plan, they could also postpone paying capital gains taxes on spiraling growths in value at the end of the ownership period. These tax-sheltering opportunities stimulated construction in many areas to the point of overbuilding; the absorption of the many empty apartments, offices, shopping centers and industrial properties continues today.

In the years following TRA '86, real estate investment lost much of its romantic appeal to the speculators who had been active in the high tax-shelter years. In most areas of the country, investment property values started falling, new construction diminished considerably and the real estate market generally went into a decline. Under the new laws, buyers of income-producing properties insisted that their investments earn a return on their own merit, not just from their tax shelter benefits. To achieve this positive cash flow, buyers applied higher capitalization rates when estimating property values, driving the sale prices down 15 to 30 percent.

Many of the lenders who had jumped on the bandwagon in the early 1980s found themselves with portfolios that, when adjusted for declining values, no longer protected their loan balances. Disaster struck in the form of numerous failed savings and loans and other financial institutions.

A severe recession was felt throughout the land during the late 1980s and early 1990s. Real estate investment activity came to a virtual halt, with those still in possession of their investments extending every effort to just hold on.

And then, in 1992, a ray of hope emerged. The Federal Reserve acted to lower interest rates enough to begin to stimulate the economy. Interest rates paid to depositors on savings fell to lows of 2 to 3 percent, allowing real estate loans to be made at 6 to 7 percent. A frenzy of refinancing activity swept the nation: nearly every mortgage outstanding at 9 percent or more was refinanced with a new, low-interest-rate loan. In addition, the surviving lenders slowly began to make loans on new construction, stimulating the real estate markets in many areas of the country.

And that's where we are today—in an environment of a slow return to an improved economy, but with very conservative attitudes toward real estate investments.

This fifth edition of *Essentials of Real Estate Investment* will examine our current real estate market and describe the various opportunities existing for real estate investors. Despite the limitations of TRA '86, real estate still provides a profitable alternative for an investor's portfolio. Much of the income can be sheltered by deductions for operational costs, interest expenses and depreciation. And, depending on local and national economic circumstances, the real estate cycle has always proven that market values rise after a decline, so the prognosis for the immediate future is good.

This text is divided into two major sections, Principles and Practices, and the chapters are presented as follows:

SECTION A: PRINCIPLES OF REAL ESTATE INVESTMENT

- Chapter 1 introduces the nature of the real estate market and includes purposes for investing in real estate as opposed to other forms of investment. It also describes the advantages and disadvantages of real estate investments.
- Chapter 2 provides an inventory of the various forms of real estate ownership, including individuals, groups, partnerships, trusts and leaseholds.
- Chapter 3 investigates the financing alternatives for leveraging real estate investments. Included are discussions of the government's role in finance, sources of funds, types and forms of real estate loans, special loan provisions for investment financing, and default and foreclosure consequences.
- Chapter 4 reviews the current income tax laws governing real estate investments. Included are a number of tax-sheltering alternatives.
- Chapter 5 describes the market and property analyses necessary to determine the feasibility of a real estate investment.
- Chapter 6 completes Section A and examines the financial requirements necessary to measure the economic feasibility of a real estate investment.

SECTION B: PRACTICES OF REAL ESTATE INVESTMENT

- Chapter 7 begins a chapter-by-chapter examination of the various types of real estate available for investments. Here, a description of single lots and acreage is presented, together with the special analysis this type of investment requires.

- Chapter 8 examines the investment requirements for residential properties and includes single-family homes, multiunit apartments and cooperatives and condominiums.
- Chapter 9 investigates investing in office buildings, including management requirements.
- Chapter 10 describes investments in commercial properties, including strip store buildings and small and large shopping centers.
- Chapter 11 presents the opportunities for investing in industrial properties, including industrial parks, warehouses and lofts.
- Chapter 12 examines a variety of alternative real estate investments, including mobile home parks, motels, amusement parks and housing for the elderly, among others.

A book such as this could not be completed without the help of numerous good people along the line. My gratitude is extended to the following people for their invaluable help in preparing the fifth edition of this book: James Sweetin, Cooke Real Estate School, Inc.; Byron B. Hinton, ASA, MAI, JDH/Austin, Valuation Consultants; Gene Campbell, Tarrant County Junior College; and Donald G. Arsenault, Key Investments Realty Advisors, Inc.

For their help with the fourth edition, I would like to thank Karen B. Abbott, Treasure Coast School of Real Estate; Richard Blyther, Southwest Los Angeles Community College; Gerald R. Cortesi, Triton College; James E. Howze, Advanced Career Training Systems; Craig Larabee, Nebraska School of Real Estate; Calvin Montgomery Sr., Prairie State College; Richard P. Riendeau, October Real Estate Group; Jeff Siebold, The Siebold Group; and Steve Williamson, Real Estate Education Specialists. Without their timely comments, this text would be far less than it is.

Thanks also are extended to the following people for their assistance in earlier editions of this book: Robert Bond, Gene Campbell, Jack Flynn, Bo Cooper, Walstein Smith Jr., Donald L. Pietz, Samuel P. DeRobertis, Peter C. Glover, William M. North Jr. and Roger W. Zimmerman.

I have the deepest admiration for their creative minds and their help in the arrangement of the material. They are largely responsible for its smooth transition and sequential development.

To my son, David B. Sirota, newly associated with me in this endeavor, I give loving gratitude for his technical competency in contributing to the HP-12C analyses of the examples presented. Thanks also to Elbert B. Greynolds Jr. of Southern Methodist College for his assistance with HP-12C calculations.

My wife Roslyn has my eternal love and devotion, not only for putting up with me during the long hours of writing, but also for correcting my tenses and "thesaurasizing" my work until my written words sounded more like my spoken ones. It is her cherished belief that I am more articulate than erudite.

This book is lovingly dedicated to my grandchildren, who provide me with the motivation for seeking to create a larger estate for their future benefit.

1
Introduction

Key Terms

betterments
bundle of rights
buyer's market
cycle
demand
discretionary funds
easy money
fixity
foregoing
highest and best use
leveraging
liquidity
market value

permanence
personal property
property
real estate
real property
relative scarcity
seller's market
supply
sweat equity
tax shelter
tight money
TRA '86
value in use

Property is anything that can be owned. **Real estate** is defined as land and all natural and man-made improvements permanently attached thereto. All other property is **personal property**. To own real estate is not only to possess the physical property but also to acquire certain legal rights to its continual peaceful utilization and redistribution. Thus, when we acquire real estate, we also acquire an accompanying **bundle of rights** in the property. These are the rights of possession, control, enjoyment, exclusion and disposition, and they change the definition of real estate to **real property**.

The ownership and control of real estate is very much a fundamental part of our lives. We depend on real property to feed and clothe us and to provide us with shelter. In our country, these essential needs are met in various ways. Because technological achievements have advanced our living standards, we are no longer individually dependent on the ownership of land for the fulfillment of our basic needs. We rent or own apartments or houses serviced by utility companies and financed by lending institutions. We work in office buildings, manufacturing plants and shops, and we purchase our goods in stores, play in parks and consume the products of far-off farms and ranches.

Many persons now have the financial capability to step beyond using real property only to supply their basic necessities. These individuals acquire real estate as an investment, a storehouse of value, which represents the conversion of their work efforts into a tangible, valuable asset.

A real estate investment can be described as *the commitment of funds by an individual with a view to preserving capital and earning a profit.* We all make investments of various kinds throughout our lives. We invest time, energy and money in educating ourselves and our children, in purchasing cars, in obtaining good health care, in accumulating savings and in pursuing other ventures necessary to ensure a better quality of life.

In many instances, investment also represents the **foregoing** of some present comforts in anticipation of future benefits. Foregoing is sometimes even more important than money, and it often involves the expenditure of time and energy. This personal hands-on approach to an investment is known as **sweat equity.**

Investment in real estate, however, extends beyond our everyday activities and concerns the commitment of free money, money accumulated in excess of funds required to secure life's necessities. This free money, often referred to as **discretionary funds,** can be viewed as money available for investment.

THE NATURE OF THE REAL ESTATE MARKET

Characteristics of Real Property Investments

Each parcel of real estate is unique and thus requires an individual investment analysis of its specific locational attributes. However, all real property has certain common characteristics that affect its value. These characteristics include fixity, longevity, permanence, risk and market segmentation.

Fixity.   Real estate is fixed in location, which greatly restricts the scope of its marketability. As a result of this *fixity,* real estate values are subject to any political, economic and demographic activities occurring in the immediate vicinity.

Longevity.   Real estate is generally considered to be a long-term investment because of the durability of the improvements and the permanence of the land. This quality of *longevity* enables investors to estimate, with some degree of reliability, the present value of a future stream of income from their properties.

Permanence.   The *permanence* of real estate forms the basis of our system of long-term mortgage-debt amortization. Investment in real estate usually involves relatively large dollar amounts and is highly capital-intensive, requiring complex financial arrangements. These complexities, in turn, require the expertise of lawyers, accountants, brokers, property managers, real estate consultants and other specialists.

Risk.   Real estate investment is a relatively *high-risk venture* that reflects the uncertainties of a somewhat unpredictable market. Some of these risks include:

Business Risks: the ability to get and keep tenants;
the potential for competitive developments;
the risk of changing consumer tastes;
the danger of increasing operating costs.

Financial Risks: potential rise in interest rates;
lack of available financing;
potential foreclosure;
danger of personal guarantees.

Liability Risks: possible environmental contamination;
possible changing government regulations;
risk of social constraints imposed by neighborhood groups.

Market Segmentation.   Real estate can be segmented by type of product (houses, apartments, commercial, industrial), quality and/or geographic location.

There is no readily identifiable, organized national market for real estate as there is for stocks and bonds, although some interstate communication occurs through the Multiple Listing Services (MLS) and referral services. The realty market generally is a combination of local markets that react speedily to changes in local economic and political activities and somewhat more slowly to regional, national and international events.

The fractured aspect of this unorganized and largely unregulated real estate market is further complicated by the lack of standardization of the product and the fact that most of the market's participants react intuitively, giving little attention to formal feasibility or marketing studies. However, the investor who seeks qualified help and takes advantage of available protective measures can make real estate one of the safest investments of all.

Besides these inherent characteristics of real property, many government activities also directly or indirectly influence property values. At the federal level, income tax laws are often confusing and frustrating. So is the government's regulation and control of money. This power effectively dictates the extent of real estate activity through manipulation of the supply as well as the cost of mortgage money.

Our various levels of government also function in numerous other ways to affect real estate property values. Environmental controls and impact studies add time and costs to the development of land costs inevitably paid by consumers. Local political attitudes toward zoning and growth restrictions raise the prices of properties already developed, effectively creating a monopolistic position for their owners.

Fueling these political attitudes is the antigrowth philosophy of citizens in some areas where property taxes and other public costs are rising at an alarming rate to serve an ever-increasing population. "Not In My Back Yard" (NIMBY) and "Build Absolutely Nothing Anywhere Near Anybody" (BANANA) are becoming the slogans in these troubled cities.

Supply of and Demand for Real Estate

In the very broadest sense, the supply of land is unlimited. Although it is true that the earth represents a fixed supply, it is also true that this supply can be extended indefinitely by building *under* as well as *over* the landmasses and the open seas. Still, there are huge expanses of land that remain unusable in their present state and/or uninhabitable because of geophysical circumstances.

It is the **relative scarcity** of usable land, however, that is important to real estate as an investment vehicle. Relative scarcity is what establishes the basic value for real estate. The economic worth of property fluctuates with the effective demand for strategically located and thus, by definition, relatively scarce parcels of land. Even more important than the supply of and demand for *unimproved* land are the interactions of these economic factors as they affect the existing stock of *improved* real estate.

One of the principal components of **demand** is *population,* not only in terms of numbers of people but also in terms of subgroupings according to age and financial ability to purchase real estate. Migrational trends and locational economic-base analyses can be developed to estimate variations in the demand for real estate within a given area. Changes in these trends as well as in living patterns determine where there will be growth in demand for real property next and what this demand will require in terms of housing and related real estate developments.

The current state of our financial markets also contributes to the demand for real estate because it affects the availability of mortgage money with reasonable interest rates and affordable payments. The effects of **tight money** can be devastating to the activities of a local realty market, while **easy money** can stimulate a realty boom.

Supply can sometimes be viewed as a *function of demand* when the bidding on available properties forces prices upward. Serving effective demand and anticipating its impact is a real estate supplier's most important skill, one that industry professionals and investors are vigorously striving to develop with increasing degrees of sophistication. Because most real estate developments involve a time lag which is needed to prepare raw land, get all the appropriate government approvals and construct new buildings—shrewd investors constantly study—the market to *anticipate* demand.

Often, supply itself may be viewed as an accelerator of demand. The imposition of building moratoriums and/or stringent environmental controls seriously inhibits the increase of new housing stock and puts the full pressures of demand on existing property owners. This virtual monopoly affects rental rates and property prices. Thus, the available stock of improved real estate itself establishes the design, quality, price and terms for the consumer.

However you view supply, its determinants are predominantly a function of physical, economic and political factors. The costs and availability of construction labor and materials and unimproved land, as well as political attitudes regarding natural community growth versus planned growth, all affect the supply of land available for development within a particular locality.

Finally, it is important to recognize that the real estate market is segmented. As this book illustrates, real estate investors deal in such things as acreage, lots, houses, apartments, stores, shopping centers and industrial developments. While in one segment supply and demand may be in balance, another segment may be in a state of oversupply or undersupply.

Real Estate Cycles

Keeping in mind the cause-and-effect relationship between supply and demand, we can now examine the cyclical nature of the real estate market. A real estate **cycle** is frequently described as either a **buyer's market** or a **seller's market**. A buyer's market indicates a surplus of supply and a downward price trend, favoring the purchaser. In a seller's market, supply is short and demand is high; prices are forced upward by the competitive market situation.

The term *cycle* implies repetitive, ongoing fluctuations in price, and the buyer's and seller's markets are equal and opposite partners in the real estate cycle. Thus, we can begin at any stage of a real estate cycle to examine the whole cycle's fluctuation. If we enter a cycle somewhere near its peak, we can observe a shortage of supply, high prices as a result of competitive bidding and, logically, high concurrent profits for sellers. Such high profits attract new investors, who wish to capitalize on the opportunities, and it is reasonable to assume that new construction will take place, regardless of costs. With new buildings available as additional inventory to satisfy demand, the market cycle will level temporarily, then start to fall until supply exceeds demand. At this point, the cycle has reached its valley, and conditions are those of a buyer's market.

Of course, there are many other catalysts that can affect a cycle, acting to speed it up or slow it down, to raise or lower its peaks and valleys. Included among these catalysts are tax reforms, interest rate fluctuations and the onset of a depression or recession, to name only a few.

The inherent imperfections of the real estate market contribute to the perpetuation of the cyclical trend. Lack of communication among real estate building contractors and the time lag between start-up and completion of building are major factors in this problem. Another problem arises when contractors base a decision to build on gut feelings instead of market research. Entering the market at the peak of a cycle involves planning, possible rezoning and financing, as well as labor and material acquisitions in anticipation of construction. When building continues at a feverish pace to capture the profits of backlogged demand, little thought is given to overbuilding until the inevitable occurs and supply **exceeds** demand.

Then the situation is reversed, with few buyers and many alternative properties from which to choose. A concomitant lowering of prices results until little, if any, profits are left. Building ceases and market conditions continue at a low point until the excess supply is absorbed, at which time the market begins to move toward the peak again.

Despite the cyclical short-run fluctuations in any real estate market, property values, in general, rise over the long term. However, this trend is based on summarization of activities involving many properties. Any individual property may react cyclically or counter cyclically to the general activities of the marketplace, much as individual stocks gain or lose value within the stock exchange. Real estate investors should consider each purchase carefully from both its micro and macro positions in the realty market. Investors must be aware of the long-term aspect of real estate investments.

Value Theory of Real Estate

Although all of the foregoing economic principles are important for potential real estate investors to keep in mind, in the final analysis investors will be primarily concerned with the value of one particular property. Real estate has value only as one in a series of alternative investment opportunities. Value is, in reality, in the eye of the beholder, the occupier or the user.

A seller's value is, more often than not, a reflection of personal and slightly sentimental feelings. Undoubtedly, the buyer or agent will have an entirely different opinion of the value of that particular property. Likewise, the insurable value, condemnation value and taxable value of that property may differ in dollar amount.

In theory, the value of a parcel of real estate is interpreted as its **market value**, or its value as established in an exchange. As such, *value is defined as the price that a knowledgeable buyer will pay and a seller will accept for a property that has been exposed for sale to the market for a reasonable length of time.* Neither buyer nor seller in this scenario should be acting under duress or enjoying any advantage, financial or otherwise. Most real estate transactions require an estimate of the market, or exchange, value of the property involved.

However, market *value*—as estimated by the seller, the appraiser or perhaps a real estate broker—may differ substantially from market *price*, which is established by what the buyer will actually pay for the property.

In addition to its market value, real estate also has a **value in use**. This is the value on which a number of real estate investors rely and a value that could differ from the property's market value. For instance, compare the market value of a property currently used as a parking lot with its potential value as the site for a highrise office building.

When determining the value of a particular property at a specific point in time, an evaluator has several basic principles of value to use as guides. The *principle of substitution* contends that no rational, economical person would pay more for one property than for another of like design, quality and utility. This principle is the basis for the cost approach to estimating the market value of real property, and it often establishes the uppermost limit of a property's market value.

The *principle of balance* identifies the problems that result from an oversupply or undersupply of a particular type of real estate. For instance, too many condominiums of the same size, design and price in one area would act to depress the values of all of these properties within the market.

The *principle of contribution* states that the value of an addition to a property is a function of its contribution to the overall profitability of the property, not just of its construction cost.

The *principle of conformity* states that a property similar to its neighbors in design and quality has the most reasonable value, while a property dramatically different from or nonconforming to its surroundings is invariably lowered in value.

The *principle of anticipation* stipulates that most investors make their investment decisions based on the measurement of the present value of an anticipated net income stream. This principle is the basis of the income approach to realty evaluation and often establishes the lower limits of a property's market value.

The *principle of highest and best use* is fundamental to estimating the value in use of a real estate investment. This principle is defined as the legal and possible use that is most likely to produce the greatest net return to a property over a given period of time.

As we have already discussed, value is primarily a function of the interactions of supply and demand. A relatively scarce but desirable item's value may increase because of its scarcity and desirability. But remember that attitudes concerning desirability change constantly and thereby have an impact on value.

Real estate is considered just such a relatively scarce and desirable item. Its value is in a constant state of change because of a myriad of continuously operating social and economic forces. Estimators of real estate value must be acutely alert to three stages of change in property values:

1. *Integration*: a condition of developing value;
2. *Equilibrium:* a condition of stable value; and
3. *Disintegration:* a condition of declining value.

A property's value is affected by the prevailing stage of change in its city or neighborhood. Since property cannot be moved, it may go through this evolutionary cycle many times during its economic life.

PURPOSES OF INVESTING IN REAL ESTATE

To Preserve Capital

A primary reason for investing in real estate is the preservation and possible enhancement of the capital invested. On average, owners have enjoyed rising property values over the years. Consequently, the capital value of the investment is preserved. It is precisely for this reason that real estate investments are described as hedges against inflation. Theoretically, the values of real estate fluctuate with local market cycles, but prices of real estate generally tend to rise over the long term.

A real estate investment may build up additional equity for its owner through reduction of the mortgage debt. The periodic repayments of the principal amounts owed on existing financing—payments made from rents collected—increase an equity in property. This increasing equity can be secured for reinvestment either by refinancing the mortgage or by selling the property, depending on the market. In fact, one of the more important benefits of investing in real estate is this ability to reuse the capital through periodic, tax-free refinancing, while at the same time preserving the value of the investment.

Although the problems associated with tenants are legendary as well as endless, tenants often improve the properties they occupy to enhance their living environment. These **betterments** tend to increase a property's value and are invariably left behind when the tenant moves. Betterments not only preserve an owner's capital investment but actually enhance it, sometimes substantially.

To Earn a Profit

Fundamentally, all investors in real estate seek a profit on the money they invest. By definition, an investment of any kind is a commitment of funds with the intention of preserving capital and earning a profit. For real estate investors, these profits assume two forms. The income stream from the tenants' rents should generate one kind of profit. The gross amount of rent should be adequate to pay for all of the fixed and variable operating expenses of the property, with enough remaining to show a return on the investment. Thus, an investor anticipates that the *income* will provide a steady cash profit while the invested capital remains protected over time. When the property is sold, this investment will be recovered intact or, better still, a gain will be made. This gain reflects the increase in the property's value during the time it was held and is the second form of profit that can be earned by a real estate investor.

Before committing any funds to the purchase of real estate, an investor should scrutinize carefully the returns available from other opportunities. For instance, a viable alternative to investing $100,000 cash in a real estate venture is to deposit this money into a government security paying 7 percent interest per year. The $7,000 annual interest, or profit (before taxes), that would be earned on this investment becomes a benchmark against which to measure the anticipated profitability of an alternative investment. The $100,000 can be withdrawn from this arrangement at a specific time, so it meets the requirements of an investment: preservation of capital and generation of a profit.

If we analyze a real estate investment that shows a 7 percent annual return (before taxes), with the possibility of recovering the full investment within some identifiable future time period, we see a situation parallel to that of the government security. However, compared to this security, real estate investment involves a greater degree of risk. This risk includes the ongoing, day-to-day management of the property, the likelihood of actually being able to collect the rents in the amounts and at the times anticipated and the chances of fully recovering the investment in the future. In addition, unforeseeable problems might occur.

Thus, a 7 percent return on a real estate investment should not be considered equal to a 7 percent return on a government security. Something extra must be earned to offset the greater risks that are so much a part of realty ownership. In addition, to compensate for personal management efforts and lack of liquidity, real estate investments must develop even larger returns. Unlike other investments, real estate is often difficult to cash in at a specific point in time. Therefore, to be viable, a real estate investment should be designed to develop a relatively higher rate of return (profit) than is available from safer, more liquid investment opportunities.

To Develop Tax Shelters

Until the passage of the Tax Reform Act of 1986 **(TRA '86)**, tax sheltering was as important a reason to invest in real estate as was earning a profit and preserving capital. TRA '86 substantially diminished this purpose.

Prior to TRA '86, **tax shelters** were achieved in a number of ways:

- Sheltering the taxable income from the investment's cash flows;
- Sheltering other income with carryover excess losses; and
- Sheltering the taxes on profits, if any, when the property is sold (capital gains).

Under TRA '86, real estate investors may still continue to shelter the income from their investments with allowable deductions for operating expenses, interest and depreciation. Depreciation allowances, however, have been substantially reduced.

More significantly, only those investors who spend a majority of their time in active management of real estate or who earn less than $100,000 annually and manage their own properties can carry over losses to shelter other income. Passive investors, such as owners of shares in limited partnerships, are not allowed to shelter other current income. Capital gains exemptions are also eliminated. Thus, the tax-sheltering opportunities for investing in real estate have been severely curtailed.

The full ramifications of the current tax laws, as they apply to investment decision making, will be examined in later chapters.

ADVANTAGES OF INVESTING IN REAL ESTATE

Any list of available avenues of investment will include stocks, bonds, savings certificates, life insurance policies, antiques, commodities, consumer merchandise and real estate. The investment opportunities in real estate include open land, vacant lots, farm acreage, industrial properties, houses, apartment buildings, stores, shopping centers, office buildings, clinics, recreational projects, mineral deposits, securities, mobile-home parks, condominiums and airspace. Competition for the dollars available for investment is high, and each opportunity has its own particular advantages and disadvantages. The general advantages of investing in real estate, however, include its relatively high-yield possibilities, leveraging opportunities, tax flexibilities and the retention of a high degree of personal control over the capital invested.

Relatively High Yields

Yields in excess of 20 percent after taxes are common for many real estate investments. Yields can even exceed this amount, reaching infinity, in those cases, in which 100 percent or more leverage, using borrowed funds to purchase property, has been achieved. More common, though, are realty investments that regularly develop 15 to 20 percent annual returns over the life of the investment. These profits reflect the opportunities that exist in real estate and, when compared to average yields on other types of investments, explain the popularity of this investment form.

The return on a savings investment is the rate of interest paid by the bank or savings association. These rates are quite low at this time, ranging from 1.8 to 5 percent, depending on the type and duration of deposit. These are *before-tax* yields, which are eroded by the taxes paid in accordance with the investor's particular tax bracket. Stocks often pay dividends that average about 5 percent of the value of the investment; but unlike savings, for which the amount of deposit remains essentially constant over time, the value of a stock fluctuates. As a result, an element of risk is introduced for a stock investor who analyzes yield in terms of dividends received plus growth in value. If this growth is 5 percent per year and the stockholder receives 5 percent in dividends, the yield is 10 percent before taxes.

Bond yields fluctuate, sometimes dramatically, as a function of the money market. A bond owner may earn 7 percent interest but may also have to take a discount when selling in a market at more than 7 percent. Some bonds, such as municipals, are tax-exempt, and their yields are commensurately lower, depending upon the bond's rating.

It is axiomatic in real estate investment that high profits are positively correlated with high risk. Although yields on real estate investments do fluctuate from time to time and from property to property, there are guidelines on which objective decisions may be based. For instance, despite the fractured quality of the general real estate market, there are fairly definable submarkets. One such submarket is in apartment projects. An investor can usually find apartment buildings comparable in location, number of apartments and their size and decor to an investment under consideration. The investor can thus research competitive rents and estimate the income possible from an anticipated investment. This analysis and others will provide data on which an objective decision concerning the profitability of the investment can be based. There are similar submarkets for houses, stores, office buildings, shopping centers and other forms of real property.

Leveraging Opportunities

Although stocks and bonds allow a purchaser to borrow up to 50 percent of the value of the securities, real estate offers an investor the highest **leveraging** opportunities of any investment alternative. Many realty transactions require 20 to 40 percent of a property's value as a cash down payment, while others have 10 percent, 5 percent, or even no down payment cash requirements. A few investors, after completing some highly sophisticated financing strategies, may even be able to enjoy the benefits of arranging their real estate investment portfolios with greater than 100 percent leverage and end up with cash in their pockets.

High-leverage situations include transactions involving carryback mortgages, land leases, subordination, joint ventures, syndication, sale-leasebacks, wraparound mortgages, participation mortgages and other creative real estate ownership and financing arrangements. These concepts and their applications will be examined in upcoming chapters.

Income Tax Flexibility

Real estate still allows its owner some degree of tax flexibility, due in large part to the application of depreciation allowances and the ability to deduct the premises' operating costs from the gross income collected. These operating expenses include property taxes, insurance premiums, maintenance and management, and they effectively reduce the amount of income subject to taxation. Interest on loans may also be deducted, further reducing taxable income.

High Degree of Personal Control

Real estate investments provide the opportunity for a high degree of personal control. Purchase terms can be designed to reflect specific financial circumstances. Often, rents can be arranged to anticipate changes in future realty cycles. Various bookkeeping techniques can be adopted to reflect individual needs as they change over time. Property can be periodically refinanced to capitalize on the equity accumulated. And the investor usually retains the power to decide on when, how and to whom the investment will be sold, under terms that satisfy personal economic requirements.

DISADVANTAGES OF INVESTING IN REAL ESTATE

There are no perfect investments. An investor who prefers the guaranteed safety offered by United States government securities is required to forgo high yields to achieve this safety. An investor who is interested in the relatively high yields offered by real estate will have to sacrifice a certain amount of safety and

liquidity and be willing to take a more active personal role in managing such an investment.

Relatively Poor Liquidity

Although real estate is usually easy to purchase, it is frequently difficult to sell quickly, and there is little certainty about the final sale price. Unlike the stock and bond markets, where there are almost always buyers to be found if the price is low enough, sometimes real estate cannot even be given away, let alone sold at a reasonable price. For example, in good times owners are reluctant to sell, while in bad times everyone wants to sell simultaneously, reducing a property's marketability significantly.

Large Capital Requirements

Contributing to the poor liquidity of real estate income property are the relatively large sums of money needed for property acquisition, maintenance and reserves. Despite the high leveraging opportunities that exist in this field, a sound investment must be backed by adequate operating capital to protect it in the event of unforeseen major crises. An unexpected reversal in the economic cycle of a community could result in a high number of vacancies and, at the same time, eliminate any possible market for disposing of the suddenly declining investment property.

Necessity of Constant Management

Everything about real estate, as in most other areas of present-day living, is expensive. At current rates for repairs, everyday maintenance is costly, to say nothing of required replacement of worn-out items. Major maintenance expenditures such as a new roof, plumbing or an electrical system can easily amount to thousands of dollars.

Constant property maintenance is an absolute necessity for improved real estate investments. Buildings need careful attention, including perpetual nailing, patching, painting and replacement of worn parts to satisfy tenants and ensure continuing rental cash flows. In addition, the hallways, elevators and grounds also require routine upkeep.

In other words, a real estate investment requires more active participation on the part of the individual investor than do most other investment opportunities. This management activity may be passed along to a professional management agent or service, but the income from the property must then be sufficient to justify the cash paid for these services.

Landlordism

Most real estate investments require the property owner to enter into some form of personal involvement with the professional manager and/or the tenants. These interpersonal relationships are often warm and rewarding, but they can also become distressing, especially when a manager must be dismissed or a tenant evicted. People are often deterred from investing in real estate because, as landlords, they are exposed to tenants' complaints and the problems of managing property. These factors should be included in the acquisition decision.

Risk

Finally, it must be clearly understood that there are substantial risks involved when investing in real estate. It is true that there are risks in every field of endeavor, even in our daily activities. Still, it is important to reiterate that investing involves decision making: a choice of what you should buy; when and where you should buy; and, most significantly, if you should invest at all.

What makes real estate investment so hazardous is the number of agencies and events beyond the investor's control that influence the success of the endeavor. The unpredictability of the income tax code is itself a large enough detractor to discourage the most astute investor. And we cannot ignore the vicissitudes of the financial markets as interest rates fluctuate in response to the natural laws of supply and demand, as well as to the imposition of monetary controls by the Fed.

Add the other disadvantages, enumerated previously, and you can draw a clear warning: although real estate investment carries with it the potential for large rewards, there are indeed substantial risks involved.

SUMMARY

In economic terms, land is considered a relatively scarce commodity, although from a practical point of view, land is infinite in supply because it can be developed into the air and underground. Still, most of the earth's population gathers tightly in the great cities of the world, congregating where the jobs are. Thus, there is an ever-increasing demand for a limited supply of desirable real estate. This pressure of demand acts to force the prices of available real estate to new heights.

Real estate market activities fluctuate as a function of supply and effective demand. When the top of the cycle has been reached, with high prices reflecting high profits, the entry of new builders adds to the supply and reduces the prices and profits accordingly, resulting in a reversal of the cycle. The microcycle is local in character, while the long-term cycle shows an ever-increasing value for real estate over time.

In addition to the demands of a growing population, artificial limitations on the supply of real property add to the increasing costs of real estate. Concerns with pollution have led to environmental controls that limit new construction. Political attitudes regarding controlled growth have also inhibited construction in many areas of the country. Natural gas and water shortages, sewer inadequacies, central city decline and resultant suburban expansions all have placed horrendous burdens on current property owners to support their local governments on an ever-shrinking tax base.

Despite all these obstacles, real estate investors continue to seek profitable projects. Attempting to anticipate demand and, in some areas of this country, actually creating demand by the very designs of their projects, real estate developers are reducing the sizes of homes; eliminating the frills in office buildings; providing the magnetism necessary to attract customers to shopping centers; and creating new concepts in planned unit developments, mobile-home parks, office parks and industrial parks, all in an effort to bring a usable product to a receptive market.

Real estate is fixed in location, with each parcel unique. It is durable, and its longevity ensures an investor a return for a fairly long time. However, real estate ownership usually requires relatively complex financial designs that reflect its high dollar values.

The measurement of a property's value is a function of its utility, its ability to generate income in the future and its position in a spectrum of alternative investment opportunities.

Value often is based on subjective, intuitive interpretations, although a body of principles has been developed to describe property value in more objective terms. These principles include those of substitution, highest and best use, balance, contribution, conformity, and anticipation, and they describe the function of value in conjunction with the activities of a rational economic investor.

Basically, people invest in real estate with a view toward minimizing risk, preserving capital and earning a profit. Real estate investments offer relatively higher yields, greater leveraging opportunities, greater income tax sheltering strategies and a higher degree of personal control than most other types of investments.

On the other hand, real estate is definitely illiquid compared with stocks and bonds. It also requires a commitment to personal involvement in management, either through a professional manager or with the tenants themselves. The role of landlord has probably turned many away from the opportunities for profit available in real estate investments.

EXERCISE 1   (Answers may be checked against the Answer Key.)

1.   From a rational point of view, an investor in real estate must consider all of the following analysis aspects, *except*

    a.   yield.
    b.   risk.
    c.   pride.
    d.   value.

2. Real estate investments should be considered first and foremost from the viewpoint of the

    a. economic soundness of the project.
    b. unique financing techniques available.
    c. tax shelter opportunities.
    d. unlimited growth potential.

3. Real estate investments have all of the following advantages, *except* high

    a. yields.
    b. leverage.
    c. liquidity.
    d. personal control.

4. Which one of the following statements is true regarding the characteristics of real estate?

    a. It has a central and controlled market.
    b. It is a short-term asset.
    c. Each parcel is similar to each other parcel.
    d. Its market condition is seldom in balance with supply and demand.

5. Supply and demand theory indicates that if both increase at the same rate, prices will

    a. go up.
    b. go down.
    c. first go up and then go down.
    d. remain constant.

6. A "buyer's market" indicates all of the following circumstances *except*

    a. excess supply.
    b. lower prices.
    c. high demand.
    d. flexible terms.

7. Of the following approaches to value, which one reflects the actual price that a knowledgeable buyer will pay?

    a. Value in use
    b. Highest and best value
    c. Appraised value
    d. Market value

8. To increase the use of leverage when buying a real estate investment is to

   a. decrease its yield.
   b. increase its risk.
   c. decrease its operating expenses.
   d. increase its beginning book basis.

9. Because of the fractured quality of the market, a real estate investment is frequently considered highly

   a. profitable.
   b. illiquid.
   c. transferable.
   d. valuable.

10. When slum properties start attracting investors, they are entering a period of

   a. integration.
   b. equilibrium.
   c. disintegration.
   d. urban renewal.

DISCUSSION

1. Investigate the economic conditions of your community and identify the point in the realty cycle at which you believe it to be.

2. Identify a specific neighborhood in your community and estimate where it is on the development spectrum: integration, equilibrium or disintegration.

2
Ownership Interests in Real Property

Key Terms

ancillary probates
blue-sky law
collapsible corporation
community property
curtesy rights
discretionary trust
dower rights
fee simple ownership
general partner
grantor retained income trust (GRIT)
inheritability
intervivos trust
investment trust
irrevocable trust
joint tenancy
joint venture
leasehold interest
limited liability company (LLC)

limited partnerships
living trust
partnership
Real Estate Investment Trust (REIT)
Real Estate Mortgage Trust (REMT)
regular corporation (C corporation)
right of first refusal
S corporation
severalty
sole and separate ownership
survivorship
syndicate
tenancy by the entirety
tenancy in common
testamentary trust
Umbrella Partnership Real Estate Investment Trust (UPREIT)

How an investor holds title to real estate has a significant impact on the degree of personal involvement in management and on the amount of profit to be earned, taxes to be paid and personal liability for debts and/or damages. This chapter includes a review of the major forms of interests in real property, including ownership by individuals, corporations, partnerships, trusts and leasehold interests.

INDIVIDUAL OWNERSHIP

Individuals may acquire legal interests in real property, called **fee simple ownership,** either singly or with their spouses. Individual ownership provides investors with the greatest degree of personal control over their real estate investments. The individual owner who holds an undivided fee simple title to a property has the largest possible interest in such an investment. Without partners to please or shareholders to impress, individuals may design their investment holdings to meet their own immediate and long-term goals.

On the other hand, individual owners assume a high degree of personal involvement, responsibility and liability for their investments as well as all the problems inherent in such tight control. For example, legal suits for contributory negligence and consequential damages can easily bankrupt an underinsured property owner. The eviction of nonpaying tenants may well become anathema to another. Individual ownership of real estate demands that the investor take an active role in investment management.

The various forms of individual ownership include tenancy by the entirety, tenancy in common, community property, joint tenancy with the rights of survivorship, sole and separate ownership and ownership in severalty.

Prior to examining each of these several forms, we must make an important distinction concerning an individual owner's rights of property control. An owner can hold a fee simple title or an undivided interest in a fee subject to the right of either inheritability or of survivorship.

Inheritability implies that the control individuals have over their estates includes the right to designate who will inherit their property. These designations are described in the owner's will, which requires a legal probate procedure before the estate can be distributed to the heirs.

The purpose of the probate process is to provide creditors of the deceased with a reasonable amount of notice and time in which to perfect their claims against the estate. To this end, a primary probate is initiated in the deceased's state of residency and **ancillary probates** are initiated in each state in which portions of the estate's assets are situated. Thus, for a deceased Michigan resident who owned property in Arizona, the primary probate proceedings would take place in Michigan, and an attorney in Arizona would supervise the ancillary proceedings in that state.

Survivorship, on the other hand, eliminates this personal control over the distribution of an estate after death. When two or more persons enter into a survivorship form of ownership, they give up their inheritable rights and designate that upon one owner's death, the other(s) in the agreement will be the recipient(s) of the deceased's portion of the property. The interests of the deceased pass automatically and immediately to the survivors in this form of ownership.

Holding title subject to the right of survivorship eliminates the necessity of probate proceedings, with concomitant savings in time and costs. However, as we shall soon see, the survivorship form may create inheritance tax problems for those estates large enough to be subject to such a tax.

Tenancy by the Entirety

Tenancy by the entirety is an arrangement limited to husbands and wives that includes the automatic right of survivorship and is not available in community property states. The owners are construed to be one entity, and when one spouse dies, the other immediately becomes the sole owner. Neither husband nor wife may unilaterally dispose of his or her interest.

The right of survivorship inherent in tenancy by the entirety is interpreted to vest the entire value of the property in each party to the arrangement. For inheritance and estate tax purposes, the United States Internal Revenue Service (IRS) considers that property held under this form of ownership belongs *entirely* to the deceased spouse. Thus, death taxes will be assessed against the net value of the demised's estate, including the *full value* of property that passes to the surviving spouse. And the entire value of the property will be taxed again when the survivor dies.

Tenancy in Common

Recognized in all states, **tenancy in common** is an arrangement in which each of several owners controls an undivided portion of an entire property. This relationship can be established between any two or more persons.

The basic components of tenancy in common are the concepts of *inheritability* and *undivided interests*. Inheritability provides individual owners with the right to designate to whom their proportionate share of the property will pass on their demise. Undivided interest implies that no single participant can claim a *specific portion* of the subject property but rather has the rights to the entire property and its benefits based on a proportionate share. Each tenant in common has an equal voice in the property's management, unless otherwise specified, and each assumes a proportionate share of the responsibilities, obligations and profits of the tenancy.

A husband and wife would normally each own an undivided one-half interest in a property. Four partners might agree on an equal ownership arrangement of one-quarter interest each. However, any proportion is allowable. For instance, one partner may have a 13/20 undivided interest, while another has a 5/20 undivided interest, and a third partner a 2/20 undivided interest. In a $20,000 cash transaction, the partners would contribute $13,000, $5,000 and $2,000, respectively.

$$\begin{array}{r} \$20,000 \\ \times\ \underline{13/20} \\ \$13,000 \end{array}$$

$$\begin{array}{r} \$20,000 \\ \times\ \underline{\ 5/20} \\ \$\ 5,000 \end{array}$$

$$\begin{array}{r} \$20,000 \\ \times\ \underline{\ 2/20} \\ \$\ 2,000 \end{array}$$

Anyone may own property as a tenant in common. It is a form of ownership whereby each participant may dispose of his or her own interest at will, unless there is a formal partnership agreement to the contrary. Each participant's undivided interest is inheritable and is distributed by will to the deceased partner's heirs. Thus, in a state that recognizes *tenancy by the entirety,* if a husband and wife wish to exercise control over their estate by will and designate some other party their heir, they should hold title to property as *tenants in common* so that each will have an undivided one-half interest.

Community Property

Under **community property**, which applies only to husbands and wives, monies earned during marriage and property purchased with these community funds belong equally to each spouse, who simultaneously maintains his or her *inheritable rights.* Thus, the spousal relationship under community property is exactly opposite to the survivorship rights of spouses who are tenants by the entirety.

As shown in Table 2.2, only eight states recognize community property, each with differing interpretations of the various intricacies inherent in this form of ownership. Most agree, however, that the participants may maintain separate personal controls under special circumstances. For instance, property inherited by one spouse can be maintained as separate property. Also, any funds flowing from this separate property may be kept separate, as long as they are not commingled with community funds in the family checking or savings accounts. If this income is deposited into a family account, the funds become community property, but the inherited real estate can still be maintained as separate property. On the other hand, if the income from separate property is kept apart from community funds, any additional property purchased with these monies will also be considered separate property, even if the acquisition occurs during marriage. Texas, however, considers *any* money earned during marriage to be community property, even those funds earned from separate property.

Joint Tenancy with Rights of Survivorship

All but four states recognize **joint tenancy**, whereby participants who are not necessarily husbands and wives can own *equal undivided interests* in property, subject to the rights of *survivorship.* Any joint tenant may sell his or her interest, but the new owner will assume the role of a tenant in common with any remaining owners, who will retain their joint tenancy relationship with one another.

Although anyone may hold title in joint tenancy, it is unusual for persons other than family members to enter into such an arrangement. Remember, survivorship effectively eliminates an owner's right to designate by will to whom property interests vest. They will automatically vest in the surviving owners.

Thus, when a father involved in a joint tenancy arrangement with his wife and son dies, the father's one-third undivided interest automatically vests in the surviving wife and son, raising each of their proportionate interests to an undivided one-half. If the wife then dies, the son automatically acquires the full interest in the property, and probate proceedings are avoided each time. However, for joint tenancy, just as for tenancy by the entirety (also a survivorship estate), the IRS considers the total property value as the deceased's when estimating the inheritance and estate tax liability after *each* participant's death.

Sole and Separate Ownership

All states recognize **sole and separate ownership** of property, which is an inheritable estate. This form of ownership vests title to property in the name of one spouse while implying that the other is still alive but has signed over his or her interest. Sole and separate ownership can be utilized to take advantage of special property tax exemptions, to simplify property management or to avoid inheritance taxes.

For instance, in Arizona, as in several other states, a qualified veteran is eligible for special tax exemptions on his or her portion of a property. If a wife quitclaims her interest to her veteran husband, he can then claim the tax exemption for the entire property, not just his half. Although Arizona is a community property state, the veteran would own this particular property as separate property because, as described previously, property inherited or received as a gift by one spouse in a community property state may be held as his or her sole and separate property.

Often, one spouse will quitclaim his or her interest in a property to the other for ease of management. This same purpose can be achieved if one spouse executes a power of attorney that legally grants the other full authority over the property.

In addition, sole and separate ownership is often utilized to transfer one spouse's share of a property to the other as a gift to avoid probate costs and inheritance taxes. However, a transfer of this nature may be subject to gift taxes. The impacts of inheritance and gift taxes will be examined in chapter 4.

Severalty Ownership

Finally, all states acknowledge that single persons—whether unmarried, divorced or widowed—own their real property in **severalty**, also known as sole ownership. Severalty is an inheritable estate because a survivorship estate requires two or more persons. Thus, owners in severalty should designate by will to whom they wish property to be distributed after their death. Corporate ownership is also in the form of severalty.

Dower and Curtesy Rights

Most states recognize the legal rights of a surviving spouse in the real estate of a deceased husband or wife. The rights of a widow in the property of her deceased husband are called **dower rights**, while the rights of a widower in the property of his deceased wife are called **curtesy rights**. The degree to which these rights are respected varies from state to state.

Table 2.1   Real Property Ownerships

Type	Relationship	Consequences Upon Death
Tenancy by the Entirety	Husband and wife, *only*	Automatic Survivorship
Tenancy in Common	Anybody	Inheritable
Community Property	Husband and wife, *only*	Inheritable
Joint Tenancy	Anybody, although usually family members	Automatic Survivorship
Sole and Separate	A married person in his or her own right, but implying a living spouse	Inheritable
Severalty	Unmarried or divorced persons, widows and widowers	Inheritable

Adapted from *Modern Real Estate Practice* by Galaty, Allaway and Kyle, Real Estate Education Co., Chicago.

Table 2.1 summarizes and compares pertinent data concerning the individual ownership forms discussed in this section. All the forms of individual ownership and the states in which they are recognized appear in Table 2.2.

It is important that investors be familiar with the laws of all states in which they anticipate purchasing real estate. These specific laws will prevail for all transactions concerning their property regardless of their principal state of residence. Any income derived from property is subject to the laws of the state in which it is situated as well as to federal income taxes. In addition, as previously described, although a deceased's main probate originates in the state of primary residency, ancillary probate proceedings are required in each state wherein owned property is located.

GROUP OWNERSHIP

In addition to individuals who own real estate investments singly, with their spouses or with others as tenants in common, there are more formal arrangements for group ownership of realty. Two important property ownership types are the corporation and the formal partnership.

Corporations

A **regular corporation**, now also known as a C corporation, is a separate entity created under the authority of the laws in the specific state of its incorporation. It is composed of any number of persons who join together for mutual purposes and is considered to have a personality and existence distinct from that of its members. Corporations are endowed with the capacity for continuous succession despite changes in membership, and they act as individuals in matters relating to the common purposes of the association. These actions must remain within the bounds of its powers, as outlined in the corporate charter, and within the laws of the various states in which it is licensed to operate. As a legal individual, a corporation can hold title to real property in its own right.

Participation in a corporation is evidenced by stock certificates that are traded by various means, mostly in organized stock exchanges. Certain classes of shareholders have the right to vote but usually take a passive role in the activities of their corporations. The actual operation of a corporation is often left to professional managers, who serve together with the company's president and board of directors for the shareholders' benefit.

Corporations formed for the purpose of investing in real estate are designed primarily as *capital-accumulating vehicles*. Utilizing a public stock offering, a corporation may attract funds "looking for an investment," giving smaller investors an opportunity to expand their participation far beyond their individual financial capabilities.

Corporations have five general characteristics: (1) continual life, (2) centralized management, (3) limited personal liability, (4) easy transferability of interests and (5) double taxation.

Continual Life.   Corporations only "die" when they are disbanded intentionally, are absorbed into another company by merger or become bankrupt. Otherwise they function perpetually, with new managers replacing those who retire.

Centralized Management.   Large corporations can afford to attract talented professional people. A corporation's functional design lends itself to centralized management, in which trained and experienced teams are directed by and held accountable to a board of directors.

Limited Personal Liability.   One of the most important characteristics of a corporation formed for real estate investments is its ability to shield a shareholder's personal estate from the debts of the corporation. Unlike a general partnership, in which each participant is personally responsible for a proportionate share of a venture's liabilities, a corporation limits its shareholders' risks to the extent of their investment in the company. In the event of a bankruptcy, other personal assets of the shareholders are not subject to attachment for any of the corporation's debts. This immunity does not cover those corporate loans for which officers are required to be personally liable.

Easily Transferable Interests.   Because of the efficiency of organized public exchanges, corporate stock ownership is relatively easy to transfer. This characteristic is particularly desirable for real estate investors, who normally face a difficult situation when they need to sell their holdings.

Double Taxation.   Clouding the efficiency of corporate ownership for real estate investments is the problem of double taxation. The corporation is subject to income taxes on the profits it generates, and the shareholders must pay taxes again when these profits are distributed to them as dividends.

This double tax has made corporations less desirable for real estate investors and has led to the popularity of the limited partnership and the real estate investment trust as alternative ownership forms. As we shall see later, these latter forms of ownership act as investment conduits, by-passing double taxation.

TABLE 2.2   Chart of Ownership

| State | Sole | Concurrent | | | |
	Individual	Tenancy In Common	Joint Tenancy	Tenancy by the Entirety	Community Property
Alabama	•	•	•		
Alaska	•	•		•	
Arizona	•	•	•		•
Arkansas	•	•	•	•	
California	•	•	•		•
Colorado	•	•	•		
Connecticut	•	•	•		
Delaware	•	•	•	•	
District of Columbia	•	•	•	•	
Florida	•	•	•	•	
Georgia	•	•	•		
Hawaii	•	•	•	•	
Idaho	•	•	•	•	•
Illinois	•	•	•		
Indiana	•	•	•	•	
Iowa	•	•	•		
Kansas	•	•			
Kentucky	•	•	•	•	
Louisiana*					•
Maine	•	•	•	•	
Maryland	•	•	•	•	
Massachusetts	•	•	•	•	
Michigan	•	•	•	•	
Minnesota	•	•	•	•	
Mississippi	•	•	•	•	
Missouri	•	•	•	•	
Montana	•	•	•	•	
Nebraska	•	•	•	•	
Nevada	•	•	•	•	•
New Hampshire	•	•		•	
New Jersey	•	•	•	•	
New Mexico	•	•	•		•

*In Louisiana, real estate can be owned by one person and by two or more persons, but these ownership interests are created by Louisiana statute. There is no estate comparable to those of joint tenancy, tenancy by the entirety or community property, nor is there any statutory estate giving surviving co-owners the right of survivorship. Two or more persons may be co-owners under indivision, or joint, ownership.

TABLE 2.2   Chart of Ownership (continued)

State	Individual	Tenancy In Common	Joint Tenancy	Tenancy by the Entirety	Community Property
	Sole	Concurrent			
New York	•	•	•	•	
North Carolina	•	•	•	•	
North Dakota	•	•	•		
Ohio*	•	•		•	
Oklahoma	•	•	•	•	
Oregon	•	•		•	
Pennsylvania	•	•	•	•	
Rhode Island	•	•	•	•	
South Carolina	•	•	•		
South Dakota	•	•	•		
Tennessee	•	•	•	•	
Texas	•	•	•		•
Utah	•	•	•	•	
Vermont	•	•	•	•	
Virginia	•	•	•	•	
Washington	•	•	•		•
West Virginia	•	•	•	•	
Wisconsin†	•	•	•		
Wyoming	•	•	•	•	

*Ohio does not recognize joint tenancy, but permits a special form of survivorship by deed through an instrument commonly called a "joint and survivorship deed."
†As of 1986, Wisconsin recognizes "marital property" that is similar to community property.
Reproduced from *Modern Real Estate Practice* by Galaty, Allaway and Kyle, Real Estate Education Co., Chicago.

S Corporations

A special form of corporation called an **S corporation** (S corp) is available for small businesses. This form is established to pass through profits or losses but not dividends to its shareholders. It offsets the onerous double tax while preserving the advantage of limited personal liability intrinsic in the corporate design. However, under the S corp format, a company might earn profits without passing them along to shareholders in time for them to pay taxes.

S corps are a creation of the tax laws. To qualify, a company must file an election form with the IRS and meet the following criteria:

- It must be a domestic corporation.
- It must not have more than 35 shareholders. A husband and wife are treated as one shareholder.
- The stock must be owned by individuals, not other corporations.

- Nonresident aliens or foreign trusts are not eligible to participate.
- It must have only one class of stock, although designations for voting or nonvoting stock may apply, making the S corp as flexible as a limited partnership.

Until the passage of the Subchapter S Revision Act in 1982, S corps could not have more than 20 percent of gross receipts in the form of passive investment income, such as rents. The elimination of this rule has broadened the use of this ownership vehicle to include income property investment as well as properties held for growth.

The major advantages of an S corp include limited personal liability, ease of transferability of ownership shares, centralized management and comparative ease of formation. Its basic disadvantage is that aggregate losses may be passed through to the individual shareholders in an amount equal only to cash paid for the stock, plus any loans made to the company. Thus, the S corporation's most efficient application for real estate investment is for projects designed for purposes other than tax shelters.

Collapsible Corporations

A corporation formed for a single purpose and then disbanded when the goal is achieved is termed a **collapsible corporation**. For instance, a corporation may be formed for the specific purpose of owning an unimproved property until building is completed on the site. During the course of construction, certain operating expenses, such as management salaries, mortgage interest, placement fees and title insurance premiums, are treated as ordinary costs. Because there can be no rental income from the property until the building is completed, these expenses are in effect *active losses* and, as such, can be utilized to offset other active income. This usually results in a substantial tax shelter for the corporation's owners. And, when the building is finally completed and the property is sold, profits from the sale of the improved property are also considered active income. This technique now has added meaning with the elimination of special capital gains tax treatment.

Partnerships

Under the aegis of the Federal Uniform Partnership Act, real estate may be owned by individuals and/or corporations in **partnership**, with every partner considered a tenant in common with each of the other partners. The various forms of this type of ownership include general partnerships, limited partnerships (syndicates) and joint venture partnerships. Because of the legal complexities involved in forming a partnership, it is important to employ an attorney's services in preparing a partnership agreement.

General Partnerships.   Many general partnerships are relatively informal arrangements wherein some friends and/or family members join together and purchase an investment property as tenants in common. The only evidence of the partnership is the names of these people on a deed specifying their proportionate ownership interests in the property. Other general partnerships can be designed with a formal contractual agreement that specifies in detail the various rights, duties and obligations of each member and whether their ownership interests are freely transferable. Some agreements require that a participant's interest be offered to the remaining partners prior to being sold outside the partnership. This condition is called a **right of first refusal**.

Under the general partnership form of ownership, each partner assumes an active management role. As a result, there must be unanimous agreement each time a decision is made, regardless of the proportions of ownership. Thus, a general partnership with unequal shares still allows each of the owners an equal voice in management.

General partnerships are usually designed to join together compatible persons with similar goals for real estate investments, thereby enlarging their individual capabilities to acquire property. Although the management votes are equal, the distribution of earnings and the mortgage and property tax obligations are based on each participant's proportionate percentage of ownership. Partners are then personally responsible for their own income tax liability.

In a general real estate partnership, members are personally liable for all debts and obligations of the partnership, regardless of their proportionate share. In the event of bankruptcy, other personal assets of the partners may be attached to satisfy creditors. However, the partnership itself is not responsible for the private debts of any one partner. In the event of a personal bankruptcy, only the proportionate interest of the troubled partner may be attached by creditors.

Many formal general partnership agreements specify what the surviving partners' relationship with the heirs of a deceased partner will be. Recognizing the need for continuing compatibility in a general partnership in which each participant has an equal voice in management, most formal realty agreements grant the remaining partners an option to purchase the ownership interest of a deceased partner.

A buy-out formula is devised at the inception of the partnership, usually based on the fair market value of the share at the time of death. The funds for the purchase option may be secured from the proceeds of a partnership life insurance program or from contributions made by each surviving partner. In the absence of a buy-out agreement, or if the remaining partners do not exercise the option that does exist, the heirs assume the deceased's partnership position and the realty investment continues to function.

Limited Partnerships.   Unlike general partnerships, in which each participant takes an active management role and is also subject to the personal liabilities involved, **limited partnerships**—also known as syndicates—attract real estate investors who prefer to take a passive role in management and who wish to limit their personal liability to the extent of their specific cash investments. However, court decisions have held that this personal liability is protected only as long as the individual investor does not become involved in the day-to-day partnership activities.

A limited partnership is formed when a real estate promoter, assuming the liability and responsibility of a **general partner,** purchases or takes an option to purchase an investment property. Members of the public are then invited to participate as limited partners by buying ownership shares in various denominations. The result is a relatively large group of investors, often more than 100, who rely on the management expertise of the general partner for promised profits.

The limited partners take a passive role in management and enjoy the security of protecting their other personal assets from liabilities incurred by the partnership. Any losses are limited to the extent of the individual's investment in the group. However, if a limited partner agrees to purchase $100,000 worth of units in the project, payable in five $20,000 increments over time, the exposure is for the entire amount of the investment, regardless of how much has been invested to date.

Limited partnerships are investment conduits that pass profits directly through to the investors in proportion to their ownership shares. Any annual income tax liabilities are thus imposed at the investor's level. When the property is sold, the proceeds are also distributed proportionately to each investor. Because excess losses can no longer be passed through to the passive investors in a limited partnership, these ownership entities have lost their efficacy as tax shelter investments.

Each share in the limited partnership is the individual property of the investor and is inheritable. The shares are evaluated according to current market prices at the time of the owner's death and then distributed to the heirs after payment of any required inheritance taxes.

Many smaller realty investors are attracted to this form of ownership. They can not only limit their personal liability and avoid the burdens of active property management but also expand their individual investment capabilities by becoming part of a group that invests in larger, more efficient and hence potentially profitable realty ownership ventures.

Limited partnerships have become popular vehicles for real estate ownership because they offer a wide latitude of investment opportunities, the ability to attract large sums of venture capital and great flexibility in organizational design. Their organizational flexibility stems from their ability to design investments that can fulfill individual investors' requirements. To illustrate, one investment may be organized to attract persons interested in receiving income in the form of regular cash flow from one single specific property, such as an office building. Other limited partnerships can be designed to attract investors who prefer to purchase shares in a diversified investment portfolio consisting of a variety of properties, much like a mutual fund in the stock market.

As an investment conduit and to preserve its single-tax profile, a limited partnership must actively avoid displaying, *at any one time*, five characteristics of a corporation: continuity, central management, limited liability, easy transferability of interests and double taxation. In fact, the IRS looks with disfavor on any limited partnership in which more than two of these characteristics exist at any one time.

As a result, since centralized management and limited liability are absolutely basic to this form organization, limited partnerships are designed to terminate at a specified time, and certain restrictions are placed on the transferability of ownership shares. In the first instance, the termination date is often established in advance. In the second instance, the organizational agreements usually include the general partner's right of first refusal to purchase any shares before they are offered to the public.

Because limited partnerships are concerned with selling *units* of ownership in an enterprise, they come under the definition of a securities dealership and, as such, are subject to Regulation D of the Uniform Partnership Act, more commonly known as the **blue-sky law.** This law requires every general partner to prepare a comprehensive prospectus to distribute to potential investors. In addition to describing the physical property, the terms and the conditions of the investment, the prospectus must include full disclosure of the names and histories of each general partner, as well as a clear indication of all of the risks inherent in the proposition.

When investors consider forming or joining a limited partnership, they must know precisely what is required in the way of organization, costs and potential benefits. A comprehensive outline for a limited partnership offering is shown in the exhibit at the end of this chapter.

The dissolution of a limited partnership occurs on the expiration of its term or on the first occurrence of one of the following:

- election by the general partner(s) to dissolve or discontinue the partnership, which is approved by a majority vote;
- bankruptcy of the partnership; or
- the sale or disposition of all or substantially all partnership assets, including the cessation of active business, the distribution of all cash and the termination of reserves for liabilities.

The benefits from this form of ownership extend beyond even the more usual income, depreciation and growth in value potentials of most real estate investments. Since termination dates must be established in advance, shrewd promoters may design a number of separate limited partnerships, each controlling an individual property. These partnerships can then be traded regularly, with each transfer resulting in new increased depreciation levels for each unit.

Joint Venture Partnership.   A special form of general partnership, the **joint venture**, brings together the skills and assets of a group of heterogeneous investors for a specific realty project. For example, a joint venture partnership might be formed by a landowner, a developer and a financier, each of whom contributes unique skills and assets to the overall project and receives, in exchange, a proportionate share of ownership.

The scope of a joint venture can be broadened to include as partners not only those persons mentioned above but also carpenters, electricians, plumbers and other artisans who contribute labor and materials as their share and who receive in return a proportionate ownership.

Joint ventures must have a definite agreement setting forth the intentions of the parties, including provisions for treatment of the cash flows. This form of ownership can be entered into by individuals, corporations and partnerships, who become tenants in common with one another and are subject to the conditions, privileges, obligations and liabilities of the full partnership discussed earlier.

Limited Liability Company. In late 1988, a new type of entity, the **limited liability company (LLC),** received a favorable IRS opinion and has become an alternative to the limited partnership. An LLC has a corporate form but the tax advantages of a partnership without the restrictions of an S corporation.

Resembling a corporation because of its shareholders' limited personal liability and an S corporation because only shareholders feel the tax impact, the LLC includes these additional benefits for its owners:

- Both gains and losses are passed through to individual shareholders.
- It may be designed to dissolve on the death or bankruptcy of one or more of its members.
- It may include in its ownership nonresident aliens or foreign investors.
- Its basis may be expanded to add the partnership's debt to its investors' capital—unlike the S corp, which limits the basis to the cash investment of its shareholders (IRS Rev. Rul. 88–76, 1988–38 IRB). For example, if an LLC is formed with $1 million contributed by its shareholders, and $500,000 is used to make a down payment on a $3 million office building, the LLC's basis is increased to

  $1 million
  +$2.5 million in debt
  $3.5 million.

LLCs can be organized only in states with authorizing legislation. Currently, 32 states have adopted LLC laws, and 11 more are pending. The IRS continues to rule favorably for LLCs and, under Private Letter Ruling 9226035, has consented to allow conversions of existing limited and general partnerships to LLCs.

For more information about this interesting ownership format, read "LLCs May Be a Better Investment Vehicle" in the May 1993 issue of *The Real Estate Investing Letter,* Management Resources, Inc., 861 Lafayette Road, #5, Hampton, NH 03842-1232, (603) 929-1600.

TRUST OWNERSHIP

A *trust* is an arrangement whereby one person or entity legally holds title to a property and manages it for the benefit of another. The creator of a trust is the *trustor*, the holder of legal title is the *trustee* and the receiver of the benefits of the trust is the *beneficiary*. Under some agreements, the beneficiary may also be the trustor.

Trusts may be classified as **discretionary trusts** or **irrevocable trusts.** The former can be altered or discontinued at the discretion of the participants. The latter are established for a specific purpose and cannot be changed until this purpose is achieved.

Trust agreements pertinent to real estate investments include the **testamentary trust**, the **living trust** and the **investment trust**. These real estate trusts are created for many reasons, including to

- provide continuity in ownership over several generations;
- enlist the expertise of professional management;
- eliminate repetitive probate costs; or
- hide the identity of beneficiaries.

Testamentary Trusts

A trust may be established by the provision of a decedent owner's will specifying that certain portions or all of the property in the estate be placed into a trust for the benefit of designated heirs. This form of ownership is a **testamentary trust** and vests control and management of a deceased's property in the name of a trustee. In this manner, an estate may be kept intact through one or more generations of heirs and enjoy the benefits of professional management during the intervening years until its final distribution per the terms of the deceased's will.

Living Trusts

A living trust is also known as an **intervivos trust.** In this form of real estate ownership, a trustor executes an agreement with a trustee to hold property in trust for the trustor's benefit and under the trustor's direct control for a certain time until specific goals have been attained. The living trust is terminated when these goals are achieved. Such a trust is originated by naming the trustors as primary beneficiaries during their lifetimes. Upon death, the living trust changes to a testamentary trust, and the decedents' heirs move from secondary beneficiary position into primary position.

A living trust is often employed by land developers when acreage is purchased under the terms of an installment contract. The seller of the land is required to place the receivable contract in trust with a bank or title company together with instructions to release certain portions of the collateral land as stipulated payments are made to the trustee by the purchaser-developer. The trust ends when the contract is paid in full. Thus, the land seller becomes the beneficiary of this living trust as well as the trustor. The trustee accepts payments, issues releases and sends the proceeds from the payments to the beneficiary.

This trust arrangement guarantees the developer periodic releases of parcels from the contract. These timely releases are vital to the success of the project because they ensure a constant flow of land for development. In the absence of such an intervivos trust agreement, the developer would need to find the seller each time a payment was made to secure a release of the needed property from the lien of the contract. Since the trustee—usually a corporation—is the legal owner of the contract, the developer can quickly and efficiently secure the periodic releases when needed.

In the event that the seller dies during the term of the contract, the trust will continue uninterrupted, with the benefits passing through to the heirs under the testamentary provisions. Thus, the trust continues to function until the contract is satisfied, the property fully distributed and the goals achieved.

Investors sometimes make use of the anonymous ownership advantage of an intervivos trust to hide their names as beneficiaries. This technique is especially effective if the revelation of a property owner's name might have an adverse effect on the negotiations for the purchase, sale or refinancing of a specific property.

Intervivos trusts established to become testamentary trusts and to control property over several generations eliminate the costs of repetitive probate proceedings because the secondary beneficiaries automatically advance each time the primary beneficiary dies. Generation-skipping trusts have been eliminated under the tax laws, and currently the value of a trust's assets is included in the total value of an individual's estate for inheritance tax purposes.

However, an irrevocable trust can still be established to avoid inheritance taxes. To create such a trust, a property owner must make an irrevocable gift of property to a trustee, with the property to be held on behalf of the named beneficiaries until the donor's demise. Thus, the donor may enjoy the income from the property and, at death, have the income accrue to the benefit of the heirs. The gift is subject to appropriate gift taxes at the time the trust is established but is exempt from inheritance taxes, unless it is made within a period of three years prior to the trustor's death. In that case, it will be included in the total value of the estate.

Grantor Retained Income Trust (GRIT)

The **grantor retained income trust (GRIT)** is useful for a family with considerable real estate assets. The grantors, usually the parents, transfer titles to income-producing properties in trust to a trustee for the benefit of the grantee, usually the child or children, for a period of years. During the term of the trust, the income flows to the grantors, but at the end of the trust period, the property vests outright in the grantees.

The benefit of a GRIT is that all appreciation in the values of the properties after the trust is created is removed from the estate of the grantors, provided they survive the trust term.

The Technical and Miscellaneous Revenue Act of 1988 (TAMRA) imposed the following limitations on the use of a GRIT.

- The grantor, not any other person(s), must be the beneficiary of the income from the trust.
- The grantor must not be a trustee of the trust.
- Only the grantor may receive income from the trust property.
- The trust term must not exceed ten years.

Other family and charitable trusts may be created to satisfy unique ownership requirements. It is vital to seek the help of an attorney and an accountant thoroughly familiar with both federal and state tax laws to avoid the many pitfalls inherent in this relatively complicated form of property ownership.

Investment Trusts

In addition to the individual trust forms for property ownership already described, trusts can also be designed to act as investment conduits for small investors, enabling them to pool resources to participate in the field of real estate. By subscribing to and meeting the specific IRS requirements listed below, these investment trusts avoid the double tax burden imposed on corporate earnings. The IRS requirements are:

- Transferable beneficial shares must be issued to at least 100 persons.
- More than five persons must own more than 50 percent of the beneficial shares of the trust.
- At least 75 percent of the trust's assets must be in real estate.
- At least 90 percent of the trust's earnings must be distributed to shareholders each year.
- The trust itself must be a passive investor, hiring others to manage and operate its investments.

The three common types of investment trusts are the equity trusts known as real estate investment trusts, real estate mortgage trusts and a hybrid form of these two.

In addition to these basic real estate trust forms, special investment trusts can be designed for the development and ownership of medical buildings, mobile-home parks, recreational condominiums, miniwarehouses and other unique real estate developments. A synopsis of a trust offering is shown in Figure 2.1.

Real Estate Investment Trusts.   More commonly known as **REIT**s, trusts of this type use the accumulated funds of investors to purchase real estate income and speculative properties as long-term investments. A REIT is primarily an income generator for a group of small investors and is similar to the stock market's mutual funds.

REITs give the small investor the opportunity for broad-based participation in real estate equity investments, offering both regular income from rentals and long-term gains in property value as incentives. By law, REITs must pay out most of their income each year as dividends to their beneficiaries. Unlike other

---

FIGURE 2.1   Synopsis of a Trust Offering

Synopsis of a Trust Offering
(Subject to State Securities Division Approval)
REGENCY APARTMENTS
100 Real Estate Investment Trust Units
Minimum Investment $30,000

This offer may be considered speculative and there is no assurance that the property will increase in value or that the Trust will realize a profit from the operation or upon the sale thereof. There is no public market for the Trust interests and none can be expected to develop.

The Regency Corporation shall be the manager of the Trust. No dealer, salesperson or any other person has been authorized to make any representations other than those contained herein. This publication does not constitute an offer to sell or the solicitation of an offer to buy any of the securities offered hereby to any person to whom it is unlawful to make such an offer. The Trust intends to sell only those number of interests described herein.

The Regency Investment Trust is acquiring the Regency Apartments under an agreement executed with Allied Investment Corporation (the sellers). The purchase price is $3 million, to be paid in cash upon closing. It is the intention of this Trust to generate positive cash flow income to its investors for five years, then capital gains profits when the project is converted to condominiums and sold.

The Property. The Regency Apartments consists of 100 two-bedroom, 13/4 bath, unfurnished rental units. It is located at the intersection of Bell and Center Streets, close to Monterey Plaza Shopping Center. The complexes is composed of ten individual two-story red brick buildings on a three-acre lot. There are two heated swimming pools, saunas, whirlpool baths, dressing rooms and improved patios. Each apartment has its own carport and storage area, as well as small private patios or balconies. The apartments are all 900 square feet and include built-in kitchens, paneling, wallpaper, separate air-conditioning, drapes and carpets.

Pro-Forma Statement.

Income:

100 apartments @ $300 per month	$ 360,000

Expenses:

Vacancy 5%
Management 5%
Reserves 5%
Taxes 7%
Insurance 3%

Maintenance 15%	Total (40%)		144,000
		NET:	$ 216,000
			(7.2% on $3 million invested)

(Note: Projected growth in value is to $5 million in five years [$50,000 per apartment as a condominium]. This reflects a 12% additional annual return for a total overall projected annual yield of 19.2% before income taxes.)

All books and records shall be housed at the office of the Regency Corporation and shall be open to inspection by all members of the Trust during regular business hours. Monetary distributions shall be made monthly and all profits shall be distributed equally to each unit of the Trust (1/100). No unit owner shall bear any financial loss in excess of the original contribution.

forms of real estate ownership, REITs *may not* pass losses through to their beneficiaries. Thus, their use as tax shelters is limited. Their greatest appeal is to those investors who can absorb additional active income but do not have either the financial capability or the inclination to invest directly in real estate.

Because of the decline of investments in real estate for tax sheltering purposes, the popularity of REITs has increased dramatically, eclipsing to a great degree the use of the limited partnership as an ownership vehicle for small investors.

Real Estate Mortgage Trusts.   Commonly known as **REMT**s, trusts of this form attract participants who prefer the benefits offered by real property financing activities (a somewhat more stabilized form of cash flow) to the often-volatile activities of the real estate equities market.

A REMT utilizes the monies secured from the sale of beneficial interests to establish a substantial line of credit with its bank or a similar financial institution. Then the REMT uses this credit to participate in the real estate financing market as a lender of second mortgages, wraparound loans, gap loans, participation loans and other sophisticated and often esoteric financing forms.

Hybrid Trusts.   Often REITs and REMTs are established as interlocking trusts, with the REIT dealing in property equities and the REMT financing these investments. In effect, this combination creates a *hybrid trust* arrangement and offers beneficiaries a greater opportunity for investment diversification.

The Umbrella Partnership REIT.   A new structure for the ownership and management of real estate investments is known as the **Umbrella Partnership Real Estate Investment Trust (UPREIT)**. The UPREIT is a REIT that invests together with other non-REIT investors in a partnership that itself owns a portfolio of substantial partnership interests in high-quality investment real estate. Its advantages include

- lowering the tax burden to existing owners on formation of the UPREIT;
- allowing public shareholders to access institutional-grade real estate investments; and
- providing greater flexibility in the acquisition of additional institutional real estate by REITs.

Taubman Centers, Inc., was the first publicly traded REIT to adopt the UPREIT format, raising $294.8 million in an initial public offering in November 1992.

An UPREIT typically owns a managing general partner interest in the umbrella partnership. In turn, the partnership owns several interests in other commonly managed partnerships owning institutional-grade real estate, such as the Taubman superregional shopping malls.

For further information on the UPREIT, read "How Umbrella Partnership REITs Work" in the May 15, 1993, *Mortgage and Real Estate Executives Report,* Warren Gorman Lamont, 210 South Street, Boston, MA 02111, 1-800-950-1203.

LEASEHOLD INTERESTS

A real estate investor may be involved with leasehold interests as a tenant-developer leasing vacant land for the construction of a large commercial or residential project and/or as a landlord of the improvements so constructed. As a tenant of vacant land, an investor can exercise tremendous leveraging capabilities by pledging the landlord's land, in addition to the improvements, as collateral to obtain a construction mortgage. As landlords of the improved property, most investors will hire professional managers, although some take a direct role in management.

An understanding of land leases, subordination, completion bonds and leasehold insurance is a prerequisite to sound investment planning. Leases, rents and special rental clauses will be examined in later chapters as they apply to specific types of investments.

Land Leases

In Maryland, and especially in Baltimore, land leases have been used since colonial times as a form of interest in property. In earlier years, *perpetual leases* were granted by landowners to tenants. The owner, now a *lessor,* retained title to the land and, for an agreed-upon annual rent, transferred its possession and use to a tenant, or *lessee.* The tenant, in turn, pledged this **leasehold interest** to a lender in exchange for the money needed for improvements made to and on the land.

The perpetual quality of these early ground leases created difficulties for the tenants. They could never acquire clear title to the land and had to negotiate with the landlord if they wished to escape from the continuous liability imposed by these never-ending ground leases. Therefore, in 1884, the Maryland legislature passed a law requiring that ground leases for periods of more than 15 years include a lessee's purchase option.

At about this same time, a parallel system of perpetual land leases was developing in Pennsylvania. In this state, equitable title to a property was passed to the tenant under a land lease by a contract for a deed (land contract) on which the payment schedule was designated by the word *forever.* In 1885, the Pennsylvania legislature prohibited the use of perpetual contracts and required that specific termination dates and redemption rights for long-term tenants be included in land contracts. These latter rights were designed to protect tenants against any arbitrary or capricious eviction proceedings by landlords.

Even though financial institutions in Maryland and Pennsylvania have long been granting mortgage loans secured by a tenant borrower's leasehold interest, land-lease financing has never been widely accepted in our country. In the event of a default on the part of the mortgagor, a lender succeeds to the position of the borrower under the terms of the ground lease, which does not satisfy the property ownership requirement of many fiduciary lenders.

Recently, however, and especially in Hawaii and California, net ground leases have gained wider acceptance for major new commercial real estate developments. In addition, some leaseholds are eligible for Federal Housing Administration (FHA) and Department of Veterans Affairs (VA) mortgage insurance and/or guarantees. The FHA requires underlying leases for 99 years from their insured lessee-mortgagors, while the VA will approve guaranteed loans that must be repaid at least 15 years prior to the expiration date of the ground leases.

Subordination.   The major sources of funds for financing leasehold improvements are the financial fiduciaries—banks, savings associations and life insurance companies. Because of their conservative lending policies, these financial intermediaries must be in first priority lien position to receive full legal title to *the land* as well as to *the building* thereon in the event of a foreclosure. Therefore, a leasehold mortgage granted by one of these primary fiduciary lenders invariably includes a covenant from the landowner that places the legal fee in a *subordinate* position to the mortgage lien. Thus, in the event of a default, a lender does not merely succeed to the position of the tenant under the terms of the land lease contract. Instead, the lender recovers the entire property, not just the improvements. (See Figure 2.2, Subordination Agreement.)

An exception to the requirement for landlord **subordination** is sometimes made for a tenant-developer whose credit is so strong that consideration of the value of the collateral property is almost incidental to a loan transaction. If a tenant such as JC Penney or Sears wished to secure financing to construct its own store or warehouse on leased land, the company could secure the necessary funds simply by affixing authorized signatures to the loan documents. Such an arrangement is called a *credit loan*.

Protective Covenants

Most leasehold mortgages are designed to include both the land and the improvements as collateral for the loan, thereby requiring the landlord's subordination of legal fee. Because landowners who subordinate face the risk of losing their properties if a developer-tenant fails, they often insist that certain special risk-minimizing terms and conditions be included in the land lease contract. Such protective covenants include partial subordination, completion bonds, mortgage underwriting requirements and commercial leasehold insurance.

Partial Subordination.   An agreement for partial subordination requires the *tenant-developer* to invest a portion of the improvement's construction costs as a down payment, thereby preventing 100 percent leverage. An experienced landowner-lessor understands that a lessee's cash participation will surely create a positive work incentive at the same time that it creates an equity cushion in the event of a default on the leasehold mortgage.

One technique for participation could require the developer to invest, in cash, at least 20 percent of the building costs, thus limiting the leasehold mortgage amount to 80 percent of the construction costs. In the event of a default, the landowner would be in a cushioned equity position when forced to assume the developer's role. Any equity participation formula acceptable to both lessor and lessee can be used as the basis for partial subordination. The amount of cash required from the developer depends on a good credit rating, and the better the track record for past ventures, the lower the cash requisite.

FIGURE 2.2   A Sample Subordination Agreement

Agreement to Subordinate Fee Interest to Tenant's Mortgage

Lessor acknowledges that Tenant intends to erect a structure on the demised premises for the purpose of operating a _____, complete with paved parking area and, accordingly, expresses its consent thereto. Lessor also acknowledges that it will be necessary for Tenant to secure mortgage financing for the project, and that in order to facilitate such mortgage financing, Lessor's interest as owner of the fee simple in the land must be subordinated to a mortgage lien of the lender. Therefore, Lessor agrees that it will subordinate at any time during the term of this lease, its interest as owner and Lessor, to an institutional mortgage loan to be obtained by Tenant on the demised premises, providing that such institutional mortgage does not exceed_____dollars ($_____). Lessor shall not be obligated to subordinate its interest unless Tenant invests twenty (20%) percent of the total amount of the cost of the improvement project for which the institutional mortgage loan is set.

The following conditions and terms shall apply to effectuate Lessor's subordination:

1.   Lessor covenants and agrees to execute, deliver, and join in with Tenant, at Tenant s written request, a mortgage or other form of agreement subordinating Lessor's fee interest in the demised premises, Lessor realizing that such financing institution may require such an executed document from it, in order that Tenant may acquire funds for the sole purpose of improving the demised premises of Lessor, and thus carry out the purpose of this agreement.

2.   Likewise, Lessor will promptly endorse, without recourse, any drafts, checks, or disbursement documents, representing payment to Tenant of the proceeds of such financing, in the event that Lessor's name appears thereon, such endorsement to be made solely as procedural in making such funds available to Tenant.

3.   Lessor shall not be required, nor does it in any way agree, to subject itself to personal liability, by the execution of the mortgage or other document of subordination, in that the sole and limited purpose of such execution by Lessor of the required documents, is to subject the fee simple interest of Lessor to an institutional mortgage lien for the sole purpose of improving Lessor's demised premises.

4.   Lessor shall not, without the written consent and approval of Tenant, modify, alter, or change any of the terms of any mortgage, or any instrument appertaining thereto, so long as the limitations set out herein have been complied with by Tenant.

5.   Tenant agrees to pay all costs and expenses, without any liability, obligation, or contribution thereof from Lessor which are incurred in connection with the obtaining of any such mortgage, and further agrees that it will make all payments of amortization, principal, and interest of the mortgage, as and when they become due, and to perform and comply with all the other terms, covenants, and conditions of the mortgage, and in the event of a failure so to do, Lessor may, at its option, do so, and Tenant shall pay any amount which Lessor so pays, upon the demand of Lessor, with interest at eight percent (8%) per annum, or Lessor may, at its option, treat the amount so paid by it as additional rent due and payable on the date provided for the next ensuing rent payment, and Lessor shall have all the rights and remedies for failure to pay the same at that time, as it shall have for failure to pay rent.

6.   Lessor also covenants that in the event the mortgage lender discovers a defect in the title of Lessor, or discovers an encumbrance of any sort which effectively prevents the lender from giving a mortgage loan to Tenant, for the aforesaid purpose, Lessor shall be obligated to remove or eliminate, at its sole expense, the title defect or encumbrance, as the case may be, within a reasonable period of time. provided Lessor exercises all due diligence to cure such defect, or to eliminate any such encumbrance, but, in any event, such defect or encumbrance shall be cured or eliminated within ninety (90) days from that date that Tenant communicates to Lessor the existence of any such title defect or encumbrance on the property subject to this lease and the documents Tenant requires. For the period of time in which Lessor will be endeavoring to cure or remove the title defect or encumbrance, the amount of rent that shall be payable by Tenant to Lessor will be _____dollars ($_____) month, and not_____ dollars ($_____) per month, as called for elsewhere herein. If, after the expiration of ninety (90) days, Lessor has not caused to be cured the title defect or defects, or caused to be removed the encumbrance or encumbrances, as aforesaid, then Tenant shall have the option to declare this lease agreement as null and void, in which event both parties shall be discharged and released from all further performances hereunder, except that Lessor shall refund to Tenant any prepaid rents.

Tenant s rights under this entire paragraph shall, however, be subject to the following conditions:

1.   The subject mortgage shall be obtained from institutions such as banks, trust companies, insurance companies, savings and loan associations, pension funds, or other recognized public lending institutions.

2.   The mortgage shall not be for a sum greater than the value of the buildings and improvements to the demised premises, less twenty percent (20 percent) thereof. Such value is to be determined by an appraisal of the premises as secured by the institution committed to make the permanent loan. In the case of a construction loan, the appraisal shall cover only the value of the prospective buildings and improvements to be made. All funds derived thereunder, from the lending institution, shall be expended only for capital improvements upon the subject demised premises of Lessor.

3.   No such mortgage loan shall extend for a term longer than the unexpired primary term of the lease, and provisions of any such mortgage loan shall require that it be paid, or prepaid, principal, and interest, in equal payments, at least annually, in an amount sufficient to fully amortize it within its term. It is contemplated and covenanted between the parties that the word "mortgages" shall mean one construction mortgage, if necessary, and one permanent mortgage resulting therefrom, and no more, anything to the contrary herein notwithstanding.

4.   All such mortgages shall affirmatively provide that Lessor joins therein for the sole purpose of subjecting the fee title to the demised premises therein, and not In any way to create personal liability upon Lessor, and duplicate copies of any notice by the mortgagee of default shall be sent to Lessor; Lessor shall have a period of two (2) weeks from any such notice to cure the default, and the Lessor shall have the right to assume the position of tenant under the mortgage, and to perform the same should this lease be properly terminated by Lessor, on account on account of Tenant's default.

Completion Bond.   Another protective covenant for a landlord is a clause in the land lease that requires the developer to secure a completion bond from an insurance company. This bond guarantees completion of the project with insurance funds in the event of a developer's bankruptcy or death. Before issuing this bond, an insurance company carefully examines the financial credit and technical capability of the developer and the general building contractor. Thus, the bonding company in effect acts as the landowner's credit-clearing agency. If the developer or the contractor is not granted a bond, the land lease will probably not be granted either.

Mortgage Underwriting.   In addition to the preceding risk-minimizing techniques of partial subordination and completion bond requirements, a landowner is frequently protected by a leasehold mortgagee's loan underwriting requirements. Before agreeing to issue a new loan on a commercial real estate venture, a lending institution investigates the prospective borrower's financial position and the economic feasibility of the proposed project. Before a leasehold mortgage will be granted, a borrower's credit must be acceptable and the project itself must have the potential to generate enough cash flow to be self-supporting. The techniques for assessing the financial feasibility of a realty investment are examined in Chapters 5 and 6.

If the results of the feasibility study are positive, the developer is required, under a rental achievement clause, to secure as many firm rental commitments from tenants as are necessary to meet the project's break-even requirement. Once enough advance leases with acceptable tenants are developed to generate income adequate to cover the expenses of property taxes, insurance premiums, maintenance fees, utility charges and debt service costs, a lender usually feels secure enough to provide necessary financing. Thus, the landowner benefits indirectly from the underwriting requirements of the mortgagee.

Commercial Leasehold Insurance.   In the event that developers are not able to secure enough national tenants to satisfy a project's break-even requirements, they may seek to secure leases from good *local* tenants. To raise the credit rating of these local tenants to the equivalent of the AAA-rated national tenants, commercial leasehold insurance is often purchased. Under this form of insurance, the insurer guarantees the payment of rent in the event the insured cannot pay it. This guaranty usually meets the lender's requirements, and a combination of leases from national as well as local tenants can be pledged to the lender—in addition to the real estate—as security for issuing the leasehold mortgage.

Currently, the largest leasehold insurer in this country is the Commercial Leasehold Insurance Corporation (CLIC), a subsidiary of the Mortgage Guarantee Insurance Corporation (MGIC). CLIC provides leasehold insurance for tenants in shopping centers, office developments and industrial parks. Numerous insurance plans are available, with the required premium corresponding proportionately to the extent of the insurance risk. Under a typical plan, CLIC might begin to pay rent 30 days after an insured tenant's default and continue this payment for a specified time, such as 18 months. This plan recognizes that landlords usually collect at least one month's rent in advance and allows them the opportunity to find another tenant with no interruption in the flow of cash rental receipts.

The underwriting process of the leasehold insurer is yet another indirect protective device for the landowner and for the project's developer. A refusal by the insurer to issue a policy for a prospective tenant provides the developer and landowner with a reliable indication of the tenant's poor credit ability.

SUMMARY

This chapter has presented an overview of the various types of ownership interests in real property. Ranging from individual ownerships to corporate forms, partnerships, trusts and leaseholds, real estate investors have many ownership formats to choose from to satisfy their specific personal preferences.

Real estate can be owned individually with either survivorship or inheritability as a goal. Although ownership forms can be changed during a lifetime with the agreement of all parties thereto, it is the distribution of property after death that dictates its lifetime ownership design. Thus, in most states, husbands and wives may own property as tenants by the entirety, with the result that the deceased's portion will automatically vest in the surviving spouse. This eliminates the time and cost of probate but also eliminates the rights of the deceased to designate an heir other than the spouse.

To preserve the prerogative of designating by will to whom an estate will pass, an inheritable estate must be established. Toward this end, the community property form of ownership is recognized in only eight states, while the tenancy in common format is available in every state to provide spouses with an alternative to tenancy by the entirety.

For those who want to avoid probate costs in the community property states and also in those states that do not recognize tenancy by the entirety, the available form of ownership is joint tenancy with the rights of survivorship. This type of estate can be utilized by any two or more persons, but because it effectively eliminates inheritability, it is usually limited to use by family members.

For the married individual who wishes to maintain control over property, sole and separate ownership is available. And finally, for the single person, ownership in severalty is the format under which to own real estate. Each of these forms—sole and separate, and severalty—is inheritable, since only one person is involved.

An alternative to the individual ownership of property is the establishment of a corporation for this purpose. Here, personal liability is limited to the corporation's assets. In addition, the corporate form provides a basis for attracting a pool of investment funds from many smaller investors through the sale of stock. Its design guarantees continuity and affords the means for hiring professional management. Corporate earnings are subject to double taxation and, as such, are limited in use as real estate investment ownership formats. However, S corporations can be used as investment conduits and to avoid double taxation.

Often real estate investors enter into partnerships to share in a potentially profitable venture. A full, or regular, partnership gives each participant an equal voice in the management, despite the proportionate share of ownership. In addition, each partner is personally responsible for the liabilities of the partnership.

On the other hand, limited partnerships and syndicates shelter passive investors' individual liabilities. In this form of ownership, the general partner, or syndicator, assumes full responsibility for management in addition to full liability for the success of the investment.

Property ownership in the form of a trust is established to create continuity in the management of an estate and to avoid repetitious probate costs. Living, or intervivos, trusts, which after death become testamentary trusts for the benefit of the heirs, can be established to control property during the life of a beneficiary. This form of ownership directs a trustee to hold the legal title to property in trust for specified beneficiaries and to follow the directions established in the trust agreement for the management of the properties involved.

Investment trusts such as REITs and REMTs are established on this living trust basis, as are family and special trusts. However, REITs and REMTs serve as investment conduits for many smaller investors and qualify under specific IRS regulations to act as trustees in purchasing, managing and financing real properties. Because of these special requirements, profits from these activities are taxed only once—at the beneficiary level—not twice as in the corporate ownership form.

Real estate developers are often involved in leasehold interests as a form of property ownership. Many larger commercial ventures, such as office buildings and shopping centers, are constructed on leased land.

Landlords of vacant land are often required to subordinate their legal fee interests to the liens of new mortgages secured by developers for the construction of their projects. To minimize the risks inherent in subordination, in which the landowners may lose their property in the event of a developer's bankruptcy, many landlords insist on a partial subordination agreement requiring the developer to invest, in cash, a portion of the building costs.

In addition, most land leases designed for the construction of new buildings require the developer or the building contractor to secure a completion bond and advance rental commitments from AAA-rated tenants. The total amount of these rental commitments must be adequate to cover the basic operating expenses and debt service requirements of the project. Thus, a subordinating landowner is doubly protected as a result of the underwriting specifications of both the bonding company and the construction financiers.

EXERCISE 2   (Answers may be checked against the Answer Key.)

1. Automatic survivorship is intrinsic in which of the following forms of realty

    a. Sole and separate ownership
    b. Tenancy in common
    c. Tenancy by the entirety
    d. Community property

2. An S corporation

    a. requires 100 or more shareholders.
    b. is subject to double taxation.
    c. is available to foreign investors.
    d. limits the personal liability of its shareholders.

3. Tenancy in common includes which of the following?

    a. Automatic survivorship
    b. Married persons only
    c. Undivided ownership
    d. Equal ownership shares only

4. Participants in a general partnership usually take title as which of the following?

    a. Joint tenants
    b. Tenants in common
    c. Tenants by the entirety
    d. Tenants in severalty

5. Corporations are formed to own real estate for all of the following reasons, *except*

    a. to avoid double tax on profits.
    b. for broad-based capital accumulation.
    c. to limit shareholder personal liability.
    d. to develop continuity of ownership.

6. Which of the following is *not* an attribute of a limited partnership?

    a. The personal liability of the partners is limited to their investment.
    b. Taxes on profits are imposed at the investor's level.
    c. Each partner takes an active role in management.
    d. Operating losses are passed through to the partners.

7. A father, mother and daughter own a property in joint tenancy. The daughter sells her interest to a friend for cash. How is the ownership changed?

   a. The friend becomes a joint tenant with the parents.
   b. All three parties now own as tenants in common.
   c. The friend is a tenant in common with the parents, who remain joint tenants.
   d. The daughter cannot sell her joint tenancy interest.

8. When constructing a commercial building on leased land, the developer will probably need to secure all of the following items *except*

   a. financing.
   b. subordination.
   c. a release clause.
   d. tenants.

9. A living trust usually evolves into a/an

   a. intervivos trust.
   b. testamentary trust.
   c. collapsible trust.
   d. limited partnership.

10. The blue-sky provisions of the Uniform Partnership Act cover all of the following items *except*

    a. the experience of the syndicators.
    b. an indication of the potential risk of the investment.
    c. a guaranteed return on the investment.
    d. a description of the property, terms and conditions of the investment.

DISCUSSION

1. Investigate your state laws regarding the distribution of the assets of an estate left by a person who dies intestate and without any discoverable heirs.

2. Secure a copy of an offering on a syndicated property and compare its form and content with the outline provided in the exhibit at the end of this chapter. Would you recommend an investment in the enterprise?

EXHIBIT   Syndicate Offering (Limited Partnership)

Article I. General Provisions
- Formation
- Name
- Purposes
- Place of business
- Term
- General partner
- Certificate of limited partnership
- Agent for service of process
- Exhibit of limited partners

Article II. Definitions
- Acquisition expenses
- Acquisition fees
- Adjusted invested capital
- Affiliate
- Assignee
- Cash available for distribution from operations
- Cash from sales or refinancing
- Closing date
- Distribution
- Finders' fees
- General partner(s)
- Gross offering proceeds
- Gross property revenue
- Limited partners
- Managing general partner
- Majority vote
- Net proceeds
- Offering and organization expenses
- Offering memorandum
- Operation expenses
- Original invested capital
- Partners
- Partnership
- Partnership properties
- Property Management fee
- Sales commission
- Subscription agreement
- Subordinated real estate commission
- Total outstanding units
- Unit
- Unit holders
- Working capital reserve

Article III. Capital Contribution and Related Matters
- Capital contributed by general partner(s)
- Capital contributed by limited partners
- Payment for units
- Subsequent offerings of addition units
- No action or consent necessary by limited partners for admission of other limited partners
- Remedies for default in capital contributions
- Subscriptions and admissions
- General partner(s) may purchase units
- No assessments or additional contributions
- No withdrawal of capital contributions
- Return of capital
- No interest on capital
- No priority
- Securities laws
- Temporary investment of partnership capital

Article IV. Allocation of Distributions, Income, Losses and Other items Among the Partners
- Distribution to the partners
- Capital accounts
- Obligation of general partner(s) to make up negative capital accounts
- Allocation for tax purposes
- The limited partners' share of allocations and distributions among themselves
- The general partner or partners' share of allocations and distributions among themselves
- Allocation between assignor and assignee
- Timing of distribution
- Express consent of allocations
- Limitations on distributions
- Special allocation for tax-exempt and foreign investors
- Tax withholding

Article V. Management of Partnership
- The management powers of the general partner(s)
- Restrictions on powers of the general partner(s)
- Actions requiring consent of all general partners
- The limited partners have no management powers
- Duty of the general partner(s) to devote time
- General partner(s) may engage in other activities
- Dealing with the partnership
- Liability of the general partner(s) and their affiliates
- Decisions
- Consent of the limited partners not required
- Liability of general partner(s) for capital contributions
- Reserves

Article VI. Compensation to the General Partner(s) or Affiliates
- Property management fee
- Real estate brokerage commission on acquisition
- Partnership management fee
- Real estate brokerage commission on resale of property
- Standby loan commitment fee
- Loan guaranty fee
- Fee for initial property management and marketing advice and rental marketing structure
- Development supervision fee
- Limitation on compensation to general partner(s)
- Initital partnership, tax advice and administration fee
- Farm property management fee
- Investment advisory fee
- Mortgage brokerage commission
- Subordinated interest
- Sales commission
- Incentive management fee
- Rental consulting fee
- Fees payable on removal

EXHIBIT Syndicate Offering (Limited Partnership) (continued)

Article VII. Books, Records, Accounts and Reports
  Books and records
  Limited partners' rights regarding books, records
    and tax information
  Accounting basis and fiscal year

Reports
Tax matters partner
Bank accounts
Designated person

Article VIII Assignment of Interests in the Partnership
  Assignment of interest in the partnership of the
    general partner(s)
  Assignment units
  No assignment allowed under certain
    circumstances

Substituted limited partner
Death, insanity, incompetency or bankruptcy of a
  limited partner

Article IX. Dissolution and Termination of the Partnership
  Dissolution
  Continuation of the business of the partnership
  Authority to wind up
  Accounting

Winding up and liquidation
No recourse against general partner(s)
Claim of limited partners or assignees

Article X. Termination of a General Partner
  General partner(s) ceasing to be a general partner(s)
  Removal of a general partner(s)
  Continuing interest of terminated general partner(s)

Termination of executory contracts with general
  partner(s) or affiliates
Reports after removal

Article XI. Meetings and Voting Rights
  Notice of meetings
  One vote per unit

Voting rights of the limited partners
Consents

Article XII. Partnership Expenses
  Reimbursement to general partner(s)
  Expenses of general partner(s)—nonreimbursable

Direct payment of partnership expenses
Payment of expenses of the partnership

Article XIII. Amendments of Partnership Documents
  Amendments in general
  Amendments requiring greater than a majority rule

Amendments by the general partner(s)

Article XIV. Borrowings
  Loans by the general partner(s) to the partnership
  Loans by the partnership to the general partner(s)
    or others

Commercial loans

Article XV. Representations and Warranties of the Partners
  General partner(s)
  Limited partners

Indemnification by limited partners

Article XVI. Miscellaneous Provisions
  Notices
  Article section headings
  Construction
  Severability
  Choice of venue and law
  Counterparts
  Entire agreement
  Amended certificates of limited partnership
  Power of attorney to the general partner(s)
  Further assurances
  Successors and assigns

Waiver of action for partition
Attorneys' fees
Creditors
Remedies
Authority
Tax elections
Legends
Signatures
Election to be governed by successor or different
  limited partnership law
Arbitration

Exhibits
  Description of property to be acquired
  Name, address, number of limited partnership units
    and capital contributions of each limited partner

3
Financing for Real Estate Investments

Key Terms

all-inclusive loan
amortization
ARMS
assumable
CAPS
ceiling
collateral
construction loans
contract for deed
deed of trust
default
draws
due on sale
exculpatory clause
FHA
foreclosure
graduated payment loans
hypothecation

index
interim loans
leverage
lien
lis pendens
mortgage
negative amortization
note
other people's money (OPM)
sale-leaseback-buyback
split-fee financing
subject to
take out loans
term loan
VA
variable interest rate
work out
wraparound loan

The importance of finance in real estate investments is axiomatic. The profitability of most transactions is based primarily on financial arrangements designed to enlarge the returns on investments. The appropriate application of **leverage** may dramatically increase investors' profit margins—but often their risks as well.

In its simplest form, real estate finance includes the pledge of real property as **collateral** to back up a borrower's promise to repay a loan. If a default occurs, the lender is legally entitled to acquire full ownership of the pledged property and sell it to recover the balance owed.

In a broader sense, the financing relationship is described in terms of *rights* pledged as collateral for a loan. Borrowers *hypothecate* (pledge) their rights to a lender but continue to own and control the property throughout the term of the loan. In this relationship, the lender holds equitable title to the property, which can be perfected into full legal ownership if the borrower defaults.

Hypothecation implies that a borrower may acquire or continue occupancy and control of the real estate pledged as collateral for a loan. Thus, a borrower may live in, rent out, farm and otherwise continue to use and benefit from property that is itself encumbered by the lien of a real estate loan, as long as the terms of the loan are followed.

This, then, explains one of the basic attractions of real estate as an important investment vehicle. An owner may control a large, valuable property with relatively small amounts of money. This process, known as *leverage,* is the use of small amounts of money to control valuable properties through financing. Thus, with a 10 percent cash down payment, a purchaser might conceivably be able to buy a $100,000 property with an investment of only $10,000 and a $90,000 loan.

$$\begin{array}{r} \$100,000 \\ \times \quad 10\% \\ \hline \$\ 10,000 \end{array}$$

$$\begin{array}{r} \$100,000 \\ -\ 10,000 \\ \hline \$\ 90,000 \end{array}$$

Leverage gives investors a powerful tool for the potential accumulation of large estates in their lifetimes. In fact, many investors strive to apply leverage to the greatest extent possible in order to control many highly valued properties with a minimum amount of their own money. This approach preserves an investor's other liquid assets, which can then be used to solve the specific problems that inevitably arise in the course of property ownership and management.

Leverage also acts to increase yields substantially, as revealed in the following examples:

Impact of Leverage			
Purchase Price	Down Payment	Net Sale Profit	Yield
$100,000	$100,000	$20,000	20%
100,000	50,000	20,000	40%
100,000	20,000	20,000	100%
100,000	-0-	20,000	infinite

Leverage couples high returns with high risks. Since large mortgages require large payments, rental cash flows need to be carefully maintained at levels adequate to meet these obligations. Any slight rental decrease could adversely affect a highly leveraged investor's safety position.

SOURCES OF FUNDS

Generally, our economy is based on the power of credit—using **other people's money (OPM)**. The philosophy of "buy now and pay later" is precisely what real estate finance is all about. However, despite the pressures for increased use of credit in this country, the need for savings should also be emphasized, since without savings there would be no credit! Most lending is based on savings accumulated through accounts and certificates at banks and savings institutions, premiums paid to life insurance companies and pension and retirement fund contributions. Table 3.1 illustrates the amount of loans outstanding at a point in time by various types of lenders. Note that the total amount of loans exceeds $4 trillion, a dramatic testimony to the importance of real estate finance in our economy.

The inventory of lenders for real estate finance may be divided into three general categories: fiduciary, semifiduciary and nonfiduciary. These groups are distinguished by the degree of responsibility exercised by the specific lenders in each category.

Fiduciary Lenders

Fiduciary lenders, charged with expressing the highest degree of responsibility to their principals, include commercial banks, savings institutions and life insurance companies. Displaying a generally conservative attitude toward real estate finance, these fiduciaries, also called *financial intermediaries,* are charged with preserving the quality and quantity of their depositors' and premium payers' monies. This responsibility is manifest in the careful screening of each loan applicant's credit and the studious examination of the collateral property's value.

Commercial Banks.   Originally designed to serve only the commercial checking needs of their customers, commercial banks now offer a full spectrum of checking and savings accounts as well as other services, including real estate loans. However, they prefer to participate in relatively short-term loans to maximize their market position.

The short-term real estate mortgages that attract commercial banks include construction loans, home improvement loans and mobile-home loans. **Construction loans**, also known as **interim loans**, are designed to finance real estate developments during their construction stage. These interim loans are replaced by more permanent types of financing, called **take out loans**, once construction is completed. A construction lender usually requires a borrower to secure a written take out loan commitment before issuing an interim loan.

Usually, the contractor for a new building requires regular funding during the course of construction to meet the payroll and purchase the materials necessary to the building process. However, because the contractor has no building to pledge as collateral for a loan at the outset of the development process, a lender cannot be expected to issue a check for the full amount of the loan until the collateral is actually constructed in the manner and quality specified in the plans.

TABLE 3.1   Mortgage Debt Outstanding

1.54   MORTGAGE DEBT OUTSTANDING[1]

Millions of dollars, end of period

Type of holder and property	1990	1991	1992	1992 Q4	1993 Q1	Q2	Q3	Q4P
1 All holders	3,761,525	3,923,371	4,042,645	4,042,645	4,059,199	4,099,591	4,155,690	4,218,693
By type of property								
2 One- to four-family residences	2,615,435	2,778,803	2,953,527	2,953,527	2,975,134	3,024,789	3,085,698	3,146,381
3 Multifamily residences	309,369	306,410	294,976	294,976	294,042	291,178	290,679	292,052
4 Commercial	758,313	759,023	713,701	713,701	708,966	702,210	698,299	699,488
5 Farm	78,408	79,136	80,441	80,441	81,057	81,414	81,014	80,772
By type of holder								
6 Major financial institutions	1,914,315	1,846,726	1,769,187	1,769,187	1,753,045	1,765,176	1,768,931	1,777,772
7 Commercial banks[2]	844,826	876,100	894,513	894,513	891,755	910,989	922,492	940,547
8 One- to four-family	455,931	483,623	507,780	507,780	507,497	526,817	538,906	556,778
9 Multifamily	37,015	36,935	38,024	38,024	37,425	38,058	37,621	38,150
10 Commercial	334,648	337,095	328,826	328,826	326,853	325,519	325,124	324,749
11 Farm	17,231	18,447	19,882	19,882	19,980	20,595	20,841	20,870
12 Savings institutions[3]	801,628	705,367	627,972	627,972	617,163	612,458	609,584	603,559
13 One- to four-family	600,154	538,358	489,622	489,622	480,415	480,722	478,297	472,492
14 Multifamily	91,806	79,881	69,791	69,791	70,608	68,303	68,649	68,533
15 Commercial	109,168	86,741	68,235	68,235	65,808	63,111	62,318	62,214
16 Farm	500	388	324	324	332	322	320	319
17 Life insurance companies	267,861	265,258	246,702	246,702	244,128	241,729	236,855	233,667
18 One- to four-family	13,005	11,547	11,441	11,441	11,316	11,195	10,967	10,814
19 Multifamily	28,979	29,562	27,770	27,770	27,466	27,174	26,620	26,248
20 Commercial	215,121	214,105	198,269	198,269	196,100	194,012	190,061	187,403
21 Farm	10,756	10,044	9,222	9,222	9,246	9,348	9,206	9,201
22 Federal and related agencies	239,003	266,146	286,263	286,263	287,081	298,991	309,579	321,907
23 Government National Mortgage Association	20	19	30	30	45	45	43	43
24 One- to four-family	20	19	30	30	37	38	37	37
25 Multifamily	0	0	0	0	8	7	7	7
26 Farmers Home Administration[4]	41,439	41,713	41,695	41,695	41,529	41,446	41,424	41,386
27 One- to four-family	18,527	18,496	16,912	16,912	16,536	16,133	15,714	15,303
28 Multifamily	9,640	10,141	10,575	10,575	10,650	10,739	10,830	10,940
29 Commercial	4,690	4,905	5,158	5,158	5,187	5,250	5,347	5,406
30 Farm	8,582	8,171	9,050	9,050	9,156	9,324	9,533	9,739
31 Federal Housing and Veterans' Administrations	8,801	10,733	12,581	12,581	13,027	12,945	11,797	12,215
32 One- to four-family	3,593	4,036	5,153	5,153	5,631	5,635	4,850	5,364
33 Multifamily	5,208	6,697	7,428	7,428	7,396	7,311	6,947	6,851
34 Resolution Trust Corporation	32,600	45,822	32,045	32,045	27,331	21,973	19,925	17,284
35 One- to four-family	15,800	14,535	12,960	12,960	11,375	8,955	8,381	7,202
36 Multifamily	8,064	15,018	9,621	9,621	8,070	6,743	6,002	5,284
37 Commercial	8,736	16,269	9,464	9,464	7,886	6,275	5,543	4,797
38 Farm	0	0	0	0	0	0	0	0
39 Federal National Mortgage Association	104,870	112,283	137,584	137,584	141,192	151,513	160,721	166,642
40 One- to four-family	94,323	100,387	124,016	124,016	127,252	137,340	146,009	151,310
41 Multifamily	10,547	11,896	13,568	13,568	13,940	14,173	14,712	15,332
42 Federal Land Banks	29,416	28,767	28,664	28,664	28,536	28,592	28,810	28,860
43 One- to four-family	1,838	1,693	1,687	1,687	1,679	1,682	1,695	1,698
44 Farm	27,577	27,074	26,977	26,977	26,857	26,909	27,115	27,162
45 Federal Home Loan Mortgage Corporation	21,857	26,809	33,665	33,665	35,421	42,477	46,859	55,476
46 One- to four-family	19,185	24,125	31,032	31,032	32,831	39,905	44,315	52,929
47 Multifamily	2,672	2,684	2,633	2,633	2,589	2,572	2,544	2,547
48 Mortgage pools or trusts[5]	1,079,103	1,250,666	1,425,546	1,425,546	1,462,181	1,473,323	1,514,002	1,546,818
49 Government National Mortgage Association	403,613	425,295	419,516	419,516	421,514	413,166	415,076	414,066
50 One- to four-family	391,505	415,767	410,675	410,675	412,798	404,425	405,963	404,864
51 Multifamily	12,108	9,528	8,841	8,841	8,716	8,741	9,113	9,202
52 Federal Home Loan Mortgage Corporation	316,359	359,163	407,514	407,514	420,932	422,882	430,089	439,029
53 One- to four-family	308,369	351,906	401,525	401,525	415,279	417,646	425,154	434,494
54 Multifamily	7,990	7,257	5,989	5,989	5,654	5,236	4,935	4,535
55 Federal National Mortgage Association	299,833	371,984	444,979	444,979	457,316	465,220	481,880	495,525
56 One- to four-family	291,194	362,667	435,979	435,979	448,483	456,645	473,599	486,804
57 Multifamily	8,639	9,317	9,000	9,000	8,833	8,575	8,281	8,721
58 Farmers Home Administration[4]	66	47	38	38	34	32	30	28
59 One- to four-family	17	11	8	8	7	6	6	5
60 Multifamily	0	0	0	0	0	0	0	0
61 Commercial	24	19	17	17	16	15	14	13
62 Farm	26	17	13	13	11	11	10	10
63 Private mortgage conduits	59,232	94,177	153,499	153,499	162,385	172,023	186,927	198,171
64 One- to four-family	53,335	84,000	132,000	132,000	137,000	145,000	158,000	164,000
65 Multifamily	731	3,698	6,305	6,305	6,665	7,407	7,991	8,701
66 Commercial	5,166	6,479	15,194	15,194	18,720	19,616	20,936	25,469
67 Farm	0	0	0	0	0	0	0	0
68 Individuals and others[6]	529,104	559,833	561,649	561,649	556,892	562,101	563,178	572,196
69 One- to four-family	348,638	367,633	372,708	372,708	366,998	372,645	373,805	382,288
70 Multifamily	85,969	83,796	85,430	85,430	86,023	86,140	86,428	87,000
71 Commercial	80,761	93,410	88,538	88,538	88,396	88,412	88,956	89,438
72 Farm	13,737	14,994	14,973	14,973	15,474	14,904	13,990	13,471

1. Based on data from various institutional and governmental sources; figures for some quarters estimated in part by the Federal Reserve. Multifamily debt refers to loans on structures of five or more units.
2. Includes loans held by nondeposit trust companies but not loans held by bank trust departments.
3. Includes savings banks and savings and loan associations.
4. FmHA-guaranteed securities sold to the Federal Financing Bank were reallocated from FmHA mortgage pools to FmHA mortgage holdings in 1986:Q4 because of accounting changes by the Farmers Home Administration.

5. Outstanding principal balances of mortgage-backed securities insured or guaranteed by the agency indicated.
6. Other holders include mortgage companies, real estate investment trusts, state and local credit agencies, state and local retirement funds, noninsured pension funds, credit unions, and finance companies.
SOURCES. Based on data from various institutional and government sources. Separation of nonfarm mortgage debt by type of property, if not reported directly, and interpolations and extrapolations, when required, are estimated mainly by the Federal Reserve. Line 64, from Inside Mortgage Securities.

To solve this dilemma, the interim loan is funded through a series of **draws**. Whenever a specified stage of construction has been completed to the lender's satisfaction, a portion of the entire loan is released to the contractor, providing the funds to pay for the services and materials used to date. Each time another stage is completed, another draw is issued, until the building's completion, when the final draw is paid.

When construction is completed to everyone's satisfaction, the interim loan is usually replaced by a permanent long-term mortgage. In this manner, the increasing value of the collateral matches the growing balance of the loan as draws are issued, thereby protecting the lender. In the event of a default during the construction period, the lender will foreclose on the collateral, even though it is unfinished, and either sell it to recover the monies already distributed or complete the project, depending on the market.

To ensure this recovery, an interim lender usually requires that the underlying land be free and clear of any financial encumbrances and that it be pledged as collateral for the loan. In this manner, the lender acquires a margin of safety, called an *equity cushion*. In a situation involving a leasehold mortgage, the lender requires a subordination agreement, as discussed in chapter 2.

Home improvement loans are another short-term lending activity engaged in by commercial banks. These loans are of particular significance to those investors who purchase rundown properties for repair and resale. Issued to cover the costs of room additions, swimming pool installations or other remodeling requirements, home improvement loans usually take a second lien position behind an existing first lien. Some lenders have made available combination loans for purchase and rehab.

Mobile-home loans are usually of shorter duration, and they appeal to commercial banks and finance companies. These loans have become particularly successful because the FHA and VA have accepted them as eligible for mortgage insurance and guarantees. Some of these loans are for the mobile units only, while others include the land as well (Landpak).

Savings Institutions.   Mutual savings banks, savings and loan associations and savings banks provide most of the long-term loans for single family, owner-occupied housing. Dealing primarily in conventional loans, these institutions invest most of their assets in real estate financing.

In the past, limitations imposed on savings institutions by federal and state regulating agencies restricted their service areas. Savings institutions invariably developed as neighborhood banks, with their lending capacity limited by the quantity of deposits they attracted. In today's real estate market, any limitations on area have been eliminated by participation in the secondary mortgage market.

Life Insurance Companies.   The nation's life insurance companies invest approximately one-third of their assets in long-term mortgage loans and participate predominantly in the financing of large commercial real estate developments. These companies provide most of the funds needed to develop apartment and office buildings as well as shopping centers and industrial projects.

Over the past few years, many of this nation's banks and savings institutions have suffered terrible setbacks caused by declining markets, inflated appraisals, loss of economic and employment bases and TRA '86. Although not all banks and thrifts have been affected, those that have been are gradually being reorganized or absorbed by healthy institutions.

In the process, the Federal Reserve has emerged as the governing body for all financial fiduciaries and has established a strong depositors' insurance program under the Federal Deposit Insurance Corporation (FDIC). The FDIC has effectively replaced the bankrupt Federal Savings and Loan Insurance Corporation (FSLIC).

Many of the problems of the troubled organizations originated in the loosened controls following banking deregulation in 1980, which allowed these financial fiduciaries the opportunities to expand their profit potentials by making direct investments in business and real estate ventures. In the excitement generated by this newfound power, many inexperienced and some dishonest financiers became involved in high-risk investments that failed. The bailout of these failed institutions is an ongoing situation and, it is estimated, will cost taxpayers hundreds of billions of dollars.

Semifiduciary Lenders

Semifiduciary lenders act somewhat independently from principal depositors and premium payers. Included in these sources for real estate finance are retirement and pension funds, mortgage brokers and bankers, issuers of improvement district and industrial development bonds, credit unions and real estate investment and mortgage trusts. These companies retain a high degree of internal discretion regarding their investment decisions and are not regulated as closely as the primary fiduciaries.

Retirement and Pension Funds. Although federal legislation has imposed greater controls over the financing activities of these entities, they are still able to make many independent decisions regarding the kinds of real estate loans they issue. Their autonomy allows them to participate in financing speculative land-development projects as well as to invest in more stable real estate ventures.

As with the full fiduciaries, retirement and pension funds often invest in real estate financing through the services of mortgage brokers and bankers.

Mortgage Brokers and Mortgage Bankers. Acting as representatives, or correspondents, for their investors, mortgage brokers and bankers are semifiduciary sources of real estate finance. These companies are not primarily responsible to depositors or premium payers but are directly accountable to their investors, who rely upon these loan originators and servicers to underwrite new loans carefully and according to established lending standards.

Mortgage brokers bring together borrower and lender, confirm the loan arrangement, charge the borrower a placement fee and move on to the next transaction. Mortgage bankers, on the other hand, not only originate loans and secure fees for these activities but also *service* these loans by collecting payments, periodically inspecting the collateral and supervising any necessary foreclosure actions. In effect, a mortgage banker becomes the lender's local representative, responsible for a loan from inception through satisfaction, whereas a mortgage broker primarily acts as a catalyst in the creation of a new loan.

Real Estate Bonds.   Many communities finance municipal, industrial and housing developments with the issuance of bonds. These debts are repaid from property taxes, rental receipts and mortgage payments collected from tenants and owners of the various properties.

Individual subdivision developers may also be eligible to finance the installation of off-site improvements—including sewer and utility lines, street paving, sidewalks and similar items—by issuing improvement district bonds. In some areas of the country, these bonds are the specific obligation of the property owners within the district. In other areas, these bonds can become general obligation bonds, to be paid by the community through property taxes.

Real Estate Investment and Mortgage Trusts.   REITs and REMTs are semifiduciary sources of money for real estate finance. Acquiring their funds through the sale of beneficial interests to the public, these trusts make loans for construction mortgages as well as for permanent long-term mortgages on improved income properties. Acting mainly through the services of mortgage brokers and bankers, the trusts provide the extra flexibility in loan placements often vitally needed for the completion of complex realty projects.

Credit Unions.   Although credit unions are primarily active in financing personal property acquisitions for their members, their increasing popularity is allowing them to expand their investments to include short-term and long-term real estate loans.

Nonfiduciary Lenders

In addition to these financial intermediaries, there is a third category. This group includes title insurance companies and private lenders who often become financiers when carrying back loans to help sell their own properties. Because these lenders maintain complete discretion over their loan decisions and are not responsible to anyone but themselves, they are called *nonfiduciaries*.

Title Insurance Companies.   The title insurance companies are a relatively untapped source for financing real estate subdivision developments. These firms have a natural attraction to real estate investments as potential sources for the development of new title insurance business.

Although some arrangements might include financing the purchase of raw acreage, a title company would be more inclined to finance off-site improvements in a subdivision, such as streets, sidewalks, sewers and so on. This financing would normally be in the form of a blanket mortgage secured by all of the lots in the project. The mortgage would be repaid gradually as each lot was sold, with a portion of the proceeds applied to reducing the balance owed.

In exchange for this loan, the title company would expect to receive a fair-market interest return on its investment plus exclusive representation as the title insurer for the entire project. In addition, it is often expedient to arrange for the title company to act as the closing escrow agent for all subdivision sales and mortgage loans.

Individuals.   Another important source of real estate financing is the seller who, to facilitate the sale of property, agrees to accept a portion of the equity in the form of a carryback mortgage, land contract or wraparound agreement.

Other individuals enter into mortgage lending by forming companies designed specifically for this purpose. These private lending companies generally provide junior mortgage loans to property owners who wish to capitalize on their equity.

To balance and manage an investment portfolio more efficiently, real estate investors should be fully acquainted with all the various mortgage loan opportunities in their specific geographic areas, including lender attitudes, loan costs and availability of funds.

FORMS OF REAL ESTATE FINANCE

When property is pledged as collateral for a loan, three basic forms are utilized to establish the desired lender-borrower relationship, depending on the area of the country. The basic forms are the note and mortgage, deed of trust and contract for deed or real estate contract.

Note and Mortgage

The note and mortgage form of financing requires that the borrower-mortgagor pledge the property and all the rights therein to a lender-mortgagee in exchange for a loan. The borrower retains legal fee ownership, while the lender secures an equitable interest in the collateral, an interest that can be expanded into a full legal fee if the borrower defaults.

Because borrowers retain legal fee title, they enjoy certain redemption privileges in the event of a foreclosure action depending on the laws of the state in which the property is located. For instance, in the state of Alabama, a borrower may combine equitable and statutory redemption periods for up to two years, during which time the property can be redeemed and ownership continued. Other states have varying redemption periods under the note and mortgage form, with most averaging approximately six months before a defaulted borrower's legal ownership is foreclosed.

In this form of finance, the **note** is the actual contract for the repayment of the debt, while the **mortgage** is the pledge of real estate to secure the promise to pay. A note by itself is legal evidence of a debt and stipulates the conditions of the loan and the terms of repayment. A mortgage, which always needs a note to be legally enforceable, describes the collateral and rights being pledged.

Deed of Trust

With one exception, the note and deed used to establish a **deed of trust** financing relationship parallel the note and mortgage. With the deed of trust, the borrower-trustor actually deeds the legal fee in the collateral to a third-party trustee to hold in trust subject to the lien of the lender-beneficiary. When the loan is paid in full, the trustee reconveys the property to the trustor. State laws vary regarding the use of deed of trust. In California, for instance, it is not absolutely necessary for a note to accompany the trust deed. In Washington, the trust deed arrangement is worded so that the property vests in the trustee only in the event of a default.

The deed of trust financing arrangement acts to shorten a borrower's redemption period from as long as one year (under a note and mortgage) to as little as 90 days. In the event of a default, the trustee is empowered by the terms of the trust agreement to sell the collateral at public auction after having followed the letter of the law. This procedure includes provisions for adequate notice to all concerned parties and prescribed time periods for all events of default through foreclosure.

As with a mortgage, any proceeds from the auction sale must first be applied to the costs of the sale. The remaining funds are then distributed to the beneficiary, to all junior lienors and finally, but rarely, to the trustor.

The deed of trust is currently being used in the District of Columbia and the following states:

Alaska	Idaho	Tennessee
Arizona	Mississippi	Texas
California	Missouri	Virginia
Colorado	Nevada	Washington
Georgia	North Carolina	West Virginia

Contract for Deed

Known by many other names—such as real estate contract, land contract, bond for deed, agreement of sale and contract of sale—this form of financing instrument is utilized primarily between individual sellers (lenders) and buyers (borrowers), not with banks or savings institutions. A **contract for deed** is not accompanied by a note but is a single complete agreement, granting physical possession to the buyer-borrower-vendee at the same time that it establishes the financing agreement with the seller-lender-vendor.

Contracts for deed are usually employed in situations in which the seller of a property is helping the buyer complete the purchase by carrying back a loan for a portion of the seller's equity in the property. In such a case, a contract for deed is executed between the buyer and seller for the amount of the seller's equity.

The legal fee remains in the name of the *seller*, while the buyer secures an equitable title in the property as well as its possession and control. When the terms of the loan contract are met, the seller delivers a deed to the buyer, the recording of which is evidence of the loan's satisfaction.

A variation of this form of financing is the wraparound contract, in which there is existing underlying financing that the purchaser will not assume and that will continue to be the responsibility of the contract holder.

Some pitfalls of the contract for deed form of financing include

- providing for transfer of title on the seller's demise prior to contract's satisfaction. (Frequently this can be accomplished through the establishment at the time of the sale of a collection escrow where the vendor places the deed until the terms of the contract are fulfilled. Placing the deed into escrow means that the deed theoretically has already been transferred, it is out of the vendor's possession, and it is free from liens and judgments.);
- providing for protection of title in case of litigation against the seller; and
- determining priority of intervening liens.

Maintaining legal title in the collateral during the term of the loan gives the seller certain foreclosure powers not available in either the mortgage or deed of trust forms. Basically, the buyer's redemption periods are dramatically reduced, sometimes to as little as 30 days. Certain states, fearful that this foreclosure power may be used arbitrarily or capriciously, prohibit or seriously inhibit the use of contracts for deed as a form of financing.

TYPES OF REAL ESTATE FINANCE

The three forms of finance—the note and mortgage, deed of trust and contract for deed—may be used to serve the particular needs of the principals in a real estate transaction. Generally, the mortgage and trust deed forms are used by financial fiduciaries and are designed to be in senior loan position, with priority over any and all intervening liens. The contract for deed can also be a senior loan when the seller-vendor owns property free and clear and carries back such a contract. However, most land contracts are established as junior loans.

A **lien** is a legal claim against a specific property, whereby the property is made the security for the performance of some act, usually the repayment of a debt. A lien can be either voluntary, as with a mortgage, or involuntary, as with a tax lien or judgment.

A mortgage loan becomes a voluntary lien as of the precise time of its recording at the office of the recording official of the county in which the property is located. The property's recorded history will be carefully reviewed prior to the granting of a new loan, and all prerecorded encumbrances will have to be satisfied. This procedure establishes that the new lender's rights are superior to the rights of any subsequent lien holders. Thus, the legal doctrine of "first in time, first in right" acts to protect a lender's senior lien position.

Senior Loans

The financial fiduciaries described previously—the commercial banks, savings institutions and life insurance companies—are required by their licensing and regulating agencies to practice the highest possible degree of financial responsibility. They are totally prohibited from placing their customers' funds in jeopardy when making investment decisions. Consequently, the real estate financing activities of these fiduciaries are normally limited to senior mortgages and deeds of trust. They usually adopt a conservative approach to lending, including a thorough analysis of a borrower's credit and a complete evaluation of the property to be pledged as collateral.

In the event of a foreclosure, these fiduciaries will seek to recover any funds still unpaid through the sale of the collateral. To exercise their primary fiduciary responsibility, these lenders must be in senior lien position against the subject property at all times. The creation of any intervening liens jeopardizes a fiduciary lender's chances of recovery at a foreclosure sale and constitutes a breach of the loan contract. Generally, senior loans are either conventional, insured or guaranteed loans.

Conventional Loans.   Although many conventional loans are insured by private mortgage insurance companies (PMI), some do not have any insurance or guarantee by a third party. These uninsured conventional loans rely completely on the borrower to meet all obligations when due.

To offset the risk implicit in this arrangement, a conventional lender will not only qualify both borrower and property conscientiously but will also require that a borrower have a prescribed amount of personal funds invested in cash in the property. This equity investment provides the lender a safety cushion in the event of a default.

The amount of this equity cushion establishes the loan-to-value ratios employed by lenders to determine the amounts of loans to be made. Historically, lenders required that a borrower pay 50 percent of a property's value as a cash down payment before a loan for the balance would be issued. These equity requirements gradually diminished from 50 percent to 33 percent to current requirements of between 20 and 25 percent, thus allowing a conventional mortgage to be placed at about 80 percent of a property's value.

This equity requirement acts to protect lenders by tightly tying borrowers to their property ownership. A borrower who has invested personal funds of 20 to 25 percent would be unlikely to undermine the value of the property or walk away from it. The periodic decrease in the loan balance each month, coupled with a possible rise in the property's value because of inflation and physical improvements, increase an owner's equity from the very first payment. A conventional senior first mortgage, therefore, is most unlikely to go into default.

Insured or Guaranteed Loans.   Unfortunately, a conventional lender's requirement of 20 percent equity effectively eliminates many potential property owners who cannot meet these cash reserves but are financially responsible and capable of meeting payment requirements. To solve the dilemma of reducing down payments yet preserving the fiduciary integrity of the institutional lenders, a system of mortgage insurance and guarantees has been developed. Loans can be insured either by the Federal Housing Administration (FHA) or by private mortgage insurance companies, or else they can be guaranteed by the Veterans Administration (VA).

The **FHA** *home loan insurance program*, under section 203(b)—which accounts for three-fourths of all FHA-insured mortgages—currently uses the following formula for determining insurable loan-to-value ratios on owner-occupied, single-family residences:

- The down payment is 3 percent on acquisition prices of $50,000 or less.
- For more expensive properties, the down payment is 3 percent of the first $25,000, 5 percent of the amount between $25,000 and $125,000 and 10 percent of the amount over $125,000, up to the maximum amount allowable in different areas of the country.

For example, the buyer of a $50,000 home would need a down payment of $1,500,

$$\begin{array}{r} \$50,000 \\ \times \quad 3\% \\ \hline \$\ 1,500 \end{array}$$

whereas the buyer of a $200,000 home would need a down payment of $13,250.

$$\begin{array}{r} \$25,000 \\ \times \quad 3\% \\ \hline \$\quad 750 \end{array} + \begin{array}{r} \$100,000 \\ \times \quad 5\% \\ \hline \$\ 5,000 \end{array} + \begin{array}{r} \$75,000 \\ \times \quad 10\% \\ \hline \$\ 7,500 \end{array} = \$13,250.$$

The **VA** stands behind eligible veterans and guarantees a lender that the loan balance will be repaid in the event of a default. Although the VA guarantee and FHA mortgage insurance programs are alike in principle, they differ in one important respect: unlike the FHA program, which insures the total balance due throughout the term of a loan, the VA plan covers only the top portion of a loan's balance.

The FHA charges an insurance premium, currently at the rate of 2.25 percent of the loan amount. This can be paid in cash at loan closing or added to the loan and amortized over the loan period. In addition, the borrower pays an annual premium of 0.5 percent, which is payable monthly. If the loan is prepaid, with the proper application, the borrower may recover the unused portion of the premium. The VA charges a funding fee ranging between 1 percent and 2 percent, depending on the down payment, to be paid in cash at closing or added to the loan amount.

The VA guarantee varies from 25 percent of the loan balance to a maximum amount of $46,000. Thus, lenders can seek reimbursement from the VA for only a portion of any defaulted loan. However, because most lenders are willing to absorb 80 percent of a property's value as an in-house risk, as evidenced by the conventional mortgage loan-to-value ratio, the top portion of a loan is specifically what a lender needs to have guaranteed. As a result, a qualified veteran can utilize the VA guarantee in place of the standard 20 percent down payment and purchase a property for up to $184,000 with no down payment.

There is no upper limit to the value of a property eligible for a VA loan guarantee. The veteran would simply pay cash down to any mortgage amount acquired. This VA program is applicable to owner-occupied, single-family homes and owner-occupied apartment buildings of four units or less.

Private mortgage insurance companies participate in guaranteeing the top 5 to 25 percent of a conventional senior loan. The borrower pays an insurance fee commensurate with the risk—the higher the loan-to-value ratio, the greater the risk and the larger the premium. In the event of a default, the lender looks to the guarantor for the amount of compensation agreed upon, forecloses on the property and sells it at auction to recover the difference. Private mortgage insurance (PMI) may be described as "default insurance" or "equity insurance" since it does not protect the borrower, just the lender.

Income Property Loans

When making loans on residential income, commercial and industrial properties, lenders must evaluate many variables. In addition to the property's value and the credit characteristics of the borrowers, the lenders must consider the possibility that they may wind up managing the property in the event of a foreclosure.

Following guidelines established by the Federal National Mortgage Association (FNMA) for purchase of commercial loans, lenders carefully examine the ability of the income from the property to support the debt service required to amortize the loan. Thus, the amount of the loan is established as a function of the property's net income and down payment, and debt ratios are adjusted accordingly.

To qualify for an income property loan, the following items require examination:

- personal financial statements,
- property income statements,
- appraisals and feasibility studies and
- the borrower's management track record.

Junior Loans

Most real estate transactions are finalized when a buyer secures a new senior loan for the major portion of the property's value, with the balance paid as a cash down payment. Frequently, however, a buyer will require additional financing in the form of a second mortgage or contract for deed to offset the burdens of heavy front-end cash requirements. These junior loans are usually established between the individual parties to a real estate transaction, with the seller carrying back a portion of the equity in the form of a second mortgage.

With the increasing costs of real estate, junior loans are often necessary to complete many sales. In some areas of this country it is virtually impossible to complete a sale without a second mortgage, and sometimes a third encumbrance is required.

Alternative Types of Finance

The three basic forms of real estate finance—the note and mortgage, trust deed and contract for deed—are employed as either senior or junior loans. The structures of these instruments are flexible and therefore adaptable to fit almost every contingency. In addition, special forms of these instruments can be designed to finance unique real estate situations, such as the wraparound, the sale-leaseback and the joint venture.

Wraparound Encumbrances.   One of the most useful forms of junior loans is the **wraparound loan,** also called an **all-inclusive loan**. The unique feature of a *wrap* is that it creates a new loan that encompasses any existing loans without disturbing the legal priority of any underlying encumbrances. The wraparound loan cannot be used to bypass a due-on-sale clause, but it can be drawn at a higher rate of interest than the underlying encumbrances.

EXAMPLE: Assume that a property is to be sold for $100,000, with a $10,000 (10 percent) cash down payment made by the buyer and a $90,000 wraparound mortgage carried back by the seller at 10 percent interest. The seller's existing mortgage has a $70,000 balance, which is payable at 8 ½ percent interest. Thus, the seller actually has a $20,000 equity in the wrap and will be earning a full 10 percent on this amount plus a 1 ½ percent override on the first mortgage balance.

Property Sales Price	$100,000
Buyer's Cash Down Payment 10%	− 10,000
Wraparound Mortgage (to be carried back by Seller) Interest on Wraparound Loan 10%	$ 90,000
Seller's Existing Mortgage Interest Rate 8 1/2%	$ 70,000
	$ 20,000 Seller's Equity

Seller earns 10% on Equity Amount PLUS
1½ % on First Mortgage Balance

$$\begin{array}{cc} \$10,000 & \$35,000 \\ \times\quad .10 & \times\ .0150 \\ \hline 1,000 & 525 \end{array} + \quad 525 = \$1,525 \quad + \quad \$10,000 = .1525$$

OR an effective annual earning rate of 15.25%

Obviously this yield, which is as high or higher than that offered by many alternative investments, may go a long way to relieve the reluctance of a seller who must carry back a junior loan to complete a sale of a property.

A wrap can assume any of the three major financing forms—a mortgage, a deed of trust or a contract for deed. It can be designed to incorporate any and all of the special clauses to be discussed later in this chapter. Because of its relative simplicity, it allows great flexibility in its design.

Sale-Leasebacks.   Another useful tool of real estate finance, the sale lease-back, is utilized primarily in large-project real estate transactions. In this situation, the owners of a property sell it to investors and, simultaneously, lease it back. The rents established in the lease are based on a fair and prearranged return of the investment over the lease period. Thus, the investors are actually purchasing a guaranteed return on their investment while insuring its recovery.

The advantages of this form of finance to the seller-tenant include the immediate use of the cash proceeds from the sale and the opportunity to deduct the entire rental amount as an operational business expense. This deduction is particularly advantageous, because the rent is based on the value of the land *and* the buildings. If the seller were to retain ownership of the property, only depreciation on the buildings would be allowed as a deductible business expense. Thus, the sale-leaseback technique is used most effectively with properties already fully depreciated.

An additional advantage for the seller-tenant in this arrangement is that the obligation for the lease appears on the firm's balance sheet as an indirect liability, whereas a mortgage would be considered a direct liability that would adversely affect the firm's debt ratio in terms of obtaining future financing.

When the lease includes an option for the tenant to repurchase the property at the end of the lease term, it is called a **sale-leaseback-buyback**. However, care must be taken to establish the buyback price for a fair-market value at the time of sale. Otherwise the arrangement is considered a long-term installment mortgage and any income tax benefits that might have been enjoyed during the term of the lease will be disallowed. The buyback option is an important tool for the tenant because it effectively reestablishes a new depreciable basis when the property is repurchased.

Joint Ventures.   Also of great value as an investment financing tool for acquiring real estate is the joint venture. This technique is a form of equity participation that teams lenders, who advance most or all of a project's funds, with the developer, who contributes time and expertise, as partners and co-owners. Some joint venture participation arrangements can be expanded to include the landowner and the construction contractor as well as the financier and the developer.

A variation of this arrangement is **split-fee financing**. Here the *lender* purchases the land under the project and leases it to the developer while at the same time financing the improvements to be constructed on this leasehold. The land-lease payments are established at an agreed-on base rate plus a percentage of the profits from the building's revenues. Under this arrangement, the lender-investor benefits by receiving a fixed return (interest) on the loan investment, a flexible return on the land investment and possible residual benefits when the lease expires and clear ownership of the property is acquired. The developer has the advantage of high leverage and a fully depreciable leasehold asset.

SPECIAL PROVISIONS FOR INVESTMENT FINANCING

The variety of possible loan terms and conditions is virtually inexhaustible, complementing the sought-after quality of personal control usually required in real estate investments. Special financing clauses of particular importance to investors include prepayment arrangements, due-on-sale provisions, assumption privileges, exculpatory clauses and what are often called *creative financing arrangements*.

Prepayment Clauses

Prepayment provisions in a real estate loan may include the right to pay the debt in full before it is due, to impose penalties for any prepayment, to completely restrict prepayments for some designated time period or to make any combination of these terms.

Prepayment Privileges.   In the absence of any reference to prepayments in a loan contract, a borrower may satisfy the balance of the debt at any time without restriction or penalty. Some loans include a provision stipulating the total prepayments that may be made in any one year without penalty. Such a clause establishes a partial prepayment privilege.

Prepayment Penalties.   Normally, a lender will not want a high-interest-rate loan to be repaid prematurely. Hence, controls are established on prepayments of high-yield loans. One form of control is the inclusion of a prepayment penalty clause in the loan terms. This clause imposes a penalty on any prepaid sums, thereby compensating a lender for any loss in earnings caused by early repayment. These penalties generally range from 3 percent to 5 percent of the loan balance. In extreme cases, these percentages could be applied to the original loan amount. Some states have laws restricting such penalties.

Lock-in Clauses.   Some loans include a clause that prohibits any prepayment for a specified time period, often for as long as ten years. This stringent form of control, known as a lock-in clause, is placed on very high-yield loans to preserve a lender's earning position.

Often, combinations of prepayment conditions are incorporated into a single loan. For instance, a loan could restrict any prepayment for a certain time period, then allow proportionate prepayments to be made annually, and finally allow the balance of the loan to be repaid without restriction at the expiration of a specified term. Any deviations from the agreed-on formula would result in the imposition of penalties.

Due-on-Sale Clauses

Lenders usually include a due-on-sale clause in their loan contracts. Also known as a *call clause* or *transfer clause,* this provision stipulates that a borrower may not sell, transfer, encumber, assign, convey or in any way dispose of the collateral property or any part thereof without the express written consent of the lender. The **due-on-sale** clause goes on to state that if any of the foregoing events should occur without the lender's consent, the loan balance would immediately become due in full, with true jeopardy of foreclosure if not so paid.

The due-on-sale clause is designed to protect a lender from default by a subsequent buyer of property who assumes the original loan. Studies have shown that far fewer defaults and foreclosures occur against original borrowers than against second or third owners, a testimony to the credit-underwriting procedures of lenders.

Thus, in an assumption of an existing loan, the due-on-sale clause subjects the credit of a potential new owner to the rigorous scrutiny of a credit analyst. If the buyer's credit is found lacking, some adjustments in the loan provisions will be suggested. If these adjustments are not acceptable to the parties involved, the lender simply calls in the balance of the loan, requiring the parties to seek financing elsewhere.

A lender's imposition of this call power can seriously affect the easy salability of an encumbered property. The legality of the due-on-sale clause was challenged and, after conflicting high court decisions in many states, was ruled legally enforceable by the United States Supreme Court on June 28, 1982. However, the case, *Fidelity Federal Savings and Loan v. de la Cuesta,* pertained only to federally chartered savings associations and banks. On October 15, 1982, President Reagan signed into law the Garn-St. Germain Depository Institutions Act of 1982. Known as the Garn Bill, it defined clearly that all due-on-sale clauses are enforceable for all real estate loans.

Assumption Versus Subject-to Provisions

In the absence of a due-on-sale clause, existing financing is **assumable** by the buyers. A buyer who assumes an existing mortgage agrees to accept responsibility for repayment of the balance of the loan. In fact, the purchase of a property and the assumption of the existing loan legally place the buyer in the same liability position as the original makers of the note and mortgage and all intervening owners who had assumed the same loan. In other words, a lender can look to any and all persons who have assumed the loan for repayment and, in the event of a default, can hold them all personally liable for complete satisfaction of the balance of the loan

---

TABLE 3.2   Monthly Principal and Interest Per $1,000

Rate	15-Year Loan	30-Year Loan
5.00	7.91	5.37
5.50	8.17	5.68
6.00	8.44	6.00
6.50	8.71	6.32
7.00	8.99	6.66
7.50	9.28	7.00
8.00	9.56	7.34
8.50	9.85	7.69
9.00	10.15	8.05
9.50	10.45	8.41
10.00	10.75	8.78

To avoid the imposition of this personal liability when buying a property with an existing mortgage, and in the absence of a clause prohibiting such an approach, a purchaser may stipulate in the contract that the purchase is being made **subject to** the existing loan balance. This approach effectively eliminates this particular buyer's contingent personal liability in the event of a future default. Only the original borrower and any intervening assumers would be liable.

Exculpatory Clauses

An effective technique used to minimize a borrower's personal liability when creating a new loan is the inclusion of an **exculpatory clause** in the contract. This clause is designed to limit a borrower's personal liability exclusively to the property being pledged as collateral, thus eliminating any possible attachment of other assets in the event of a default. Most exculpatory clauses are between individuals because lending institutions avoid their use.

Alternative Financing Arrangements

Under most circumstances, a real estate loan is paid in regular monthly payments of principal and interest over a specified time period. This system is called **amortization.** Every payment is a function of the interaction among the loan amount, rate of interest and time of payments. Books of amortization tables are available for determining the monthly payments for any real estate loan. (See Table 3.2.)

The lack of money for real estate loans and the relatively high interest rates on what money is available combine to stimulate many innovative forms of finance. These alternative financing techniques include variable payment schedules as well as variable interest rates. They flourish as a way to enhance lenders' earnings while providing borrowers with affordable payments. Following are some of the more popular forms of creative financing.

Variable-Payment Schedules.   Under a loan contract, payments can be arranged to reflect the specific needs of the parties thereto. For instance, some borrowers require lower payments in initial loan periods, while others prefer to pay higher amounts during the early years. In the first instance, persons with limited earnings could enjoy the privilege of lower payments for a few years; in the second instance, higher-wage earners might choose to repay their loans earlier in anticipation of retirement.

Most variable-payment schedules are designed as *escalating loans,* also known as **graduated payment loans,** with lower early payments that gradually increase to reflect a borrower's improving economic status.

Most loans are designed to amortize the amount owed over a prescribed period of time. When payments are varied to reflect the needs of the loan participants, both interest and principal can be adjusted. To the extent that the principal portion of the payment is waived, an interest-only amount can be derived. Under this arrangement, the amount owed remains constant over time, and some provision must be made for this balance to be paid in full as a *balloon payment* at a specified *stop date*. This loan is then called a **term loan**.

When a portion of the interest is waived in addition to the principal, the loan amount owed will increase from payment to payment. This is called **negative amortization**, and unless some provisions are made for the payments to increase to include some principal as well as interest, the balloon payment will be higher than the original face amount of the loan. Negative amortization has fallen into disfavor in many parts of the country. However, it can be an excellent financial tool when properly managed.

Variable Interest Rates.   Most real estate loans are arranged to be repaid over relatively long periods of time at fixed interest rates. This procedure has proved to be somewhat less than efficient because interest rates fluctuate over time, sometimes quite dramatically.

As a result, a number of lending institutions are including **variable interest rate** clauses in their mortgages. This technique involves the development of a formula for payment computations based on an acceptable measuring unit called an **index** (such as the U.S. Treasury Bill Index or Cost of Funds Index), as an indication of current interest rates. Lenders will usually add a small margin amount to the index. If the index moves up a point, then the interest rate on the loan will be adjusted upward about 1½ percent. Likewise, if the index drops, so will the loan's interest rate.

Obviously, there are faults in this program. Any substantial change in the index could result in chaotic conditions for both the borrower and the lender. To offset the potential problem of drastic changes in interest rates, annual and lifetime **caps** are imposed on most variable rate loans. Thus, a 5 percent loan could include a two-point annual cap plus a six-point lifetime cap and the interest rate could be adjusted by two percentage points for each of three years, for a maximum rate of 11 percent.

A *shared appreciation mortgage* (SAM), also known as a *participation mortgage*, allows a lender to secure a share in the growing value of the property being financed. Normally, a lender will reduce the interest rate on a new loan in exchange for 25 to 50 percent of the property's increased value in five to seven years. Ownership remains in the borrower's name, but the note attests to the partnership agreement.

A *pledged account mortgage* (PAM) is another approach to lowering payments in the early periods of a loan. A PAM provides graduated payments for the borrower, full cash to the seller and level payments to the lender. The buyer-borrower under a PAM makes a down payment to the lender, not to the seller. This money is deposited into an interest-bearing account and is utilized to subsidize the borrower's payments over a period of time. The lender issues a 100-percent-of-value loan, cashing out the seller. The borrower then makes low payments in the first 12 months, subsidized by draw-downs from the reserve account to equal the normal payment needed to amortize the loan. Each year thereafter, for up to five years, the borrower's payments go up gradually each month while the subsidy diminishes accordingly. Ultimately the reserve is used up and the borrower's payments rise to adequately amortize the balance of the loan over its remaining period.

A *buy-down mortgage* is a variation of the PAM. A seller, builder, buyer, buyer's parents or any third party or combination of parties makes a lump-sum payment to the lender at the time the loan is originated. In exchange, the interest rate is lowered, making the payments more affordable.

A *rollover loan* is another effective technique for adjusting payments and interest. Long-term payout schedules are established, but three-year, four-year, or five-year stop dates are included. This forces the borrower to refinance accordingly and allows the lender to adjust interest rates and payment amounts.

Zero percent financing (ZPF) features loans at no interest. Offered by sellers who agree to carry back these loans to sell their properties, this arrangement requires that only principal payments be made until the loan amount is satisfied. The IRS imputes an interest rate on these transactions both to the borrower and to the seller, allowing the borrower a commensurate income tax deduction while charging the seller-lender tax on the imputed interest. The interest rate imputed is the current Treasury bills rate, adjusted twice a year.

A slight variation on this theme is the *growing equity mortgage* (GEM), in which the borrower regularly increases the principal portion of the payment over the required amortizing amount, reducing the loan term substantially.

The biweekly mortgage is an illustration of the GEM. By making one-half the loan payment twice a month, the borrower actually makes one full month's extra payment per year. This entire amount is applied to the principal and acts to reduce the amortization period.

A *lease-purchase-option* is still another form of creative financing. Here a lease is designed to include the terms and conditions of a purchase option at the expiration of the lease period. Often, portions of the rental payments are credited to the purchase price. If the rental payments are considered option payments, a seller can postpone income tax impacts until the option becomes due. If the option is exercised, the payments are treated as capital gains. If the option is not exercised, the payments are considered ordinary income (*Carl E. Koch*, 67 T. C. 71, 1977).

DEFAULTS AND FORECLOSURES

The basic responsibilities of the parties to a real estate financial contract are clear-cut. In exchange for money loaned, a borrower is obligated to

- repay the loan according to the conditions stipulated;
- preserve the value of the collateral; and
- protect the priority lien position of the lender.

In the event the borrower breaches any of these obligations, the lender can exercise powers of acceleration and insist that the loan balance, plus accrued interest and costs, be paid immediately and in full.

Defaults

A **default** is the breach of one or more of the conditions or terms of a loan agreement. When a default occurs, the acceleration clause found in all loan contracts is activated, allowing the lender to begin actions to cure the default, which could include foreclosure.

Payment Delinquencies.   The most common default is the nonpayment of principal and interest when due. Although most loan payments are due "on or before" a specified date, most lenders respect a reasonable *grace period*, usually 15 days. Longer delinquencies usually result in a reminder phone call or letter, and a continuing lack of response will generally trigger the foreclosure process. Payments over 30 days late could negatively affect a borrower's credit standing.

Property Tax Delinquency.   The nonpayment of property taxes is a technical default under a real estate loan. Property taxes represent a priority lien over existing loans: if a tax lien is imposed, the lender's position as a priority lien-holder is jeopardized. The collateral property may be sold for taxes in some cases, eliminating the lender's safe lien position. As a consequence, all realty loans include a clause that stipulates the borrower's responsibility to pay property taxes in the amount and on the date required. Many loans include a portion of the taxes in the payments to be held in escrow until due.

Other Property Liens.   Defaults also occur when a borrower allows federal or state income tax liens to vest against the property. In some jurisdictions, mechanics' and materialmen's liens also take priority over preexisting loans, and a borrower is in default if these liens are recorded against the collateral property.

Hazard Insurance Premiums.   Nonpayment of hazard insurance premiums also constitutes a default because the protection of the collateral is placed in jeopardy. Often the insurance premium is included in the loan payment.

Neglected Property Maintenance.   Finally, a borrower is considered in default if the property is allowed to physically deteriorate to a point at which its value falls below the balance of the loan.

Foreclosures

If any of the above defaults occurs, most lenders would rather **work out** the problems of a loan with the borrower than enter the **foreclosure** procedure. For instance, if the monthly payment is delinquent, the lender may offer some provision for a moratorium on a portion of the payment, or even on the entire payment, to solve the problem in the short run. If this is not successful, or if any of the other reasons for default cannot be remedied, then formal foreclosure is the only alternative.

Voluntary Conveyance of Deed (Deed in Lieu of Foreclosure).   To avoid the complications and expenses of pursuing a formal foreclosure, a defaulting borrower may voluntarily convey the property to the lender. This strategy may keep the borrower's credit clear and put the collateral into the hands of the lender quickly and efficiently. Depending on the circumstances, some lenders may not accept a voluntary conveyance.

Judicial Foreclosure and Sale.   If the voluntary conveyance procedure is not possible, as in cases of abandonment, then more formal procedures are followed. The most common foreclosure method under a note and mortgage format is the judicial procedure. A complaint is filed in the court for the county in which the property is located, and a summons is issued to the mortgagor indicating the foreclosure action.

Simultaneously, a title search is made to determine the identities of all parties with an interest in the collateral property, and a **lis pendens** filed with the court, giving public notice of the pending foreclosure. Notice is sent to all parties involved, allowing them to defend their positions. If they do not do so, they will be forever foreclosed from any future rights by judgment of the court.

After the appropriate number of days required by the jurisdiction for public notice, a foreclosure suit is held before a presiding judge and a sale of the property at public auction is ordered by means of a judgment decree.

A public sale is necessary to establish the actual market value of the property. If the proceeds from the auction sale are not sufficient to recover the outstanding loan balance plus costs, the lender may, in most states, sue on the note for the deficiency.

Power-of-Sale Foreclosure.   Under a deed of trust, the foreclosure process is the power-of-sale method of collateral recovery. In the event of a default, the beneficiary (lender) notifies the trustee of the trustor's (borrower's) default and instructs the trustee to foreclose.

Notice of default is recorded by the trustee at the county recorder's office and a public notice is placed in the newspaper stating the total amount due and the date of the public sale, usually 90 to 120 days from the recorded default.

A holder of a deed of trust may elect to pursue a judiciary foreclosure in order to secure a deficiency judgment and acquire other assets.

Strict Foreclosure.   Under a contract for deed, some states allow a strict foreclosure process to prevail when the borrower's equity is small. Designed to protect lenders under low down payment transactions, strict foreclosures can take place in as little as 30 days when the borrower has paid less than 20 percent of the purchase price.

Redemption Periods

An errant borrower has certain redemption rights under the law. In the judicial foreclosure process, the borrower can redeem the property by making outstanding payments plus interest and penalties *prior* to the auction sale. This is known as *equitable redemption.* In some states, the borrower has the right to pay the loan in full, plus interest and expenses, up to six months *after* the auction sale and redeem the property. This is known as *statutory redemption.*

Under the power-of-sale procedure, the borrower has the right to pay the balance in full only *prior* to the sale date to preserve ownership.

SUMMARY

The funds for financing real estate emanate from savings, both personal and corporate. These savings are held in the form of deposits in banks and savings institutions and as premiums paid for life insurance policies and into retirement and pension funds.

Basically, the funds for financing real estate investments originate from the financial fiduciary intermediaries in this country—the banks, savings associations and life insurance companies. Either directly or through their correspondent mortgage bankers or representative mortgage brokers, these institutions provide most of the monies for short-term construction or home improvement loans; owner-occupied, single family home mortgages; and large-project, long-term financing, respectively.

The financing system involves hypothecation, in which a borrower pledges the subject property as collateral to back up a promise to repay a loan while still retaining possession and control of the property. The loans issued adopt the form of a note and mortgage, a deed of trust or a contract for deed. Under the note and mortgage, the borrower-mortgagor has the longest periods of equitable and statutory redemption if the lender-mortgagee forecloses. These redemption periods are shortened somewhat in the deed of trust format, which requires a borrower-trustor to transfer the property's title to a holder-in-due-course trustee, who will maintain this title in trust for the lender-beneficiary. In the contract for deed or land contract format, the buyer-borrower-vendee does not receive title to the property from the seller-lender-vendor until the terms of the contract are met, thus creating the possibility for even shorter redemption periods.

The mortgage, trust deed or land contract can be arranged as either a senior or a junior loan. A senior loan is a lien in first priority position; no other liens are allowed to exist or to be created to jeopardize this protected position. The financial fiduciaries participate in the senior loan market.

Junior loans, established in subordinate lien positions to senior loans, are utilized by title companies to finance the costs of off-site improvements for land developers in exchange for the title insurance business on the properties sold. These loans are usually designed as blanket liens, with individual lots released as required payments are made.

Individuals are also using junior loans with increasing frequency to finance the disparity between a new or an existing senior mortgage and the price of the property being transferred. Because of the spiraling values of real estate, it is becoming increasingly necessary to utilize a carryback junior loan to complete a sale.

One of the more flexible types of junior encumbrances is the wraparound contract, which encompasses existing liens. When the wrap is drawn at a higher interest rate than the one that exists on the underlying mortgage, the wrap holder can effectively raise the yield.

Among the variety of special provisions that may be included in a real estate loan contract, those that are of primary importance to investors are the lock-in, right-to-sell, assumption and exculpatory clauses. Often a lender wishes to enjoy the yield from high-interest mortgages for a prescribed time period. To ensure this continuity, the lender prohibits the borrower from repaying the loan for the number of years stipulated in the agreement.

In addition, a currently popular technique for lenders seeking to control their yields is the due-on-sale provision. Here, the borrower must inform the lender in writing of the possible sale of all or a portion of the collateral property and obtain the lender's permission before the sale can be consummated. In this process, the lender may adjust the terms of the loan to reflect more readily current money market conditions.

Investors may avoid any extended personal liability obligations when purchasing a property with an existing loan by arranging the terms to include the words *subject to,* rather than *assume and agree to pay.* This format limits the investor-buyer's personal liability to the collateral property, thus protecting other assets from attachment in the event of foreclosure and a subsequent deficiency judgment.

This same limitation can be created by designing an exculpatory clause into the format of a new loan secured when purchasing a property.

Real estate loans can be established with an almost infinite variety of terms and conditions, each loan representing the manifestation of the bargaining positions of the participants. Thus, payment schedules, interest rates, stop dates, balloon payments, placement fees and loan amounts reflect the status of the money market at the time a loan is originated. And a borrower, given the personal control intrinsic in realty ownership, can refinance property periodically to provide the cash flows necessary to pursue the highest possible profit potentials.

Creative financing techniques, incorporating any number of versions of variable interest rates and variable payment schedules, are currently available to finance real estate purchases. Variable payment arrangements allow lenders and borrowers to manipulate both interest and amortization rates. Variable interest rates protect lenders from holding low-interest loans when rates are rising sharply. They are generally indexed to government securities rates or the cost of money.

The shared appreciation mortgage (SAM) and its variations, including the equity participation mortgage and pledged account mortgage, allow the borrower-buyer to pay lower interest rates and/or make smaller payments in return for a share in the property's appreciation over a specific number of years. The rollover loan allows lenders to periodically alter interest and payment terms, whereas zero percent financing eliminates interest and acts as an inducement to buy. The growing equity mortgage market allows for regularly increasing proportions of principal in monthly payments, thereby reducing the term of the loan. The lease option treats monthly payments as rent with an option to buy at the expiration of the lease period.

A borrower is in default when regular payments are delinquent, property taxes are not paid, income tax liens are allowed to vest, hazard insurance premiums are neglected and maintenance is ignored. If the borrower does not or cannot cure these problems in a reasonable time and does not give the lender a voluntary deed in lieu of foreclosure, a formal foreclosure procedure is pursued.

Judicial foreclosure is utilized under a note and mortgage format. Here a lis pendens is filed and a judgment sought to sell the collateral property at a public auction. Under a trust deed, the power-of-sale foreclosure allows the lender to record notice of default and schedule a public sale in 90 to 120 days. Some states allow strict foreclosure under a contract for deed when the borrower's equity is low and can be wiped out in as little as 30 days.

An errant borrower has six months to redeem a property prior to the auction under a judicial sale by bringing the payments current. In addition to this equitable right of redemption, some states allow the borrower an additional six months after the sale to redeem the property by paying the balance of the loan in full. Under the trust deed, the borrower must pay the balance in full prior to the auction sale to maintain ownership.

EXERCISE 3   (Answers may be checked against the Answer Key.)

1. When an institutional lender makes an 8 percent real estate loan while it is paying an average of 3 percent to its depositors, the lender is actually earning which of the following returns on its investment?

    a.   3 percent
    b.   5 percent
    c.   8 percent
    d.   infinite

2. The basic difference between a deed of trust and a note and mortgage is the

    a.   interest rate.
    b.   redemption period.
    c.   length of the loan.
    d.   size of the loan.

3. Which of the following relationships is *incorrect*?

    a.   Private mortgage insurance—insures the top 10 percent of loan
    b.   FHA mortgage insurance—can be eliminated when borrowers reach 20 percent equity
    c.   VA loan guarantee—guarantees the top 20 percent of a loan
    d.   Private mortgage insurance—can be eliminated when borrowers reach 20 percent equity

4. When assuming the balance of an existing loan

    a.   the original borrower is relieved of any further personal liability on the loan.
    b.   the new borrower does not incur any personal liability on the loan.
    c.   the new borrower is buying the property subject to the terms of the loan.
    d.   the original borrower and the new borrower are jointly liable on the loan.

5. All of the following terms refer to a real estate financing transaction *except*

    a.   collateralization.
    b.   agglomeration.
    c.   subordination.
    d.   hypothecation.

6. The real estate loan form under which the lender always maintains legal ownership is a

   a. deed of trust.
   b. note and mortgage.
   c. contract for deed.
   d. certificate of title.

7. The principal portion of the *second payment* on a $100,000 loan for 30 years at 7 1/2 percent is (use a $7 per $1,000 amortization factor):

   a. $ 75.00.
   b. $624.53.
   c. $ 75.47.
   d. $700.00.

8. A wraparound financial encumbrance implies all of the following conditions *except*

   a. an existing underlying encumbrance.
   b. a possible override profit.
   c. an all-inclusive loan.
   d. a priority lien position.

9. A seller under a sale-leaseback arrangement benefits from all of the following results *except*

   a. immediate cash receipts.
   b. release of liability under existing assumed mortgage.
   c. tax-deductible rent payments.
   d. continued possession of the property.

10. With a $60,000 wrap loan payable at 10 percent interest-only around an existing $50,000 loan balance at 8 percent, the wrap holder's annual yield is

    a. 8 percent.
    b. 10 percent.
    c. 20 percent.
    d. 56 percent.

DISCUSSION

1. In light of the recent banking crisis, have the lending institutions in your area tightened their loan underwriting requirements? If so, how?

2. Examine the laws in your state covering the redemption periods allowed an errant borrower under the various real estate financing forms: mortgage, trust deed and land contract.

4

Income Taxes and Real Estate Investments

Key Terms

active income

alternative minimum tax

boot

capital gains income

deferred exchange

depreciation

exchange

installment factor

ordinary income

passive income

portfolio income

pyramiding

realized gain

recognized gain

taxable income

tax shelters

The Tax Reform Act of 1986 (TRA '86) eliminated most of the excess carryover loss deductions and capital gains exemptions for real estate investors. It also extended depreciation cost-recovery periods. This dramatically changed investment strategies regarding tax shelters and firmly established positive cash-flow profits as the primary reason for investing in real estate.

Prior to 1986, in a frenzy of tax shelter investments, construction of every type of income property proceeded at a feverish pace. Negative cash-flow apartment buildings, shopping centers, industrial parks and other developments proliferated in local markets all over the country. This resulted in overbuilding, which contributed greatly to the crash of the late 1980s and early 1990s. Currently, the country is emerging from this recession, which included the bankruptcies of many investors and the savings and loan associations and banks that funded them.

It is important to understand, however, that not all of the shelter has been removed from real estate investments. In fact, real estate income property is probably the only investment alternative that allows an owner to shelter most of its income. Deductions are allowed from gross income of operating expenses, interest costs and a modicum of depreciation allowances. And, depending on individual circumstances, some growth in value is possible under our current economic recovery. However, verifiable positive cash flows from the investment property under consideration should continue to be the pivotal point for rational investment decision making.

Unlike property taxes, which are imposed to support the various services of local government structures, income taxes provide the revenues necessary to pay for the operations of the federal and state governments. The earnings of most individuals and businesses in this country are subject to an income tax, although there are a number of exceptions to this rule. For example, persons who earn less than a minimum gross annual income, some of the elderly and qualified charitable and religious organizations are exempt from paying income taxes.

This chapter will examine the important income tax considerations for real estate investors. The handling of various tax alternatives has a direct effect on the profitability of real estate investments. On one hand, the rents from investment property or the profits from the sale of real estate increase the owner's taxable income. On the other hand, operating expenses, depreciation, refinancing, installment sales and exchanging can all provide the investor with a shelter for this income. In addition, developing an appropriate management strategy can result in a tax shelter for some of an investor's income from other sources.

INCOME SUBJECT TO TAX

For the purpose of computing tax liability, gross income earned can be divided into two general categories—ordinary income and capital gains income.

Ordinary Income

All monies earned in the normal course of working or conducting a business are identified as **ordinary income.** The bulk of ordinary income is derived from wages, salaries, commissions, interest, dividends and annual operating profits from businesses and investments. Other earnings included in this category are tips, prizes, awards, alimony, royalties, gambling winnings, jury duty fees and similar income.

Capital Gains Income

Monies earned as profits on investments made *outside* the ordinary course of work and business are identified as **capital gains income**. Such income includes profits made on the sale of real property, stocks, equipment and other assets not held for regular business purposes. In other words, noninventory assets produce capital gains income when sold for a profit. This category also includes property held for the *production of income,* such as apartment buildings and machinery in a plant, but specifically excludes all property held as inventory stock *for resale* to customers. Capital gains profits are the difference between the net sales price of the property and its remaining book value.

A property's remaining book value (also known as the adjusted book value) is a function of its purchase price plus the costs of any capital improvements made during ownership less allowable depreciation to the date of its sale. Only improvements on a property may be depreciated, not the land itself.

For example, consider a commercial property purchased for $200,000 on January 1, 1988, and sold for $200,000 net on December 31, 1993. No capital improvements were made to the property during the intervening years. Assume further that the owner allocated $40,000 of the purchase price to land value and the balance of $160,000 to the building to be depreciated at the rate of 3.17 percent per year. (This reflects the 31 1/2 year straight-line rate established by TRA '86 on nonresidential real estate, that is, 100 / 31.5 = 3.1746, rounded to 3.17).

Thus, the remaining book value at the time of the sale was $169,568.

$$
\begin{array}{rl}
\$\ 160,000 & \text{balance} \\
\times\ \ 0.0317 & \text{depreciation rate} \\
\hline
\$\ \ \ \ 5,072 & \text{per year} \\
\times\ \ \ \ \ \ \ \ 6 & \text{years} \\
\hline
\$\ \ \ 30,432 & \text{total depreciation}
\end{array}
$$

$$
\begin{array}{r}
\$\ 160,000 \\
-\ \ \ 30,432 \\
\hline
129,568 \\
+\ \ \ 40,000 \quad \text{land value} \\
\hline
\$\ 169,568
\end{array}
$$

The seller enjoyed a capital gain go $30,432.

$$
\begin{array}{rl}
\$\ \ 200,000 & \text{investment} \\
-\ 169,568 & \text{remaining book value} \\
\hline
\$\ \ \ 30,432 &
\end{array}
$$

$$
\begin{array}{rl}
\$\ \ \ 30,432 & \text{capital gain} \\
\times\ \ \ \ \ \ 0\ .28 & \text{tax rate} \\
\hline
\$8,520.96 &
\end{array}
$$

This is the exact amount of the total depreciation deducted over the six-year period. Notice that the sale price equals the earlier purchase price, indicating that no *real* depreciation (loss in value) occurred during the intervening years. Thus, the owner is charged with the *recovery* of the amounts deducted for depreciation and must pay a capital gains tax on this "profit."

Income tax on capital gains is applied at the taxpayer's rate, up to a maximum of 28 percent. If we assume that the owner in our example is in this 28 percent bracket, then the tax on the gain will be $8,520.96. Note that investors in improved real estate enjoy a major benefit of being allowed to recapture depreciation allowances for a maximum of 28-cent dollars.

Capital losses occur when a seller sells a property at *less* than its remaining book value. These losses may be used by the taxpayer to offset other capital gains made in the year, with any excess capital losses becoming ordinary losses, but only to the extent of $3,000 per year until used up.

TRA '86 preserved the right of a person 55 years old or older to take a one-time $125,000 exemption on the gain in the sale of a personal residence. If the property is owned jointly, only one spouse need be 55. However, only one such exemption is allowed per couple. This gets complicated when the surviving spouse remarries and the new spouse is "tainted" by the one who has already received the tax advantage. In this case, it may be wise to sell before marrying.

The Technical and Miscellaneous Revenue Act of 1988 (TAMRA)

TAMRA was passed to make some corrections in the TRA '86 laws. The changes affecting real estate are as follows:

- A married couple had been allowed to defer paying income tax on the gain in the sale of a personal residence if they reinvested in another home within two years. However, if one spouse died during the interim period, the deferral was lost. TAMRA now allows the surviving spouse the same deferral opportunity.
- A person over 55 years old could exclude up to $125,000 of gain from the sale of a principal residence if he or she had lived in the home for three of the preceding five years. TAMRA amended this regulation to residency of only one year in the previous five years if the taxpayer had spent the other four years in a nursing home or other facility for those incapable of self-care.
- Owners in cooperative housing corporations that converted to condominiums were obligated to pay a tax on the increased value of their units. TAMRA amended this rule to allow a tax-free conversion, provided that the units are the owners' principal residences.

The Omnibus Budget and Reconciliation Act of 1993 (OBRA)

The government's propensity to tinker with the income tax laws continued in 1993. Passage by Congress of OBRA brought more changes to the tax code. This act targeted high earners, raising their tax rates.

It also extended straight-line recovery periods on nonresidential properties from 31.5 years to 39 years, effective for properties acquired after May 13, 1993. Any properties purchased prior to this date remain depreciable at the established rates. Residential income property remains depreciable at 27.5 years, costs of land improvements at 15 years and personal property used in business at 7 years. Commercial tenant's improvements have been extended to 39 years.

All rental activities are considered passive, regardless of owner participation. However, OBRA reintroduced the concept of granting qualified investors the opportunity to deduct all passive losses from other ordinary income. To qualify, taxpayers must spend at least 50 percent of their working time (against a total of at least 750 hours per tax year) in development, redevelopment, construction, reconstruction, acquisition, conversion, rental, operation, management, leasing or brokerage activities. This rule became effective January 1, 1994, and earnings prior to this date cannot be changed from passive to active. All other passive rules remain unchanged.

OBRA also extended permanently the tax credits on low-income housing developments and mortgage bond programs. It reduced deductions for entertainment expenses to 50 percent and disallowed any deductions for club dues or a spouse's travel expenses to business meetings.

In a mortgage workout, when a lender forgives part of a mortgage debt to avoid a foreclosure, the IRS considers this amount a "phantom income," meaning that it is taxable in the current year. OBRA allows a postponement of this tax until the property is sold, but the owners must deduct this amount of debt forgiveness from their book basis.

INCOME TAX RATES

Taxes are imposed only on **taxable income**, which is the net amount remaining after all allowable deductions and adjustments have been made to the gross amount of income earned in a specific year. The tax rates are incremental—that is, all earnings listed under a specified rate are taxed at that rate, whereas earnings over the stipulated amount are taxed at the next rate, and so on.

1993 Individual Tax Rates

The income tax rates for individuals in 1994 follows:

1994 Taxable Income Brackets

Rate	Singles	Joint Return
15%	$ 0– 22,750	$ 0– 38,000
28%	22,751– 55,100	38,001– 91,850
31%	55,101–115,000	91,851–140,000
36%	115,001–250,000	140,001–250,000
39.6%	over 250,000	over 250,000

Corporate Tax Rates

The corporate tax rates effective for 1994 follows:

Corporate Income Tax Rates

Rate	Taxable Income
15%	$ 0– 50,000
25%	50,001– 75,000
34%	75,001–100,000
39%	100,001–335,000
34%	335,001–10 million
35%	10 million–15 million
38%	15 million–18.33 million
35%	over 18.33 million

Remember that corporate income is subject to double taxation, as described in Chapter 2—once as corporate earnings and again as dividends distributed to shareholders. To avoid this double tax, realty investments may be held by individuals as an S corp, as a partnership or in a trust.

All tax rates will be adjusted for inflation in subsequent years.

Alternative Minimum Tax

The **alternative minimum tax** (AMT) is a special levy on high-income investors and corporations who take so many deductions and credits that they would pay little or no tax.

To calculate the AMT, follow these five steps:

1. Determine regular taxable income in accordance with current IRS regulations.
2. Add the tax preference items designated by law, such as excess accelerated depreciation over straight-line rates, defined excess passive losses and interest received on tax-exempt bonds issued for nongovernmental projects.
3. Deduct $22,500 for married couples filing separately and for estates and trusts; $33,750 for individuals; or $45,000 for joint filers or corporations.
4. If the taxpayer's alternative minimum taxable income exceeds $112,500 for individuals or $150,000 for joint filers and corporations, then the deductions must be reduced by 25 percent of the excess income until phased out. Thus, the exemption is totally phased out on a joint income of over $330,000.
5. Finally, the AMT rate is applied: 26 percent up to $175,000 ($87,500 for married persons filing separately) and 28 percent on any excess AMT income. The taxpayer must pay the alternative minimum tax amount if it is higher than the regular tax amount.

REAL ESTATE INVESTMENTS AS TAX SHELTERS FOR ORDINARY INCOME

Real estate investments continue to be defined as **tax shelters**, although many of the benefits have been severely limited—if not eliminated entirely—by TRA '86. Although special capital gains treatment is gone and depreciation allowances have been minimized, all income from every real estate investment can be sheltered by operating expenses as well as interest charges and depreciation. In addition, certain *active* investors may benefit up to $25,000 in excess loss carryover against other ordinary income.

Passive Versus Active Investors

All business and investment activities are identified in one of the following three categories:

1. Active trade or business
2. Portfolio activity
3. Passive activity

Active Trade or Business.   The taxpayer who materially participates in a trade or business on a regular, continuous and substantial basis is defined as being active. A tax loss generated by an active trade or business may be used to offset outside income, such as salary. All real estate rental activity is considered passive, no matter how involved the owners are, except corporation-owned rentals and the operation of a hotel, motel or inn, which are considered active.

Portfolio Activity.   Portfolio activity includes interest, dividends, royalties and annuity income, as well as gains or losses from the sale or exchange of portfolio assets. Portfolio income is reduced by deductible expenses directly allocated to such income.

Portfolio activity of concern to real estate investors includes real estate investment trust dividends and income from a real estate mortgage investment conduit, both of which cannot be sheltered by passive losses.

Passive Activity.   Passive activities are trades or businesses in which a taxpayer does not materially participate; that is, all activities carried on for a profit *except* an active trade or business or portfolio activity.

Losses from passive trade or business activities each year may be used to offset income from other passive activities for the year, but *cannot offset other* **active income or portfolio income**.

This **passive income** rule applies to individuals, estates, trusts, personal service corporations, partnerships and S corporations. It does not apply to regular corporation-owned real estate and equipment. Limited partnerships are intrinsically passive because limited partners do not participate in management.

This provision attempts to match income with expenses and eliminates, to a large degree, the tax sheltering aspects of real estate investments.

The $25,000 Exception.   The single exception to the strict classification of real estate rental activities as passive rather than active permits an individual taxpayer to use up to $25,000 of real estate losses to offset other income—active or portfolio. However, the investor must actually participate in the rental activity by engaging in management decisions and maintaining or arranging for maintenance of the property. The taxpayer must own more than 10 percent of the investment to qualify for this exception.

The $25,000 allowance is reduced by 50 percent of the amount by which the taxpayer's adjusted gross income (AGI) exceeds $100,000. The AGI is the total of all

FIGURE 4.1   Summary of Income Definitions

Active Income	*Passive Income*	*Portfolio Income*
Wages, salaries, profits from ownership of trade of business and operations of motels and hotels	Profits from rental operations, limited partnerships, hobbies	Interest, dividends, royalties, annuities, gains from sale or exchange of portfolio assets

All expenses allocable to individual activities are deductible in that column only. No excess losses in any one activity may be used to shelter income from other activities, except as to the $25,000 rule and the $3,000 annual excess capital loss carryover.

sources of income, each adjusted by its own allowable deductions, and is found on the last line of the first page of the income tax form. Thus, $125,000 AGI reduces the $25,000 allowance to $12,500, and $150,000 AGI reduces it to zero, even though the taxpayer qualifies in every other manner. Figure 4.1 summarizes the income definitions for quick reference.

Operating Costs and Interest Expenses

Investors in income-producing real property are allowed to deduct all operating expenses and interest paid on property loans from the investment's gross income. Every real estate investment incurs operating expenses in one form or another and to varying degrees. Vacant unimproved land is subject to property taxes; improved property develops a multitude of operating costs, including property and sales taxes, insurance premiums, maintenance charges, management fees, bookkeeping, advertising, pest control and snow removal. Any investment purchased with a loan also incurs interest expenses.

These and other charges are all deductible from the gross annual income when determining the net income, which is subject to tax at the owner's rate. In addition to these operating and interest expenses, improved income property may enjoy another deduction—depreciation of the improvements.

Depreciation

Depreciation is described by appraisers as a "loss in value from any cause." This loss can result from a physical wearing out or from functional and economic obsolescence.

From an accounting standpoint, depreciation is a recovery of investment costs; prior to TRA '86, depreciation for income tax purposes was named *cost recovery*. To the extent allowable, many investors accelerated their cost recovery accounting to take advantage of high amounts of such depreciation.

TRA '86 eliminated most of the favorable depreciation provisions introduced by prior tax laws. Esoteric methods such as double-declining balances, component units and accelerated cost-recovery techniques have been replaced by the following simplified methods:

- Residential rental properties placed in service after January 1, 1987: 27 1/2 years straight-line (3.63 percent per year).
- Nonresidential real estate: 39 years straight-line (2.564 percent per year).
- Autos and light trucks: five-year write-off, 200 percent declining balance allowed
- Personal property and manufacturing equipment: seven-year write-off, 200 percent declining balance allowed
- Land improvements (sidewalks, etc.): 15-year write-off, 150 percent declining balance allowed
- Rehabilitation tax credit for nonhistoric structures placed in service before 1936: 10 percent
- Rehabilitation tax credit for certified historic structures: 20 percent

---

Example: To illustrate how real estate investments act as tax shelters, consider the following analysis:

$50,000	gross annual income
−20,000	annual operating expenses
$30,000	cash flow before debt service
−25,000	interest paid on loan (limited to investment income)
$ 5,000	cash flow before depreciation
−10,000	depreciation allowance
($5,000)	net paper loss

The gross annual income reflects income from all of the property's sources, such as rents, vending machines and laundry. The operating costs include property taxes, insurance premiums, maintenance, utilities and management. The $30,000 cash flow is profit but is sheltered from income tax by the allowable interest expense and depreciation deduction. Thus, this investment generates a $5,000 passive loss. This loss can be used to offset the owner's other passive profits or, if the owner qualifies, to reduce other active or portfolio income accordingly, saving tax dollars.

REAL ESTATE INVESTMENTS AS TAX SHELTERS FOR CAPITAL GAINS

With the elimination of preferred treatment of capital gains profits, real estate investments have lost much of their glamour as tax shelters. Whereas in the past accelerated depreciation allowances resulted in large annual shelters recaptured at 40-cent dollars when the investment was sold (60 percent of gain exempt, 40 percent taxed at ordinary rates), all profits are now taxed at ordinary rates, not to exceed 28 percent.

The tax law *has* preserved other sheltering aspects, including tax-free refinancing, installment-sale deferment, exchanges and inheritance tax exemptions.

Tax-Free Refinancing

Refinancing involves the securing of a new loan to replace an old loan. Logically, the new loan should be sufficient not only to satisfy the balance of the existing loan but also to pay all of the placement costs involved *and* generate new cash the borrower can use for additional investments. *Any money acquired by refinancing is not subject to tax,* even if these funds exceed the original purchase price of the specific property. This money is considered borrowed money and, as such, is not taxable.

In this regard, a distinction should be drawn between two types of gains: **realized gain** is the actual profit derived from a transaction, such as the money received from refinancing; **recognized gain** is that portion of the profit subject to tax. In the case of refinancing, a taxable capital gains income from this transaction exists only when the realized gain becomes recognized gain *upon the sale of the property.* In the meantime, property can be financed and refinanced repeatedly over time to generate tax-free cash that can be invested and reinvested for additional profits.

Pyramiding Through Refinancing

One way to acquire a substantial amount of real estate is to periodically refinance those properties already owned and then use the proceeds to purchase new properties. This procedure is called **pyramiding** through refinancing.

Unlike pyramiding through selling (in which an investor purchases a property, improves it for resale at a higher price and then purchases additional properties with gains from the sale), pyramiding through refinancing is based on *retaining* all properties acquired. By not selling, the investor is constantly increasing the refinancing base while avoiding capital gains taxes.

Pyramiding through refinancing begins with the purchase of one property. If more than one property can be purchased to start the plan, then the refinancing base will be enhanced at the outset. The type of property to be purchased should be improved income property that has the ability to generate at least enough cash flow to cover all operating costs plus mortgage payments.

It is in the best interests of the investor to purchase better properties in stable or growing areas. An older property in a declining neighborhood would make a poor investment with which to pyramid through refinancing. Rents and values of such buildings might actually decrease and thus destroy the refinancing cycle.

With the appropriate application of deductible allowances, most—if not all—of the net income earned during the years of ownership could be sheltered, while capital gains taxes can be avoided through the refinancing process. The estate can then be left to the investor's heirs without the investor ever having paid capital gains tax on any profits derived from ownership of this property.

Although pyramiding to avoid capital gains taxes is a practical strategy, sometimes the sale of a property is unavoidable. As indicated, any gains made in such a sale are subject to income tax.

A seller may postpone the tax liability on the gain from the sale of a primary residence by investing in another home of equal or greater value within 24 months of the date of the sale. Any gain on the sale is thus carried along to the new purchase and may disappear entirely if this investment pattern is maintained throughout the taxpayer's life and the property is left to heirs. A *commercial* property owner, however, does not have this privilege of postponement. And, as noted earlier, an owner 55 years old or older is limited to one $125,000 exclusion on capital gains earned on the sale of a primary residence.

Installment-Sale Deferment

Capital gains taxes can be postponed by the application of an installment sale plan, available to both residential and commercial property owners provided the sale price is $5 million or less. For more expensive properties, special rules prevail. Dealers in real estate may not sell under installment deferment but must pay any tax on gains at the time of sale. Dealers are persons or companies that have real estate as their stock in trade—for example, subdividers who sell lots or builder/developers who sell houses.

A gain on an installment sale is computed in the same manner as the net capital gain on a cash sale: gross sale price minus costs of sale minus adjusted book basis equals net capital gain. However, under an installment sale, the seller can elect either to pay the total tax due in the year of the sale or to spread the tax obligation over the length of the installment contract.

The installment sale provision in the tax law is intended as a relief provision for owners who can sell their property only by agreeing to accept payments in installments. A seller might receive less cash in the year of the sale than the tax required on the total gain. Therefore, the law allows tax payments to be made as installment payments are received.

Example: Consider a property sold for $100,000 net. On a noninstallment sale, the buyer pays $40,000 cash and assumes an existing loan balance of $60,000. The adjusted book basis on the date of the sale is $80,000. Given these facts, a cash transaction would result in a taxpayer in the 28 percent bracket taxpayer paying $5,600 tax on this property in the year of the sale:

```
$100,000   net sale price
- 80,000   adjusted book basis
$ 20,000   capital gain
×    0.28  tax rate
$   5,600
```

An installment sale can be designed to postpone portions of the seller's tax liability. For instance, the sale can be structured to require $8,000 as a cash down payment and $32,000 as a junior loan back to the seller. The buyer then assumes the $60,000 existing loan. The installment contract is payable in four equal annual principal payments plus interest at an agreed rate.

Computation of the seller's tax liability under the installment contract first requires a determination of the **installment factor** (gain/equity) to identify what portion of the principal payment is profit and what portion is return of the equity buildup. In this case, the seller's gain is

```
$100,000   net sale
- 80,000   adjusted book sale
$ 20,000
```

and the equity is

```
$100,000   net sale
- 60,000   loan balance
$ 40,000
```

Thus the installment factor is

```
$ 20,000   gain
+ 40,000   equity
      .50, or 50 percent.
```

The seller's annual tax liability is

```
$8,000   cash down payment
×  .50   installment rate
$4,000
×  .28   tax rate
$1,120
```

for a total of

```
$1,120   annual tax
×    5   years
$5,600   over five years
```

This is exactly the same total tax that would be paid if the property were sold for cash. The installment treatment allows the seller to pay this sum over the term of the contract as the principal is received. All interest received by the seller is declared as portfolio income.

The installment plan allows a seller to pay tax in amounts proportional to the gain collected each year. Thus, a seller whose tax bracket *decreases* over the term of an installment contract will pay *less* tax than if he or she had elected to pay the full tax in the year of the sale. This arrangement is particularly advantageous to a seller nearing retirement age who will enter a lower tax bracket during the term of the installment contract. On the other hand, there is the possibility that a seller's tax bracket could rise over the installment term, which would lead to the payment of *more* tax. Consequently, a seller is allowed to pay the full amount of tax due on a capital gain any time it becomes expedient during the installment contract period.

Exchanges

An alternative method for tax-deferred pyramiding can also be accomplished by up-side trading or the property **exchange** technique. Section 1031 of the Internal Revenue Code provides for the recognition of capital gain to be postponed under the following conditions:

- Properties to be exchanged must be held for productive use in a trade or business, or for investment.
- Properties to be exchanged must be "like kind"—similar in nature or character.
- Properties must actually be exchanged.

Property held for productive use in a trade or business includes such things as machinery, automobiles, factories and rental apartments. Property held for investment may include such items as vacant land and antiques. "Like kind" means that a machine can be exchanged for a machine or real estate for real estate. Improvements on the land are considered differences in the *quality* of the real estate, not in the type. Thus, a vacant lot can be exchanged for a store property or an industrial property for a highrise office building. Often, unlike property, called **boot**, is included in a real estate exchange and must be accounted for separately. Boot may include cash, jewelry or other personal property.

There are at least six basic mathematical computations involved in the exchange process:

1. balancing the equities;
2. deriving realized gains;
3. deriving recognized gains;
4. determining tax impacts;
5. reestablishing book basis; and
6. allocating the new basis.

These computations are illustrated by the simple two-party exchange recorded in Table 4.1.

TABLE 4.1   Two-Party Exchange

STEP 1.   *Balancing the Equities*

PROPERTY A		PROPERTY B
$100,000	EXCHANGE PRICE	$150,000
− 60,000	EXISTING MORTGAGE	− 80,000
40,000	OWNERS' EQUITY	$ 70,000
+ 30,000	CASH REQUIRED	
$ 70,000		

STEP 2.   *Deriving Realized Gains*

PROPERTY A		PROPERTY B
$100,000	EXCHANGE PRICE	$150,000
− 70,000	ADJUSTED BASIS	− 90,000
$ 30,000	REALIZED GAIN	$ 60,000

STEP 3.   *Deriving Recognized Gains*
(Recognized gain equals the sum of unlike properties)

-0-	CASH REQUIRED	$30,000
-0-	BOOT	-0-
-0-	MORTGAGE RELIEF	+20,000
-0-	RECOGNIZED GAIN	$50,000

STEP 4.   *Determining Tax Impacts*
(Taxable income is the realized gain or the recognized gain, whichever is *less*)

$30,000	REALIZED GAIN	$60,000
-0-	RECOGNIZED GAIN	50,000
-0-	TAXABLE GAIN	$50,000

(Note: *B* will pay income tax on $50,000. *A* will pay no tax.)

STEP 5.   *Reestablishing Book Basis*

$ 70,000	OLD BASIS	$ 90,000
+ 80,000	NEW MORTGAGE	+ 60,000
+ 30,000	CASH AND BOOT PAID	+ -0-
+ -0-	RECOGNIZED GAIN	+ 50,000
$180,000	TOTAL	$200,000

LESS

60,000	OLD MORTGAGE	$ 80,000
+ -0-	CASH AND BOOT RECEIVED	+ 30,000
$ 60,000	TOTAL	$110,000
$120,000	NEW BASIS	$ 90,000

STEP 6.   *Allocating the New Basis*
(Each party will decide which portions of the new basis to allocate to land
and to improvements to establish new depreciation schedules.)

A two-party, like-kind property exchange will not qualify if

- the parties are related;
- either party sells the property within two years of the exchange; or
- a property in the United States is exchanged for a property outside this country.

For purposes of this regulation, related persons are immediate family members, lineal descendants, corporations in which the exchangers own more than 50 percent of the stock, two corporations that are members of the same holding group and a grantor or fiduciary of a trust.

The two-year disposition rule is waived in the event of death or involuntary conversion.

It is not often that each of two potential exchangers owns property that is desired by the other. More frequently, exchanges involve three or more property owners. The element of timing is thus an important factor to be considered. The process requires two contracts: one between the first two parties, structuring the exchange; and a second contract in which the third party buys the unwanted property. Each contract is conditional upon the closing of the other, and they must be closed simultaneously.

Deferred Exchange.   A federal court decision in 1979, *Starker v. United States* (602 F.2CD 1341, 9th Circuit), introduced the **deferred exchange** to expand the tax-free exchange provisions in the tax law. Section 1031 of the Tax Code was amended to include the deferred exchange, which, for the first time, allowed traders to set up an exchange for properties not yet available but to be found within certain time constraints.

The law allows properties to be identified no later than 45 days after the exchange is established and closed not later than the earlier of (1) 180 days after the initial transfer or (2) the due date of the exchangers' tax returns for the year of the transfer.

For example, assume that Jones and Smith agree to exchange like-kind properties. Jones already owns the property to be traded and transfers title to Smith. In exchange, Smith agrees to transfer to Jones, at some time in the future, a specific type of property. If Smith does not acquire the property and consequently cannot make the transfer, Smith must pay Jones the price in cash.

When designing the deferred exchange, keep in mind the number of days from the date of the initial transfer. Title to the second property must be transferred within the 180-day period.

Distribution to Heirs

The ultimate capital gains tax shelter is to maintain ownership of investment property until death. At death, the property is appraised for inheritance tax purposes, and the deceased's heirs acquire title, with the new book value of the inherited property being the value established at the time of death.

Although capital gains taxes can be avoided, certain estates are subject to the imposition of inheritance taxes. But with the appropriate application of tax-free gift giving, even these taxes can be avoided.

Inheritance Tax.   The federal tax laws established exemptions for the values of estates subject to federal inheritance taxes. In addition, every state except Nevada has its own inheritance tax. These state rates vary and should be reviewed in conjunction with investment planning.

The current exemption for federal estate tax purposes is $600,000 per person. To qualify for inheritance taxes, then, a deceased's estate would have to be evaluated at more than $600,000 net, or $1.2 million if owned jointly with a spouse. In other words, the gross value of the entire estate is estimated; debts against the estate, as well as all probate costs, are deducted; and the balance (or one-half if jointly owned) must exceed $600,000 before it is subject to federal estate taxes. The tax rate is currently 37 percent after the initial exemption, 53 percent on estates between $2.5 million and $3 million, and 55 percent on larger estates.

In addition to the estate tax exemptions, operators of farms and ranches can deduct $750,000 more from their net estate values. This special farmland exemption is designed to protect family farms from the impact of inheritance taxes.

Gift Tax.   With proper planning, investors may be able to distribute their entire estates by using tax-free gifts to avoid inheritance taxes.

The law provides gift exemptions of up to $10,000 for each donor per donee every year. Thus, a husband and wife can give $20,000 tax-free each year to each heir. Gifts in excess of the exemptions are subject to tax at the federal level and at the state level in the following states: California, Colorado, Louisiana, Minnesota, North Carolina, Oklahoma, Oregon, Rhode Island, Tennessee, Virginia, Washington and Wisconsin.

SUMMARY

Ordinary income is derived from wages, salaries, commissions, interest, dividends and profits earned from year-to-year activities of businesses and investments, in addition to other earnings. Ordinary income in excess of allowable deductions is taxed at the federal and state levels at progressive rates established by Congress and state legislatures.

Ordinary income is sheltered to the extent of such allowable deductions as medical care, moving costs and charitable donations, if itemized. The ordinary income from real estate investments is sheltered by operating expenses, interest charges and depreciation deductions. Operating expenses include management and maintenance fees plus charges for utilities, advertising, property taxes, insurance premiums, bookkeeping services and similar costs. Interest charges are deducted from a property's gross earnings before deriving the taxable income.

Current depreciation allowances are a 27 1/2-year straight-line rate for residential income property and a 39-year straight-line rate for commercial property.

Capital gains income is composed of profits (or losses) on noninventory assets held as investments for relatively long periods of time and then sold. All gains are now treated as ordinary income.

In the past, excess losses from business and investments could shelter earnings from any source. Now, losses from active trades or businesses can only be used to shelter earnings from these activities, while losses from passive activities are limited to sheltering earnings from passive activities.

All real estate rentals are considered passive activities, and any losses are limited to the investment's income. The exception is a $25,000 excess loss carryover given those individuals who earn less than $100,000 adjustable gross income and take a clearly defined active participation in a real estate investment in which they own more than a 10 percent interest.

In addition, full-time real estate professionals may now use passive losses to shelter other income.

Investors often capitalize on their equity by refinancing and securing tax-free dollars from the new mortgage proceeds. Property equities grow through inflation and as a consequence of the regular repayment of existing mortgages. Funds secured from refinancing are not subject to income tax, even though these monies may exceed the original price paid for the property. Thus, investors may refinance regularly and secure new cash assets that enable them to acquire additional properties and expand their investment portfolios.

Taxes on profits from capital gains can be deferred through installment sales or the exchange process. When trading like properties, owners can carry their old book values over to the new properties, effectively deferring taxes on any gains. Depending on the terms of the transaction, an up-trader can usually shelter the entire gain, while the down-trader will have to pay taxes on the portion of the equity recovered.

EXERCISE 4   (Answers may be checked against the Answer Key.)

1.   By definition, portfolio income includes all of the following items *except*

   a.   stock dividends.
   b.   oil and mineral royalties.
   c.   investment sales profits.
   d.   savings account interest.

2. Ordinary income consists of earnings from all of the following sources *except*

   a. wages.
   b. business profits.
   c. stock dividends.
   d. capital gains.

3. On improved income property, all of the following items are allowable expense deductions *except*

   a. interest charges.
   b. maintenance costs.
   c. principal payments.
   d. depreciation.

4. When investment property is sold for less than its remaining book value, its depreciation was

   a. approved by the IRS.
   b. underestimated.
   c. overestimated.
   d. estimated correctly.

5. When an investment property purchased for $150,000 is refinanced with a new loan for $175,000, the $25,000 is

   a. taxed as portfolio income.
   b. taxed as active income.
   c. taxed as passive income.
   d. not taxed until the property is sold.

6. Under the current tax law, capital gains exemptions are

   a. limited to $25,000.
   b. taxed at 15 percent.
   c. eliminated completely.
   d. applied only to commercial property.

7. The losses sustained when selling an investment property must first be deducted from any capital gains made in the year, with any excess losses

   a. allocated to shelter active income at the rate of $3,000 per year.
   b. marked off the books.
   c. carried forward to shelter any future capital gains.
   d. deducted as an operating expense.

8. Passive income is derived from which of the following?

    a. Interest on savings
    b. Dividends from stocks
    c. Income from rentals
    d. Royalties from oil leases

9. A commercial property was purchased for $100,000 with 20 percent allocated to the land. At a straight-line depreciation rate of 3.1746 percent per year, what is the adjusted book basis of this property at the end of the tenth year?

    a. $ 2,540
    b. $25,400
    c. $68,254
    d. $74,600

10. Which of the following is the installment factor for a property sold for $100,000 net subject to a loan balance of exactly $40,000 with an adjusted basis of $60,000?

    a. 33 1/3 percent
    b. 66 2/3 percent
    c. 100 percent
    d. 150 percent

DISCUSSION

1. The reinstatement of some form of capital gains exemptions was initiated by ex-President Bush. He said it would generate more income tax, whereas Congress generally felt it was really a bonus for high earners. What do you think?

2. Research the reason the federal and most state governments tax the estates of deceased persons. Investigate your state's inheritance tax requirements.

Market Analysis and Property Analysis of Real Estate Investments

Key Terms

deed restrictions   *plat*
EPA   *setback*
market analysis   *subdivision restrictions*
minimum housing standards

Many real estate investments are made in a relatively informal manner. A real estate broker offers a particular property to an interested buyer, who inspects it and briefly analyzes its income potential. Sometimes the services of an appraiser are sought to verify the market value of the property. If the investment meets the buyer's criteria and the terms of the purchase can be arranged to satisfy both parties, the transaction is completed.

Often, however, a more intensive analysis of the possible financial success of an investment is desired to satisfy the requirements not only of the investor but also of the financier and potential tenants. These formal market studies are generally undertaken with large projects, such as subdivisions, office buildings, shopping centers, industrial parks and mobile-home complexes. Market studies consist of three broad analyses: market analysis, property analysis and financial analysis. This chapter will examine the first two; with the financial analysis will be discussed in the following chapter.

MARKET ANALYSIS

Although each study is designed to meet the needs of a particular development, all investigations include analyses of the community, the market, the site and the property.

Community Profile

Most new real estate projects begin with an available piece of property, an investor looking for a property and a broker acting as a catalyst to unite the two.

Thus, a project starts with a predetermination of use—for example, a shopping center. The market study must then include an analysis of the community this center is intended to serve.

Market analysis is predominantly concentrated at the local level. To determine the potential income that can be realized from an investment, a careful investigation must first be made of the economic climate of the community and, more particularly, of the neighborhood in which the project is located.

This analysis generally begins with an on-site tour of the area. The investors obtain copies of maps of the locale, zoning ordinances, applicable building codes and statistical data concerning the area's population. They then examine at least five major factors in the neighborhood: land usage, transportation and utility services, economic climate, occupancy rates and available services and facilities.

Neighborhood Boundaries and Land Use.   A neighborhood can be defined as an area within which common characteristics of population and land use prevail. There is no predetermined size for a neighborhood. In rural areas it may consist of three square miles, while a city neighborhood may be five square blocks.

The investor must determine the boundaries of the area before a market analysis can be made. Rivers, lakes, mountains, parks, railroad tracks or major highways help delineate the boundaries of a neighborhood. Particular note should be made of natural and artificial boundaries that may curtail the future growth of a neighborhood.

In the absence of any obvious physical boundaries, an investor must determine the extent of land that is under common usage and that shares a similar population. Any variances or restrictions in zoning should also be noted. Depending on the type of property involved, these zoning regulations may have a positive or negative effect on a real estate investment. Commercial and industrial enterprises would be adversely affected by a zoning restriction limiting the area to residential or multifamily use. On the other hand, the desirability of a residential neighborhood could decline severely if a zoning ordinance favorable to industrial development were granted for the area.

The physical and political boundaries of a neighborhood help to set the trade areas, the market from which the investment project will draw its customers. A larger project would normally draw customers from a greater area.

Neighborhood Economy.   Various sources of statistical information are available to an investor for assessing the economic climate of a neighborhood. The local chamber of commerce accumulates data concerning the number and types of businesses in the area, the volume of their activity and general trends in their growth or decline. A neighborhood with a well-diversified business sector is usually more economically stable than an area that depends on a single major industry for its support.

Information secured from local financial institutions also provides a reliable indication of an area's economy. The volume of mortgage loans outstanding and being issued reflects the overall confidence in the real estate market. If lenders will not initiate loans for which property in the area serves as collateral, that may indicate a decline in neighborhood property values.

Interest rates charged for loans act as a measurement for local business activities. Theoretically, there is an inverse relationship between interest rates and business activities—as interest rates climb, economic activity declines; as interest rates drop, economic activity increases. Such information is vital to developers who anticipate financing their projects both during construction and after completion, when a permanent, long-term mortgage loan will be required. The amount of interest will directly affect the rate of return from the project.

Competitive rental prices currently charged for residential, commercial and industrial space in the neighborhood offer an accurate measurement of the area's economy. Low rents indicate an oversupply of rentals relative to a limited demand, whereas high rents indicate a shortage of rental space. The Consumer Price Index, published by the Bureau of Labor Statistics, provides information concerning trends in rental schedules.

Occupancy Rates.   The occupancy rates for a particular type of property also reflect the relationship between supply and demand in the neighborhood. Occupancies constantly change and vacancy rates fluctuate accordingly, and this affects rents.

A high occupancy rate indicates a shortage of space and the possibility of rent increases. A low rate, as reflected by many "For Lease" signs posted in a neighborhood, results in tenant demands for lower rents and other concessions from landlords.

The oversupply of space that results in low occupancy rates can be either technical or economic in origin. Technical oversupply occurs when there are more available units than potential tenants; economic oversupply reflects asking prices beyond the purchasing power of potential tenants. Statistics on vacancy rates can be obtained from the U.S. Census Bureau or from current housing reports, which are published by the Department of Commerce and list vacancies by region. Local utility companies often provide information regarding vacancies, with the number of nonoperating meters corresponding roughly to the number of vacant apartments, stores or offices, as the case may be.

The investor-developer must also be able to predict whether future occupancy levels will rise or fall and how quickly these transitions will take place. To answer these questions, existing competitive space must be inventoried according to building type, age, size of units and rental schedules. In addition, careful attention should be devoted to securing an inventory of all new construction, both under way and contemplated.

To a great extent, accurate prediction of occupancy rates depends on matching the composition of the local populace to the available space. The investor-developer should know the number of potential tenants and their ability and willingness to purchase or rent the properties being developed. The stability and trends of their incomes must also be determined.

Statistics issued by the Department of Labor list the total number of employed persons by region and also provide the investor with information regarding unemployment ratios. Information obtained from the chamber of commerce can furnish investors with a clear picture of local employment opportunities and the median income of the community's population. In addition, local financial institutions can provide information about the population's savings habits as an indication of economic stability. These employment and income data should provide some reliable benchmarks for establishing appropriate rental schedules.

To plan efficiently for the number and type of housing units needed, investors in residential rental properties must determine the most common individual family size and composition, in addition to the total number of people within the area. For example, the prospects for financial success of a highrise apartment complex composed of studio and one-bedroom units in an area composed mainly of families with two children would be quite different from those prospects for a similar property in a neighborhood of young singles or childless couples. Local marriage, birth and divorce records will provide investors with information regarding the structure of family units within the area.

In addition to the family structure, investors in residential real estate must be aware of current shifts in population. When changes in the composition of a neighborhood are detected, these alterations must be carefully analyzed in terms of land use and income level. An increase in population due to an influx of middle-income families into an expanding community has a considerably different meaning from an increase in population due to overcrowding in lower-rental areas. The implications for the future use of the neighborhood are quite different in each case.

Transportation and Utilities.   Regardless of the type of development contemplated, transportation facilities are of prime importance to future tenants and must be included in the market analysis of the property. In large cities, close proximity to public transportation is vital to apartment dwellers, who may not own cars. Employees in many office buildings often rely on public transportation to get to work. Traffic patterns, street networks and traffic counts in a neighborhood are significant to such commercial ventures as strip stores or shopping centers. Industrial developments require convenient access to railroads, expressways or airports for receiving and distributing goods.

In addition to public transportation facilities, access and linkage to various parts of the community are essential components of the market analysis process. It is crucial to examine not only the *distance* to work but also the roads and freeway networks to determine the amount of *time* it takes to reach various destinations.

For example, a housing project constructed some distance from the center of a community on less expensive land might be successful if a connecting freeway allows potential buyers to get to work faster than if the project were built in town with only surface transportation available. Thus, a time-distance study should be included in feasibility reports.

Residential, commercial and industrial property users are also deeply concerned with the availability of adequate parking facilities. The aggravation of over-crowded curb space in urban areas can be relieved by off-street tenant parking. Commercial enterprises need adequate parking facilities for their customers, and industrial concerns require dockside space for loading and areas for employee parking.

The costs and availability of utility services are having an increasingly impor-tant effect on profits from investment properties. Commercial and industrial users are particularly concerned with heavy-duty power lines, adequate sewer-age systems, access roads and other special services required by the nature of their businesses.

Neighborhood Facilities.   Although the existence of neighborhood amenities is of greater significance to residential investors, any improvements that help to attract potential residents will indirectly benefit commercial and industrial developers by providing a local pool of potential consumers and employees. When inspecting a neighborhood, an investor should note the location and num-ber of parks, playgrounds, theaters, restaurants, schools, colleges, churches and other social or cultural organizations and facilities that will be attractive to future inhabitants.

Community Acceptance.   Finally, the increasingly important community involvement with any major new real estate development must be recognized in a market study. The type of development must be compatible to the neighbor-hood. In addition, any rezoning effort will probably involve the immediate neigh-bors of the subject property and other concerned citizens. They will have to be satisfied.

Environmental impact studies are also required in many areas of the country. These studies describe the effects of the project not only on the immediately sur-rounding properties but also on the community and region as a whole. Project plans must be approved by various government agencies, including street and road, water, sewer, fire, building inspection and other departments charged with protecting the health, safety and welfare of citizens.

Any time lags necessary to satisfy these requirements must be included in the study. This information helps the investor develop the strategy necessary to com-plete the project and enter the market in a timely manner.

Evaluating the Data

Once the community profile is complete, the investor-analyst must combine the information collected concerning transportation facilities, economic conditions, type and number of similar spaces, rental schedules and population composition and evaluate it as a whole. When reviewing the data, the investor should remain aware of the special needs of the particular type of property for which the investigation was made.

Industrial property developers should pay specific attention to the opportunity for physical expansion, transportation facilities, special utility services, availability of raw materials and the quality and quantity of the potential labor pool in the area. Commercial property developers must be informed about traffic patterns, car and pedestrian traffic flows, location of competitors, public transportation facilities, adequate parking space and the income profile of the market-area populace. Of special interest to residential property developers are the size of family units, median income levels, trends in family composition and locational movements, and sociological and cultural compatibilities.

Reconciliation of the neighborhood survey data with the specific qualities of the property to be developed allows the investor to estimate the optimum rental rates that can be secured for the space offered. From this estimate, the investor will be able to calculate the profitability of the project after deducting expected operating expenses, interest on loans and depreciation. Thus, a project will receive a "go" or "no go," depending on the rate of profitability and its acceptance by the investor.

The market analysis is only as reliable as the judgment of the person making the evaluation. An inexperienced investor should seek the services of a professional property analyst who is fully knowledgeable about the nature of business and economic cycles and who can accurately assess their influences on the character and future trends of the subject market area.

Local Government Regulations

Just as the various agencies of the federal government have an impact on real estate investment activities, so local agencies affect the investment process. Following are some more specific ways in which the regulating bodies of local governments control the growth and development of communities.

Subdivision Regulations.   Most major communities in this country have adopted laws to regulate the subdividing of land. The purpose of these laws is to prevent the unplanned and haphazard division of large parcels of land into small building lots, which has been the prevalent practice in the past. City and county officials are now charged with the duty of supervising the orderly growth of their communities. As a result, an investor who wishes to develop a parcel of land must present an application for plat approval and required zoning changes to the special local agency in charge of subdivision control, such as a local planning and zoning department.

Plat Approval.   In order to control the design of a new subdivision, a developer must submit a plat for approval by all of the various departments involved in community services. A **plat** is a drawing of the subdivision by an engineer or architect that shows lot sizes, street widths, easements and so on. The proposed lot sizes must conform to acceptable standards. The street design must link up to existing roadways and incorporate special safety features, such as proper

FIGURE 5.1 Pima County, Arizona, Summary of Zoning Classifications and Principal Users

		Minimum Lot Area (sq.ft.)	Width (ft.)	Min. Area Per Unit (sq. ft.)	Minimum Yards Front (ft.)	Side (ft.)	Rear (ft.)	Stories; Bldg. Height (ft.)
SR: Suburb Ranch	1-family residences, agricultural, hospital, recreational uses	144,000	None	144,000	50	10	50	2; 30
CR-1: Single Residence	1-family residences and home occupations; horses permitted	36,000	100	36,000	30	10	40	2; 30
CR-2: Single Residence	CR-1 uses, one family residence, home occupations	16,000	80	16,000	30	10	40	2; 30
CR-3 Single Residence	1-family residences and home occupations	8,000	60	8,000	20 or on a corner lot 20	8 18	40 10	2; 30
PR-3: Planned Res. Dev.	1-family residences in CR-3 zone only	40 acres		8,000	50	50	50	2; 30
SH: Suburban Homestead	SR uses, duplexes, two trailers on one lot; professional or semi-professional offices	36,000	100	18,000	30	10	40	2; 30
CR-4 Multiple Residence	CR-3 uses, duplexes, multiple dwellings (not more than 4 units in one building)	7,000	60	3,500	25 or on a corner lot 25	8 18	35 10	...; 30
CR-5: Multiple Residence	CR-3 & CR-4 uses multiple dwellings, boarding & rooming houses	7,000	60	2,000	25 or on a corner lot 25	7 17	35 10	...; 30
TR: Transitional	CR-3, CR-4, CR-5 uses, tourist court or hotels, profess. offices, clinics	10,000	60	1,000	20 or on a corner lot 20	7 17	25 10	...; 30
TH Travel: Tra. Court	Trailer Court Accessory Uses	18,000		2,000	30	10	30	2; 30
GR: General Rural	Commercial agriculture, residence, mobile home, trailer court	36,000	60	36,000	30	10	40	2; 30
RVC: Rural Village	Retail business	None	None	None	Architectural review by committee & P/Z required			2; 30
CB-1: Local Business	Retail business; any TR use	None 10,000 (Res)	None 60 (Res)	None 1,000 (Res)	20 20 or on a corner lot 20	None 7 17	25 25 10	...; com'l 35, res. 30
CB-2: General Business	CB-1 uses, billboards, light manufacturing wholesale, bars	None 7,000 (Res)	None 60 (Res)	None 1,000 (Res)	15 20 (Res)	None 7 (Res)	10 25 (Res)	...; 35

FIGURE 5.1 Pima County, Arizona, Summary of Zoning Classifications and Principal Users (continued)

		Minimum Lot		Min. Area Per Unit (sq. ft.)	Minimum Yards			Stories; Bldg. Height (ft.)
		Area (sq. ft.)	Width (ft.)		Front (ft.)	Side (ft.)	Rear (ft.)	
MU: Multiple Uses	Business*; residence, trailer or mobile home court	None 7,000 (Res)	None 60 (Res)	None 3,500 (Res)	20 (Res)	7 (Res)	25 (Res)	2; 30
CI-1: Light Industry, Warehouse	Limited CB-1, CB-2 uses, warehouse and light industrial uses	None	None	None	15 Ind. buffer	None Ind. buffer	10 Ind. buffer	...; 35
CI-2: Industry	Limited CB2, CI-1 uses, other uses subject to conditional permit, warehouse	None	None	None	15 Ind. buffer	None Ind. buffer	10 Ind. buffer	...; 35 50
CI-3 Industry	Limited CI-2 uses, other uses subject to conditions	43,560	None	None	10% of lot depth	35	30	None
A	Airport Approach Zone	(Regulations & Height Limits as per Article 37)						
A-2	DM Airport Appr. Zone	(Regulations & Height Limits as per Article 38)						
A-3	Ryan Airport Appr. Zone	(Regulations & Height Limits as per Article 41)						
CMH-1: Co. M. Home	Mobile home subdivision (cluster dev.)	20 acres	60 None	8,000 8,000	30 25	10 25	40 25	2; 30
MH-2: Co. M. Home	Mobile home park	5 acres	None	5,445	25	10	25	2; 30

*MU business must have 30-day notice.

widths, gradients for curves, access for fire-fighting equipment and turnarounds in cul-de-sac streets.

Adequate drainage must be provided to avoid potential flood damage. Utility installations must be situated in proper easements and be readily accessible for continuing maintenance. Adequate solid and liquid waste disposal systems must be developed to prevent pollution of underground or surface water streams.

Prior to plat approval, any special circumstances surrounding each particular project must be solved to the satisfaction not only of the community agencies but also of neighbors and other citizens whose rights are involved.

Zoning Codes. In addition to subdivision regulations, most communities have local zoning ordinances that designate allowable land usage for particular purposes. Historically, zones were separated according to types of use: single-family residential, multifamily residential, commercial, industrial and special purpose (such as an airport or hospital). It was felt then—and still is in most parts of our country—that to maintain their separate integrity, these different divisions should not be mixed. See Figure 5.1 for an example of one area's land uses.

Over time subdivisions have been designed with an inner core of space for single-family housing surrounded by areas intended for more intensive uses, such as apartments and store buildings. Industrial land is usually located along the highways and railroads to facilitate shipping requirements and minimize the effects of pollution on residential areas.

Zoning designations are usually based on a system of code letters that stand for certain allowable uses and specify the amount of land that can be utilized for construction. These zoning codes also include specifications for spaces that must be left vacant between adjoining lots. This type of specification is referred to as a **setback** requirement.

For instance, a county CR-4 designation (see Figure 5.1) could indicate a multiple residence use requiring a minimum of 7,000 square feet of total lot area per unit and construction setbacks of 25 feet from the front lot line, 35 feet from the rear lot line, 8 feet from each side lot line and not more than 30 feet building height.

Of course, these requirements vary from jurisdiction to jurisdiction and depend to a great degree on the type of development anticipated for the specific location. It is important for a real estate investor to be thoroughly familiar with local zoning codes, which—in some high-growth areas—can change rapidly.

Rezoning a property from its present use to a more intensive use, such as changing a vacant lot zoned for a single house to a zoning that would permit four units, may result in substantial profits for an investor, as we will discover in later chapters. The rezoning process involves application by the professional staff of this agency and a public hearing in front of a commission and/or a city council or county board of supervisors, who rule on the acceptability of the professional staff's recommendations. Public hearings allow petitioners to state their cases and also permit neighbors and other interested citizens to make their feelings known. Participants have recourse to the courts if they feel rezoning decisions are unfair.

Since each jurisdiction follows its own specific techniques for conducting the rezoning process, investors interested in this form of activity would be well advised to know the requirements in their particular area.

Deed and Subdivision Restrictions.   Restrictions are covenants that run with the ground: once recorded, they remain in effect into the future. Each new owner of the property buys "subject to" the restrictions. All of the owners affected would have to agree in order to have them removed or changed. Restrictions specify what the property can or cannot be used for or what can or cannot be built on the land. Restrictions supersede any zoning on the property.

Individual deed restrictions are usually imposed by a landowner on property to be split off and sold separately from the main parcel. By restricting the new parcels, the original owner can maintain the integrity of the main parcel.

Subdivision restrictions, on the other hand, are usually established by the developer on all of the lots in a new subdivision in order to maintain their homogeneity of use as well as value. Subdivision restrictions generally run for 50 years or longer. Thus, buyers in the subdivision can rely on their investments maintaining their values for long periods of time.

For example, restrictions may include a minimum number of square feet per residence and prohibit any other than residential use in the subdivision. Other restrictions may also be included (see chapter 11).

However, all restrictions are only as strong as the persons who will be responsible for their enforcement. In the case of deed restrictions, when the original owner dies or moves away, the split property owners may not observe the requirements. If the new owner of the main property does not object, the restrictions are broken. Similarly, the enforcement of subdivision restrictions relies on a strong neighborhood association that is not afraid to sue those who do not observe the requirements.

Investors must not only be aware of what the zoning codes are but also be alert to check with a title company or lawyer about any existing restrictions on the property in question.

Planned Unit Developments (PUDs). Many communities are experimenting with an innovative form of subdivision known as the planned unit development. A PUD involves the elimination of the side-yard setback requirements and allows mixed land uses. Thus, apartments and town houses can be joined together with common walls, while retail businesses and "clean" industrial plants can be incorporated right into the subdivision.

Example: If a 100-acre tract can hold 400 individual single-family detached houses under a zoning designation of four house lots to the acre, a PUD can be designed to include four separate 100-unit complexes. Elimination of the side-yard setback requirements makes it possible to construct a 100-unit building that includes highrise and lowrise apartments joined by common walls. Each 100-unit building would be surrounded by open space containing lawn areas, playgrounds, swimming pools, bicycle and walking paths, tennis courts, golf courses and similar recreational facilities.

Mixed land-use PUDs can incorporate retail businesses, office buildings and even acceptable industrial plants into their designs. These PUDs become entirely self-contained small communities. For instance, Reston, Virginia, has store buildings, apartments, a lake and various employment centers built right into exclusive single-family home areas. Residents of this community can walk or ride a bicycle to work, school, shopping or recreational areas.

Minimum Housing Standards.   Many communities have adopted uniform building and housing codes that designate **minimum housing standards** required for new construction as well as for older homes.

Requirements for new housing include minimum specifications for foundations, underflooring, wood framing, roofing, and weatherproofing and general requirements involving exit facilities, light, ventilation and sanitation. Some jurisdictions also require provisions for off-street parking facilities and fire warning systems.

Most cities maintain inspection staffs charged with determining the safety of existing properties. If a building or a portion of a building is found to be unsanitary and/or unsafe, these inspectors have the power to issue appropriate citations to the owner, specifying failings that need to be corrected and penalties if they are not. At the same time, a sign is posted indicating that the building is unsafe and advising against entry. Ultimately, if the faults are not corrected, the structure may be condemned and destroyed as a public nuisance.

In great part, these minimum housing standards are a result of the activities of mortgage lenders. Historically, lenders have fought for better building codes for potential enhancement of the value of their collateral. The FHA has been a pioneer in these efforts by standardizing appraisal techniques, which led to the establishment of new housing codes in the mid-1930s.

Planned Growth.   Many communities throughout the country compete with one another to attract new industry by offering tax waivers, free land and other incentives. Industrial development foundations are formed by local businesspeople and given carte blanche and large budgets with which to lure desirable industries away from other communities. New industry means new jobs, higher earnings, more taxes and, generally, growth, expansion and prosperity.

In some areas, communities have lost control of their growth as a natural consequence of burgeoning population. City planners and citizens alike are displeased over these developments, and, reflecting the attitudes of their constituents, politicians are moving to advocate a *no-growth policy*. Some have yielded to pressure from the construction industry and have modified their views to form a policy of *planned growth*. This policy vests more power in the bureaucratic agencies that control land use and development and seriously inhibits new construction.

As a direct consequence of slowing new building, the values of existing properties have risen. A dramatic case in point is the increased values of coastal and lakeside properties in areas that have imposed building moratoriums and that enforce severe controls on new developments.

Environmental Protection Agencies.   Increased pollution of our natural environment led to the passage of the National Environmental Policy Act of 1969 which established a federal administrative division called the Environmental Protection Agency (EPA). Among its other duties, the **EPA** determines environmental control guidelines for the development of real estate projects. In practice, the EPA encourages the individual states to adopt and enforce local controls of their own and steps in only when the states do not act to implement the minimum federal guidelines.

The broad objectives of the federal environmental control guidelines are to develop and maintain a high-quality environment now and in the future. Toward this end, the EPA was created to take all action necessary to protect, rehabilitate and enhance the environmental quality of the country. Its goals are to provide the people with clean air and water; to protect aesthetic, natural, scenic and historic environments; and to ensure freedom from noise.

To make sure that long-term protection of the environment is the guiding criterion in public decisions, the EPA guidelines require government agencies at all levels to consider qualitative factors as well as economic and technical factors, long-term benefits and costs in addition to short-term benefits and costs, and alternatives to proposed actions affecting the environment.

In those states that have adopted environmental controls, the government agencies are guided in their analyses by the results of individual environmental impact studies. Each major political jurisdiction in these states has an environmental quality division. As a prerequisite to the development of a new real estate project, an application for environmental review must be filed by the developer with the appropriate agency. An investigation is conducted and an environmental impact report is released. Contributions to this report are made by the various governmental groups involved in the decision, such as the local zoning board, building inspection department, sewer department and city transportation division. Figure 5.2 outlines San Diego's process.

If the application is approved, development proceeds to completion. If defects in the plan are revealed in the impact study, the applicant is informed and may resubmit the application together with proposed remedies. If the project is categorically denied because of potential serious damage to the environment, the applicant may appeal through appropriate legal channels.

PROPERTY ANALYSIS

An investor needs to examine carefully the physical characteristics of the parcel of land to be utilized in a new construction or the nature and condition of the existing building considered for purchase. In the first instance, the land's geological and surface characteristics are investigated, as well as the costs of their probable modification and of the installation of utilities, roadways and landscaping. In the second instance, the physical condition of the existing building, its functional capability and the costs of modernization must be analyzed for potential repair and maintenance expenses.

The Site

Besides the locational characteristics described in the market analysis, a site's physical attributes must be examined to determine its capacity to support the structures the investor intends to build.

FIGURE 5.2   Review Process

This chart shows the city of San Diego's environmental review process and time requirements for proposed real estate developments. In practice, the time requirements have proven to be seriously understated.

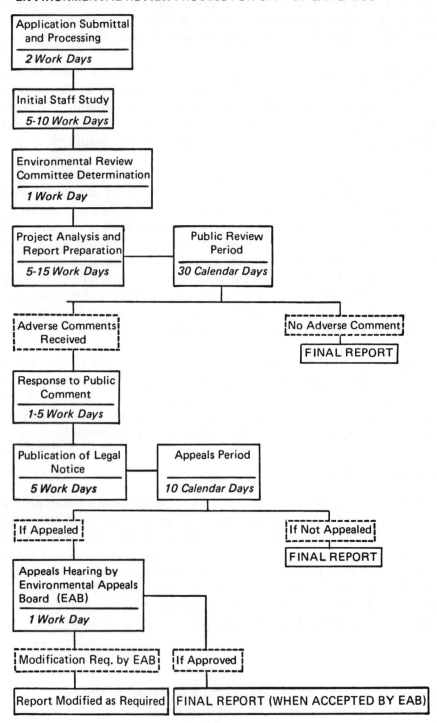

ENVIRONMENTAL REVIEW PROCESS FOR CITY OF SAN DIEGO

Surface Attributes.   The use of a parcel of real estate may be limited by its topography, vegetation, size, shape or exposure. These surface attributes include wetlands, hilly terrain, the absence of fertile topsoil, woods, boulders, irregular shapes, narrow dimensions, obnoxious odors and oppressive sounds. To cure any of these problems and to prepare a parcel of land for new construction involves expenditures that must be included in a feasibility study for a complete picture of total investment costs.

While physical irregularities may be corrected with the services of landscaping engineers, it is often more difficult to acquire the amount of land necessary to ensure adequate areas for building and parking. Residential lots need ample frontage exposure to serve the tastes of modern high-income home buyers who are seeking the quiet and protection of a suburban or rural location. Commercial property must be easily accessible to people on foot or in cars. Industrial property must have access to railroads, highways and adequate utility services, including solid and liquid waste-disposal facilities.

Subsurface Attributes.   The ability of a parcel of land to support new construction is of paramount importance to developers of highrise apartment or office buildings. Soft or slippery subsoil conditions can result in high costs if a builder has to sink support piers to firm bedrock, which is often far below the surface. New construction techniques allow buildings to *float* and are opening up formerly unusable marshy lands for building purposes, but the costs of these techniques are high.

If the land is rocky and the subsoil hard and impenetrable, there will be additional costs for excavation. In areas in which basements are desired, these costs may adversely affect the sale of houses. If substantial foundations and a number of subsurface floors are included in the building's design, rocky subsoil creates physical barriers often difficult to offset.

High subsurface water tables and areas subject to flooding often make it difficult to provide sanitary sewage disposal and adequate drainage runoff. Pollution of underground water streams is a serious problem in these areas.

Hazardous Waste.   As a result of our emerging awareness of the deterioration of our environment, there is increasing pressure to preserve the integrity of our living space. Many states have become stricter in enforcing EPA-suggested guidelines. California's Superfund Law is continually imposing new requirements on landowners, tenants and developers to ensure that their properties are free of contaminants and hazardous wastes.

A recent amendment to the California Health and Safety Code requires that an owner of nonresidential real property who knows or has cause to believe that release of a hazardous waste substance has contaminated the land give written notice of such to a buyer or be subject to a substantial civil penalty. Conversely, any tenant causing or knowing of such a problem must inform the landlord. Because California legislation influences other states, these changes may soon be significant to investors throughout the nation.

The Property

The purpose of a property analysis is to familiarize the investor with the nature and condition of the particular property under consideration and its position relative to similar properties in the neighborhood. On completion of the property analysis, the investor should know what expenditures will be needed to make the property competitive with the best units available in the area and what the average operating costs for the project will be.

Exterior Attributes.   The *visual image,* or initial impression, created by a building is of considerable importance to prospective tenants. Many investors refer to the external physical characteristics of the building as "curb appeal." Thus, an investor should note the age and style of the property as well as the condition of the walkways, the landscaping and the overall exterior appearance of the building itself. Any improvements required should be noted.

In addition, the investor should be alert to any major repairs deferred by the previous owner. The masonry, windows, eaves and trim, roof, porches, parking area, pool and other amenities and building parts must be carefully examined for defects that may require immediate attention and capital outlay.

The investor should also thoroughly inspect the quality of construction and the superstructure of the building itself. During periods of high growth, many builders cut costs by not following sound building principles and standards in the construction of their buildings. While these substandard practices may be difficult to observe, it is critical that the investor get a structural engineer's report on the quality of the construction.

Interior Attributes.   The investor should carefully examine the interior of the building, including the number of individual apartments or offices and their layouts, size, number of rooms, closets, bathrooms and views. Also, property must be renovative to accommodate the diverse uses of the tenants. Securing optimum rents is a function of desirability of design and location in the building as well as of physical quality.

When inspecting individual units, the investor should examine the condition of the hardware, plumbing, walls and electrical fixtures. In apartment units, appliances, carpets and drapes should be checked and an estimate made of the expense of repairing or replacing worn or obsolete items.

The condition of entry ways, halls, laundry rooms, storage rooms and other common interior areas should also be checked. Any redecorating and replacement that may be required to improve the general appearance of the building should be noted. This inspection should include the appliances, heating and cooling systems, plumbing fixtures, water heaters, elevators and swimming pool and other tenant amenities, as well as the machinery required for snow removal and lawn and pool maintenance.

Operating Expenses.   The investor should verify the amount of property taxes with the local tax assessor and the amount of insurance premiums with an agent. Constant attention must be paid to adequate insurance coverage, both casualty and liability, in the face of inflation and ever-increasing financial settlements. Frequently, an investor can secure relatively accurate utility cost information by calling the local providers.

Asbestos and Hazardous Waste.   In addition to considering the presence or absence of hazardous waste on the site, it is important for purchasers of existing structures to address the possibility that construction materials containing asbestos or other hazardous waste material, such as lead-based paint, may be present. The cost of removing these items could affect the profitability of the venture.

Removing asbestos or other hazardous wastes can be current deductible expenses only if it can be shown that

- removal is necessary to keep the property in an ordinarily efficient operating condition and
- the costs will not materially add to the value of the property or appreciably prolong its life.

Otherwise

- the costs must be capitalized as a permanent addition to the existing basis of the property, to be recovered at its sale; or
- the costs must be depreciated independently for 27.5 or 39 years, depending on whether the property is residential or commercial; or
- the investor must identify which portion of the costs would increase the value of the building and capitalize that portion. The balance can then be deducted as a repair cost.

However, a recent review has concluded that hasty and careless removal of asbestos may cause more harm to the removal workers than leaving it in place would cause to the building occupants. Researchers using sophisticated new techniques have discovered that when existing asbestos materials have not been disturbed, the concentration of airborne asbestos is comparable to the level of concentration in outdoor air. The EPA agrees that when asbestos is not damaged or disturbed, it probably should not be removed.

Because of the many and varied problems that may exist within structures, investors are advised to enlist the services of a qualified private building inspector for a professional opinion of the structure's condition.

An investor must accurately estimate ongoing maintenance expenses, in addition to monies earmarked for future replacement of major items, such as the roof, furniture, carpets and elevators. Together with the payments necessary for debt service, the investor is then ready to do a financial analysis to complete the feasibility study.

SUMMARY

Many real estate investments are made in a somewhat informal manner, with a buyer purchasing a property after a cursory examination of its physical condition and a rudimentary analysis of its profit potential. Other realty transactions require more definitive feasibility studies, including analyses of the market that the project will serve, an in-depth examination of the property itself (both land and buildings) and a complete financial analysis of the quantity and quality of the income stream to be derived.

A market analysis initially consists of the development of a community profile in which the project's market and its composition are clearly defined. Often, there are no clear-cut physical boundaries, such as mountains, streams or roadways, to delineate a market neighborhood. Rather, the area is described as that which is under common usage and shares a similar population. The economic climate of the neighborhood is then examined to discover types of business activity, volume of sales and general trends of growth or decline. Included in the trend analyses are the interest rates charged on loans, the availability of money for mortgage and business loans and competitive rental prices charged for properties similar to the projected investment. High interest rates generally indicate a tight money market and a probable shortage of funds for loans. High rents indicate a probable shortage of space and, therefore, a good rental market.

Occupancy rates aid in measuring the economic quality of the market that a realty project will serve. High current occupancy rates, or low vacancy rates, indicate a shortage of space and the possibility for rent increases. An oversupply of space, on the other hand, indicates a weak market and the possibility of developing less cash flow from the project than anticipated. Careful projections must be made of future trends in the development of comparable rental space from new construction, both under way and contemplated.

A complete profile of the neighborhood's population is included in the economic analysis. In addition to the number of persons located in the area, information about their family structure and financial positions can be helpful in planning the number and types of housing units needed or the composition of a shopping center. Current population shifts must be diagnosed for an indication of potential changes that may affect the investment.

Once the economic profile of the market neighborhood is finished, the locational qualities of the area should be identified. These attributes include the type and availability of transportation facilities and utilities, as well as neighborhood amenities that would enhance a contemplated project.

A careful investigation must be made of the community acceptance of a major new realty development. In addition to the immediate neighbors' attitudes, the requirements of all the various public agencies that will be involved in the project's supervision prior to and during construction must be analyzed. Any substantial negative points of view will have to be met forthrightly before the project is undertaken.

An in-depth study of the physical qualities of the land on which a project will be constructed—or in the case of a used property, of the building itself—must be coupled with the economic analysis of the market the realty project will serve. Both surface and underground attributes of the site must be analyzed in terms of their ability to support a new project. An already existing building must be inspected in terms of its appearance and functional efficiency so that the owner can learn of potential refurbishing costs and ongoing operating expenses.

EXERCISE 5   (Answers may be checked against the Answer Key.)

1. The primary purpose of subdivision regulations in most states is to

    a. enable developers to profit from rezoning.
    b. divide large parcels of land into small lots.
    c. prevent unplanned and haphazard subdividing.
    d. inhibit growth in developed areas.

2. Which of the following describes a mixed-use subdivision?

    a. A racially integrated neighborhood
    b. Proportionate grouping by population age
    c. A legally prohibited method of development
    d. Different but compatible developments in one designated area

3. Fundamentally, a planned unit development (PUD) is designed to

    a. attract members of one racial or religious group.
    b. eliminate side-yard restrictions for more efficient land use.
    c. relegate housing developments to the suburbs.
    d. discourage mixed-use subdivisions.

4. In a market analysis, the occupancy rates for a particular type of property should be compared to the

    a. community's overall occupancy factor.
    b. nation's occupancy factor for that type of property.
    c. community's occupancy factor for that type of property.
    d. U.S. Department of Labor's employed persons list.

5. When analyzing the site for a new commercial investment project, all of the following factors must be considered *except* the site's

    a. surface attributes.
    b. possible contamination.
    c. subsurface attributes.
    d. fertility.

6. When examining the building included in a proposed commercial investment, all of the following factors must be considered *except* the propert's

    a. appearance.
    b. location.
    c. physical condition.
    d. square footage.

7. How many units can be built on an apartment site 220 feet wide by 385 feet deep, where the zoning requires a total side-yard setback of 20 feet, a front yard of 25 feet, a rear yard of 10 feet, a height limit of two floors and a minimum of 3,500 square feet of usable lot area per unit?

    a.   16 units
    b.   20 units
    c.   24 units
    d.   40 units

8. All of the following statements about residential subdivision restrictions are true *except* they are

    a.   enforceable only against the original home owner.
    b.   covenants that run with the land.
    c.   effective as long as they are enforced.
    d.   established to maintain the homogeneity of property use and value.

9. A feasibility analysis is primarily designed to provide an investor with information appropriate to

    a.   avoiding payment of income taxes.
    b.   guaranteeing a profit on the investment.
    c.   making an economically rational investment decision.
    d.   satisfying various government regulatory agencies.

10. The Environmental Protection Agency (EPA) establishes guidelines for the prevention of all of the following circumstances *except*

    a.   air pollution.
    b.   soil contamination.
    c.   water impurities.
    d.   property accessibility.

DISCUSSION

1. Secure a copy of a recent feasibility study of a property in your area, and examine it in relation to the material in this chapter.

2. With the increasing awareness of the effects of uncontrolled growth on the environment, a trend toward a no-growth attitude seems to be emerging nationally. Investigate the attitudes in your community from both citizens' and politicians' points of view.

6
Financial Analysis
of Real Estate Investments

Key Terms

amortization

annuity

break even

compound interest

discounted cash flow

discount rate

effective interest rate

fixed costs

interest factor (IF)

internal rate of return (IRR)

nominal interest rate

operating expense

opportunity cost

present worth

reserves

return on investment (ROI)

time value of money

variable costs

FINANCIAL ANALYSIS

After reviewing the market in which an investment is contemplated and the physical attributes of the property itself, as described in the prior chapter, an investor should undertake a thorough financial analysis to attempt to estimate the value and potential profitability of the investment. Although such a financial analysis appears to be a relatively simple matter of comparing income with expenses to derive a net cash flow and a return on the investment, in reality it requires a dedication to honestly examine all of the facts before making a decision to purchase the property.

The most difficult part of a financial analysis is the gathering of complete and accurate data pertinent to the project. No matter how sophisticated and complex, no analysis is valid without clear and accurate inputs. Owners typically understate expenses and overstate occupancy. Few include management fees or reserves for replacements, while others brag about 100 percent occupancy when in reality their rents are too low. Deferred maintenance is common.

Conservative investors recognize that because of credit losses and intervals between tenants for normal maintenance, 95 percent occupancy *is* full occupancy. Also, depending on the age and condition of the property, at least

5 percent of the gross income should actually be set aside as **reserves** for replacement of major building components such as roofs, boilers, and so on. Many investors have faced financial ruin because there were no reserves available for such expenses. A reasonable amount must also be allocated to management no matter who actually manages the property.

A financial analysis requires a diligent effort to gather real information about the property in order to come as close as possible to an accurate opinion of the investment's potential.

The following summary is a typical example of the information required to make an analysis of an income property.

WESTWOOD SQUARE APARTMENTS SUMMARY, 1994
Scheduled Gross Income

Bedrooms	Baths	No. Units	Rent-Range	Total
1	1	18	$350–415	$ 6,830
2	1½	32	$450–505	15,002
				21,832
Monthly Laundry Income				600
Monthly Storage Income				150
Monthly Parking Income				320
Monthly Misc. Income				425
				23,327
			×	12
				279,924
Less 5% Vacancy Factor				13,996
Effective Gross Annual Income				$265,928

Scheduled Annual Operating Expenses

Real Estate Taxes	$ 21,015
Hazard and Liability Insurance	4,062
Electricity	1,900
Water	5,820
Sewer	14,350
Garbage	5,988
Resident Managers	12,000
Professional Managers	13,996
Maintenance and Repairs	15,835
Advertising	3,050
Supplies	6,800
Telephone	720
Replacement Reserves	5,000
Total Expenses	$110,536
NET OPERATING INCOME	$155,392

The net operating income is an indication of the property's value. For instance, if the area's market capitalization rate for these types of apartments is 10 percent, then the property's value would be $1.5 million.

$$\begin{array}{l} \$ \ \ 155,392 \ \ \text{net operating income} \\ + \ \ \underline{\hspace{1.2cm}.10} \ \ \text{capitalization rate} \\ \$1,553,920, \text{ or approximately } \$1.5 \text{ million} \end{array}$$

An interested investor can make an offer predicated on this financial analysis. This offer would probably include securing a loan on the property, the payment for which would come from the net operating income.

The net operating income also provides the basis for analyzing the potential before-tax and after-tax returns on the buyer's investment. However, these analyses depend on an understanding of the effects of the costs of money and the impacts of time on the value of money.

Interest

An understanding of the principles of interest as they apply to real estate investment is basic to any financial feasibility study for income property. Interest may be described as rent paid for the use of money. Just as rent is paid for the use of an apartment, office or store, so interest, together with principal, is paid on a real estate mortgage as a condition of the terms of the loan agreement. The investor borrows (leases) money at a certain interest rate (rent) for a specified time period, during which the amount borrowed is systematically repaid (amortized).

The amount of rent that a landlord can charge for the use of property is a function of the rental market for that particular type of real estate. Similarly, the rate of interest that a lender can charge is a function of the money market as it affects that particular type of loan. A rational borrower-investor will not pay a lender more interest than the lowest interest rate available on a specific loan at a particular time. Unlike most charge account interest rates, which are based on a *monthly rate* of 1 or 1½ percent (12 or 18 percent per year), real estate loans are established at *annual rates* that are currently between 7 and 10 percent per year.

Simple Interest.   Most loans made on real estate are established at a simple rate of interest. Simple interest is paid only for the amount of money (principal) that is still owed as of the date of computation; that is, interest is not paid on the money that has already been repaid to the lender.

The formula for computing the amount of simple interest is:

$$I = PRT$$

$$I = \text{interest}$$

$$P = \text{principal}$$
$$R = \text{rate}$$
$$T = \text{time}$$

EXAMPLE: Using this formula, the interest on a $1,200 loan to be repaid in one year at a 10 percent annual rate is $120.

> $ 1,200 principal
> ×   .10 annual rate
> ‾‾‾‾‾‾‾
> 120 per year

If this $1,200 loan were to be repaid in 12 equal payments of $100 *plus* simple interest at the rate of 10 percent per year, the interest portion of the first monthly payment would be $10.

> $ 1,200 principal
> ×   .10 annual rate
> ‾‾‾‾‾‾‾
> 120 total interest at this rate
> ÷   12 months
> ‾‾‾‾‾‾‾
> $ 10

The total amount of the first month's payment in this example is $110.

> $ 1,200 principal
> ÷   .12 months
> ‾‾‾‾‾‾‾
> 100 principal
> +   10 interest
> ‾‾‾‾‾‾‾
> $ 110

The second month's payment is $109.16.

> $ 1,100 new principal
> ×   .10 annual rate
> ‾‾‾‾‾‾‾
> 110 total interest at this rate
> ÷   12 months
> ‾‾‾‾‾‾‾
> 9.16 monthly interest
> +100.00 principal
> ‾‾‾‾‾‾‾
> $109.16

The third month's payment is $108.33.

> $ 1,000 new principal
> ×   .10 annual rate
> ‾‾‾‾‾‾‾
> 100 total interest at this rate
> ÷   12 months
> ‾‾‾‾‾‾‾
> 8.33 interest
> +100.00 principal
> ‾‾‾‾‾‾‾
> $108.33

The last payment is $100.83

> $ 100 new principal
> ×   .10 annual rate
> ‾‾‾‾‾‾‾
> 10 total interest at this rate
> ÷   12 months
> ‾‾‾‾‾‾‾
> .83 monthly interest

<u>+ 100.00</u> principal
$100.83

This illustrates the fact that simple interest is charged only on the remaining amount of principal owed and only for the time that the amount is unpaid.

Amortization.   The payment schedule just described is an illustration of **amortization**—the systematic repayment of a loan.   Most real estate mortgages are established for 15 to 30 years and require a regular payment to be made annually, semiannually, quarterly or, more usually, monthly basis (see Table 6.1).

For example, consider a $50,000 loan at 7 percent for 30 years with a payment of $333 per month, principal and interest. Its amortization table would appear as follows:

EXAMPLE:

Period	Interest	Principal	Balance
1			$50,000.00
2	$291.66	$41.34	49,958.66
3	291.43	41.57	49,917.09
4	291.18	41.82	49,875.27
etc.			

Add-on Interest.   Although the simple interest rate is used for most real estate loans, some lenders occasionally employ an add-on interest rate. This method involves the computation of interest on the total amount of the loan for the entire time period. This amount of interest is then added onto the principal owed for repayment over the term of the loan *before* the monthly payments are calculated. Add-on interest has the effect of almost *doubling* the simple interest rate. This form of interest computation is used for some home improvement loans and junior liens created by private mortgage companies.

EXAMPLE: In the case of a $1,200 loan for one year at an interest rate of 10 percent, if the add-on method of computation is employed, first the total interest on $1,200 for a one-year period is derived at the rate stated in the loan agreement:

$1,200 principal
<u>×   10</u> annual rate
$ 120 interest

Next, this amount is added to the total principal owed:

$1,200 principal
<u>+ .120</u> interest
$1,320 total

Finally, this sum is divided by the number of required payments, to arrive at a monthly payment of $110.

$1,320 total
÷   12 months
$ 110 per month

In formula form, the add-on interest rate is calculated as follows:

$$A = \frac{2IC}{P(n + 1)}$$

A = add-on interest rate
I = number of installment payments per year
C = total loan charges including all interest over contract term
P = principal
n = total number of installment payments in contract

EXAMPLE: Substituting figures from the example, the add-on interest rate would be computed as follows:

A = 2IC/P(n + 1)
A = 2(12) ($120) ÷ $1,200(12 + 1)
A = $2,880 ÷ $15,600
A = 0.1846 or 18.46%

At add-on interest rates, the borrower in this example pays a level $110 per month for 12 months until the loan is satisfied. An inspection of this schedule reveals that although the first month's payment is a true reflection of the 10 percent per annum simple interest charge, the second and subsequent months' payments are not. The interest charges in these months do *not* stop on the portion of the principal that has been repaid. Examine the sixth payment of $110. The $100 principal portion of this payment repays exactly half the total loan:

$100 principal
×   6 payments
$600, which is half of $1,200.

However, the 10 percent portion still reflects the interest charged on the entire $1,200. Thus, the 10 percent add-on interest rate is really about 18 percent, as seen from the formula calculations.

Nominal and Effective Rates of Interest.   The relationship between simple interest and add-on interest should now be quite clear. At a simple rate of 10 percent interest, the **nominal interest rate,** the rate contracted for, is the same as the **effective interest rate,** the actual rate paid by the borrower. However, add-on interest, which has a nominal, or contracted, rate of 10 percent, results in an actual, or effective, rate of approximately 18 percent.

TABLE 6.1   The Cost of a Mortgage Monthly Principal and Interest per $1,000 of Loan

Rate	15-Year	30-Year
6.00	8.44	6.00
6.50	8.71	6.32
7.00	8.99	6.66
7.50	9.28	7.00
8.00	9.56	7.34
8.50	9.85	7.69
9.00	10.15	8.05
9.50	10.45	8.41
10.00	10.75	8.78

Note: Multiply the cost per $1,000 by the size of the loan (i.e., $80,000 at 8 percent for 30 years; 7.34 × $80 = $587.20 per month principal and interest).

Even with simple interest loan agreements, the nominal rate may not always be the effective rate. For instance, when a borrower executes a new mortgage loan for $100,000 and has to pay a one-point fee of $1,000 plus $500 of other costs, only $98,500 will be received at the closing.

$100,000   total
−   1,000   fee
−   500   costs
$ 98,500

However, this borrower will still have to pay interest on the full $100,000 contracted for, which, in effect, raises the interest rate.

Compound Interest.   **Compound interest** is interest paid on interest earned.

EXAMPLE: At the beginning of a year, if $1 is deposited in a savings account at 10 percent interest, the account will have a balance of $1.10 at the end of the year.

$1.00   principal
× .10   annual interest rate
.10   interest
+1.00   principal
$1.10

If this new $1.10 balance is allowed to remain on deposit and the interest rate continues at 10 percent, then the balance in the account at the end of the second year will be $1.21 and so on.

$ 1.10   principal
× .10   annual interest rate

.11   interest
+ 1.10   principal

$ 1.21

Compound interest may be computed using the following formula:

$$CS = BD (1 + i)^n$$

CS = compound sum
i   = interest rate per period
BD = beginning deposit
n   = number of periods

EXAMPLE: At the end of ten years, the balance of a savings account with $1,000 deposited at the beginning of the period at 10 percent interest, compounded annually, would be computed as follows:

$$CS = BD (1 + i)^n$$
$$CS = \$1,000 (1 + .10)^{10}$$
$$CS = \$1,000 (1.10)^{10}$$
$$CS = \$1,000 (2.59374)$$
$$CS = \$2,593.74$$

If interest is compounded more frequently—say, monthly or even daily (as advertised by many banks and savings associations)—then the *effective* rate of interest earnings is slightly higher than the *nominal* rate.

The concept of compounding forms a basis for most investment decisions. A savings account at the current interest rate is a constant investment alternative, and this interest rate constitutes a safe return on such funds. In other words, the compound interest earned on a savings account is a safe and viable investment yield against which potential earnings from other investment opportunities can be measured.

Within this framework, an investor will measure the *risk* of alternative investments, assigning a required return to each alternative as a function of its specific risk. Thus, an investment in an apartment project might require at least a 15 percent return, or yield, as a function of a 10 percent *safe rate* plus a 5 percent *risk rate*.

Compound Worth of an Annuity. The effects of compound interest on a single deposit provide an investor with a fundamental basis for investment comparison. However, an owner of income property is more concerned with the compounding of a series of deposits, which would more closely resemble a property's cash flow in terms of rents. Any series of regular annual receipts or payments is termed an annuity.

The formula for calculating the future compound worth of an annuity deposited into an interest-earning account at the *beginning* of each period is:

$$CS = RD [(1 + i)^{n-1} + (1 + i)^{n-2} + (1 + i)^{n-n}]$$

CS = compound sum
i = interest rate per period
RD = regular deposit
n = number of periods

EXAMPLE: A regular deposit of $1 made at the beginning of each year for three years at 10 percent annual compound interest will be worth $3.31 at the beginning of the third year, as shown:

$$CS = \$1[(1 + .10)^{3-1} + (1 + .10)^{3-2} + (1 + .10)^{3-3}]$$
$$CS = \$1[(1.21)^2 + (1.10)^1 + 1]$$
$$CS = \$1[3.31]$$
$$CS = \mathbf{\$3.31}$$

Using the same formula, compare the future value of a ten-year series of $100 annual deposits at 10 percent annual compound interest, with a single $1,000 deposit made at the beginning of the period.

EXAMPLE:
$$CS = \$100 [(1.10)^9 = 2.3579]$$
$$+(1.10)^8 = 2.1435$$
$$+(1.10)^7 = 1.9487$$
$$+(1.10)^6 = 1.7715$$
$$+(1.10)^5 = 1.6105$$
$$+(1.10)^4 = 1.4641$$
$$+(1.10)^3 = 1.3310$$
$$+(1.10)^2 = 1.2100$$
$$+(1.10)^1 = 1.1000$$
$$+(1.10)^0 = \underline{1.0000}$$

Total   **15.9372 at the beginning of tenth year**

$$CS = \$100 [15.9372]$$
$$CS = \mathbf{\$1,594 \text{ (rounded)}}$$

And

$$CS = BD (1+i)^n$$
$$CS = \$1,000 (1.10)^{10}$$
$$CS = \$1,000 (2.5937)$$
$$CS = \mathbf{\$2,594 \text{ (rounded)}}$$

TABLE 6.2   Annual Compound Interest at the Rate of 10%

Years	Future Worth of $1 (Deposited Beginning Period)	Future Worth of Annuity of $1 (Deposited End of Period
1	1.1000	1.0000
2	1.2000	2.1000
3	1.3310	3.3100
4	1.4641	4.6410
5	1.6105	6.1051
6	1.7715	7.7156
7	1.9487	9.4871
8	2.1436	11.4358
9	2.3579	13.5794
10	**2.5937**	**15.9372**
15	4.1772	31.7724
20	6.7275	57.2749
25	10.8341	98.3470
30	17.4494	164.4940

The difference of $1,000 represents the annual compounding effect on the whole $1,000 deposit during the entire period versus the systematic $100 deposited at the beginning of each year.

The mathematical calculations to determine the compound worth of a single sum of money or of an annuity involve the use of an **interest factor (IF).** In the example of the compound sum of a *single amount* of $1,000 at 10 percent annual interest for ten years, the beginning deposit ($1,000) is multiplied by an IF of 2.5937. Similarly, in the example of a $100 *annual annuity* for 10 years at 10 percent per year, the regular deposit ($100) is multiplied by an IF of 15.9372. Thus, the portion of the equation represented by $(1 + i)^n$ *equals the IF.*

These interest factors are a function of interest rates and time, and they can be derived for any combination of these inputs. Table 6.2 represents the interest factors for the future worth of $1 and of an annuity of $1, compounded at an annual rate of 10 percent.

In Table 6.2, note the ten-year IF of 2.5937 for the future worth of a single sum of $1 and the interest factor of 15.9372 for the future worth of an annuity of $1, both compounded annually at the rate of 10 percent. These are the interest factors developed algebraically in the previous examples. Most interest factors are available in tabular form; still, a student of investments should be familiar with the derivations of the information in the tables as well as with the use of the tables themselves.

Time Value of Money

From the previous examples of compound interest, it can be seen that money grows in worth over time if it is employed in an earning situation. The amount of growth is a function of the rate of interest, or yield, earned on the deposit or investment. By the same logic, money *not* received until some future time must be worth *less* today. How much less it is worth is also a function of yield coupled with time.

The **time value of money** is particularly significant for real estate investors whose yields are a function of rents to be received in the future. A lease, after all, is a promise to make a series of payments (annuities) called rent. Since these monies are not immediately available for reinvestment, they are worth less now than they will be when they are received.

For instance, at a yield rate of 10 percent, a dollar that will not be received for one year is really worth only $.90 today. If the dollar could be deposited today at 10 percent per annum, it would be worth $1.10 at the end of the year. Waiting a year to receive the dollar precludes the opportunity to earn $.10.

Thus, the $.10 can be interpreted as the **opportunity cost,** or **discount rate,** which diminishes the **present worth** of the subject dollar to be received at the end of the year to $.90.

Present Worth of a Dollar.   The present worth of a dollar is, in mathematical terms, the reciprocal of its compound worth. The formula for its derivation is:

$$PW = A \left(\frac{1}{(1 + i)^n} \right)$$

PW   = present worth
i   = interest rate per period
A   = amount
n   = number of periods

EXAMPLE: The present worth of $1 to be received 10 years from today at a discount rate of 10 percent is computed as follows:

$$PW = \$1 \left(\frac{1}{(1 + .10)^{10}} \right)$$

$$PW = \$1 \left(\frac{1}{2.5937} \right)$$

$$PW = \$1 \ (.3855)$$

$$PW = \$.3855 \text{ or } \$.39 \text{ rounded}$$

To verify that the present worth of $1 to be received in ten years at a discount rate of 10 percent is worth only 39 cents today, reverse the situation. Place this latter sum of money into a 10-percent, annually compounding savings account and observe its growth to $1 in ten years ($.3855 × 2.5937 = $1; see Table 6.2).

Present Worth of an Annuity.   Just as the present worth of $1 is the reciprocal of its compound rate, so the present worth of an annuity is reciprocally related to its compound formula. The present worth of an annuity in which the payment is to be received at the *end* of each period is expressed as follows:

$$PW = RA \left[\frac{1}{(1+i)^n} + \frac{1}{(1+i)^{n-1}} + \cdots \frac{1}{(1+i)^{n-n}} \right]$$

PWA = present worth annuity
i   = interest
RA = regular amount
n   = number of periods

EXAMPLE: The present worth of $1 to be received at the end of each year for three years at 10 percent interest would be $2.49, as shown below:

$$PWA = \$1 \left[\frac{1}{(1.10)^3} + \frac{1}{(1.10)^2} + \frac{1}{(1.10)^1} \right]$$

$$PWA = \$1 \left[\frac{1}{1.331} + \frac{1}{1.210} + \frac{1}{1.10} \right]$$

$$PWA = \$1 \ [.7513 \quad + .8264 \quad + .9091]$$

$$PWA = \$1 \ [2.4868]$$

$$PWA = \textbf{\$2.4868 or \$2.49 rounded}$$

Note in Table 6.3 that the present worth of $1 to be received in ten years is $.3855, and the present worth of an annuity of $1 to be received over three years is $2.4868. These are the same interest factors that were derived mathematically in the two previous examples. These tables, and others, can be purchased in various booklet forms for use in estimating the value of an investment.

Profitability Measures

An estimate can be made of an investment's value based on the anticipated amounts of rent to be collected over a period of time. This estimate of value then forms the basis for determining whether the purchase price is competitive and the investment is economically sound.

Most investors are primarily concerned with the relationship of the value of a property to its ability to generate cash flows. They will consider purchasing only properties that are self-supporting and that also develop an acceptable return on the cash invested. The required amount of this investment return is as personal a choice as is the type of property. For instance, some investors may be satisfied with a 10 percent return, while others insist on a property that develops a yield of at least 20 percent. Some investors are content to derive a lower return in exchange for the security of a long-term lease with a national tenant. Others are willing to speculate with higher risks in anticipation of higher profits.

TABLE 6.3   Annual Compound Interest at the Rate of 10%

Years	Present Worth of $1	Present Worth of Annuity of $1 Per Period
1	.9091	.09091
2	.8264	1.7355
3	.7513	**2.4868**
4	.6830	3.1699
5	.6209	3.7908
6	.5645	4.3553
7	.5132	4.8684
8	.4665	5.3349
9	.4241	5.7590
10	**.3855**	**6.1446**
15	.2394	7.6061
20	.1486	8.5136
25	.0923	9.0770
30	.0573	9.4269

There is some confusion over the meaning of the term **return on investment (ROI)**. The confusion stems from a lack of agreement among investors and accountants regarding the definition of the word *investment*. Is the investment the total price of the property? Is it the cash down payment plus the growth in equity and value from year to year? Or is it just the specific amount of money paid by the investor to purchase and develop the project?

For our purposes, we will define *investment* as the amount of cash used in the purchase of the property plus the cash costs of any capital improvements made during its ownership. All profits generated by the investment will then be utilized to measure the return on this investment.

For example, if a property shows an after-tax cash flow of $10,000 on a $100,000 cash investment, it indicates a cash-on-cash ROI of 10 percent.

$$\begin{array}{rl} \$\ 10,000 & \text{cash flow} \\ +\underline{100,000} & \text{investment} \\ .10, & \text{or 10 percent} \end{array}$$

If the analysis is expanded to include a $3,000 paydown on the mortgage and a verifiable $5,000 increase in the property's market value, then the bottom line ROI is 18 percent.

$$\begin{array}{rl} \$\ 10,000 & \text{cash flow} \\ +\quad 3,000 & \text{paydown} \\ +\underline{\quad 5,000} & \text{increase in market value} \\ \$\ 18,000 & \text{return} \\ +\underline{100,000} & \text{investment} \\ .18, & \text{or 18 percent} \end{array}$$

Notice that the "investment" did not increase by the amount of the equity buildup or the rise in value. These profits are considered *soft profits* while they are being earned. Only the cash profits are *hard profits* because they are real and in hand. However, these same soft profits can be made hard when refinancing and/or selling the property.

Break-Even Analysis.   Whatever the investor's personal profit orientation may be, a project's **break-even** *point* is used as a primary indicator of potential profitability. The break-even point occurs when gross income equals a total of **fixed costs** plus the **variable costs** incurred to develop that particular gross income. Only when gross income exceeds the amount needed to break even will a project begin to show a profit.

Every property has fixed costs that continue regardless of income. Such costs include property taxes, insurance premiums, maintenance fees, utility charges and mortgage payments, all of which must be paid regularly. A property also incurs costs that vary according to the income generated. Such variable costs include managerial fees, special maintenance services, additional utility charges, bookkeeping and advertising costs. For ease of analysis, these variable costs are usually expressed as a ratio of rental income, such as 20 percent of every rental dollar collected. This *variable cost ratio* is usually applied at a set rate over all levels of income.

The formula for calculating a property's break-even point is expressed as follows:

$$PW \quad = \frac{FC}{1 - VCR}$$

BE   = break even
FC   = fixed costs
VCR = variable cost ration

EXAMPLE: A break-even point for a property that incurs $100,000 in fixed costs and has a variable cost ratio of 20 percent would be:

BE   = $100,000/1 − .20
BE   = $100,000/.80
BE   = **$125,000**

The occupancy rate required to generate the income necessary to break even can be expressed as the ratio of the potential income to the break-even point.

If the property consists of 30,000 square feet of rentable space at a fair-market rent of $5 per square foot per year, maximum occupancy would result in income of $150,000.

30,000	square feet
× $5	per square foot
$150,000	per year,

The break-even point would occur at 83 percent occupancy.

$125,000   break-even amount
+150,000   maximum occupancy rate
.8333, or 83%

The break-even analysis provides an investor with a clear perspective to study the financial feasibility of a particular project. If a reasonable break-even point is determined, such as the 83 percent calculated previously, then the property should be acquired by the investor. If, on the other hand, it is estimated that 95 percent occupancy must be achieved just to break even, an investor will probably decline the opportunity. In such a situation, the investor should analyze the possibilities of reducing taxes, adjusting mortgage payments and/or lowering variable costs before making a final decision.

Return on Investment.   The only absolutely reliable ROI analysis would be one of a triple net lease with an AAA-rated corporation for a specified period of time. In this case the rental income would truly be a net amount because the tenant-corporation would be paying all of the property's operating expenses, taxes and maintenance. And if the tenant was so highly rated, the rental payment would be a guaranteed income, all things being equal. Under these circumstances, the ROI can be ascertained with a high degree of certainty, with little left to guesswork.

However, the ROI analysis of other investments includes many educated guesses. The questions that permeate such analyses include, among others: Will the tenant remain in business for the term of the lease? Will operating expenses rise? Will the tenant exercise the renewal option? Does the operating statement reflect accurate data on which an informed decision can be made?

It has been customary to carefully examine the income and expense statement for one year's operation to discern what the cash flows will be. This analysis then becomes the benchmark for future years, with the investor hoping to offset any increase in operating expenses with commensurate increases in rent.

And this is where the risk factor enters into the financial analysis. Is it worth buying this property to make a 10 percent return while being exposed to all of the risks and investment demands? Or should the return be 20 percent, 30 percent or higher to make it worthwhile? Or should the investor consider an alternative opportunity?

For example, consider an 18-unit apartment project generating $100,000 gross annual income. Total operating expenses, including a vacancy factor, reserves for replacements, property taxes, insurance premiums, utilities, maintenance and management, are estimated to be 50 percent of the gross income. This leaves $50,000 for debt service and cash flow. The property is offered at $500,000 (a 10 percent capitalization rate) with $200,000 cash down and a loan for the balance for 30 years at 7½ percent fixed interest. The mortgage payment will be $25,200 per year principal and interest. The building would be booked for $400,000 for 27 ½ years straight-line. The ROI analysis for this example appears in Table 6.4.

TABLE 6.4　Return on an Investment of $20,000

$100,000	Gross Annual Income
− 50,000	50% Operating Expense Ratio
50,000	Net Operating Income
− 25,200	Annual Principal and Interest
24,800	Net Cash Flow
+ 3,000	Principal Add-Back
27,800	Taxable Before Depreciation
− 14,500	Depreciation
13,300	Taxable Income
× 0.31	Investor's Tax Bracket
4,123	Income Tax
24,800	Net Cash Flow
− 4,123	Income Taxes
20,677	10.33% Cash-on-Cash ROI
+ 3,000	Equity Growth
23,677	11.83% Broker's Net ROI
+ 10,000	2% Market Value Growth
$ 33,677	16.83% Bottom-Line ROI

Considering the facts presented in the example, should an investor buy this property? This is not an easy question to answer. It depends on as many variables as there are investors. For example, does the investor want to put $200,000 in this one project, or could two projects be purchased for $100,000 down each? (Note: Analyze this same investment with $100,000 cash down and observe the Cash-on-Cash ROI jump to 18.3 percent from 10.33 percent.) Other questions for the investor might include: Is this property located in an area where the rents could be maintained and even improved? Are the improvements in good shape? Is the ROI enough to warrant taking the risk?

Discounted Cash Flows. A more sophisticated approach to estimating the return on an investment is the **discounted cash flow method.** Unlike the traditional approach, which assumes that rents will be received far into the future and that the property will probably never be sold, the discounted cash flow procedure recognizes that income streams are finite and end at a projected point in time.

Included in this approach is the recognition that income fluctuates from time to time and that properties are usually sold or traded at an appropriate time. Even more important, this method recognizes that monies to be received in the future are discounted to their present value by a rate that reflects an investor's required return on the investment. Essentially, then, the discounted cash flow analysis is an application of the principle of the present worth of an annuity, as described earlier.

A series of straight rental payments over the lease term creates an annuity for a property owner–investor. The present worth of this annuity is calculated using the formula given earlier in this chapter.

TABLE 6.5   Annual Compound Interest at the Rate of 12%

Period	Present Worth of $1	Present Worth of an Annuity of $1
1	.8928	.8928
2	.7972	1.6900
3	.7118	2.4018
4	.6355	3.0373
5	.5674	3.6048
6	.5066	4.1114
7	.4523	4.5637
8	.4039	4.9676
9	.3606	5.3282
10	.3220	5.6502
11	.2875	5.9376
12	.2567	6.1943
13	.2292	6.4235
14	.2046	6.6281
15	**.1827**	**6.8108**

EXAMPLE: Assume a regular net annual cash flow of $5,000 under a 15-year lease, with a projected future net sales price of $150,000 for the property at the expiration of the lease. At a 12 percent required annual return rate, the IF for this annuity is 6.8108, and the IF for the residual value of the property, also known as the "reversion," is .1827. (These interest factors appear in Table 6.5).

The present worth of the income stream is $34,054.

$$\begin{array}{r} \$\ \ 5,000 \quad \text{cash flow} \\ \times\ \underline{6.8108} \quad \text{IF for annuity} \\ \$34,054 \end{array}$$

The present worth of the proceeds from the future sale is $27,405.

$$\begin{array}{r} \$150,000 \quad \text{projected net sales price} \\ \times\ \underline{\ \ .1827} \quad \text{reversion} \\ \$\ 27,405 \end{array}$$

Thus, the present worth of this investment is the total of the present worth of the annuity and the present worth of the reversion, or $61,459.

In other words, an owner can invest approximately $60,000 in cash and earn 12 percent annually on this money if the $5,000 net annual cash flow remains constant for 15 years and the property is sold for $150,000 at the expiration of the lease term.

Although rents can be fixed at a constant annual amount for the term of a net lease, the basic weakness in this analysis is the estimate of the value of the property at a point in the future. Most investors use a *capitalization rate* (cap rate) for

TABLE 6.6   15-Year Graduated Lease at the Rate of 12% Return

Period	IF	Annuity	Amount
	3.6048	$ 4,000	$14,419
First 5 years	2.0454	5,000	10,227
Second 5 years	1.1606	6,000	6,963
Third 5 years	.1827	$150,000	27,405
Reversion		Total:	$59,014

this purpose. A market cap rate is derived by dividing the net operating incomes of properties that have been sold recently by their sales prices.

The present-worth analysis can also be employed to measure the value of a series of *irregular* cash flows developed by a stepped-up, or graduated, lease.

EXAMPLE: Assume a 15-year lease with $4,000 net annual cash flows for the first five-year period, $5,000 for each of the next five years and $6,000 annually for the final five-year period. Again assume that the property will be sold for $150,000 net cash at the end of the lease term. The present worth of this investment is $59,014, at a 12 percent return rate, derived as in Table 6.6.

The IF of 3.6048 shown in Table 6.6 is the present worth of a five-year annuity of $1 at 12 percent. The IF of 2.0454 is the ten-year IF of 5.6502 minus the five-year IF of 3.6048. The IF of 1.1606 is the 15-year IF of 6.8108 minus the ten-year IF of 5.6502. The IF of .1827 is the present worth of $1 to be received in 15 years at a 12 percent return (Table 6.5).

The sum total of $59,014 can also be derived by discounting each year's net cash flow by its appropriate IF, as illustrated in Table 6.7.

Internal Rate of Return.   Real estate investors place a high reliance on **internal rate of return (IRR)** analysis in their decision making. Based primarily on discounted cash flow analysis, which in turn is based on present-value analysis, the IRR approach has achieved its importance with the advent of widely used personal calculators and advanced microcomputers, which enable investors to calculate the IRR more quickly and efficiently than ever before.

One way to measure the IRR is by calculating the present worth of each projected year's profits after assigning the investor's required opportunity rate to the analysis. This rate is fixed over the investment term. If the discount rate chosen is too high or too low, it will bias the investment decision between an investment with a high early yield and one with a high end-of-investment yield.

TABLE 6.7   15-Year Graduated Lease at the Rate of 12% Required Return

Period	IF	Net Income	Amount
1	.8928	$ 4,000	$ 3,571
2	.7972	4,000	3,188
3	.7118	4,000	2,847
4	.6355	4,000	2,542
5	.5674	4,000	2,269
6	.5066	5,000	2,533
7	.4523	5,000	2,261
8	.4039	5,000	2,019
9	.3606	5,000	1,803
10	.3220	5,000	1,610
11	.2875	6,000	1,725
12	.2567	6,000	1,540
13	.2292	6,000	1,375
14	.2046	6,000	1,227
15	.1827	6,000	1,096
Reversion	.1827	$150,000	27,405
		Total	$59,011

(Difference to $59,014 in rounding)

The IRR offsets these distortions by automatically making the net present value (NPV) of the total cash flows equal to zero. In other words, the return on one investment is compared to the normal returns on all others.

The IRR process starts with the amount of cash investment required. The analyst then takes the net returns projected over the term of the project and *searches* for the appropriate interest rate that will discount these returns to zero. This is the project's IRR.

EXAMPLE: Assume a $100,000 cash investment requirement, a $10,000 net annual cash flow for ten years and a cash reversion of $100,000 at the end of the lease period when the property is sold. The IRR is 10 percent.

$ 10,000 × 6.1446 (Table 6.3) $ 61,446
$100,000 ×   .3855 (Table 6.3)   38,550
                     Total: $100,000 (rounded)
                     Investment: $100,000
                     NPV.:   -0-

If the project time frame is shortened to five years, the IRR will remain 10 percent.

$ 10,000 × 3.7908 (Table 6.3) $ 37,900 CWA
$100,000 ×   .6209 (Table 6.3)   62,090 PWR
                     Total: $ 99,990 (rounded $100,000)
                     Investment: $100,000
                     NPV.:   -0-

Although the IRR is quickly reported on the microcomputer after the appropriate entries have been made, it is not the final answer to all investment questions. The IRR approach forces guesstimates of future net cash flows (it works best with a fixed net lease with a AAA tenant) and net sales proceeds. It also has built-in value deceptions. For example, three different investments showing the same IRR may not be equal choices for every investor. One investment may show high initial yields and another high end yields; the third may be balanced over the project's holding period.

In other words, each investment must be analyzed individually to see how it fits into the overall strategy of a specific investor. Thus, to maximize the use of the computer, an analyst should plug the IRR of the contemplated investment into a client's entire portfolio to see if the overall IRR is affected positively or negatively.

The example presented here can be modified to incorporate more complicated analyses as the analyst's skill in computer operations increases. For example, a modified IRR analysis will take into consideration the possibility of negative cash flows for a number of years in a project's start-up time. These out-of-pocket amounts must be discounted appropriately and added to the investment amount to estimate a more reliable IRR.

The Realtors National Marketing Institute (RNMI) advocates an even more intensive analysis for investors called The Financial Management Return on Investment. This approach not only adds discounted negative cash flows to the investment total but also adds the compounded values of the positive cash flows (as they in turn are invested year after year) to the discounted values of these net annual receipts over the investment term.

CALCULATORS AND MICROCOMPUTERS

These more complicated analytical techniques generally require the aid of a microcomputer or even a mainframe computer. Although the best hardware for electronic investment analysis depends mainly on personal choice, finding the appropriate software to achieve individual requirements is often more difficult. References for software information is listed at the end of this chapter.

Some of the more advanced computer programs available today allow the analyst almost unlimited latitude in treating the myriad of variables included in a real estate investment. For example, some have provisions for handling changing tax brackets, minimum tax impacts and tax payables under almost every circumstance. Also available are hundreds of programs designed to do real estate investment studies and forecasts, as well as property management software.

Despite the excitement currently surrounding the increased use of the computer in real estate analysis, a word of caution is in order at this point. However sophisticated the software, the hardware and the programming, it's the thinking behind them that really counts. Tax brackets change over time, and after-tax sale proceeds can be deceptive. Annual net cash flows can be affected dramatically by the new financial arrangements available in today's market. Negative amortization, variable interest rates, multiple balloon payments, shared appreciation loans and wraparounds are only a few of the problems analysts must consider in their attempts to measure investment returns.

Today's analyses are infinitely more sophisticated than the old six-times-gross approach. With the addition of probability theory, giving the investor good odds that the analyst's projections will be proved correct, more relevant decisions are being made daily by those willing to take the time and trouble to check on their instincts.

Figure 6.1 shows a typical spreadsheet analysis for IRR. The program allows any single change to be reflected automatically throughout the analysis.

SUMMARY

The data collected in a financial study are utilized to estimate gross annual cash flows, operating expenses, depreciation allowances and returns on investment. These mathematical analyses apply the concepts of interest, time value of money and various measures of profitability, and they complement the information secured in the feasibility study.

Interest is defined as rent paid or received for the use of money. Thus, a deposit in a savings account earns the depositor interest, or rent. Similarly, an investment (deposit) in an income property will generate a yield (interest), called a return on the investment.

Because interest, or yield, is earned on monies deposited or invested, those funds not currently available for investment are actually worth less than their face amounts. How much less is a function of time and the rate of interest, or yield, desired by the investor. Thus, $100 to be received in one year is worth approximately $90 today at a 10 percent yield, or discount rate. The $10 difference is the lost earnings or opportunity cost for not having the $100 on deposit or invested for the year.

Many feasibility studies utilize a traditional approach for estimating returns on investment, while others use the discounted cash flow method, based on the concept of the present worth of money. Traditionally, gross annual earnings are reduced by operating costs, debt payments and depreciation to arrive at a net income figure. Depending on the owner's tax bracket, this net amount is adjusted to develop a bottom-line return on the owner's cash investment. This traditional approach assumes that the income stream will continue into perpetuity.

The discounted cash flow method, on the other hand, identifies a finite period for rent flows and assumes that the property will be sold. Thus, the future net cash flows and property sales receipts are discounted at the investor's required yield rate to derive the present worth of the investment. When the discounted amount equals the investment amount, it is said that the property is generating the owner's required internal rate of return. Microcomputers and sophisticated mainframe computers are often used to analyze and present this information more efficiently.

FIGURE 6.1   Spreadsheet Analysis for IRR

Given: Purchase price = $5,000,000
Mortgage = $4,000,000 @ 12% interest, 20-year monthly amortization
Mortgage payment = $44,043,45
5% growth in base rent and expenses
Sale at end of year 5 based on 10% Capitalization rate on NOI
Land/Building allocation is $1,000,000/$4,000,000
Depreciation is straight-line for 27.5 years (use 0.03636)
Tax rate on ordinary income is 36%, on capital gain is 28%

Description	Year 1	Year 2	Year 3	Year 4	Year 5
Income					
Gross Potential	$600,000	$630,000	$661,500	$694,575	$729,304
Occupancy Factor	85%	87%	90%	93%	95%
Adjusted Gross	510,000	548,100	595,350	645,955	692,839
Recoverable Expenses	12,750	13,703	14,884	16,149	17,321
Total Income	$522,750	$561,803	$610,234	$662,104	$710,160
Expenses					
CAM Expenses	$ 15,000	$ 15,750	$ 16,538	$ 17,364	$ 18,233
Owner Expenses	5,000	5,250	5,512	5,788	6,078
Total Expenses	$ 20,000	$21,000	$ 22,050	$ 23,152	$ 24,311
NOI	$502,750	$540,803	$588,184	$638,952	$685,849
Calculation of Tax					
NOI	$502,750	$540,803	$588,184	$638,952	$685,849
less Interest	477,240	470,737	463,408	455,150	445,845
less Depreciation	145,440	145,440	145,440	145,440	145,440
Taxable Income	($119,930)	($75,374)	($20,664)	$ 38,362	$ 94,564
Tax @ 36%	(43,175)	(27,135)	(7,439)	13,810	34,043
Calculation of Cash Flow after Tax					
NOI	$502,750	$540,803	$588,184	$638,952	$685,849
less Interest	477,240	470,737	463,408	455,150	445,845
less Principal	51,281	57,785	65,113	73,371	82,677
less Tax @ 36%	(43,175)	(27,135)	(7,439)	13,810	34,043
Cash Flow after Tax	$ 17,404	$ 39,416	$ 67,102	$ 96,621	$123,284
ROI after Taxes	1.740%	3.942%	6.710%	9.662%	12.328%

Sales Analysis

Year 5 NOI	$ 685,849
10% Cap Rate	+ 0.10
Gross Sale Price	$6,858,494
Closing Expenses (10%)	685,849
Net Sales Price	$6,172,645
less Mortgage Balance	3,669,773
Cash Proceeds before Tax	$2,502,872

FIGURE 6.1   (Continued)

Calculation of Tax

Purchase Price	$5,000,000
less Accumulated Depreciation	727,200
Adjusted Book Basis	$4,272,800
	$6,172,645
Net Sales Price	4,272,800
less Adjusted Book Basis	$1,899,845
Taxable Gain	
Tax (@ 28%)	$ 531,957

After-Tax Cash Flow from Sale

Cash Proceeds before Tax	$2,502,872
Less Tax	531,957
After-Tax Cash Flow	$1,970,915

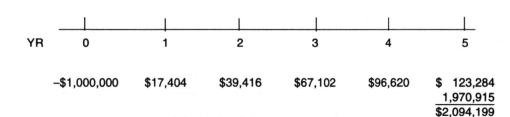

YR	0	1	2	3	4	5
	–$1,000,000	$17,404	$39,416	$67,102	$96,620	$ 123,284
						1,970,915
						$2,094,199

IRR on the $1,000,000 invested in this projected = 19.20%

Source: Allen B. Atkins, PhD, University of Arizona.

EXERCISE 6   (Answers may be checked against the Answer Key.)

Problem A

Answer the first three questions from the following information.

An investor in the 28 percent bracket purchases a residential income property for $350,000 with a $100,000 cash down payment. The loan for $250,000 is payable at 10 percent interest-only for ten years. The property generates $50,000 annual gross income. Its operating expense ratio is 30 percent. The land is booked at $50,000 and the improvements at $300,000 under a 0.036 annual straight-line rate. The property is sold for $385,000 net at the end of five years.

1. The annual after-tax cash-on-cash return on this investment is

    a. 3.6 percent.
    b. 10 percent.
    c. 28 percent.
    d. 30 percent.

2. All of the following statements are true *except*

    a. the investment throws off an $800 annual loss.
    b. this is a fully tax-sheltered investment.
    c. this is a negative cash flow property.
    d. the interest is a deductible expense.

3. What is the investor's overall average annual return after the sale at the end of the fifth year? (*Hint: Watch out for carryover loss.*)

    a. 10 percent
    b. 12.24 percent
    c. 22.24 percent
    d. 29.44 percent

Problem B

Use the information in the table to answer the next five questions.

12% Annual Compound Interest

Years	Future Worth $1	Future Worth Ann. $1	Present Worth $1	Present Worth Ann. $1
5	1.7623	6.3528	.5674	3.6048
10	3.1058	17.5487	.3220	5.6502
15	5.4736	37.2797	.1827	6.8109
20	9.6463	72.0524	.1037	7.4694
25	17.0001	133.3339	.0588	7.8431
30	29.9599	241.3327	.0334	8.0552

4. What *single* investment must be made in an account earning 12 percent annual compound interest to accumulate $100,000 in 25 years?

    a. $ 4,000
    b. $ 5,882
    c. $12,750
    d. $17,000

5. What regular *annual* payments must be made to an account earning 12 percent annual compound interest to accumulate $100,000 in 25 years?

    a. $ 750
    b. $ 4,000
    c. $ 5,882
    d. $12,750

6. What regular annual payments must be made to amortize a loan of $100,000 over 25 years at 12 percent interest?

    a. $ 4,000
    b. $ 5,882
    c. $12,750
    d. $17,000

7. At a 12 percent yield requirement, what is the present value of a $10,000 net annual income stream to be received at the end of each year for 15 years plus the cash value reversion from the sale of the property at the end of the fifteenth year for $150,000?

    a. $ 82,141
    b. $ 95,514
    c. $218,109
    d. $400,202

8. At a 12 percent yield requirement, what is the present value of an annual income stream to be received at the rate of $5,000 at the end of each year for five years, $10,000 for each of the next five years and $15,000 for each of the final five years, plus a net cash reversion from the sale of the property at the end of the 15th year of $87,500? (Answers are rounded.)

    a. $ 43,391
    b. $ 71,874
    c. $192,675
    d. $237,500

9. When analyzing the expenses incurred in operating a commercial investment property, which one of the following items is generally overlooked?

    a. Maintenance
    b. Reserves
    c. Utilities
    d. Management

10. Most financial analyses of investment property profit potentials are based on

a. dependable facts.
b. educated guesses.
c. computer inputs.
d. verifiable information.

DISCUSSION

1. What happens to the ROI if an investor refinances a positive cash flow property and recaptures all of the original monies invested?

2. Investigate the application of computer analyses to real estate investment feasibility studies. Discuss with a computer expert the application of "canned" programs designed to accommodate standardized sets of data. Secure a copy of a printout showing a computer analysis of a real estate investment and examine it for material presented in this chapter.

EXHIBIT   Information for Computer Users

Arrays Inc.: 6711 Valjean Ave., Van Nuys, CA 91406-5819, (818) 004-1899.

Boston Computer Society: One Center Plaza, Boston, MA 02108, (617) 367-8080.

Guide to Real Estate and Mortgage Banking Software: Real Estate Solutions Inc.,

Dept. F, 2609 Klingle Rd., NW, Washington, DC 20008, (202) 362-9854.

Information Sources Inc.: 1173 Colusa, Box 7848, Berkeley, CA 94707, (800) 433-6107.

Macintosh Buyer's Guide: Redgate Communications, 660 Beachland Blvd., Vero Beach, FL 32963, (407) 231-6904.

Real Data: 78 N. Main St., S. Norwalk, CT 07854, (203) 255-2732.

Real Estate Center: Texas A & M University, College Station, TX 77843, (409) 845-2031.

Real Estate Software Information Bank: 25 Parker Ave., Rodeo, CA 94572, (415) 799-6156.

7

Investing in Land

Key Terms

agglomeration	*plottage*
assemblage	*recognition clause*
build to suit	*Regulation Z*
factoring	*release clause*
growth management	*rezoning*
hobby tax rules	*spot zoning*
land banking	*subdivision restrictions*
location	*topography*
opportunity costs	

There are numerous and diverse investment opportunities in real estate, including land, residential developments, office buildings, shopping centers, industrial projects and mobile-home parks. In this portion of the book, the principles presented in the prior chapters will be applied to an examination of these various types of investments.

Of all the forms of real estate ventures, investment in vacant land probably provides the greatest opportunity for creativity and profit. Simultaneously, it is no doubt the riskiest real estate investment, requiring the most good luck. From the simple purchase of an improved lot in a subdivision by an individual who wishes to build a home, to the more complicated accumulation of hundreds of unimproved acres to hold for future development and subdividing, to the acquisition of a tract of land in anticipation of rezoning for more intensive use, land is the real estate developer's and speculator's playground.

This chapter examines methods for estimating the profitability of investing in vacant lots and acreage as a portion of a total property ownership portfolio. The goal of most land buyers is to own the right property in the right place at the right time to command the highest possible return on an investment. Depending on an individual's investment strategy, vacant land can provide a viable alternative to the ownership of improved income property. Raw acreage presents the investor with an opportunity to diversify holdings, earn high profits and offset the risks of loss from other investments.

However, high profits are inevitably balanced by high risks, and vacant land investments are probably more affected by uncontrollable outside events than any other type of real estate. Furthermore, land is not depreciable for tax purposes, and a beginning investor is well advised to start a portfolio with an improved income property. In this way, the investor can maximize profits through the use of the tax shelters, however limited, that improved property provides. When income taxes have been somewhat minimized through investment tax shelters, the investor is in a stronger financial position to speculate with vacant land.

ESSENTIALS OF LAND INVESTMENT FEASIBILITY STUDIES

Whether the investor in vacant land is a speculator or a developer of buildings, the property's location and physical quality will have a significant impact on the success of the investment. Development costs, community attitudes and timing strategies also affect the land investor's potential profits.

Property Location

The **location** of land primarily determines its potential future growth in value. Although some enterprising promoters have earned large profits from the sale of parcels of relatively isolated land, well-situated property is more likely to increase in value. For instance, land lying within a three-mile area on either side of a major highway connecting two neighboring communities is almost certain to increase in value over time. Generally, communities tend to grow toward one another, creating increased demand and higher values for intervening properties. And as a rule, the closer to the highway a parcel of land is situated, the higher its potential value.

Similarly, the purchase of raw acreage at the periphery of a community by an investor who wishes to hold the land for appreciation requires an educated prediction of the direction in which the city will expand. An incorrect estimate of future growth patterns will cause the investor to wait longer for profit realization. And as the waiting period increases, the time value of money affects the average annual rate of return.

This relationship of location to value is equally applicable to single lots and large tracts of land. For example, a lot purchased on a major arterial street in anticipation of future rezoning for a more intensive use may prove to be an extremely profitable investment if the neighborhood grows in that direction. Another example would be a lot that is located on the exterior boundary of a subdivision and that overlooks a large, vacant parcel of land. If the lot is to be used for the construction of a home, then the development of a shopping center, office building or other commercial activity on the larger parcel may diminish the lot's value.

Property Features

The physical features of vacant land, such as **topography** and soil composition, are as important as location in terms of future profitability. A land parcel's physical features may be economically advantageous to one owner and disadvantageous to another. For instance, sloping foothill land is inefficient for farming but desirable for high-priced homes with attractive views. Likewise, unimproved acreage near a large city may be less useful for cattle grazing than for development as a suburban bedroom community.

Purchasers of single lots within a city must also be aware of the physical characteristics of their land. A lot's location, contours, drainage, soil quality and rezoning potential affect its value. Interior subdivision positions are essential to the buyer of a house lot, while railroad tracks and highways are significant features of an industrial parcel. Retail and office developments require access to major traffic arteries with high traffic counts, while apartment and mobile-home dwellers seek public transportation facilities and neighborhood serenity.

Timing

"Buy low and sell high" is axiomatic to any investor seeking a profit, and proper timing has a great deal to do with both of these accomplishments. Timing is a particularly important factor in real estate investments because, by their very nature, these investments are long-term. In fact, real estate is often considered a nonliquid investment. Often, it is easy to buy real estate but quite a bit more difficult to sell it; in some unfortunate instances, it can become impossible even to give it away.

Land speculation requires a greater awareness of timing than many other real estate investments because most land does not produce income during the holding period. It is held by the investor pending a rise in value. The longer this interim holding period, the lower the investment's annual yield will be.

In addition to the land's initial purchase price, the investor must make cash expenditures for mortgage payments, property taxes and improvements to the land. Unless the property can be leased for some income-generating activity, vacant land requires constant financial support during its investment life.

Depending on a lot's location and characteristics, some owners seek to minimize their holding costs by renting their properties as parking or used-car lots during the interim period. Owners of larger parcels have found it expedient to develop farm or ranch operations while waiting for the property to appreciate in value. Leasing the land to tenant farmers on a profit-sharing basis will often produce enough tax sheltered income to carry an investment, and the property tax rates on agricultural land are often much lower than those on land otherwise designated. Other interim uses include leasing the land for a vegetable stand, a flea market or a swap meet or—for longer waiting periods—a mobile-home park, a drive-in movie theater or a ministorage facility, to name a few.

FIGURE 7.1   IRS Hobby Tax Rules

The IRS defines farming and ranching for profit, not as a hobby, based on the following criteria

- The activity must be currently and clearly pointed to making a profit.
- The owners/operators must have experience in the activity.
- Considerable personal time and effort must be expended in the activity.
- There must be legitimate hope for value appreciation.
- The owner's or operators' other activities must be limited.
- A continued series of annual losses cannot be tolerated.
- Occasional minimum profits are not acceptable.
- The activity must be the owners' or operators' main source of income.
- Farming and ranching solely for enjoyment makes it a hobby.

The IRS has become strict about enforcing these **hobby tax rules** in an effort to close the tax loop-holes that became prevalent in the 1970s and early 1980s. Some farming and ranching enterprises had been designed for large operating losses to allow their investors the opportunities for abusive tax shelters.

Farming Losses

Although we have passed from a primarily agricultural society to a highly indus-trialized one and are now entering an era of services and informational systems, many parcels of land in this country are still used for farming and ranching. When these activities are the main occupations of their owners, the income acquired is considered ordinary income and is treated as active income for tax purposes.

However, numerous investors who are not clearly defined as active farmers or ranchers come under IRS Code Section 183, which limits the deductions that can be taken by any individual or S corp (active or passive) that is involved in these activities as so-called hobbies. Deductions are limited to gross income. Any excess losses cannot be carried forward to future years but are lost forever. The IRS has also qualified the differences between farming or ranching for a profit and doing so for a hobby (see Figure 7.1).

Opportunity Costs

Whereas mortgage payments and property tax cash outlays during the holding period are fairly obvious, **opportunity costs** for the equity invested in the land are all too often ignored. While the interest paid on a debt can be easily identi-fied as a cost for maintaining the investment, the interest *not earned* on the cash invested in the property must also be included as a holding cost. The rationale for this practice is based on the present-worth principle. If this money were invested, it would generate a profit. Therefore, the money not earned on the cap-ital invested should be considered a carrying cost.

For most real estate investors, the opportunity cost on invested capital forms the basic measuring unit for determining investment acquisitions. If, when sold, a property cannot develop a return on the investment that substantially exceeds the loss of earnings during the holding period, then these monies should be left on deposit or invested more profitably elsewhere.

Community Acceptance

An investor in vacant land must become acutely aware of the legal and political attitudes of local governing bodies. As noted earlier, local government may have a direct effect on the future development of a specific parcel of land. Some communities have passed **growth management** legislation that requires developers to have their infrastructure (streets, sewers, sidewalks utility lines and so on) in place before they offer their properties for sale. Other communities have raised other barriers to development. For example, if a community practices a no-growth policy, it may be difficult—if not impossible—to secure the cooperation necessary to have subdivision plans approved and/or necessary utility services installed.

The future value of land often depends greatly on the availability of roads, utilities and waste disposal facilities. Some communities control their growth by refusing to issue permits for the installation of these utilities. Because a local moratorium on gas, sewers or other utilities can destroy the timing strategy for a particular development, an investor in land should carefully select those parcels that can be developed with as few potential difficulties as possible. In the long run, growth management may result in ever-increasing prices for developments and serious shortages of land for housing.

SINGLE-LOT INVESTMENTS

The opportunities for single-lot investments include those individual parcels purchased for residential construction and those that have the rezoning potential for more intensive, and therefore more profitable, use. In the first instance, the investor acts as a developer, albeit on a small scale. In the second, the investor is a speculator seeking to profit from the gain in value of the rezoned lot.

Residential Lots

Many people purchase a lot in anticipation of building a house on it in later years. By acquiring a homesite at current costs, such a buyer hopes to profit from its growth in value over time. Simultaneously, many of these buyers, unable to purchase a lot for cash, enjoy the opportunity to make affordable payments over time so that the debt on the lot will be paid in full prior to construction. The free and clear land then becomes the equity necessary to secure a mortgage on the building.

Speculative Lots

In addition to residential lots purchased for future use, investors also buy strategically located vacant lots in anticipation of a rise in value and a profitable resale. Generally, these speculative lot purchases are based on the possibility of a successful **rezoning** of the property for more intensive use than single-family residences. Included in this inventory are lots physically suited for multifamily apartment projects and office structures as well as for commercial and industrial developments.

Rezoning residential land for a more intensive use usually raises the value of the property, sometimes quite dramatically. For instance, in one community, when a 600-foot block of residential property was rezoned for retail commercial use, its value increased immediately from $200 per front foot to $500 per front foot. No physical changes were required to make the land more usable, nor were any additional monies invested.

The success of a rezoning request depends largely on whether the subject property is located in an area of use compatible with that being sought by the property owner. Good land-control practices usually prevent any **spot zoning** and require the applicant to prove conformity to the general land use plan and to follow adopted pollution-control ordinances.

Rezoning activities are sometimes costly and time-consuming. Any rezoning proposal requires the satisfaction of numerous individuals who hold vested interests in the outcome of the proposed change, as well as the approval of the community's planning agency. Any objections by adjoining property owners and other affected persons, sometimes expressed eloquently and often vehemently at public hearings, must be overcome by the applicant. If enough surrounding owners object to the change, the public officials may not grant the new zoning. However, the rewards are usually worth the efforts required to obtain rezoning.

When purchasing vacant lots with possibilities for growth in value, an investor must make a careful examination of the community to identify potential areas of expansion. Once these neighborhoods are discovered, a meticulous search should be made to discover those particular vacant parcels of land with rezoning potential.

Lease Versus Resale

It is important for investors who purchase lots for resale to carefully evaluate their personal financial positions before actually selling. It may be more advantageous to *lease*, rather than *sell*, the property.

A lease holds certain advantages for both the landowner and the tenant. The owner benefits by securing an income stream into the future. In addition, at the expiration of the lease, the owner retains the reversionary rights to the land as well as any improvements made thereon by the tenant. Long-term land leases also provide the landowner with an asset—the lease—that can be capitalized on. By pledging the lease as collateral, the landlord can secure cash from a lender—tax-free cash that can be used to purchase additional investments. Thus, the landlord continues to own the leased land and can expand the investment portfolio accordingly.

The primary benefit to a land-leasing tenant is leverage: the leasehold interest acquired under a long-term land lease can be pledged as collateral for a mortgage to construct a new building. With a loan sufficient to pay for the costs of construction, the developer may be able to leverage 100 percent and avoid investing personal funds in a project. In addition, the rent paid by the tenant for the use of the land is considered an operating expense in the year that it is incurred. Thus, by paying rent on land rather than owning it, a tenant is effectively gaining the benefits of "depreciating" the land over the life of the lease. Remember that land is not specifically depreciable.

Build to Suit

In an attempt to convert a vacant lot into income-producing improved property, owners sometimes advertise that they will construct a building on a lot to satisfy the particular requirements of a potential tenant. On the signing of a long-term lease and the construction of the building, the landowner becomes a landlord in the traditional sense. At the expiration of the lease, the landlord continues to own both the land and the vacant building, which can be rerented or converted to a new use.

The difference in economic positions between an owner of a vacant parcel of land and an owner of a vacant building is of critical importance to an investor deciding whether to **build to suit**. In the first instance, the property owner pays relatively low property taxes and faces no continuing property maintenance problems. In the second, the owner's taxes are higher because they are based on the value of the building as well as of the land. In addition, the empty building requires continuous care, repair and protection.

The economic position of a building owner is more vulnerable, so the landowner who solicits a tenant on a build-to-suit basis will negotiate rather firmly for a lease that will completely satisfy investment requirements over the term of the initial lease period. To provide adequate protection against the increased risk, the rent will have to be arranged to develop an acceptable *return on the investment* as well as a timely *return of the investor's cash outlay*.

As a further precaution, a build-to-suit landowner will generally avoid the construction of a *single-purpose* building if at all possible. Such buildings are usually difficult to rerent and expensive to remodel. Nevertheless, many single-purpose buildings for fast-food franchises or 24-hour minimarkets are being constructed for strong, A-rated national tenants.

ACREAGE

Like purchasers of small lots, investors in raw acreage can be classified as either speculators or developers. A larger land parcel can be bought for resale as a single unit or for subdivision into either improved or unimproved lots. In the former situation, the investor acts as a speculator, holding the land for growth in value, then selling the tract intact.

When raw acreage is subdivided, the investor who sells the land in small parcels after few or no improvements have been made is speculating in land promotions.

The subdivider who improves the raw acreage with roads, sewers, water and other utilities and amenities before selling lots is a land developer.

Land is often worth more as one wholly integrated and cohesive unit than it is as a number of individually owned separate parcels. This concept is called **agglomeration**, **plottage** or **assemblage**. To apply this principle of ownership and value, a major farming or ranching enterprise would seek to control as many adjoining acres as possible to attain more efficient production. Similarly, the total of the individual values of lots in a block could be worth less than the entire block as a single site for a large shopping center. However, in this case, the value increase is a function of a change in use as well as the efficiency of single ownership.

Plottage can have a reverse effect on the value of acreage for speculators and developers. When quantities of land are accumulated for investment purposes, the total value of the individual smaller parcels is usually less than the value of the total property when finally acquired. However, if the speculator or developer decides to subdivide this wholly owned property, the sum of the sales prices of the individual lots often greatly *exceeds* the value of the property as a single unit. This concept will be examined in the next chapter in a discussion of conversion of rental apartments into condominiums.

Acreage for Resale in One Unit

In regions of the country in which the land is fertile, very little acreage speculation takes place. Productive land is usually held by individual farmers or ranchers. On the death of the owner, the land is passed to family heirs. Speculation in acreage is most common in areas of the country in which the land is relatively unproductive.

The value of land is not based merely on its productive capacity. Depending on intended use, location can become the key factor in determining value. Land speculators are not as concerned with soil fertility as they are with locational advantages or disadvantages that will affect the future desirability of the land for developers and/or builders. Accessibility to nearby major highways and communities; availability of water, gas and electricity; and proximity to natural and constructed amenities such as lakes, woods, golf courses or ski slopes all increase the profit potential of investments in raw acreage.

Speculators in unimproved land range from the small investor, who might buy 5 to 40 acres located on the periphery of an expanding community, to large investment syndicates, which purchase thousands of acres to hold for future resale. Regardless of the size of the investment, however, the philosophy is always to buy *right* to net a large profit.

Large profits are often less than they appear to be. For example, throughout its holding period, raw acreage requires the payment of such basic carrying charges as property taxes, interest and opportunity costs. Although taxes on vacant acreage are relatively low, the compounding effects of opportunity costs must be included when analyzing the feasibility of an investment in acreage. Remember, there is usually no cash flow to provide offsetting income during the years between purchase and sale.

Assuming a property tax of 1 percent per year plus an opportunity (interest) cost of 9 percent per year, the value of the land will have to increase at least 10 percent annually just for the investor to break even when the property is sold. When an investor's desired profit rate and an appropriate percentage ratio to cover monies needed for the costs of a sale (for example, commissions, title policy premiums, legal fees, income taxes) are added to this 10 percent rate, required annual increases in property value of 15 to 20 percent are not unreasonable.

This rate of increase means that the property must double in value every five to seven years if the costs of investment plus a profit are to be earned. For example, even if the value of the land increases 100 percent over a ten-year holding period and the property owner sells for an amount twice what was originally paid, the annual rate of return would be only

$$\frac{\begin{array}{ll} 100 & \text{percent total increase} \\ +10 & \text{years} \end{array}}{10 \quad \text{percent}}$$

At a 10 percent annual value increase, the investment may not yield an amount of return adequate to cover both carrying costs and anticipated profits. Thus, it is vital for an investor to make an effort to identify future value-growth patterns by carefully investigating trends in local property values.

Evaluating Land

The evaluation of raw land depends to a great degree on its future, rather than its present, use. Thus, an investor must be able to predict the type of eventual use as well as the time when this use will become feasible—not an easy task.

The most popular basis for evaluating land is the comparative approach, in which similarly zoned parcels of land that have been sold recently are said to establish the value of property. This approach includes adjustments for location, size and date of sale.

A more comprehensive approach is advisable because the existing zoning of the land may not be its highest and best future use. The time value of money must also be considered. Analyzing an area's demographics, employment centers and traffic counts can help an investor form an opinion about the land's future use. This information helps an investor project the number of acres that will be in demand for each use classification—residential, business, industrial and so on.

In addition, a careful forecast should be made of when the property will be ready for development. The factors to consider in this analysis include supply, demand, availability, growth patterns and distance from existing development. Some effort should be made to project building costs and rents to estimate what a developer might pay for the land in the future.

Finally, to derive the present value of the land, an appropriate investment return must be established. When improved properties are being sold for close to a 10 percent cap rate on an all-cash basis, raw land requires a higher return rate because of the special risks involved in land investments. For example, a 20 percent annual return requirement could be applied to project the future sale price.

EXAMPLE: Suppose a 15-acre tract of raw land is available for sale to an investor who anticipates its use as a neighborhood shopping center within five years. The present commercial rents in the area average $12 per square foot, and a 5-percent annual inflation factor is anticipated.

If the land were ready for immediate development, its value would be worth approximately half the anticipated rents or, in this case, $6 per square foot. At 5 percent annual growth, the land will be worth $7.66 (rounded) per square foot in five years. For an investor who requires a 20 percent annual return, the price for the parcel today will be $3.08 (rounded) per square foot.

USING THE HP-12C:

Future Value: Given: $6 per square foot today
             5-year term
             5% annual growth

1.	Clear financial register	f	FIN
2.	Keystroke 6		
3.	Change sign, press	CHS	
4.	Press	PV	
5.	Keystroke 5, press	n	
6.	Keystroke 5, press	i	
7.	Press FV = 7.65769 or $7.66 rounded		

Present Value: Given: 7.65769 future value
             5-year term
             20% required return

1.	Leave 7.65769 on viewer	
2.	Keystroke 20, press	i
3.	Press PV = –3.07745 or –$3.08 rounded	

Note: Answer is negative because an outlay of $3.08 is required today to earn $7.66 in five years at 20% annual compound interest.

Subdividing for Speculation: Land Promotions

Many land promotion schemes are the consequence of speculation in raw acreage. The promoter buys a large tract of vacant acreage at wholesale prices, divides it into smaller parcels and resells these smaller, usually unimproved, lots at retail prices to buyers scattered throughout this, as well as other, countries.

These lots are marketed through various promotional plans and advertising media. One of the more common marketing methods is to invite prospective buyers to a free dinner during which salespeople extol the virtues of the property through lecture and film. Often, these dinners are followed by an offer of a trip to the site, with any costs for traveling reimbursed by the promoters after purchase of a lot. Generally, the various large companies involved in such land promotions follow a format of marketing the individual lots as second, or retirement, homesites.

The financing designs of both the original purchase of raw acreage by the promoter and the subsequent sales of lots to individuals are the most important elements in this form of real estate investment. A purchase of land for use in a sales promotion usually requires the seller of the raw acreage to carry back a substantial portion of the sales price as an installment land contract or purchase-money mortgage. Thus, after the promoter makes an agreed-on cash down payment, usually about 5 percent to 10 percent of the purchase price, the landowner will accept a lien on the acreage involved for the remainder of the sales price. This balance is to be paid by the promoter on some regular amortization schedule. Under a land contract, the seller retains legal title to the acreage until the terms of the contract are met, usually with the requirement that the balance be paid in full.

Most land promotion property is sold to subsequent small-lot owners with any underlying financial arrangements left intact. As a result, each individual sale is made subject to the lien of at least one existing encumbrance, the installment contract or purchase-money mortgage between the promoter and the seller of the acreage. The existence of an underlying encumbrance poses a serious threat to the purchaser of an individual lot if the promoter does not make payments as required. The small-lot owner may be financially hurt in a subsequent foreclosure of the master lien. To offset this problem, most legitimate promoters secure a **recognition clause** in their original financing agreement. The vendor or mortgagee agrees in advance that if the promoter should default during the term of the agreement, the lender will respect the rights of subsequent lot owners and honor their contracts.

Alternatively, a **release clause** may be inserted in the land contract. Under the terms of the contract, individual lots may be released from the master lien after a certain agreed-on percentage of its balance has been paid by the vendee.

The sales of lots to individual purchasers are generally designed as installment land contracts. Most buyers of these promotional lots make small cash down payments and the balance is carried back by the selling company to be paid in regular monthly installments. Frequently, the *seller's* signature is not notarized, and, consequently, the contract is unacceptable to the appropriate county office for recording.

A promoter hopes that the initial sales campaign will generate enough individual sales to quickly develop the cash flows necessary to meet the required underlying contract payments. Sometimes it takes a few years to reach this break-even point, and the promoter must be prepared to meet payments and operating costs with other funds. A promoter can offset a cash shortage either by selling the individual contracts secured through early sales, a process called **factoring**, or by pledging these contracts as collateral for a bank loan to meet operating expenses. Once a break-even point has been met, however, continued sales will generally result in substantial profits.

Because they recognize the complexities and possible pitfalls for the consumer in this form of land promotion, both federal and state regulatory agencies carefully supervise such programs. All interstate land sales must conform to the requirements of the federal government's **Regulation Z**. The promoters must prepare and distribute to all prospective lot purchasers a full disclosure report describing the subject property and the complete financial arrangements of the transaction. In addition, many states require that the promoter post bonds in amounts adequate to complete any promised improvements to the land, such as roads, golf courses, club houses and lakes, *before* granting the promoter permission to market the lots.

Interstate Land Sales Regulations

The Department of Housing and Urban Development (HUD) engages in the regulation of interstate land sales. HUD's activities in connection with the Interstate Land Sales Full Disclosure Act are of particular significance for those investors contemplating large-scale land sales promotions.

Authorized under Title XIV of the Housing and Urban Development Act, the interstate land sales law is administered by the Office of Interstate Land Sales Registration, U.S. Department of Housing and Urban Development, Washington, DC 20411.

This law requires anyone engaged in the interstate sale or leasing of 25 or more improved lots to register the offering with HUD and to make available to each prospective lot purchaser or lessee all facts pertinent to the legitimate use of the land. The terms and conditions of any financing in existence at the time of the sale or lease must be stated, and the existence of any other liens must be revealed. The probability for completion of promised off-site improvements such as paving, parks, golf courses and marinas must be given.

In addition to this data, the disclosure must also provide information about distances to nearby communities over paved or unpaved roads; provisions for placing contract payments into a special escrow fund set aside for the purchase of the property; the availability of recreation facilities; sewer and water services or septic tanks and wells; the present and proposed utility services and charges; the number of homes currently occupied; soil and foundation conditions that could cause problems in construction or in the use of septic tanks; and the type of title the buyer will receive.

A buyer is protected in several ways against failure to comply with the provisions of the full disclosure requirements. If a prospective buyer has not been furnished with a property report before signing, the contract may be canceled and a refund obtained. Furthermore, the buyer must receive a property report at least 48 hours *before* a contract is signed and must have seven calendar days *after* for a "cooling off" period. If the buyer wishes to cancel the contract during this period, a full refund of any payments will be made.

Criminal penalties of up to five years' imprisonment, a fine of up to $5,000 or both may be imposed if a developer willfully violates the law, makes an untrue statement or omits any material fact required in the statement of record or in the property report. In addition, the purchaser may sue for damages not to exceed the purchase price of the lot, plus any improvements made thereto and reasonable court costs.

Complementing HUD's requirements, a number of states have enacted their own interstate land sales regulations. Administration of such state laws is usually placed in the office of the state real estate or land commissioner. In Nebraska, for instance, a developer wishing to sell land located in other states must file an application for permission to sell with the Nebraska Real Estate Commission. The developer must pay a filing fee commensurate with the number of lots in the subdivision and post a bond to guarantee the timely completion of the off-site improvements promised in the sales.

Prior to granting approval for interstate land sales in Nebraska, the director of the commission, or a deputy, visits the land at the developer's expense to verify personally the facts presented in the application.

Both the federal Interstate Land Sales Act and the various state laws regulating such sales have been developed to curb the fraudulent activities of unscrupulous promoters of vacant land. Although land promoters invariably earn relatively high profits, the purchasers of these lots often can barely recover their investments.

CASE 7.1:   **1,280-Acre Land Promotion.**   The profit potentials in a land promotion program can be illustrated in the case of a two-section (1,280-acre) parcel of land, to be subdivided into 2,560 one-half-acre lots. These lots will then be marketed within the state in which the property is located.

The purchase price of the raw acreage is $1,000 per acre, and it is estimated that it will cost an additional $500 per acre to improve the land with roadways and basic utilities. An additional $500 per acre will be needed for interest charges, carrying costs and promotional fees. The sales price of the half-acre lots will average $3,000 each, with 10 percent of the total sales to be received as cash down payments. These monies will be allocated for sales commissions and closing costs. The land contracts to be secured from the sales will be discounted and sold by the promoter for 75 percent of their face value. It is anticipated that the project will take three years to complete. The financial analysis appears below.

CASE 7.1   1,280-Acre Land Promotion

Costs:

1,280 acres @ $1,000 per acre		$1,280,000
1,280 acres improvements @ $500 per acre		640,000
1,280 acres carrying costs @ $500 per acre		640,000
	Total Costs:	$2,560,000

Income:

2,560 one-half-acre lots @ $3,000 each	$7,680,000
Sales and closing @ 10%	768,000
Sales contracts face amount	$6,912,000
25% discount	1,728,000
Net cash receipts	$5,184,000
Less costs (above)	2,560,000
Net profit before taxes	$2,624,000
28% taxes (ordinary income)	734,720
Net profit after taxes	$1,889,280
Return on total investment	73.80%
($1,889,280 + $2,560,000)	
Average annual return	24.60%
(73.80% + 3 years)	

Note that this case includes discounting the contracts in an amount of $1,728,000, a substantial sum of money. If the promoter were to hold the receivables, the returns would increase dramatically. However, the face amount of those receivables would not be immediately available for reinvestment, as is the discounted sum. Thus, an opportunity cost would have to be applied for the loss of earnings during the contracts' holding periods, offsetting to a great degree the higher profits.

However, note that the returns in this analysis are based on the full amount of the investment, assuming they are paid in cash. More realistically, considering a leveraging investor, the cash expended over the three years would include only the $1,280,000 costs for land improvements and carrying charges, plus a portion of the purchase price represented by an acceptable down payment, such as 10 percent ($128,000). The balance of $1,152,000 would be carried back by the seller of the raw acreage and would be paid over time by the receipts collected from the subsequent individual land contracts.

Therefore, the face amount total of the sales contracts—$6,912,000— must be decreased by the $1,152,000 owed to reflect the promoter's equity prior to discounting. The difference is $5,760,000, and a 25 percent discount ($1,440,000) will result in a $4,320,000 cash flow before costs and income taxes. Applying the more realistic cash investment figure of $1,408,000 ($1,280,000 + $128,000 = $1,408,000), the returns are now as follows:

Total gross income	$7,680,000
Sales and closing costs	768,000
Sales contracts face amount	$6,912,000
Less underlying encumbrance	1,152,000
Promoter's equity in contracts	$5,760,000
25% discount	1,440,000
Net cash receipts	$4,320,000
Less costs (adjusted)	1,408,000
Net profit before taxes	$2,912,000
28% taxes	815,360
Net profit after taxes	$2,096,640
Return on cash invested ($2,096,640 ÷ $1,408,000)	148.90%
Average annual return (148.90% ÷ 3 years)	49.64%

Thus, leveraging actually doubles the bottom-line return of this investment.

Subdividing for Development: Land Bankers

Speculation in acreage places an investor in a somewhat passive role while waiting for values to rise to the point at which profitable sales can be made. On the other hand, development of acreage into subdivisions requires an investor to play a more active role in order to effectively market the inventory of lots. Often, investors or builders purchase raw acreage situated on the boundary of an expanding community, improve the property, subdivide it and sell lots or build houses, apartments, offices or shopping centers on the land.

A developer who improves raw land for construction purposes and maintains an inventory of lots as a function of this ongoing business is called a *land banker*. Besides the purchase price of the unimproved acreage, the costs of **land banking** include property taxes, interest, off-site and on-site improvements, engineering, site development, plat acceptance, sales commissions, insurance and costs incurred because of timing constraints. The skills, risks and responsibilities required of the land banker–developer make this a very specialized segment of real estate investment.

To begin the development process, a land banker purchases a parcel of raw land, usually 160 acres or more, and prepares plats and maps of the property designating street locations, lot sizes and the general plan for the entire proposed development.

These plats, usually drawn by civil engineers or licensed surveyors, are submitted to the appropriate community regulating agencies for approval of design and zoning. After meeting local governmental requirements, including submission of a full environmental impact study (if applicable), the subdivider proceeds to physically prepare the land and sell lots to both individuals and builders.

Depending on the amount of acreage involved in the development, the resulting subdivision may follow the style of surrounding neighborhoods or may acquire a distinct character of its own. Many large-scale developments include land designated for the location of a school and/or a park, including a swimming pool, tennis courts, a clubhouse and perhaps, even a golf course.

Most well-planned subdivisions include a set of restrictions itemizing the type, design and quality of the improvements to be constructed on the lots therein. These **subdivision restrictions** are recorded and become covenants that run with the land so that each lot buyer and subsequent homeowner is required to observe them. Their enforcement becomes the responsibility of the neighborhood association formed after the project is completed. The restrictions are designed to create an economic and physical homogeneity within a neighborhood, which is important for maintaining property values. Restricting lots to residential construction eliminates incompatible land uses. Requiring a minimum square or cubic footage for each house creates an economic *floor*, limiting the neighborhood residents to those who can afford to purchase a home of the specified size.

Many builders do not have the financial capacity, the expertise or the inclination to become involved in land development. Such builders prefer to leave this type of real estate investment opportunity to those with proven skill in the field. Smaller builders are usually content to purchase lots from a developer–land banker, either singly or in packages of from 5 to 50 lots, depending on their needs. The prices paid for these lots reflect the developer's costs of acquisition and preparation and desired rate of return on the investment. For smaller builders, this technique of land acquisition is much less costly and demanding than an active entry into the field of subdividing.

CASE 7.2:   **160-Acre Mixed-Use Subdivision.**   The profit potentials in land banking can be illustrated in the development of a 160-acre parcel of land as a subdivision that will contain a park, a school, apartments, offices, stores and house lots.

Assume a purchase price of $1,120,000 ($7,000 per raw acre) plus $1 million allocated for engineering, platting, rezoning, improvements, interest charges and other carrying costs. The project is expected to sell out in two years because of its strategic location and strong market demand. Of the total parcel, 15 acres will be donated to the city for a park and roads, and 10 acres will be sold to the local school board for $100,000. This price reflects the developer's break-even costs for the 10 acres and, together with the donated park site, establishes the amenities necessary to attract potential home-buying families.

Anticipating a successful sellout of residential lots, contracts for the sale of a 10-acre apartment site at $20,000 per acre, a 10-acre office site at $30,000 per acre and a 15-acre shopping center site at $40,000 per acre have been arranged in advance. The balance of the land, 100 acres, will be subdivided into 400 individual house lots to be sold for an average price of $6,500 each. Sales commissions and closing costs for all properties are estimated to be 10 percent of the total receipts. The financial analysis follows:

CASE 7.2   160-Acre Mixed-Use Subdivision

Costs:

160 acres @ $7,000 per acre		$1,120,000
Improvements		1,000,000
	Total:	$2,120,000

Income:

15 acres Donated for park		-0-
10 acres School site		$ 100,000
10 acres Apartment site @ $20,000 per acre		200,000
10 acres Office site @ $30,000 per acre		300,000
15 acres Commercial site @ $40,000 per acre		600,000
100 acres @ 400 house lots @ $6,500 each		2,600,000
160 acres	Total:	$3,800,000
Less sales costs @ 10%		380,000
Net cash receipts		$3,420,000
Less costs (above)		2,120,000
Net profit before taxes		$1,300,000
28% taxes		364,000
Net profit after taxes		$ 936,000
Return on total investment		44.15%
($936,000 ÷ $2,120,000)		
Average annual return		22.08%
(44.15% ÷ 2 years)		

Note that in this case, as in Case 7.1, the bottom-line return is a function of the fact that the entire investment has been paid in cash. With the appropriate application of leverage, the returns for the mixed-use subdivision developer can be increased substantially.

In this particular investment, the monies generated by the advance sales of the school site plus the apartment, office and commercial parcels ($1.2 million total) would more than cover all of the $1 million cost of the land improvements. Then, if the purchase could be arranged on an installment basis, the investor's cash outlay could be reduced to zero and the excess $200,000 used as a down payment. With this high leverage, the investor's returns would climb indefinitely, creating exciting possibilities for land banking profits.

However, it must be clearly understood that investment in unimproved land is a high-stakes gamble. It is the most unpredictable of all types of real estate investment. No one can accurately estimate when it will sell or for what amount. As the RTC can attest, the bulk of losses suffered by investors, lenders, and ultimately taxpayers, during the recent banking crisis was in unimproved land. In an economic slowdown, it is the first to suffer and the last to recover.

FOREIGN INVESTORS

Much has been written about foreign investment in the United States. Although these reports give the impression that foreigners are owners of a large percentage of American real estate, the facts reveal an entirely different story. A study by the National Realty Committee and the Government Research Corporation indicates that non-American investors own a little more than 1 percent of our real estate. These foreign investors include groups from Japan, Taiwan, Vietnam, the Middle East, Canada, Latin America, Korea and some European countries. Anyone involved with foreign transactions is responsible to report large cash payments to the IRS; furthermore, such persons are liable for unpaid federal taxes. So, investors and brokers be wary.

Generally, foreign investors purchase American property because of:

- the appreciation in the values of their currency when compared to the dollar;
- highly inflated values of real estate in their countries;
- easing of restrictions on foreign investments by their governments; and
- perceived security of investments in the United States, based primarily on the stability of our government.

SUMMARY

This chapter examined some of the opportunities for investing in vacant land. Depending on a property's location, quality, purchase price, holding costs and appropriate timing, profitable speculative land investments can be made to enhance an investor's portfolio. Because most land holdings do not produce regular income, they are recommended for the investor who has accumulated numerous improved income properties that will provide cash flows needed to carry the investment.

Land investments provide speculative opportunities that can generate high profits in relatively short time periods, depending on specific circumstances. Primarily, the location of the land determines the amount and timing of its future growth in value.

Investors must be aware of the opportunity costs, as well as the initial purchase price, when estimating the profitability of purchasing raw land. In addition, careful attention must be paid to the physical attributes of and political attitudes toward a specific land parcel and the area in which it is located. These inputs must be positive to generate the required growth in value within a reasonable time frame.

Single-parcel investments include residential lots purchased for the construction of a home at some future time as well as speculative lots for resale.

More pertinent to the accumulation of a diversified real estate investment portfolio is the purchase of residential lots with rezoning potentials. The rezoning of a parcel of land to a more intensive use often substantially raises the property's value. It is not unusual for values to double or triple when a property is rezoned from residential to commercial use. In the long run, it is sometimes more profitable to lease these rezoned parcels for new construction rather than to sell them. The rental income developed from leasing establishes an annuity for the landowner.

An alternative to leasing vacant land is constructing a building on the property and thus converting the speculative quality of the investment to a more permanent income stream. Care must be taken not to erect a single-purpose building, which may be difficult to rerent when the initial lease expires or if the tenant defaults.

In addition to single-lot investments, many persons speculate in vacant acreage in anticipation of profits through growth in value. Some investors purchase acreage to hold until it increases in value to a point at which the property can be sold profitably in one unit; others purchase acreage wholesale for subdivision purposes and then make a profit by selling the smaller parcels at retail prices. It must be clearly recognized that investing in vacant land has probably the highest risk of any real estate investment.

EXERCISE 7   (Answers may be checked against the Answer Key.)

1.   What is the value of acreage producing 6,000 bushels of grain per year worth $10 per bushel, with a cost factor of 50 percent and a market capitalization rate of 10 percent?

   a. $ 30,000
   b. $ 60,000
   c. $300,000
   d. $600,000

2.   Of the factors affecting a land parcel's future growth in value, the one that is generally considered most important is

   a.   location.
   b.   price.
   c.   quality.
   d.   timing.

3.   From a locational point of view, a growth in value over time would most likely occur in land

   a.   adjoining a school.
   b.   near an interstate highway.
   c.   adjoining a manufacturing plant.
   d.   near a railroad line.

4. An analysis of the profitability of a vacant land investment includes all of the following *except*

    a. income lost from unrented vacant land.
    b. price and terms paid for initial purchase.
    c. carrying costs, including interest and property taxes.
    d. opportunity costs on equity invested.

5. When discussing the quality of land, all of the following are included, *except*

    a. its topography and fertility.
    b. the terms and conditions of its purchase and sale.
    c. the availability of utilities.
    d. the legal and political feasibility of its development.

6. Excess loss carryover is disallowed by the IRS for

    a. wheat farmers.
    b. horse ranchers.
    c. cow ranchers.
    d. hobby farmers.

7. Investors purchase vacant lots for all of the following reasons *except* to

    a. build homes in the future.
    b. resell them at higher prices.
    c. have them rezoned.
    d. shelter income taxes with depreciation allowances.

8. Of the following, the property that will generally develop the highest rental rate is a/an

    a. existing vacant store building.
    b. newly constructed garden apartment.
    c. new store building constructed to suit a specific tenant's needs.
    d. new store constructed as a speculative investment.

9. Agglomeration, or plottage, is based on the principle

    a. of buying low and selling high.
    b. that the sum of the parts is more valuable than the whole.
    c. that the whole is more valuable than the sum of the parts.
    d. of buying wholesale and selling retail.

10. Under the Interstate Land Sales Act, a buyer of a lot in a nationally pro-
moted subdivision has how many days after signing the purchase agreement to cancel the deal?

    a.   0 days
    b.   3 days
    c.   5 days
    d.   7 days

DISCUSSION

1. Investigate whether your community encourages growth, no growth or
planned growth, and examine the implications of this attitude for real
estate investors and developers.

2. Find a vacant site for sale on the periphery of your community and analyze its present value, using the information in this chapter. How does
your appraisal compare to its asking price?

8

Investing in Residential Properties

Key Terms

common areas	*income approach*
condominium	*lease*
conversion	*market approach*
cooperative	*proprietary lease*
cost approach	*securities*
evictions	*sinking fund*
Fair Housing Act	*tax credit*
horizontal regime	*timesharing*

More people invest in residential property than in any other form of real estate. Residential investments include ownership of a single-family detached house, an apartment unit in a cooperative or condominium and multiunit apartment buildings ranging in size from duplexes to highrise complexes.

A key factor of residential real estate ownership is the management and maintenance aspects of the landlord-tenant relationship. While these relationships are usually amicable, unpleasant circumstances occasionally do arise. The necessary commitment to active management, including the resultant interpersonal relationships, inhibits many investors from participating in residential rental ownership.

This chapter includes an examination of the various forms of residential property investments, including management responsibilities and cash-flow analyses. A case describing the profit possibilities in the conversion of a 100-unit apartment complex into a condominium of individual ownerships is presented to broaden perspectives in the field of residential property investment.

SINGLE-FAMILY DETACHED HOMES

Free-standing houses on single lots compose the greatest number of individual investments in the real estate industry. Sixty percent of this nation's families own their own homes. Included in this inventory—in addition to the multitude of owner-occupied, detached, single-family homes—are houses purchased for rental, resale, rezoning and conversion into apartments.

Prior to TRA '86, sophisticated investors shunned these properties. After the recent banking fiasco, however, single family homes have gained new respectability. The RTC was able to dispose of individual houses quickly, while some apartments and office complexes remain boarded up. Even in economically distressed areas, buyers can always be found for houses under affordable terms. This is not always true for other types of properties.

Furthermore, under current conditions, single-family tenant problems are simpler than those of multiunit buildings. Evicting one tenant may solve a specific problem, while wholesale evictions may be necessary to rid apartment buildings of drug pushers and other troublemakers. If the owner fails to evict such persons, the property can be confiscated under existing "drug and organized crime" laws.

In some regions, as in East Fort Worth, Texas, numerous distressed houses exist in communities with high employment and good wages, creating a strong demand for these properties. They can be purchased for relatively low prices because of the shortage of mortgage funds for investment and the existing foreclosure stigma. This dichotomy creates a pocket of profitable rents and the probability of high capital gains when the mortgage market returns to normal.

Owner-Occupied Homes

Technically, owner-occupied homes do not meet the full criteria for a real estate investment. They are not income-producing properties and, therefore, are not eligible for the complete range of tax deductions allowed for income properties. Only property taxes and interest paid for mortgages on an owner-occupied home are deductible expenses for income tax purposes, and then only if the taxpayer itemizes on the tax return. Additional deductions allowed for rental property include depreciation along with operating expenses, maintenance costs and insurance premiums. Most owner-occupants, however, consider their houses as investments. A home is the only real estate purchase they many people will make, and if they buy low and sell high, it will come closer to an "investment" in the complete sense of the word.

The owner-occupied home has proved to be a successful means of enforced savings for many people. A commitment to long-term mortgage payments results in the accumulation of equity, which provides the basis for the measurable inheritable estates of many owners. Frequently, homeowners find that they have relatively large equities in their properties—equities that may be capitalized to accumulate additional real estate holdings.

Owner-occupied houses have also proved to be hedges against inflation for those who wish to expand or improve their accommodations. Although the costs of new construction have been rising, owners of existing houses have generally secured enough funds from the sale of their older homes to enable them to purchase new homes.

Affordable Housing

In the 1980s, the availability of affordable housing became an important social issue. Many of our working poor have become our walking poor when some personal crisis has forced them to leave the safety and comfort of their homes and become street people. For the first time, we are witnessing entire families who are dispossessed and wandering around looking for jobs and shelter.

There is a serious shortage of affordable homes and apartments for low-income and no-income people. Deep cutbacks in national welfare programs have exacerbated the problem, while state and local agencies scramble to provide temporary shelters to preserve the health and safety of the poor.

Low-Income Housing Tax Credits

One of the more socially redeeming tax shelters to survive TRA '86 is the tax credit available to owners and developers of low-income housing. This credit is also available for the costs of rehabilitating properties for low-income tenants.

Up to 1988, the credit was available only to owners who earned $200,000 or less in taxable income. Congress, in an effort to stimulate more construction in this category, removed the earnings restriction entirely, opening up this tax sheltering opportunity to high-income investors.

Tax credits are substantially better than tax deductions. A **tax credit** is directly deductible from income *taxes*. Thus, it is a 100 percent tax benefit, unlike other tax benefits, such as operating expenses, which are deducted from income. For example, a $100 *deduction* at a 28 percent tax rate is worth only $28, whereas a $100 tax *credit* can save the same taxpayer a full $100.

Low-income housing tax credits provide an owner-developer with credits over a ten-year period on the following bases:

- New construction and rehabilitation: A credit of 9 percent of the total building costs is allowed each year for the construction and/or rehabilitation of each qualifying low-income housing unit. To qualify, the costs must exceed $2,000 per unit.
- New construction and rehabilitation financed with tax-exempt bonds or other federal subsidies: A maximum credit of 4 percent is allowed each year, including projects financed with Farmers Home Association (FmHA) loans.
- Costs of acquiring existing housing: A maximum credit of 4 percent is allowed each year. To qualify, the property must not have been used for low-income housing within the previous ten years.
- Targeting requirements: To receive these credits, at least 20 percent of the units in a project must be occupied by individuals with incomes of 50 percent or less of the area's median income, adjusted for family size, *or* at least 40 percent of the units must be occupied

by individuals with incomes of 60 percent or less of the area's median income, adjusted for family size. Units may not be used on a transient basis, thus eliminating hospitals, retirement homes, hotels and so on from these credits.

The Omnibus Budget and Reconciliation Act of 1993, OBRA, extended these tax credit opportunities for an indefinite amount of time.

Homes for Rental Income

To qualify as an investment in the fullest sense, a house must be rented to someone other than the owner. Generally, single-family house rentals generate only enough funds to cover the mortgage payments, taxes, insurance premiums and minimum maintenance costs. The owner of a detached house rarely secures cash flows that exceed break-even requirements. Thus, any vacancy, even for a short time, seriously erodes the profit potential of this type of rental-income property.

EXAMPLE: Consider a house valued at $70,000 purchased with $20,000 cash and a loan for $50,000, payable at 9 percent interest. Assuming a maximum rent of $500 per month, this property will experience a $2,880 annual loss.

If the investors qualify for the $25,000 special exemption under the current IRS code, they will actually experience a $ 93.60 out-of-pocket expense for this property at a 28 percent tax level. If the investors do not qualify for the special exemption, the total annual losses will have to be carried forward until the investment is sold. In either case, the owners will not receive any return on the $20,000 invested.

$ 6,000	Gross annual income
− 2,400	40% operating expense ratio
3,600	Cash flow
− 4,500	Interest at 9% (Any principal paid does not affect this analysis)
(900)	Negative cash flow
− 1,980	Depreciation ($55,000 × .036)
(2,880)	Loss
× .28	Investor's tax level
806.40	Tax shelter, if qualified
$ 93.60	Cash out-of-pocket

An owner of a rental house must be personally concerned with the constant maintenance of the property to ensure its continuous rental appeal and the avoidance of major repairs. In addition, maintenance of a single-dwelling unit is costly, time-consuming and inefficient in comparison to larger apartment projects. The need for personal involvement of time and effort and the requirements of maintaining a one-to-one relationship with tenants inhibit the popularity and profitability of this form of investment.

Some single-family house investors have entered into partnerships with their tenants on an equity sharing basis. The investor purchases the property and, instead of rent, the tenant makes the loan payments and maintains the property. Then, at some specified time in the future, the property is refinanced or sold and the partners share in the profits.

For those who are able to personally repair and rehabilitate older, worn-down properties, higher profits are possible. By purchasing dilapidated houses at bargain prices, these investors can receive benefits in at least three ways: an income stream that often shows a high return on a small amount of invested capital; an immediate growth in property value as a result of the repairs made; and, as a result of this added value, an expanded base for refinancing and continued investment pyramiding.

Homes for Resale

Because of the increased costs of constructing new homes, speculation in older houses is a popular form of real estate investment. The anticipation of growth in value has attracted investors to buying homes, leasing them and selling them for profits. The rental income during the intervening years often contributes to the carrying costs of the investment.

Some investors pyramid their holdings by constantly buying and repairing older homes for resale at higher prices. Profits from the sales are used to purchase more properties for rehabilitation.

Homes for Rezoning

Generally, the most profitable detached-house investments include those located on potentially rezonable lots. Depending on location and physical attributes, these houses can often be renovated after rezoning and leased rather than sold. These older homes are particularly attractive to certain tenants who can capitalize on the architectural charm of such buildings to enhance their business activities. For example, law offices, antique shops and real estate offices enjoy a "home-office" environment when located in older houses.

Conversion of Homes to Apartments

A unique investment opportunity, depending on local zoning codes, is the conversion of large, older, but sturdily built houses into several rental units. Many mansion-sized homes built on the periphery of older, central, downtown areas and passed over by a city's growth have fine conversion possibilities. Often, the quality of construction in these houses is such that new partitions, bathrooms and kitchen facilities can be installed quickly and efficiently. However, some of these houses require updated wiring, plumbing and fire escapes to meet current minimum building standards.

These apartments are usually in demand because of their proximity to downtown work areas and their old-fashioned charm. The spacious rooms with high ceilings found in such buildings appeal to many people, who will pay higher rents to enjoy this environment.

In the past, many of these grand old homes were purchased and razed by builders of highrise apartment and office buildings. Now, community planners are encouraging conversion of the remaining properties into apartments or offices and requiring the retention of their historic architectural styles.

THE FAIR HOUSING ACT

The rules and regulations of the Civil Rights Act (Title VIII—Fair Housing, effective December 31, 1968, and amended, most recently in March 1989) are of significance to investors.

Upheld by the U.S. Supreme Court case of *Jones v. Mayer* (392 U.S. 409, 88 S.C.T. 2186, 20 L.Ed., 2d 1189), the act is designed to eliminate discrimination in the sale or rental of housing based on race, color, gender or national origin. Single-family homes sold without the services of a licensed real estate broker, single-family homes rented by an owner who does not own more than three such houses at the same time and rooming houses for not more than four families in which the owner resides on the property are exempt from the provisions of the act. These exemptions do not indicate that the government sanctions discrimination under any circumstances. Investors are strongly advised to avoid any and all discriminatory situations.

The 1989 amendment expanded the act to include protection against discrimination for the handicapped and families with children. The new law extends fair housing protection to both the mentally and the physically handicapped. However, it specifically excludes persons who would pose a direct threat to the health and safety of others.

The new law stipulates that apartment buildings with four or more units, ready for occupancy on or after March 1991, be accessible to persons in wheelchairs. In buildings with no elevators, only the first-floor units are covered by the provisions. All doors and hallways in the building, as well as in individual units, must be wide enough to allow passage by wheelchairs. Light switches, electrical outlets and other controls must also be wheelchair-accessible. Bathroom walls are required to be reinforced to accommodate the installation of grab bars, and kitchens and bathrooms must be designed to allow free mobility for the handicapped.

The new law also extends fair housing coverage to families with children under the age of 18, including pregnant women. As a result of this expansion of the law, all-adult communities are banned, except those that operate specifically for the elderly under state or federal programs and those projects in which all residents are at least 62 years old. Retirement housing projects in which at least 80 percent of the units are occupied by at least one resident who is 55 years old are also exempt, if special services and facilities are provided for the elderly.

Although the **Fair Housing Act** is a federal law and under the jurisdiction of HUD, its implementation is generally left to the individual states, which have inaugurated their own open-housing regulations. These state laws are usually broader in scope than the federal law, and many include prohibitions against discrimination in financing and appraising real property as well as in leasing and selling.

When a problem occurs under the open-housing laws, a complaint is filed with the local commissioner, who investigates accordingly. The commissioner attempts to solve the dilemma amicably and without litigation. If a suit is necessary, it is initiated by the complainant in the appropriate state or federal court. In addition, the United States Attorney General's office may bring an action for injunctive relief in the federal court that has jurisdiction over the dispute.

A complainant can generally expect an answer to a locally filed action within 30 days. If the action is filed at the federal court level, an answer should be forthcoming within 100 days. Violators who refuse to obey the order of the court are held in contempt and fined or sent to prison for up to six months. Persons found guilty of bringing false charges or complaints with "willful intent" to falsify are subject to five years' imprisonment or a $10,000 fine.

MULTIUNIT APARTMENT RENTALS

Rental apartments are a popular form of living unit in this country. Ranging in size from a single small room above a garage to the numerous duplexes, triplexes and giant apartment structures found in all major communities, rental units vary widely in price, design, amenities and profitability.

In general, the basic benefits and special problems associated with this type of property ownership are similar for all investors in apartment rentals. One of the primary concerns of an owner-lessor is the stability and harmony of the landlord-tenant relationship. The owner wants the apartments to be occupied by contented, responsible tenants who pay their rent on time. Tenants, on the other hand, seek peaceful occupancy of well-maintained living quarters at reasonable rates.

Nearly all states have landlord-tenant laws with which residential rental investors should be acquainted. These laws are patterned after the Federal Housing Act and include prohibitions against discrimination in rentals because of race, color, religion, gender, national origin and, in some states, age. These antidiscrimination laws may also be enforceable at the city level, as in New York City. Some cities have adopted rent-control laws as well, inhibiting to a great degree the profitability of owning rentals in these communities.

Management Responsibilities

Of all the types of real estate investment, apartments require the greatest amount of management participation in physical maintenance and continuing tenant relations. The responsibilities increase with the number of apartments owned.

An investor may take either an active or a passive role in managing apartment units. Depending on specific circumstances, an apartment property containing fewer than ten units generally does not generate enough cash flow to support a professional manager. Projects of up to 20 units can rely on the services of an off-premises manager, while those that exceed 20 units generally require the services of an on-premises caretaker who, in project sizes of up to 100 units, doubles as a manager. Apartment investments that exceed 100 units usually employ an off-premises, professional management firm to oversee the entire operation, including an on-premises maintenance engineer.

Basically, the entire apartment management process is one of human relations. Physical maintenance can be handled a do-it-yourself approach or by hiring an expert from the field. For example, a leaking faucet may require only a simple washer replacement made by an owner-manager, while major plumbing repairs become the province of a licensed plumber. Repairs to elevators, heating and cooling equipment and swimming pools, along with other technical maintenance requirements, are invariably handled by professionals.

Success in apartment investments is mainly a function of the number of occupied units and happy tenants. In most circumstances, the landlord maintains the property and collects the rents, while the tenant pays the rent on time and enjoys the peaceful occupancy of the rented premises.

Unfortunately, such relationships are not universal. This is one of the major weaknesses in this form of investment. The landlord-tenant relationship often deteriorates when one of the parties shirks responsibility. Tenants can become angered at substandard maintenance, unruly neighbors, unreasonable rent raises or combinations of any of these. Landlords become upset with tenants who are noisy, dirty, slow in paying rent or disrespectful of the terms of the lease. As a result, apartment owner–managers spend fully 90 percent of their time concerned with problems created by as little as 5 percent of their tenants. However, this is an unavoidable characteristic of this type of investment and must be anticipated by buyers of apartment buildings. For this reason, many real estate investors prefer office, commercial or industrial properties to apartment rentals.

Leases.   An apartment/project/owner does have some control over the nature of the relationship with tenants. A rental agreement describes the owner's position in relation to that of the tenants. The formal document that stipulates the specified length and the expiration of the tenancy is called a **lease**. A lease is a legally enforceable, contractual agreement between a landlord and a tenant. In exchange for a tenant's promise to pay the rent on time and to maintain the property in good condition, the landlord grants the tenant possession of the premises and guarantees the tenant's rights to the peaceful use of the property for the duration of the lease term (see the exhibit at the end of this chapter.)

As important as the term of the tenancy may be, the investor's prime concern is *the rent* that the tenant is to pay for the use of the property. Rental payments by tenants are the owner's major source of income. The implied rental obligation entered into by the tenant under the usual apartment lease is for an agreed-on amount for the total period of the contract. However, unless the lease is specifically worded, the owner-manager may have difficulty enforcing the contract.

A lease in which the rent is stated as payable at $300 per month from September 1 this year to August 31 next year is not a legally enforceable one-year lease. It is merely an agreement for a month-to-month tenancy in which the rent is established at a fixed level of $300 per month for the year. To be legally considered a one-year lease, the agreement must be worded to obligate the tenant for $3,600, payable at the agreed-on rate of $300 per month. Thus, if a tenant defaults after five months, the landlord may sue for the balance that remains unpaid. It is fundamental to the establishment of a viable lease agreement that the rent to be paid be stipulated as the total amount for the entire lease period.

Most leases require that rent be paid on some regular, fixed-amount basis, usually monthly, as in the previous example. Although most apartment leases are established for one-year periods, some larger, more expensive complexes use leases of longer duration. In these cases, rent might be payable on a graduated basis. For example, a three-year lease for $10,800 could be paid at the rate of $200 per month for the first year, $300 per month for the second year and $400 per month for the third year. This technique enables a tenant to offset the costs of moving and furnishings in the earlier period of the lease. It also raises the rent gradually, allowing an easier absorption of higher charges in the later periods.

A lease is a promise to pay a certain sum of money as rent over an agreed-on time period. However, probably more animosity is generated over broken leases than over any other aspect of the landlord-tenant relationship. Invariably, some tenants lose their jobs, are transferred, become ill, get divorced or married or purchase a house, but the binding legal nature of a lease inhibits and prohibits a tenant's freedom to change housing to suit current needs.

Still, in the broadest sense, a residential lease actually favors the tenant because, for all practical purposes, it is generally unenforceable. If tenants move in the middle of the night, the landlord would be hard-pressed to find them and sue for the balance due. Assuming the tenant is available for suit, the legal costs and time involved relative to the balance of the rent still owed usually make any prospective gain insufficient to warrant pursuit. In fact, the law requires that a landlord diligently seek a new tenant for the vacated apartment and credit the rent received against the amount owed, thus reducing the defaulting tenant's obligation. As might be expected, few, if any, landlords choose to be rental agents for errant tenants.

On the other hand, some landlords prefer a formal month-to-month relationship that places control in their hands. A formal short-term rental agreement stipulates the monthly rental amounts and other terms in a written agreement, whereas an informal, but still legally enforceable, monthly arrangement may be made through an oral commitment between the parties. These month-to-month tenancies are automatically extended into the next period when the rent is paid.

The absence of a lease may disturb some tenants because, under this arrangement, the landlord has the power to arbitrarily adjust the rents and conditions of occupancy. Some state laws establish time frames for any changes in rental agreements. Many tenants, however, are relieved at the lack of a lease and are willing to risk a rent raise in exchange for the freedom of being able to move when desired. Most nonleasing landlords observe a no-rent-raise policy for a year as an operational strategy because they also run the risk of a tenant moving to a competitor's project. In the absence of a lease, tenants should still be required to sign an agreement to observe the rules and regulations of their occupancy.

Deposits.   Most states, under statutes governing landlord-tenant relationships, stipulate that the landlord may collect a deposit under a lease, but that deposit must be maintained in a separate account with any interest accruing belonging to the tenant, unless the interest is treated as additional rent with a provision in the rental agreement. This creates a serious bookkeeping chore.

To avoid this problem, many smaller residential project managers eliminate front-end deposits and require the first and last months' rents in advance. Larger projects collect deposits and account for them as prescribed by law.

Evictions.   Although the laws governing **evictions** for nonpayment of rent vary throughout the states, the following generally prevail:

- When a tenant neglects or refuses to pay rent when due, or when a tenant violates any provision of the lease, the landlord must provide formal notice before commencing an action for recovery of the leased premises and lost rent.
- The action shall be conducted as provided for actions for forcible entry or detainer and shall be heard in court not less than five nor more than 30 days after its commencement.
- If, after judgment for the plaintiff, the defendant tenant refuses or fails to pay the rent owed and due, the landlord may, in some states, have a lien upon and may seize as much personal property of the tenant located on the premises as is necessary to secure payment of the rent. Usually, landlords sue to evict the defaulting tenants and to secure possession of the rental units, discarding the tenants' possessions.

Provisions for Amenities.   Depending on the size of the project, residential rental properties often include some amenities besides the normal landscaping and architectural style of the construction. In fact, the opportunity to enjoy a swimming pool, sauna, clubhouse, tennis court, putting green, ski slope, marina, beach or, perhaps, golf course is what many apartment dwellers now seek for the rent they pay. A tenant might not be able to afford these amenities in a detached house, and the availability of these facilities is often a deciding factor in selecting an apartment to rent. Many tenants will pay a premium for these amenities.

Many apartment complexes are designed to attract persons with similar tastes. The success of "swinging singles" apartment projects is already legendary, as are the successes of retirement villages, ski resorts, golf and tennis groupings and similar special-interest rental developments, such as those that allow only cats as pets.

The maintenance and management of these amenities generate problems and costs for a project's owners—costs usually passed along to the tenants in the form of higher rents or use fees. The larger rental projects capitalize on their amenities by providing professional recreational directors who oversee organized, planned functions within the project. Ranging from dances to bingo games, these activities bring the tenants together and encourage friendships, which, in turn, act to create that much-sought-after longevity of tenancy so important for continued successful rental operations. Many of the more active apartment complexes find that they have lists of people waiting to move in at the first opportunity, rather than the sporadically vacant apartments found in less well organized projects.

Duplexes and Triplexes

Probably the most effective starter for a real estate investment portfolio is a duplex, triplex or fourplex apartment building. A beginning investor can occupy one unit while renting the other(s). In this manner, the owner-landlord is on the premises to minimize maintenance responsibilities.

Another advantage for the owners-tenants of a duplex, triplex or fourplex is the development of a tax shelter for the rented units of the premises as investment property. This technique requires that the owners "pay" a fair-market rent for their apartment as well as collect rents from the other tenants. By including this rent in the reported annual income, the entire property becomes eligible for allowable deductions as income property, including maintenance costs, property taxes, insurance premiums, utilities (when applicable) and depreciation. Thus, the owners may be able to shelter the entire income from the investment.

CASE 8.1:   **Triplex Profitability Analysis.**   This property consists of a brick building containing three two-bedroom, 1¾-bath apartments, each renting for $400 per month. They are unfurnished except for stove, refrigerator, carpets and drapes, and the tenants pay their own gas and electric bills. Operating expenses, including an amount for vacancy, total 40 percent of the gross annual income. The property is available for $150,000 with $50,000 cash and a 15-year carryback at 8.64 percent interest-only payment. (Note: Interest-only loan payments are relatively scarce in real estate investments but this method is used in this analysis to make the math a little clearer. Other analyses will include principal amounts.) Following is a return analysis:

CASE 8.1   Triplex: First Year's Profitability Analysis: $500,000 Cash Investment

$14,400	Gross annual income
− 5,760	Operating expenses (40%)
8,640	Net operating income
− 8,640	Debt service ($100,000 @ 8.64% interest only)
0	Cash flow

− 4,545	Depreciation ($125,000 @ 3.636% annually)
(4,545)	Loss
× 28%	Tax bracket
1,273	Tax savings (rounded)
+ 7,500	Growth in value 5% annual average)
$ 8,773	Bottom-line return (17.55% on $50,000 investment, rounded)

This analysis shows the effect of a break-even cash flow. It is difficult to generate any strong positive cash flows with smaller investments without making larger down payments or financing at lower than market interest rates. Note that if the amount for growth were eliminated this investment's yield would be only 2.5 percent ($1,273 ÷ $50,000 = .02546), not enough to attract an investor. Thus, the smaller property has to be purchased at a price low enough to allow the inclusion of a growth factor.

Multiunit Apartment Projects

The number of apartments in any one project might be 10, 50, 100 or even 1,000 units or more. Depending on the nature of the specific rental complex, there are varying degrees of management responsibility that reflect the size and scope of the project. However, regardless of size, basic financial principles of rental property are essentially the same, the only significant difference being the amount of money involved.

CASE 8.2:   **100-Unit Apartment Complex Profitability Analysis.**   Now examine the economics of a 100-unit apartment complex. The apartment mix and monthly rental schedule is as follows:

100 efficiency apartments @ $190 per month:	$ 1,900
20 one-bedroom apartments @ $250 per month:	5,000
60 two-bedroom apartments @ $325 per month:	19,500
10 three-bedroom apartments @ $400 per month:	4,000
Total monthly rent:	30,400
Total annual rent:	364,800
Other sources income (laundry, parking, etc.)	10,200
Gross annual income:	$375,000

Operating expenses, including a vacancy factor, are estimated to be 35 percent of the total gross income. The property is evaluated at $2,250,000, with $250,000 allocated to the land and $2 million as the building's basis for depreciation. An investor may purchase this property with a $500,000 cash down payment to a new $1,750,000 first mortgage payable at 10 percent interest only, due in full in 15 years. Here is a first year's profitability analysis of this investment

---

CASE 8.2   100-Unit First Year ROI Analysis: $500,000 Investment

---

$ 375,000	Gross Annual Income
−131,250	Operating Expenses
243,750	Net Operating Income
−175,000	Debt Service ($1,750,000 @ 10%)
$ 68,750	Net Cash Flow
− 72,720	Depreciation ($2,000,000 % 0.03636)
$ (3,970)	Loss
× 0.36	Tax Bracket
$ 1,429	Tax Savings (Rounded)
+ 68,750	Cash Flow
$ 70,179	14 percent c/c ROI

Note the absence of any principal add-back in this analysis because of the interest-only mortgage. note also the absence of a growth factor. Its inclusion would raise the bottom-line yield substantially. However, unlike smaller properties, which generally follow the market values closely, larger properties invariably lag behind. In this case, the value of $2.25 million will probably remain constant for a while, depending on local economic circumstances. In deciding to purchase this property, an investor would concentrate on the 14 percent ROI as the measure of profitability.

COOPERATIVES

A number of people wish to combine the economic benefits of home ownership with the carefree attributes of apartment living. While home ownership provides an inflationary hedge through value growth and equity buildup plus the tax shelters of property tax and mortgage interest deductions, living in an apartment minimizes a tenant's maintenance responsibilities and usually provides a compatible community environment. In addition, apartment living often provides tenants with amenities many people cannot afford on their own, such as a pool, sauna, marina, golf course and tennis courts.

The **cooperative** apartment ownership format provides an investor with an opportunity to marry the best of two housing concepts, ownership and tenancy. As with the **condominium**, which will be examined later in this chapter, the cooperative provides an individual investor with the chance to be an owner and simultaneously enjoy the tenancy of an apartment, with both the economic and the social benefits that accompany this arrangement. However, investors should establish local market acceptance of the cooperative form of ownership prior to attempting this form of investment.

History of Cooperatives

A cooperative is a union of members formed for the achievement of a mutually satisfactory goal. The benefits of goal attainment are shared by the members in direct proportion to the labor and capital contributed to the cooperative enterprise. A real estate cooperative involves the joining together of persons for the purpose of owning real property, usually an apartment building.

The concept of community housing is as old as humanity, dating back to the group sharing of a tree or cave. Then, as now, the right to share in the living accommodations was contingent on membership in the group. Ownership of the cave was a function of the group's ability to maintain control of the area—usually by force.

Today, property control is a function of our laws defining the rights of ownership. Cooperative ownership as a legal means of holding title to property dates back to the 1880s in the United States and even earlier in Europe. Until the end of World War II, however, cooperative ventures in this country were somewhat limited. It wasn't until the postwar period, when mortgage financing and all types of housing were in short supply, that cooperative corporations were organized on a large scale to combat high rents, especially in Chicago, Los Angeles, New York and Philadelphia. Since the 1960s, the cooperative has been eclipsed in popularity by the condominium.

Ownership Design

Cooperatives fall into two general categories—those that are publicly assisted and those that are private. *Publicly assisted cooperatives* are designed to serve lower-income groups through rent and mortgage interest subsidies and Federal Housing Administration loans. FHA Section 213 provides up to 97 percent insured financing for eligible cooperative enterprises. FHA Section 221 (d)(2) provides up to 100 percent insured financing for up to 40 years at below-market interest rates to solve certain pressing inner-city housing shortages. Section 235 allows the government to make specific assistance payments directly to a Section 213 mortgagee on behalf of a needy cooperator, and Section 236 provides direct mortgage interest subsidies for low-income cooperative developments.

Private cooperatives can be designed as either trusts or corporations. A *trust cooperative* places legal ownership of the property in the name of a trust company, which then issues *beneficial participation certificates* to purchasers of units in the cooperative. Ownership of such a certificate includes the right to lease a unit subject to the cooperative's rules and regulations. Officers of the trust retain the responsibility for maintaining and managing the cooperative.

Most cooperatives are organized as private corporations. This ownership form is probably the most efficient in design, because it provides for the election of directors by the apartment owner–shareholders. These officers of the corporation then assume the responsibilities for management. At the same time, the individual shareholders are immune from direct personal liability for corporate obligations.

A corporate cooperative vests ownership of the property in the name of a corporation. Stock in this corporation is issued and sold to apartment buyers in denominations proportionate to the value of the apartments available for lease. Buyers select a specific apartment, purchase a corresponding amount of stock in the owning corporation and execute a **proprietary lease** with what is now their own company. The lessors are then subject to the rules and regulations established in the corporate charter and bylaws.

Under the terms of a proprietary lease, the specific unit is inseparable from the entire ownership format. The amount of rent to be paid is a function of the proportionate share of the apartment's value compared with the total value of the project. For example, assume a 200-apartment highrise cooperative with an overall value of $8 million. An owner of a $40,000 apartment (who has been issued stock in this amount) has a 0.005 or ½ percent obligation for operating costs.

$$
\begin{array}{rl}
\$\ \ 40,000 & \text{apartment value} \\
+8,000,000 & \text{total project value} \\
\hline
.005, & \text{or one-half percent}
\end{array}
$$

If these costs equal $300,000 for the year, this apartment owner–tenant's contribution for operating costs is $125 per month.

$$
\begin{array}{rl}
\$300,000 & \text{total costs} \\
\times\ \ \ \ .005 & \text{obligation for costs} \\
\hline
1,500 & \text{per year, or} \\
+\ \ \ \ \ \ 12 & \text{months} \\
\hline
\$\ \ 125.00 & \text{per month}
\end{array}
$$

Financing

Developers of cooperatives secure the land for the project by purchase or lease, construct the apartment building (usually in the form of a highrise or group of highrise structures), and offer the apartments for sale. The purchaser is actually sold stock in the corporation that owns the structure in an amount commensurate with the value of the apartment chosen.

The stock may be purchased for cash or on terms. If cash is paid, then the lease for the subject apartment is developed at a rent reflecting the tenant's proportionate obligation for operating costs, as described earlier. These costs include property taxes, insurance premiums and maintenance expenses. If the stock is purchased on terms, after an acceptable down payment has been made, the buyer will execute an installment contract with the corporation to include an appropriate amount for principal and interest in addition to the proportionate operating charges.

The financial success of any corporate cooperative established with a master mortgage is dependent on each shareholder's ability to make monthly payments promptly and in the amount designated so that sufficient funds can be accumulated to satisfy operating expenses and debt-service requirements. This financial interdependence represents a serious drawback to cooperative ownership. As long as the shareholders make their payments on time, everything runs smoothly. However, if any owner defaults, the other shareholders are obligated to contribute a proportionate share of any shortages to protect their own investments and avoid a foreclosure. In other words, each cooperator must rely on the others to prevent a mortgage default.

Tax Benefits

Most privately developed cooperatives allow their shareholders to benefit from any gain in the sale of their individual stock. However, government-sponsored projects limit the amount of profit a shareholder may earn to the original purchase price of the stock plus any principal paid on the mortgage and any capital improvements made to the individual apartment. The 24-month tax-deferred reinvestment privilege afforded to homeowners who have made a capital gain on the sale of their residence is also available to cooperative shareholders.

Under the provisions of Section 216 of the IRS Code, a cooperative shareholder may deduct from taxable income the monies paid for proportionate shares of the property taxes and interest paid on the corporation's indebtedness. Furthermore, if professionals or businesses use the cooperative property for the production of income, they are also eligible for depreciation allowances.

To qualify for these deductions under Section 216, 80 percent of the cooperative's income must be derived from tenant-owner rentals. Hence, a project designed to allocate space for rental income other than that from the cooperators' units, such as street-level offices or retail shops, must observe the 20 percent limitation on such income to preserve the individual shareholders' tax benefits.

CONDOMINIUMS

A natural alternative to the cooperative, the *condominium* is based on the individual ownership of space in a multiunit building, be it apartment, store, office or other real property. Unlike the cooperative, the condominium ownership design removes the risk of reliance on others who might fail to make mortgage payments and consequently jeopardize an entire project.

History

Although present to a small degree in early Rome, condominiums did not become popular until medieval times, when they effectively solved housing shortages in the walled cities of Europe. The condominium concept, as developed in the middle European countries, became known as *co-proprietary ownership* and assumed varying degrees of importance down through the centuries.

The idea was transported to South America by the immigrants of the early 1900s. Years before the United States accepted this form of ownership, many other countries—including Belgium, Brazil, Chile, Germany, Italy and Mexico—had developed statutes recognizing and defining the condominium **horizontal regime** as a legal proprietorship.

With passage of the 1961 National Housing Act, condominiums were legally recognized in this country for the first time. Section 234 of this act provided FHA mortgage insurance for apartments to be built in densely populated areas of Puerto

Rico, which was suffering from a severe housing shortage. Highrise structures were constructed and individual mortgages arranged under FHA terms for persons who wished to purchase their own apartments. The concept, however, was only slowly accepted by mainland developers. By 1968, only California, Florida, Michigan and the District of Columbia had any significant number of condominiums.

During the early 1970s, "condomania" spread throughout the nation. A national housing shortage coupled with an easy money market gave rise to an apartment building boom, and many of the apartments were sold as condominiums. In 1972, however, adverse national publicity concerning the abuses perpetrated by some unscrupulous developers slowed the condo boom considerably. There were reports of condominium developers who retained the legal ownership of the land under their projects plus the amenities constructed thereon, such as the swimming pool and clubhouse, and then charged apartment owners extraordinary land rents and exorbitant amenity-use fees. These reports quickly dampened the public's enthusiasm for condominium ownership.

As a result of purported and proven abuses, new laws controlling condominium construction and management have been adopted by most states. Condominiums are now an efficient and viable form of property ownership that offers investors great flexibility in designing their realty holdings.

Ownership Design

Condominiums can be established for any type of real property, not just for apartment buildings. Other applications of this ownership form will be examined in later chapters. The organizational design, however, is essentially the same for all condominium developments.

Most states have legislation that establishes the legal format under which a condominium can be developed. Among other stipulations, these statutes include provisions for

- recognition of divided ownerships transferable by existing title documents;
- establishment of a binding declaration of bylaws among the participants that cannot be voided or altered without mutual consent;
- restrictions against further partitioning of the property described in the condominium regime; and
- establishment of separate property-tax assessments on each clearly defined unit.

The organization of a condominium requires that the developer first file a declaration of condominium and a master deed with the appropriate local government registration office. Then each purchaser of a condominium unit secures an individual deed to an apartment, which defines a fee simple ownership plus an undivided legal interest in all **common areas** of the condominium structure.

In a highrise apartment building, the common areas include the land, roof, elevators, stairwells, interior walls, halls and all amenities, such as a pool, parking stalls, a clubhouse, tennis courts and a golf course. In a low-rise apartment build-ing, also called a town house or a garden apartment, a condominium owner usu-ally secures fee simple ownership to the land under the unit and to the roof above it in addition to title to the unit. Thus, in a lowrise condominium, the common areas are limited to the surrounding grounds and amenities.

Management

The bylaws of each condominium regime include a provision for the establishment of an association of owners to supervise the management of the project. Included in this management responsibility is care of the common areas as well as enforce-ment of the project's rules and regulations. Each condominium unit owner receives a vote in the association, and the group elects a board of directors to assume the responsibilities of management.

In addition to supervising the personnel and services necessary for the mainte-nance of the property, the board develops the association's annual budget, includ-ing the amounts required for property taxes, insurance premiums and operating costs for the common areas. The board submits this budget to the general mem-bership for approval, and its adoption forms the basis of a special assessment charged each condominium unit owner.

As in a cooperative organization, this common-area assessment fee is based on the ratio of a particular unit's purchase price to the total original value of the project. Thus, the owner of a $40,000 apartment in a $2 million project will have a con-stant assessment ratio factor of 2 percent.

$$
\begin{array}{rl}
\$\ \ \ 40,000 & \text{apartment value} \\
\underline{\div\ 2,000,000} & \text{total project value} \\
.02, & \text{or 2 percent}
\end{array}
$$

This ratio will be applied to the annual operating expenses to determine the pro-portionate share. An annual common-area operations budget of $60,000 would require a contribution of $100 per month.

$$
\begin{array}{rl}
\$\ \ \ \ 60,000 & \text{budget} \\
\underline{\times\ \ \ \ \ \ \ \ .02} & \text{proportionate share} \\
1,200 & \text{per year, or} \\
\underline{\div\ \ \ \ \ \ \ \ \ \ 12} & \text{months} \\
\$\ \ \ \ \ \ \ \ 100 & \text{per month}
\end{array}
$$

In addition to collecting the monthly common-area operating fees from the associ-ation's members, most condominium managers impose an additional charge to accumulate funds in anticipation of major repairs and replacements. To assess the owners for their proportionate contributions to this **sinking fund**, which is depos-ited into a separate interest-earning savings account, the useful lives of the major components of the common areas are analyzed. The sinking fund charges applied in a highrise project would normally be greater than those for a low-rise apart-ment building because of additional maintenance responsibilities, such as the roof and elevator(s), in the former structure. While individual owners in a lowrise might be responsible for repairs to the roof, there are no elevators.

Financing

In effect, a highrise condominium is a vertical subdivision, with each floor representing a block and each apartment or office space a lot. Likewise, lowrise condominium structures are horizontal subdivisions, with the improvements joined together by common walls, eliminating the side yards. Thus, a developer generally secures funds for a condominium development from sources that normally provide monies for subdivision site improvements and construction financing, such as commercial banks or mortgage bankers. And, as in purchasing a single-family detached house, a condominium apartment buyer generally secures a loan from a lender in the home mortgage field.

A real estate lender views a high rise condominium apartment as a "house in the air," or a cube of space circumscribed by walls. The individual apartments are collateral for specific loans, and their values are determined much as are the values of individual houses. In the event of a default, a lender can foreclose on the collateral and assume an ownership role with all of the associated duties and obligations until the apartment can be resold. Thus, all of the normal realty lending activities apply to the financing of condominium property.

Condominiums are accepted by the FHA and VA for their insurance and guarantee programs. Moreover, they are considered by these federal agencies to be important vehicles for the provision of needed housing for low-income and middle-income individuals.

Tax Benefits

Since a condominium unit is considered a basic form of real estate, all of the tax benefits accruing to property owners also apply to condo owners. Deductions for property taxes and mortgage interest are available to an owner-occupant, while operating costs and depreciation allowances are deductible if the apartment is rented as income property. If an owner wants to sell the unit, any profits secured from the sale can be sheltered from taxes by reinvestment in another home (if the seller is an owner-occupant) or postponed through the use of an installment sale or like-property exchange.

Current Trends

The condominium form of ownership is likely to continue in importance. However, in some areas of the country, condos were built for markets that never materialized. In many instances, condos proved to be poor investments when maintenance fees accelerated faster than anticipated and, as a result, resales were difficult. Still, the apartment condo retains its position in the housing market and is a viable ownership alternative for singles and empty-nesters.

In addition to apartments, the condominium format can be applied to office and commercial buildings and to industrial and mobile-home parks. Even single-family detached houses are being constructed around condominium-area amenities, such as golf courses or marina facilities. In this type of condo development, the purchaser receives a deed to the house and underlying lot plus an undivided interest in the amenities. A regular fee for the use of these facilities is assessed by the managing association and charged to the subdivision homeowners, establishing a private club atmosphere.

Retirement and recreational developments have also used the condo format, many very successfully. Retirement communities have burgeoned all over the country, primarily in the warm-weather states (see chapter 12). These developments, which cater to the tastes and physical abilities of the owners, are usually composed of a mixture of single-family detached homes and condominium apartments. Other retirement villages consist entirely of condominiums. The larger mobile-home projects, in which each person owns a lot in condo with the other lot owners, provide for shared ownership and use of the common-area roads, pool and club-house.

Recreational condominium projects have also become successful as members of our society have become more affluent and acquired more leisure time. Ski areas, ocean and lake resorts and golf courses increasingly catch the eye of the astute investor-developer as potential building sites.

Securities Rule.   Careful attention should be paid to second-home investment condominiums that are purchased with a money-back guarantee and lock-in management agreement with the selling agency. The Securities and Exchange Commission (SEC) has ruled that these purchases are not real estate per se, but rather **securities**, which their promoters and developers must register for SEC supervision. If this interpretation prevails and the investments are not real estate, then the IRS may disallow any realty tax benefits. Consequently, investors in this area of real estate would have to prove that they were taking the risks normally associated with investment activity to be eligible for income property allowances.

Timesharing.   An innovative ownership format that is a spinoff of the recreational condominium concept is **timesharing**. Under such a format, a condominium unit can be designed for multiownership, with each owner having a specific period of use. Consequently, in theory at least, 26 persons could jointly own one condominium apartment and each use it for two weeks of the year.

Expanding on this theme, the joint owner of a mountain condominium apartment could trade the time allocation with the owner of an oceanside condominium. And through the services of an association of timesharing owners, this approach has been further extended to include owners of condominiums in foreign countries. A two-week stay in a Monaco condominium may be exchanged for the use of an Atlantic City apartment.

CONVERSIONS TO CONDOMINIUMS

Although not as popular today as in the past, one of the more creative real estate investment opportunities is the **conversion** of rental properties into condominium ownerships. Depending on market conditions at the time of conversion, as revealed by a feasibility study, an owner of an apartment, office or commercial building can file the appropriate documents to declare the existing property a condominium and can proceed to sell the individual apartments, office units or stores.

The basic market of potential purchasers for the converted units consists of the tenants occupying the building.

The most successful conversions are those of properties that are successful as rentals. People want to be there and will buy. The least successful conversions are those of problem properties. A conversion will not attract buyers to an unattractive property.

Some investors are occupied solely with conversions as profit-making ventures and travel the country purchasing property specifically to convert into condominiums. In land use, the principal of agglomeration involves combining small parcels to make one large, more valuable property. Condominium conversion investors apply the agglomeration principle in reverse—the sum of the value of the units in a condominium project exceeds the value of the whole. Other investors use this technique as a means of securing a final gain for the sale of their property when all the depreciation has been used up. Still others use conversion as a means of selling their property to avoid rent ceilings placed by local government agencies. These ceilings quickly dry up rental cash flow because property taxes, utility charges and maintenance costs continue to rise unabated.

Procedure

The conversion procedure involves filing the necessary legal documents to secure approval from the appropriate local government agencies, as described earlier. Then a marketing strategy is designed to reflect the current local demand for the type of space being offered for sale. This plan includes a price schedule of the individual units as a function of their size and location within the complex. In addition, a program for financing the individual sales with local lenders must be developed in advance.

Many conversions, especially of apartment buildings, require extensive renovation and modernization to comply with current building codes, handicap provisions and mortgage underwriting requirements. Structures with more than three floors may require the installation of elevators, and others may need stairwells remodeled to meet current fire-protection standards.

When extensive repairs must be made, care should be taken to minimize disturbance of the present tenants to preserve rental cash flow during the conversion period. One of the greatest risks of the conversion technique is the possible mass exodus of tenants and the elimination of rental income before sales commence. A converter should be prepared to meet this financial contingency with adequate capital reserves and a sound marketing plan.

A natural, often readily available market for the converter-investor is the tenant who already occupies the property involved. An honest and forthright approach is required when notifying tenants of the conversion decision. A tenant's alternatives are relatively simple—purchase the unit and retain possession or be prepared to move when the unit is sold.

Often, the harshness of the buy-or-move decision can be softened with a new lease for six months or a year to enable the tenant to find other quarters. More effective from the converter's viewpoint, however, is to arrange the purchase terms specifically for the tenant-occupant so that little cash is needed and the required mortgage payment approximates the present rental amount. Thus, the tenant can become an owner with little change in financial position. This approach can overcome some of the sales resistance from tenant-occupants, but experience has shown that only 30 to 50 percent of current tenants choose to become owners.

Midconversion Difficulties

Aside from the expected difficulties encountered with condominium organization and renovation, some conversion projects undergo extraordinary problems during the marketing period.

At some point in the sales program, a mixture of tenants, resident owners and nonresident owners may all share an interest in the same project. Problems may arise, such as inconsistent payment of rent and association dues, ignored rules and noninvolvement of resident owners.

The converter must consider the solution to these problems at the outset, establish a clear and concise set of rules and regulations and devise a set of enforceable penalties to back them up. As this is a complicated process, conversion programs should be closely supervised by competent lawyers, accountants and property managers.

Problem Analysis: 100-Unit Apartment Conversion

A conversion analysis measures a property's value as an ongoing rental operation against the potential total value to be derived from the sale of the individual units, be they apartments, offices, stores or other types of space.

EXAMPLE: Examine the economics of the conversion of a 100-unit apartment complex to a condominium ownership format. The property includes 100 apartment units situated in ten separate, individual, wood-frame and stone-faced buildings, clustered around a swimming pool and clubhouse. In addition to its garages and storage facilities, the property is surrounded by high hedges and tall trees that effectively isolate it from the adjoining neighborhood. This feeling of unity is enhanced by the rustic alpine decor complementing the rolling eight-acre terrain. The project is 20 years old and fully depreciated by its owner. It includes one-, two- and three-bedroom apartments, all with fireplaces, built-in kitchens and individual central heating and cooling units.

The buildings include a total of 150,420 square feet, of which 40,420 square feet are the hallways, laundry rooms and storage spaces, leaving 110,000 square feet as the rentable area. Market rents for this property are estimated to be an average of 35 cents per square foot per month. Thus, the gross annual rent from the apartments is $462,000.

$$
\begin{array}{rl}
110,000 & \text{square feet} \\
\underline{\$.35} & \text{per square foot per month} \\
\$\ 38,500 & \text{per month} \\
\underline{\times\quad 12} & \text{months} \\
\$462,000 & \text{per year}
\end{array}
$$

Together with $8,000 as additional annual income from laundry machines and separate garage rentals, the property generates $470,000 total annual gross income. Assuming total operating expenses of $212,000, including vacancies, the net operating income before debt service is $258,000.

$$
\begin{array}{rl}
\$\ 470,000 & \text{gross income} \\
\underline{-\ 212,000} & \text{operating expenses} \\
\$\ 258,000 & \text{net operating income}
\end{array}
$$

In this example, the $258,000 net operating income indicates a market value of $2,580,000 for the property as a rental investment. This amount is derived from an application of a 10 percent capitalization rate.

100-Unit Apartment Conversion

As Rental Apartments

$ 470,000	Annual gross income
− 212,000	Operating expenses
258,000	Net operating income
+ 10%	Capitalization rate
$2,580,000	Value as a rental

As Condominium Conversion

110,000	Total square feet living area
× $40	Depreciated market replacement factor
$4,400,000	Market value
− 880,000	Marketing expenses
3,520,000	Net sales proceeds
−2,580,000	Value as rental
$ 940,000	Potential net profit before taxes

Now this value can be compared to the total amount that could be secured from the sale of the individual apartments as condominiums.

There are various appraisal methods to estimate the sales value of converted condominium apartments. One is the **market approach**, in which an estimate of value is derived by comparing the subject property to similar property recently sold. Another appraisal method is the **cost approach**, which estimates the total costs for rebuilding the property today and then deducts an amount for depreciation commensurate with the subject property's loss in value over time. The **income approach** provides an estimate of a property's value based on the capitalization of its net income stream, as applied above.

In appraising the value of the apartments as individual units, a combination of the market and cost approaches results in a comparison factor of $40 per square foot of *living area* . This amount reflects the current depreciated value of all of the improvements, including the value of the land. Thus, the total amount of money that can be secured from the sale of the individual apartments is estimated to be $4.4 million.

$$\begin{array}{rl} 110,000 & \text{square feet of living area} \\ \times \quad \$40 & \text{per square foot} \\ \hline \$4,400,000 & \end{array}$$

A 20 percent sales cost factor—including required renovations as well as commissions, legal and mortgage-placement charges, title examination and insurance fees and escrow—would equal $880,000.

$$\begin{array}{rl} \$4,400,000 & \text{total sale amount} \\ \times \quad .20 & \text{sales cost factor} \\ \hline \$\ \ 880,000 & \text{sales cost;} \end{array}$$

Therefore, the net proceeds would be $3,520,000.

$$\begin{array}{rl} \$4,400,000 & \text{total sale amount} \\ -\ \ 880,000 & \text{sales cost} \\ \hline \$3,520,000 & \text{net proceeds} \end{array}$$

This amount is $940,000 more than the $2,580,000 the project would command as a rental operation. Thus, the owner stands to make a substantial profit on such a conversion.

SUMMARY

This chapter examined the alternatives available for investments in residential properties, including single-family detached homes, multiunit apartment projects, cooperatives and condominiums.

More investments are made in residential properties than in all other forms of real estate combined. The most common ownership is of the single-family detached home. An owner-occupied home, however, does not fully fit the technical description of an investment because it does not generate income. Still, a homeowner does consider a house as an investment and profits from it through property tax and mortgage interest deductions, as well as through possible growth in value.

To qualify as an investment in the fullest sense, a house needs to be rented. House rentals usually generate only enough income to cover the minimum maintenance expenses plus mortgage payments. Detached houses situated in areas with rezoning potentials are more profitable. Here, the rental income generated during the holding period prior to rezoning acts to develop a return on an investor's initial cash outlay, and the expected increase in property value reflects potentially large profits.

For investment purposes, duplex, triplex and larger multiunit apartment projects provide investors with many tax-sheltered profit-making opportunities. Because it involves a large degree of personal commitment to management, residential rental-apartment ownership requires more of an owner's time and effort than do most other forms of realty investment. Depending on the size of the project, these responsibilities can be delegated to professional management firms.

Single apartments in a multiunit building may be owned by individuals who join together in cooperatives or condominiums to enjoy the positive attributes of apartment living while minimizing the responsibilities of home ownership. The benefits of apartment living, with friends and activities close by, appeal to a large segment of our population.

A cooperative is based on a corporate format, in which individual shareholders execute proprietary leases for apartments suitable to their needs. The corporation owns the property, but the shareholders can benefit from deductions for their proportionate payments for property taxes and interest.

In a condominium, a specific apartment is actually owned in fee simple by an individual, who also acquires an undivided ownership interest, together with the other apartment owners, in the areas common to the overall project. Such common areas include the land, parking areas, hallways, elevators, interior walls and roof.

Condominium owners are responsible for the costs of maintaining their individual apartments, including principal and interest of any mortgage, property taxes and insurance involved in the apartments' ownership. Owners are also responsible for contributing to the maintenance costs of the common areas on a basis proportionate to the value of their apartments within the overall project. Building and liability insurance may be part of the condominium association fee.

In both forms of single-apartment ownership, the cooperative and the condominium, an owner may occupy the apartment and enjoy the facilities provided or may sell or rent the apartment as desired, but must observe the rules, regulations and bylaws of the specific project. In each case, the administration of the property is the responsibility of an association whose membership comprises all of the apartment owners. The association elects a board of directors to supervise the daily operations, most often through the services of a full-time resident manager.

Another investment alternative is the conversion of improved income properties to condominium ownerships. Applicable to apartments as well as to office buildings, shopping centers and other commercial buildings, the condominium conversion technique enables an owner to capitalize to the highest degree when selling the property. Rather than offer the property for sale as an operating rental project, an owner can create a condominium regime and offer each apartment, office or store for sale to individual buyers. This strategy often results in profits in excess of the value of the property as an operating rental project.

Because of the many complexities involved, including the financing arrangements and usual renovations required by local building inspection agencies, professional advice from lawyers, accountants, building contractors and real estate brokers should be sought by a converter before conversion plans are undertaken.

EXERCISE 8   (Answers may be checked against the Answer Key.)

1. All of the following single-family housing units are considered true real estate investments, *except* the house bought for

   a. resale.
   b. rent.
   c. occupancy.
   d. rezoning.

2. Professional investors generally consider a single-family home purchase to

   a. be a speculative and specialized activity.
   b. be a desirable investment alternative.
   c. be unable to provide adequate returns.
   d. need little advance financial planning.

3. To be a profitable investment, an apartment project includes all of the following attributes *except* be

   a. well located.
   b. well designed.
   c. clear of debt.
   d. properly maintained.

4. A taxpayer in the 28 percent bracket is entitled to a $1,000 tax credit. If the tax obligation is $7,800 before the credit, how much will it be afterward?

   a. $6,240
   b. $6,800
   c. $7,520
   d. $8,800

5. An investment in an apartment building is considered economically feasible if it

   a. merely breaks even.
   b. returns a profit on the investment.
   c. returns a profit and the investment.
   d. can be converted to a condominium.

6. The conversion of a rental apartment project to a condominium includes all of the following procedures *except*

   a. evicting all the present tenants.
   b. bringing the structure up to the current building code.
   c. filing legal documents for government agency approval.
   d. arranging financing for the apartments sold.

7. All of the following entities are exempt from the provisions of the Fair Housing Act *except*

    a. private clubs renting properties to their members.
    b. private owners of four or more houses.
    c. closed cooperative corporations.
    d. a home sold without a real estate broker.

8. The recent amendment to the Fair Housing Act extended coverage to all of the following categories *except*

    a. the mentally handicapped.
    b. the physically handicapped.
    c. families with children under 18 years of age.
    d. elderly over 62 years of age.

9. The formation of a condominium requires the filing of a declaration of intentions, including provisions for all of the following items *except*

    a. recognition of divided ownerships.
    b. establishment of a binding set of bylaws.
    c. creation of a single master mortgage.
    d. restrictions against further partitioning.

10. An apartment tenant with a lease that stipulates "The rent shall be $500 per month for one year starting March 1" moves out on June 15 during the term of the lease. The landlord is entitled to recover which of the following amounts?

    a. $ 0
    b. $ 250
    c. $ 500
    d. $4,000

DISCUSSION

1. Discuss the pros and cons of a lease versus a month-to-month tenancy from both the tenant's and the landlord's points of view.

2. Investigate the requirements for rezoning a property in your community, including the various government agencies and commissions involved in reviewing the request and holding public hearings. Which agency finally grants the rezoning ordinance?

EXHIBIT   Apartment Lease

APARTMENT LEASE
APPROVED BY BUILDING OWNERS & MANAGERS ASSOCIATION

This Lease, Made this_____day of_____, 19_____ by and between

_____hereinafter referred to

as the Lessor, and _____ _____hereinafter referred to as the Lessee.

Witnesseth: That the said Lessor does hereby demise and lease unto the said Lessee, the following described property:

Apartment No. _____ in the _____ Apartment House,

located at _____ _____in the city of

to be occupied solely as a private dwelling with occupancy limited to _____persons; including hot and cold water, and janitor service in the manner customary in the building.

LEASE TERM To Have And To Hold the above described premises, with the appurtenances thereto, unto the said Lessee from

_____, 19_____ until _____, 19_____ inclusive.

And the said Lessee in consideration of said demise does hereby covenant and agree with the said Lessor as follows:

AMOUNT OF RENTAL First—To pay to said Lessor as rental for the said demised premises

the total sum of _____ ($_____) Dollars

payable in monthly installments as follows: $_____

_____

_____

per month, during the continuance of this lease, and payments to be made payable on the 1st day of each month. IN ADVANCE, to **and**

at the office of _____
or at such other place as the Lessor shall direct; and in addition thereto to pay all gas, electric and meter reading charges levied, assessed, charged against or incurred at said demised premises for and during the term of this lease and to save the said premises and the said Lessor harmless therefrom.

CONDITION OF PREMISES Second—That said Lessee is satisfied with the physical condition of the demised premises and agrees that at the termination of this lease or any renewal thereof, by lapse of time or otherwise, Lessee will yield up said premises to Lessor in as good condition as when the same were entered upon, reasonable wear and tear only excepted. The provisions of this paragraph apply also to furnishings, if the apartment covered by this lease is furnished.

_____

_____

_____

OBLIGA- TION OF LESSOR Third—That Lessor shall furnish lights for the public halls, stairways, entrances and other public portions of the building when necessary. That said Lessor shall NOT be liable for any damage occasioned by failure to keep said premises in repair or for any latent defect in the building or for failure to furnish heat through any accident to the boiler or heating plant, or any interruption occasioned by strikes, lock-outs, or any temporary failure due to any cause whatsoever, and shall not be liable for any personal injury or accident sustained by said Lessee, his family or servants, or for any damage done or occasioned by or from any boiler or by or from any plumbing, gas, water, steam, or other pipes, or sewage, or from any gas stove or electric fixture, or from the bursting of any boiler or the leaking or running of any cistern, tank, wash stand, water-closet, or waste-pipe, in, above, upon or about said building or premises, nor for damages occasioned by water, snow or ice being upon or coming through the roof, sky-light, trap-door or otherwise, nor for any damage arising from acts or neglect of other occupants of the same building, or of any owners or occupants of adjacent or contiguous property. That all property placed in the leased premises or in the store rooms or in any other portion of said building or any appurtenant thereto, or left in care of the janitor, be at the risk of Lessee, or the parties owning same, and Lessor shall in no event be liable for the loss or damage to such property from any cause whatsoever.

SUB- LETTING and USE; PETS Fourth—That Lessee will not sub-let the premises nor any part thereof, nor assign this lease without the written consent of said Lessor, and will not permit any transfer by operation of law, or otherwise, of the interest in said premises acquired through this lease; and will not permit said premises to be used for any unlawful purpose, nor permit any loud or unnecessary noise such as to disturb the tenants of such building or neighborhood; nor permit the playing of any radio or musical instrument before the hour of 8 a.m. or after 10:30 p.m.; that no parrot, dog, or other animal shall be kept within or about said apartment. In the event a pet should be desired, the lessor should be consulted regarding what type. Pet's name is_____.

EXHIBIT   (continued)

TENANT'S CARE OF PREMISES; RULES — Fifth—And the said Lessee further covenants and agrees to take good care of the apartment hereby demised and its fixtures, and to commit and suffer no waste therein; and that no changes or alterations of the premises shall be made, that there shall be no decorating, papering, painting, locks changed, or new locks installed without the consent in writing of said Lessor, that said Lessee shall pay for all repairs required to said apartment whenever damage or injury to the same shall have resulted from misuse or neglect; that said apartment shall not be used as a "Boarding or Lodging" house, nor for a school, nor to give instructions in music or singing and none of the rooms shall be offered or sub-let by placing notices on any door, window or wall of the building, nor by advertising the same in any newspaper, or otherwise; that there shall be no lounging, sitting upon, or unnecessary tarrying in public places of said building by the said Lessee, members of the family, or other persons connected with the occupancy of the demised premises; that no provisions, milk, ice, marketing, groceries, or like merchandise, or the moving of furniture or appliances, shall be delivered into or out of the demised premises through the front entrance of said building, that said Lessee, and those occupying under said Lessee, shall not interfere with the furnace heating apparatus, or with the gas, lights, wiring or plumbing of said building, nor with the control of any of the public portions of said building; and that said Lessee and those occupying under said Lessee will comply with and conform to all reasonable rules and regulations that said Lessor has made or may make for the protection of the building or for the general welfare and comfort of the occupants thereof.

CARE, CONTINUED — Sixth—That said Lessee will not permit anything to be thrown out of the windows of his apartment, or down the court or lightshafts in said building; that nothing shall be hung, shaken, or placed on the outside of the windows, in the main halls, on stairways, or balconies of said building; that Lessee will see that all pieces of furniture are moved in such a way as not to damage the floors and walls; that Lessee will not use strong soap or powders on varnished or polished woodwork, floors, painted walls or other wall covering, nor will Lessee use any preparation of varnish on the floors or paint or decorate any woodwork or finish hardware without first consulting Lessor, or his agent; that Lessee will pay the cost of opening drains and waste pipes found to have been stopped up by any substance found to have been thrown therein.

FIRE HAZARDS — Seventh—It Is Further Covenanted and Agreed by said Lessee, that there shall not be kept, or used on said premises, any gasoline, benzine, naphtha or any products in whole or in part of them, nor any burning fluid or chemical oils, other than the ordinary street gas or kerosene of lawful fire-test. In case the building in which said premises are located, shall at any time be destroyed or damaged by unavoidable casualty or by fire, so that the premises herein leased shall be unfit for occupancy or use, then the rent hereby reserved or a fair and just portion thereof, according to the nature and extent of the damage sustained in loss of occupancy of the premises, shall be suspended and so continue until said premises shall by said Lessor be rebuilt or made fit for occupancy and use or this lease shall thereby be terminated, at the election of Lessor, or in case said premises are totally destroyed or not put in tenantable condition within one month from the time of said damage, then this lease may be terminated at the election of said Lessee, upon notice given.

ACCESS TO APARTMENT SERVICE INTERRUPTION — Eighth—That said Lessee will allow said Lessor free access at all reasonable hours to the premises hereby leased for the purpose of examining or exhibiting the same, or to make any needful repairs on said premises, which Lessor may deem it fit to make.   No interruption or curtailment of any service furnished by Lessor, or re-entry by Lessor, in the manners herein stated, shall be deemed a constructive eviction.

LIEN CLAUSE — Ninth—It is further agreed that all the goods, chattels, fixtures and other personal property belonging to said Lessee which are, or may be put into the said leased premises during said term, whether exempt or not from sale under execution and attachment under the laws of the State of Nebraska, shall at all times be bound with a lien in favor of said Lessor, with power of sale, and shall be chargeable for all rent hereunder and the fulfillment of the other covenants and agreements herein contained.

WAIVER — Tenth—No assent, expressed or implied, by the Lessor, to any breach of any of Lessee's covenants herein contained shall be admitted or taken to be a waiver of any succeeding breach of the same covenant or any other covenant of this lease. It is agreed that all of the covenants and agreements in this lease shall be binding individually, severally and jointly upon the parties hereto, and upon their separate estates, and shall succeed to their respective heirs, executors, administrators and assigns without affecting the restrictions imposed by paragraph 2 hereof pertaining to occupancy. Any modification of this instrument must be in writing.

DEFAULT IN RENT; ABANDONMENT — Eleventh—Should default be made by the Lessee in the payment of the rental or any part thereof, when and as herein provided, or should Lessee make default in performing, fulfilling or keeping of any of the Lessee's other covenants, conditions or agreements herein contained, or should Lessee remove or attempt to remove furniture or effects from the leased premises, or if an execution or other process be levied on the interest of Lessee in this lease or if petition in bankruptcy be filed by the Lessee, or should the Lessee be adjudged bankrupt or insolvent by any Court, Lessor shall have the right at his option to re-enter and take possession of the leased premises and to annul and terminate this lease. It is agreed that the receipt or acceptance of the keys to the premises by the Lessor shall not constitute a cancellation of this lease.

RE-POSSESSION OF PREMISES — Twelfth—If the leased premises shall be abandoned or become vacant during the term of this lease, without Lessee having paid in full the rent as required under this lease, then in such case Lessor shall have the right at his option to re-enter the leased premises and annul and terminate the lease, or take possession of the leased premises and let the same for the balance of the term, as agent of Lessee, upon such terms and for such sums as may be readily obtained, and apply the proceeds received from such letting, after payment of expenses, toward the payment of the rent of Lessee under this lease, and such re-entry and re-letting shall not discharge Lessee from liability for rent or from any other obligation of Lessee by reason of the terms hereof. Should the Lessor choose to re-let the premises for the benefit of the Lessee, pursuant to the option hereinabove granted, the expense of re-letting shall be computed on the basis of one-half of one month's rent as provided herein and in addition, Lessee shall pay all expenses incurred by Lessor in securing new tenant.

HOLDOVER AND RENEWAL — Thirteenth—That the said Lessee agrees at the termination of this lease, by lapse of time or otherwise, to forthwith leave, surrender and yield up possession of the demised premises in good and substantial order and repair. It is understood and agreed that this lease shall not extend beyond the term herein granted, and a holding over or continuance in the occupancy of the demised premises shall not work an extension of the said lease, but in any and all such cases, the Lessee shall be a tenant at the option of the Lessor, and an acceptance of rent by the Lessor shall establish a tenancy from month to month or _____ as the Lessor may determine. During such holdover tenancy, the Lessee shall be governed by all the covenants of the lease, except that pertaining to the original term.

AIR CONDITIONING AND WATER SUPPLY — Fourteenth—It is further understood and agreed that in the event the Lessee shall decide to install any air conditioning or cooling system in the premises demised herein, during the term of this lease, the Lessee will first submit to the Lessor for his approval, all plans and specifications of such installation; and that no work shall be started on said air conditioning or cooling system until the Lessor shall have first given his written consent to the said work, in accordance with the approved plans and specifications. It is further understood and agreed that the Lessee will, at his own expense, make all necessary changes in water supply, discharge and waste lines, together

---

EXHIBIT   (continued)

---

with all changes in electrical wiring resulting from the installation of such equipment. The Lessee further agrees that said air conditioning or cooling system shall receive its cold water supply from the main supply of the building through a special meter to be installed and maintained by the Lessor at the expense of the Lessee and the amount of water shown by said meter as used by the Lessee each preceding month, multiplied by the rate charged by the Metropolitan Utilities District to the Lessor for such water, shall at the beginning of each succeeding month become due and payable to the Lessor as so much additional rent. The Lessor shall have the right of access to the said meter at the times the readings thereon are taken, and also to inspect and keep said meter in repair. The Lessee shall not connect with or in any manner interfere with any other part of the water system of the building.

DATE OF POSSES- SION   Fifteenth—It is hereby covenanted and agreed that if the demised premises above described shall not be available for occupancy at the date named in said lease as the time when the lease term is to commence, then said lease shall commence on the date when said premises shall be available for occupancy, and a pro rata abatement of the rental herein provided shall be made until said premises are available for occupancy but the expiration of the said lease shall remain the same; and, the Lessor shall not be liable for any loss or damage of any kind whatsoever that the Lessee

may sustain or claim to have sustained by reason of such delay._____

_____

_____

_____

_____

_____

_____

SIGNA- TURES REQUIRED   Sixteenth—Until this lease is executed on behalf of all parties hereto, it shall be construed as an offer of proposed Lessee to proposed Lessor. Time being of the essence, this lease must be completed on behalf of all parties on or

before _____to be effective.

FLOOR COVERING   Seventeenth—Lessee agrees at all times during the term of this lease or any extension or renewal thereof to keep the floor in the living room completely covered by carpeting, rugs, or other soft floor covering.

IN WITNESS WHEREOF, the parties hereto have executed this lease the day and year first above written.

WITNESS:

_____   _____
                                                                            Lessor

_____   _____
                                                                            Lessor

_____   _____
                                                                            Lessee

_____   _____
                                                                            Lessee

9

Investing in Office Buildings

Key Terms

acceleration
BOMA
central business district (CBD)
escalation
homogeneous tenancies

leasehold
office parks
rental concessions
sublease
tax clause

Our nation's business activities are oriented to the office environment. Each profession, government agency, financial institution, corporation or business needs an office to house its service activities. The largest industrial firms require a main office in which to centralize their management operations, in addition to branch offices located in each city in which plants manufacture their products. The General Services Administration (GSA) of the U.S. federal government is the world's largest lessee of office space. It is responsible for providing the housing for government activities, which range from post office operations through the parks service to the space program, in addition to the myriad of activities in between.

The need for office space has steadily increased over the years as our economy has changed from an agrarian to an industrial to a service-oriented society. Currently, more than 75 percent of the people in the work force are engaged in occupations that require office space in which to operate. A migration from rural communities to urban centers has accompanied this shift in occupational patterns. As cities grow and commerce expands, demand for office space increases. The need for centralized locations, combined with technical advances in construction methods, has produced the office skyscrapers so familiar in large cities today.

Although the multistoried office building dominates the metropolitan skyline, it is just one form of office space available. Numerous firms are housed in one-story to three-story buildings located in or over strip stores along business streets, in shopping centers and in suburban office or office/industrial parks.

The transportation and parking problems of a community's downtown area have provided the impetus for the growth of smaller suburban office complexes. These areas are now attracting more office centers, some of which are designed as condominiums.

The characteristics of a suitable location in the central city include adequate parking, an aesthetically pleasing ambiance and proximity to government entities, transportation, lodging, restaurants, retail businesses and other office buildings. In the suburbs, desirable characteristics include the absence of adverse influences or activities as well as access to roads, transportation, air service, parking and other office buildings.

The factors considered absolutely essential—or at least, very important—in deciding on the location of a company's headquarters were examined in a recent survey of the top executives from 400 nationwide organizations. Listed in descending order of importance, they are

- large functional space,
- quality of community life,
- room to expand,
- efficient access to market(s),
- low cost,
- good business climate,
- community image,
- available qualified labor supply,
- social climate and
- college and university availability.

This chapter investigates the management requirements common to most office buildings, large or small, and examines the varied investment opportunities in this segment of the real estate market.

OFFICE BUILDING MANAGEMENT

Whether investors in office space are large companies involved in highrise projects or private developers investing in lowrise or midrise buildings, they have similar management responsibilities. A profitable venture requires a careful market study to determine the demand for the subject space in terms of existing rentals and future needs. Rental policies and procedures must be established that will initially attract new tenants and remain flexible enough to keep these tenants for long periods of time. Included in the establishment of policies and procedures are viable rental schedules within the terms and conditions of leases.

Market Analysis

Prior to making any investment in office property, an investor should commission or conduct a market study on the availability and character of neighboring competitive properties. The direction and degree of future trends are more significant than the present status of the market. Primary consideration should be given to the demand for space by new businesses in the area, the expansion rate of existing tenants and the number and types of tenants who desire to move from

---

TABLE 9.1   General Metropolitan Areas of Selected Cities Percent Office Occupancy Rates

	End 1993		*End 1993*
Akron	84.0	Milwaukee	79.0
Atlanta	82.9	Minneapolis	84.8
Baltimore	83.1	New Orleans	73.9
Boston	82.8	New York	84.8
Buffalo	83.8	Omaha	83.6
Charlotte	82.7	Orlando	85.6
Chicago	74.1	Pittsburgh	83.2
Cincinnati	83.4	Portland	86.0
Cleveland	81.4	Sacramento	86.1
Columbus	86.2	St. Louis	82.3
Dallas	72.8	St. Paul	82.1
Denver	82.7	Salt Lake City	85.3
Detroit	80.2	San Francisco	87.3
Fort Worth	79.9	Seattle	84.4
Houston	76.4	Tucson	80.1
Indianapolis	78.1	Tulsa	78.9
Kansas City	85.5	Washington, D.C.	86.4
Los Angeles	80.3	United States	81.7
Memphis	78.9	Canada	82.9
Miami	83.5		

Source: *BOMA Skylines Magazine,* March 1994.

their present locations. This demand is determined by the absorption rate of vacant properties and the amount of new office space that comes on the market. Currently, the office market is saturated with space created in the building frenzy of the late 1980s. It will be a few more years until this space is absorbed and any new large-scale construction of offices will begin.

To gain more definitive perspectives, the investor should study the market for office space segmentally—according to age, condition, location, facilities and amenities. An overall market vacancy figure of 5 percent may actually include a more specific 10 percent vacancy ratefor new office space and a 2 percent rate for a city's central business district. Market information is available from local newspaper reports, the chamber of commerce, private research firms in their monthly reports and the local chapter of the Building Owners and Managers Association (BOMA) see Table 9.1.

The relocation of tenants from older structures to newer properties should be examined carefully to approximate the degree of movement. An estimate can then be made of the potential attractiveness of a new structure, and new uses for older buildings may be discovered. For example, in some markets, unused warehouse space has been converted to offices and apartments, while older space vacated by tenants moving to new quarters is often occupied by businesses that require relatively little customer contact. For these firms, a prestigious location is less important than convenience of layout and reasonable rent. Once the demand pattern for an area is identified, a rent schedule for a specific property within that market can be established.

Establishing a Rent Schedule

As with most rental properties, the charge for the use of space is probably the most significant factor not only in attracting tenants but also in establishing the profitability of the investment. Depending on the economic stability of the area in question, the condition of the market for the particular investment under consideration, the quality of the building and the services provided, a realistic rent schedule should be prepared and administered forthrightly by the property owner or manager. Rental rates that are unrealistically high result in vacancies and serious cash-flow shortages, while rates that are too low minimize the investment's profit potential and depress the valuation of the property.

Generally, office rent schedules are established on a base rate with extra charges for special services. Primarily, a tenant is concerned with the interior space allocated for use, although the building's location, its condition and the availability of amenities are also considered when the rent is negotiated. Because the primary concern is space, office rents are usually established as a certain dollar amount *per square foot per year of usable space.* Thus, a base rate of $12 per square foot per year for an office with 1,000 square feet of interior space will result in a rent of $1,000 per month.

$$
\begin{array}{rl}
1,000 & \text{square feet} \\
\times \quad \$12 & \text{per square foot} \\
\hline
12,000 & \text{per year} \\
\div \quad 12 & \text{months} \\
\hline
\$ \quad 1,000 & \text{per month}
\end{array}
$$

Rent is affected by many elements, including the competitive market; the location of the subject property; the quality of the building; the services provided by management; and the inclusion of partitions, floor covering, air conditioners, utilities, parking facilities and other improvements required by the tenant which are called TIs (tenant improvements). In addition, a rental rate is influenced by the location of the office within the building itself—lobby and top-floor locations usually command the highest rates.

Since the determination of rent is based on the space used by the tenant, the areas utilized for an entry lobby, hallways, stairwells, elevator shafts, bathrooms, storage bins and the like are considered nonproductive in terms of generating cash flows. The charges for their use are built into the base rate in the lease contract. As a result, an office building is described as having a specific degree of *efficiency.* For instance, if a certain building has 10 percent of its overall square feet included in these nonproductive areas, it is said to be 90 percent efficient, whereas a building with 20 percent of its space utilized as hallways and so forth is considered to be 80 percent efficient.

Applying the efficiency factor that exists for a particular building allows an investor to estimate the number of rentable square feet available and establishes a basis for making an economic analysis of an investment's potential profitability. For example, an 80-percent-efficient structure containing 50,000 total square feet has only 40,000 rentable square feet to which the rental rate can be is applied; this must be considered when evaluating the possible gross annual income from this investment.

It may appear as though a highly efficient building would generate a commensurately high gross annual rent, but this is not always the case. For instance, a building with 10 percent of its total area devoted to nonproductive space may have narrow hallways and a small, unimpressive lobby. Although the efficiency rate for this structure is higher than that of a building with a larger lobby and wider hallways, the rental rate might be lower, because it is a less prestigious building. Thus, the achievable gross rents would actually be lower than those for a comparable structure with a lower efficiency factor.

Marketing Office Space

Marketing office space requires a systematic and continuing program to attract prospective tenants and maintain their occupancy after they have moved in. Generally, new tenants are interested in getting a rental bargain while at the same time acquiring increased office and building efficiency, economy of operational expenses and a dignified and convenient location that complements their enterprise.

Managers often display great zeal and ingenuity in seeking new tenants. However, it is important to evaluate the financial ability, current needs and future growth potential of all new applicants.

Some of the most common methods employed to attract tenants to an office project are signs placed on the property; advertisements in local newspapers and regional editions of such national publications as the *Wall Street Journal, Time, Newsweek* and *U.S. News & World Report;* and promotional brochures distributed by direct mail to all businesses in the geographic area.

On-site sales centers are often included in larger projects to centralize the activities involved in renting available space and to house the management staff. The objective of an on-site manager operating out of a sales center is to present the building's features with sophisticated audio and visual productions and thereby create the appropriate environment for effective lease negotiations and closings.

Rental Concessions. In the quest for new tenants, landlords and their agents often devise creative means of generating interest in their project. A popular technique is to offer certain **rental concessions** to make leasing office space in a new building a prestigious move as well as a decided bargain.

Although it appears that simply decreasing the rent for the office space would be the most effective rental concession, the owner of an office building is often precluded from doing so by the terms and conditions of a mortgage loan. Since a net market rent is used to substantiate the granting of a mortgage loan in the first place, any reduction of the scheduled rent would reduce the value of the entire project. As a result, landlords do not reduce rent per se but offer other concessions—for example, a free rental period that allows the tenant time to get settled and adjust to the new office. However, any concessions that seriously erode the net rental income are often not tolerated by the lenders.

Additional concessions may be granted by a landlord in return for a lease commitment from a new tenant. These could include the installation of partitions, carpets, drapes and/or fixtures, as well as the inclusion of utilities costs and janitorial services in the rental rate for a certain period of time.

In one of the more intriguing concessions employed by lessors of new multistoried office buildings, an owner-developer may assume responsibility for a new tenant's remaining obligation on an old lease. Rental agents of new office space often use the telephone listings of businesses in a given area to cold-canvass and solicit new tenants. In the presentation, the agent indicates that the management of the new building will assume responsibility for the old lease. Thus, depending on the success of this form of solicitation, a developer may become obligated to pay the rent on a number of offices deserted by incoming tenants.

The alternatives for managing surplus space of this sort include keeping it empty or minimizing the carrying costs by subleasing it at any rent obtainable. Often, the developer offers the landlord a buy-out settlement based on a cash payment in exchange for the cancellation of the lease. In any event, the developer's responsibilities are relatively short-lived compared to the long-term investment in the new office project.

Lease Agreements

Generally, a standard lease agreement is used in renting office space. Depending on individual circumstances, however, special clauses may be included to satisfy the specific requirements of the parties involved.

Tax Clause.   As a result of constantly increasing property taxes in many areas of the country, a **tax clause** is becoming a common requirement in office leases, including those drawn for relatively short periods. A tax clause stipulates that the tenant will pay any increase in taxes over the base year in addition to the contract rent.

Escalation Clause.   Paralleling the rising taxes across the country is the dramatic increase in utility charges, often to the point of actually eliminating a landlord's profits on the investment. To offset this problem, most office leases are now designed to pass utility costs on to the tenant. This can be accomplished by installing individual meters for each office, an expensive and often impossible task. More likely, a lease will be arranged with an **escalation** clause, which stipulates that the rent can be adjusted annually to reflect increasing expenses for utility charges. Either the rent can be increased by some specific factor—say 5 percent per year—or the tenant may be obligated to pay a proportion of the overall increased utility cost, much as is done under a tax clause.

Services Included.   Office leases sometimes offer the tenant certain special services for which additional rent is paid. These services can include utilities as well as janitorial and maintenance care. In certain office arrangements, the services of a central receptionist and/or typing pool are included in the lease agreement. This arrangement is most common in one-person executive office suites with central reception, conference room and other shared amenities.

Assignment and Subletting.   No doubt, one of the more controversial clauses in an office lease is the provision that the tenant be allowed to assign or sublet space in the event of a change in circumstances. In effect, this is an escape clause for a tenant that obligates the landlord to accept the new tenant. In some cases, depending on the market for office space in a particular area, a tenant may be able to **sublease** a unit for a rent *higher* than that stipulated in the original lease and thus actually make a profit on the landlord's investment.

To offset this possibility and to provide protection against the assignment or subletting of space to a tenant not acceptable to the landlord, an office lease usually includes the provision that the landlord's written permission must first be secured. Because a lease is an agreement for the total rent over the term of the contract, a tenant who wishes to move but cannot find an acceptable sublessee is obligated to pay the balance of the rent to the landlord to secure a full release from the contractual agreement. This **acceleration** power is probably one of the primary reasons that most office leases are drawn for relatively short periods, usually from one to three years. Because a landlord has the right to refuse the assignment of a lease, any developer soliciting new tenants by offering to assume old leases will probably have to pay the balance of the rent on these leases in many cases.

TYPES OF OFFICE INVESTMENTS

Office building owners range from the individual owner-occupant to the large corporate conglomerate. Most central-city, multistory office buildings are owned by large institutional investors—such as Sears, IBM, Transamerica and John Hancock Insurance Company—that have the financial capability to support the investment over the initial years, when cash returns are limited. The smaller office building owner, unable to compete with the corporate giants, has turned to the suburban market for profitable office investments. These outlying developments range from converted old houses to modern preplanned office parks.

Lowrise Office Buildings

Owning a small office building is similar to owning a small apartment building in terms of tenant turnover and management responsibilities. Although office tenants generally observe their lease commitments, small offices tend to be difficult to rent on long-term leases.

A prime location is not an overriding factor for many tenants of lowrise office buildings. Consequently, profitable investments can be made in office units located on secondary streets, enabling an investor to offer somewhat lower rents. In fact, many large-parcel developments are designed to attract high-rent tenants to the more prominent street-front exposures, with smaller offices constructed toward the rear areas of the lot. Of course, appropriate access and off-street parking facilities must be provided, not only to satisfy zoning requirements but also to attract tenants.

Owners of lowrise office developments are usually able to pass the responsibility for interior maintenance to their tenants while retaining the obligation for all major repairs and exterior care. The degree of these responsibilities is a function of the size of the project. For example, the tenant in a one-office home conversion normally accepts most of the maintenance tasks. If the house contains four offices, however, the owner of the building usually maintains the exterior and provides office-cleaning services, while the tenants are responsible for interior maintenance, repairs and decorating.

Neighborhood Offices. The most popular forms of lowrise office investments are usually smaller projects designed to serve neighborhood needs. The conversion of old homes into offices is a much-favored technique in this category. The charm of spacious, high-ceilinged rooms, the generous use of fine woods and the period-piece quality of decor appeals to many business and professional tenants. When these homes are located in relatively accessible areas of a neighborhood, they attract lawyers, accountants, smaller insurance companies and real estate brokers. Frequently, the architectural beauty of these converted offices holds tenants for comparatively long periods.

Other types of neighborhood offices include those situated above street-level stores that front on main thoroughfares with a high volume of pedestrian traffic. These locations appeal to dentists, optometrists, lawyers and others who cater to an established clientele but who do not require the more impressive and expensive premises of the retailer. A modern variant of this type of office space is those small, mixed-use commercial centers constructed around an inner courtyard containing some artistic focal point, such as a fountain or sculpture. In this design, the retail shops occupy the ground-floor spaces while the offices are located at balcony level, with entrances facing the courtyard.

Clinics. Among the more profitable lowrise office investments are those housing a number of medical practitioners, such as doctors and dentists, who have joined together to offer services from one centralized location. Depending on the size and scope of the clinic, a pharmacy and a laboratory might also be included on the premises.

Although clinic designs vary, most include the doctors' offices as complete, self-sufficient units. Others are developed around the theme of a central reception and waiting room. In this case, participating doctors share the costs of a central filing and billing system, as well as a pool of receptionists, nurses, medical technicians and typists.

The additional plumbing and special electrical requirements involved in clinic construction, including ceiling-to-floor partitions, greatly exceed the costs of other forms of office construction. Therefore, the rents are higher and the leases longer than for standard office space. As a result, many doctors have formed groups to develop clinics that they themselves own, often as condominium units.

Homogeneous Tenants. Nonmedical groups of tenants may also join together in mutually beneficial relationships. For instance, an insurance agent, a real estate broker, a mortgage banker, a title insurance company, a lawyer and an accountant could form a homogeneous tenant grouping in the financial center of a neighborhood office development. A beauty salon, barber shop, physical fitness studio and health food retailer would also make a complementary group.

A variation of this approach involves attracting a group of tenants offering the same service. Thus, an office building owner can designate a property as a lawyer's building or an insurance building, where a person seeking these special services can choose from a number of practitioners housed in the same structure.

These **homogeneous tenancies** lend themselves to central receptionists, typing pools, telephone answering services and other shared office amenities. Such systems are especially attractive to both cash-poor, newly licensed professionals and thrifty old-timers. This central design enables a tenant to choose considerably smaller office space than would be necessary if the centralized services were not provided. Consequently, the rents can be commensurately less, although a proportionate contribution toward the compensation of the central staff would be stipulated in the lease agreement.

Highrise Office Buildings

In most metropolitan areas, the largest amount of office space is contained within skyscrapers constructed to house a single institutional tenant, a group of tenants or both. The financial ability to carry negative cash-flow investments for a number of years has probably made highrise offices the exclusive investment prerogative of major corporations.

Often a large company erects an office tower, occupies some of the space for its own operations and leases to others the area it does not immediately require.

Usually, the management strategy for these large developments includes the opportunity for the major tenant to expand into the leased space as the need arises. Other large corporations construct their own wholly occupied highrise towers in strategic midcity locations to enjoy the advantages of centralized services. These companies often incorporate unique architectural designs to establish publicity value, such as the pyramid shape of the Transamerica Tower in San Francisco.

There is a growing tendency for major corporations to sell their office buildings to pools of investors and then to lease back sufficient space at higher-than-market rates to ensure investors a good return.

CASE 9.1:   **Five-Story Office Building.**   A property is located at the intersection of two heavily traveled major arteries. It is a new, glass-walled, five-story office building containing 50,000 total square feet, 40,000 of which are rentable space. The other 10,000 square feet include the entry lobby, hallways, elevator shafts, bathrooms, storage space and utility rooms. A paved parking area surrounds the building. The rents vary from floor to floor but average $10 per square foot of rentable area per year. Operating expenses are 35 percent of the gross rents, including vacancy and reserves. The total cost of the project is $2.5 million, and the investors can secure a first mortgage for $1.75 million (70 percent of value) payable at 10 percent interest-only constant over 30 years. This requires a $750,000 cash investment. Depreciation is established at an annual straight-line rate of 2.564 percent (39 years straight-line), which is applied to a book basis beginning at $2 million. The land is booked at $500,000. All leases are established for five years, at which time the property will be sold. The following tabulation shows a profit analysis of this project, including its sale. All rents and operating expenses are kept constant for the five-year analysis.

CASE 9.1 Five Story Office Building Analysis
34% Tax Bracket, $750,000 Cash Investment

I. Annual Income

$ 400,000	Gross Annual Income
− 140,000	35% Operating Expense Ratio
260,000	Net Operating Income
− 175,000	Debt Service (10% interest-only on $1.75 million)
85,000	Taxable Income before Depreciation
− 51,280	Depreciation ($2 million @ 0.025464, 39 years)
$ 33,720	Taxable Income
× 0.34	Tax Bracket
11,465	Income Taxes
85,000	Taxable Income before Depreciation
− 11,465	Income Taxes
$ 73,535	Cash-on-Cash ROI 9.80% on $750,000 Investment

II. Sale at End of Five Years

$ 3,000,000	Net Sale Price
− 2,243,600	Adjusted Book Basis ($2.5 million − $256,400)
756,400	Gross Gain
× 0.28	Maximum Capital Gain Tax
211,792	Income Taxes
544,608	Net Profit
÷ 5 years	Holding Period
108,922	Annualized Gain (rounded)
÷ 750,000	Investment
14.42%	Annualized Yield on Gain
+ 9.80%	C/C Annual ROI
24.22%	Bottom-Line Annualized ROI

Note: This analysis does not consider the time value of money.

Another way to analyze the annual growth rate of the property in this example, using the HP-12C, is to include the time value of money. With the initial investment of $750,000 as the present value, the time involved as five years and the future value as $1,290,000 ($750,000 original investment plus $540,000 net profit), the annual compound growth rate is 11.457 percent.

USING THE HP-12C:

---

1.   Clear financial register | f | | FIN |

2.   Change sign, press | CHS |

3.   Keystroke 750000, press | PV |

4.   Keystroke 5, press | n |

5.   Keystroke 1290000, press | FV |

6.   Press | i | = 11.457%

Office Parks

The congestion of downtown areas and the inconvenience this crowding creates in terms of traffic and lack of adequate parking facilities often hamper efforts to provide efficient services. Many inner-city companies, following current migrational trends, have settled into buildings located in suburban **office parks.**

In addition to quick accessibility from suburban homes, many suburban office parks offer additional amenities to attract tenants. Some provide recreational, cultural or dining facilities within the complex, in addition to a preplanned and well-maintained ambience, to serve tenants and their clients. Full-range indoor gymnasiums, pools, tennis courts and health club facilities, as well as quality restaurants, are available in many modern office-park projects.

Rental Achievement Requirements.   In the development of many new commercial real estate projects, including highrise office buildings and office parks, the financing pattern requires that the investment's break-even point be met by advance lease commitments from creditable tenants. Before issuing a construction loan, an interim financier will insist that the developer secure an agreement from a permanent lender to issue a long-term mortgage at the completion of construction, the proceeds of which will *take out* the interim mortgagee.

Although many permanent loan financiers, such as insurance companies, will readily issue such standby commitments for economically sound developments, they will only *fund* their commitments when the buildings are completed according to the approved plans and specifications. In addition, and as a condition of the loan under a rental achievement clause, these lenders require enough advance leases to be secured by the developer to meet at least the investment's fixed expenses of property taxes, insurance premiums, basic maintenance costs and mortgage payments.

Thus, an investor involved in the development of a new project must solicit leases *prior* to the completion of construction. Whereas the developer of a shopping center may need advance commitments from only a few basic major tenants, an office building developer usually needs to secure leases from *numerous* individual tenants to meet the lender's rent-up requirements. Most office building managers need to produce leases for approximately 80 percent of full occupancy to reach a break-even point, a relatively arduous task.

Office Condominiums

The office condominium concept, long used by doctors and dentists in their clinics, has won widespread interest around the country as other tenants seek to become owners. This desire results from rising rental rates for all types of rental space. To guarantee a controlled cost, many office users are becoming office owners.

Ownership of an office condominium is similar to ownership of a residential condominium. A prescribed space is owned in fee simple, together with an undivided ownership of the common areas. These common areas include the land under the building, the parking area, the entry hall and other hallways, bathrooms, utility and storage rooms and the roof. The individual owners belong to a condo association that is responsible for maintenance of the common areas plus enforcement of the adopted rules and regulations. Each owner contributes a proportionate share of the common-area costs as association fees, which are adjusted by the board of directors to reflect annual fluctuations.

One of the advantages of condominium office ownership, in addition to controlled occupancy costs, is the possibility of equity growth through mortgage principal paydown plus increasing value. Although owners are allowed to deduct interest, property taxes, association fees, maintenance and depreciation, they forfeit rent as a deductible expense, so these benefits are minimized somewhat. Still, an owner, unlike a tenant, can participate in the building's management policies.

Probably the most serious problem facing a condominium office owner is the limitation on future expansion, because it may be impossible to acquire adjoining, already-owned offices. Under these circumstances, the only alternative may be to sell and move.

Conversion to Condominiums

An office building owner may find it expedient to convert the investment into a condominium. Under the concepts of conversion for apartment projects discussed in the previous chapter, tenants can be given the right to purchase their offices before the project is offered for sale to the public.

After the appropriate renovation, filing of condominium papers, arrangement of financing, sales promotion and closings, an office building can be subdivided into individual, private office ownerships that include an undivided interest in the common areas. These common areas are the roof, elevators, hallways, entry area, utility and storage rooms and the land under the project, including the parking areas. Like their counterparts in apartment condominiums, the new owners would form an association responsible for the upkeep and taxes on these common areas. An office condominium owner would be responsible for the principal, interest, property taxes, insurance and maintenance of the specific office space plus a proportionate share of the expenses for the common areas.

This raises a problem: What would happen if some unit owners lost their properties through bankruptcy? The other unit owners would have to meet the property tax, maintenance and insurance premium liabilities. This could put all of them in jeopardy. Careful attention must be paid to all contingencies and provisions made for a real estate condo conversion.

CASE 9.2:   **24-Unit Condominium Office Complex.**   As part of a larger office park development, the developers set aside three acres on which 24 condominium office suites were constructed. These garden units are arranged around a central courtyard, and each office has a private entrance. This arrangement has given the complex an aspect of separation from the other buildings in the project. The units are of contemporary design, one and two stories in height, and they include modules of 1,200, 1,500, 2,400 and 4,800 square feet (sq. ft.). Each is self-contained, with separate heating and cooling facilities, as well as individual bathrooms and utility meters.

The land under the condominium project is held under a 99-year lease rather than in fee simple. This **leasehold** arrangement, a feature of the sales package, created an unusual marketing problem for the developers. Although it allowed for a lower initial purchase price, it also required overcoming predictable customer resistance to the nonownership ramifications of the leasehold.

Each purchaser of a condominium office suite automatically becomes a member of the association organized to manage and maintain the common areas and to supervise the condominium bylaws. The member's voting rights are based on the percentage of space purchased in relation to the overall building area of the complex. The association establishes the fees to be paid by its members for common-area upkeep. These fees are shown in the tabulation.

CASE 9.2   Division of Upkeep Fees for a Condominium Office Complex

	1,200 sq. ft.	1,500 sq. ft.	2,400 sq. ft.	4,800 sq. ft.
Janitorial services	$ 45.60	$ 57.00	$ 91.20	$182.40
Insurance	7.20	9.00	14.40	28.80
Ground lease	129.60	162.00	259.20	518.40
Land taxes	26.40	33.00	52.80	105.60
Common area services	16.80	21.00	33.60	67.20
Accounting fees	14.40	18.00	28.80	57.60
Total monthly payment	$240.00	$300.00	$480.00	$960.00

SUMMARY

This chapter examined various aspects of office building ownership, including management concerns common to such projects, regardless of size. A review of the various types of offices available to an investor was included.

Typically, an office building investor will make careful market studies before becoming involved in a specific project. Not only the existing trends in supply and demand for offices but more particularly the segment of the office market that pertains to the building under consideration will be scrutinized. Primary consideration will be given to the demand for space by new businesses in the area as well as to the expansion and movement of existing tenants.

Probably the most significant factor in the success of an office building investment is the establishment of a competitive but profitable rental schedule. Based on an annual rate per square foot of usable space, a required lease payment is a function of many variables, including competitive rents, the location and quality of the subject building, the services provided by management and the floor in the building on which the space is located.

Often landlords will offer concessions when soliciting new office tenants. Unable under many circumstances to lower rents, a landlord may provide a free rental period to offset some of the tenants' move-in costs. Additional inducements offered to attract new tenants include the installation of interior partitions, floor covering, and heating and cooling equipment; payment of utilities costs; and provision of janitorial services. Developers of highrise office projects sometimes offer to assume liability for tenants' old leases to induce them to move into the new building.

Invariably, an office lease includes special clauses designed to solve specific problems. Often a tax clause is inserted that specifies the tenant's responsibility to pay any increase in taxes over the base year in addition to the stipulated rent. Some leases include an escalation clause that allows the rent to be raised automatically to cover increased utility and maintenance expenses. An office building owner may include a subletting privilege in the lease but invariably will reserve the right to approve the new tenant.

The widespread popularity of lowrise buildings provides investors with innumerable opportunities to participate in this form of real estate ownership. Ranging from the converted house to the modern office park, these offices can be leased to small and large companies alike. Many small offices are found above stores along major arterial streets as well as in spaces allocated for this use within the arcades of large shopping centers. The most popular forms of lowrise office investments are found in smaller projects designed to service neighborhood needs.

Some specialty small-office groupings are designed as clinics and house a number of medical practitioners. These homogeneous tenants complement one another's activities through referrals and cooperation. Other homogeneous tenancies include the complementary services of professionals such as financiers, lawyers and insurance agents.

Most highrise office buildings are found in the central areas of cities, although some communities allow skyscrapers in other sections as well. Typically, a highrise structure is designed around a single major tenant; in some cases, this tenant actually owns the entire building. Other highrise office structures enjoy a mixed use, with some located in preplanned suburban office parks. The modern office park also includes such amenities as on-site parking and recreational and dining facilities.

EXERCISE 9   (Answers may be checked against the Answer Key.)

1.   Our nation's trend toward service-oriented business activities is

   a.   decreasing but requiring more office space.
   b.   increasing but requiring less office space.
   c.   decreasing and requiring less office space.
   d.   increasing and requiring more office space.

2.   For most small, lowrise office building investments,

   a.   financing is usually difficult to secure.
   b.   rents are generally higher than for larger projects.
   c.   major arterial locations are not of prime importance.
   d.   securing tenants is generally a difficult task.

3.   Small, lowrise office developments are mostly designed

   a.   to serve the needs of the community.
   b.   to serve the needs of the neighborhood.
   c.   as preplanned office parks.
   d.   as potentially high-rent operations.

4.   Highrise office developments are usually designed for all of the following reasons *except*

   a.   to serve the community.
   b.   as institutional, owner-occupied buildings.
   c.   to serve the neighborhood.
   d.   as an office park complex.

5.   Rental concessions usually include all of the following items *except*

   a.   free rent for a specified time.
   b.   carpets, drapes and partitioning.
   c.   lowering the rent.
   d.   purchase of a prospective tenant's existing lease.

6. All of the following sets of terms match *except*

   a. mutually beneficial tenants: doctors, dentists, laboratories.
   b. rent-up requirements: preconstruction lease commitments, break even, creditable tenants.
   c. office parks: highrise buildings, off-street parking, open spaces.
   d. sale-leaseback: free rent, paid move-in costs, carpets and drapes.

7. Which one of the following definitions is correct?

   a. Tax clause: The landlord pays any increase in property taxes.
   b. Acceleration clause: The tenant pays an increase in rent to offset rising utility and maintenance charges.
   c. Escalation clause: The balance of rent is due in full prior to the expiration of the lease.
   d. Subleasing clause: The tenant has the right to rent the office space to someone else.

8. While studying the market for office space to establish the feasibility of a new project, an analyst should segment the market by all of the following attributes *except*

   a. zoning.
   b. location.
   c. age.
   d. amenities.

9. Which of the following locational requirements for a company's headquarters received top priority in a recent survey run by BOMA?

   a. Low cost
   b. Qualified labor supply
   c. Large functional space
   d. Social climate

10. The establishment of a rental schedule for an office building depends *least* on which of the following?

    a. The economic stability of an area
    b. The owner's desired return on the investment
    c. The physical condition of the building
    d. The services provided

DISCUSSION

1. Discover what concessions are being offered to prospective tenants from the manager of a highrise office building in your area.

2. Secure an inventory of the tenants in a nearby office park and analyze their mix on the basis of the services they offer and percentage of the

total space they occupy. If possible, also secure the schedule of rents paid and compare these charges to the rents for similar office space available outside an office park environment.

10

Investing in Strip Stores and Shopping Centers

Key Terms

anchor tenants
common-area fee
community shopping center
graduated lease
mall
megacenters
necessary goods
neighborhood shopping center

off-street parking
option
percentage lease
regional center
strip store
super-regional centers
tenant mix

A long-range goal of many real estate investors is to own at least one regional shopping center. The appeal is that it requires minimal personal involvement if there is a management team in place, and it offers relatively high, risk-free yields. With a Sears, Montgomery Ward's and/or Penney's as an anchor tenant in a shopping mall, there is little chance for failure.

Other investors content themselves with the acquisition of small shopping centers or individual store buildings along the major streets of a community. Although in most cases management responsibility is inversely related to the size of an investment (the smaller the project, the greater the required effort), even a small property of this type is attractive because commercial tenants are the most likely to remain in one place for relatively long periods of time. In fact, the success of an entrepreneur leads directly to locational longevity—a landlord's dream!

Whereas the acquisition of strip store buildings is usually financed by local commercial banks and savings institutions, the various types of shopping center developments generally receive permanent loans from insurance companies and pension funds. As discussed previously, these lenders are primarily interested in substantial, long-term mortgage investments that include little, if any, risk. A well-rounded portfolio of real estate holdings includes store buildings as well as apartments and office buildings. This chapter examines commercial investments available for profitable returns.

STRIP STORE BUILDINGS

In most American cities and towns, small store buildings line both sides of the community's busiest streets. These stores offer commodities and services of every nature and description and serve the neighborhood, as well as the entire city, with their wares. Like the smaller apartment and office buildings previously described, **strip store** buildings are found everywhere.

Their general availability and rectangular design permit great flexibility for a variety of tenant uses. The relatively simple installation of carpeting, draperies and partitions can convert a standard 20- by 60-foot module into an inviting office. The attachment of a counter and the appropriate stoves, refrigerators, tables and chairs would create a restaurant in this same space. Shelves and display counters might transform it into a dress shop, pants store or family shoe center, while chairs and booths could make it into a barber shop or beauty salon. Housing—among other things—art galleries, flower stores, jewelry shops and boutiques, strip stores offer continuing tenancies and unlimited conversion possibilities.

In many cities in this country, strip stores were hit hard during the recent recession. A great many vacancies resulted from the failure of small businesses housed in these buildings. With the slow return to a better economy, it is expected that these stores will again attract the tenants that make these investments so viable.

Appeal to Small Investors

It usually costs very little more to purchase two or three store buildings than it does to buy a small multiunit residential building or a small office structure. Primarily because of the longevity of commercial tenants and the lesser management responsibilities (compared to residential rentals), these opportunities are attractive to the small investor. In the past, mortgage loans were relatively easy to secure on this type of investment. Today, it requires some effort to find financing on the smaller units and a lot of seller financing to make sales.

A typical strip store is a 60' by 60' building divided into three 20' by 60' bays constructed on a commercially zoned neighborhood lot. If the building is designed so that the entry doors and bathrooms adjoin each other and store-separating partitions are not constructed until the areas are leased, a tenant needing 40 front feet of space can be accommodated as well as one requiring 20 feet or even 60 feet. In fact, by constructing the shell of a 60-foot-square building and attempting to rent it before completing the interior, a landlord may also attract tenants who require special installations. A liquor store owner who would need the special plumbing and electrical installations associated with a walk-in cooler or a barber who would require appropriate plumbing are two such tenants.

MANAGEMENT REQUIREMENTS

Most strip store leases are designed to run three to five years with options to renew included to protect the tenant. Once a tenant has established a clientele in a neighborhood, the lease is likely to be renewed indefinitely.

Short-term strip store leases usually designate fixed rental terms and include renewal options providing for rent increases to offset rising operating expenses—utilities, property taxes, insurance premiums and maintenance costs. Although commercial tenants will often accept the responsibility for minor interior maintenance, major repairs and exterior upkeep usually remain the landlord's domain. With this in mind, a financial analysis of a strip store investment should include reserves for replacement of the roof, furnace, cooling systems and other major property components.

When a tenant requires an **option** to renew a lease, it should be clear to the landlord that this entails giving up control of the property for both the lease period *and* the option period. In addition, an option may or may not be exercised when it becomes due. A tenant may ignore the option and move or decide to negotiate with the landlord for new terms, depending on market conditions at renewal time. Consequently, the terms of any renewal become a function of market conditions as they change from time to time.

Except for strip stores that have some unique quality of design or location, most rents are established on a regular payment basis over the term of the lease. Some special circumstances require the inclusion of a percentage clause. (For example, a gas station lease might have a fixed rent plus a penny or two per gallon override.) Some leases also contain a property tax clause, which requires the tenant to pay any future taxes exceeding the base amount in effect at the inception of the lease.

The owner of strip store buildings often finds that the success of the investment is very much a function of the success of the tenants as entrepreneurs. If tenants cannot show a profit in a particular location, they will probably be unable to pay the rent, no matter how low it is. On the other hand, if the tenants are doing well, rent is the least concern.

As a general rule, then, a landlord's profits are very closely related to a tenant's success. In the case of a small store lease, the landlord-tenant relationship is one of interpersonal dependency, not just a legal binder. It is in the best interests of a landlord to help a tenant succeed, even to the point of decreasing rent during the start-up period to enable the tenant to become established. A **graduated lease** is extremely useful in this instance because it starts with a low rent in the initial period and gradually increases to accommodate a successful tenant's ability to meet a higher payment schedule. If the tenant fails, even at the lower rents, it is just as well, since the sooner the unfortunate mismatch is recognized, the sooner the landlord can lease the building again.

CASE 10.1: **Strip Store Development.** This block-long property consists of 600 feet of frontage on a major thoroughfare and is 150 feet deep to a 20-foot alley. The investors rezoned the parcel to commercial from apartment zoning by inviting adjoining neighbors to participate in its design. They quickly eliminated any fast food franchises, gas stations or all-night markets to control noise and traffic. The architecture was to conform to the neighborhood, and no unsightly signs or disturbing lights were erected. The alley was paved, and a seven-foot wall was built on the house side of the alley to help buffer noise. All stores were set 40 feet back from the main street to allow for front parking.

The 43,200-square-foot building was designed to be built in nine stages of 60 by 80 feet each, starting from one corner. The building code required a 30-foot setback at each corner to allow for traffic visibility. The 60-foot modules were designed to be rented in multiples of 20 feet, with the tenants choosing the space they needed. Once the construction started, the buildings filled quickly and were rented out in nine months. The final **tenant mix** is as follows:

Kinney Shoes,	100 feet
Baskin-Robbins ice cream,	40 feet
Bicycle shop,	80 feet
Lamp shop,	40 feet
See's Candy,	60 feet
Barber shop,	40 feet
Carpet shop,	60 feet
Beauty shop,	40 feet
Real estate office,	40 feet
Insurance office,	40 feet

NEIGHBORHOOD SHOPPING CENTERS

A **neighborhood shopping center** is designed to provide for the sale of **necessary goods** (food, drugs, sundries) and personal services (laundry, dry cleaning, barbering, shoe repairing) for the daily needs of the people in the immediate neighborhood. This type of center is usually situated on a four-acre to ten-acre site and normally serves a trade-area population of 5,000 to 40,000 persons within a six-minute driving distance.

Tenant Mix

The neighborhood center usually has as its major tenant a supermarket or national drug-discount store, or both, which occupies approximately 30 percent of its 30,000 to 100,000 square feet of gross leasable area. Other tenants may include a general merchandise store; clothing, shoe and furniture stores; financial offices; and other service businesses.

The grouping is arranged on a readily accessible site and offers ease of shopping through adequate **off-street parking** facilities and agreeable surroundings. The other stores are generally arranged in a straight line that doglegs toward the streets, with parking spaces in front of the building. Thus, shoppers may drive directly to the store of their choice, park briefly while completing their purchases and pull away quickly and efficiently. Because this is so much more convenient than the curbside parking required around strip stores, neighborhood centers have made serious inroads into the strip store's ability to compete for the shopper's dollar.

Percentage Leases

Neighborhood centers are generally located at the intersections of major streets on corners of land designated for this use when the raw acreage was originally subdivided. Sometimes a neighborhood center is constructed off the corner, on a parcel of land situated in the middle of a block but facing a major thoroughfare. This off-corner location acts to relieve the traffic congestion normally associated with a major intersection and improves the accessibility to the parking area. When vacant sites are not available and an investor seeks to acquire a number of improved property sites to build a shopping center, two to three years are often needed to satisfy the community's land use regulations and, in some cases, to overcome the neighbors' objections.

Wherever the center is located, its development creates a small monopoly for commercial tenants wishing to capitalize on the consumer traffic that it generates by its very existence. A landlord can secure a bonus from tenants who want to locate in the center. This bonus is secured in the form of a **percentage lease** in which a tenant agrees to pay a fixed minimum rent *plus* or *against* a specified percentage of the gross business. The minimum rent develops a basic return on the property owner's investment, and the percentage override ensures the owner a share in the tenant's success as a result of locating in the center.

For example, a supermarket may execute a lease with a minimum rent imposed as a function of the number of square feet occupied *plus* 1 percent of the gross sales above a designated amount. A dress shop may lease space on the basis of a minimum rent *against* 4 percent of the gross, or a jeweler might agree to a 10 percent overage.

The percentages charged fluctuate as the economy changes. When business is booming, percentages rise, but when things are slow, as they were in the early 1990s, percentages are lowered and often eliminated. Currently, percentage leases are rarely used, except in regional or super-regional centers where the monopoly concept still prevails. The exhibit at the end of this chapter shows a sample shopping center lease agreement.

Condominium Conversions

Although the process is rarely attempted, the neighborhood shopping center lends itself to conversion to condominiums. The sale of individual store buildings would probably produce more profit than would selling the center as a whole to a single investor.

The beginning legal procedure is the same as that for an apartment or office conversion. The tenants can be approached with an offer to purchase their own store buildings and receive an undivided interest in the common-area parking spaces as well.

A variation on this theme is an arrangement by which a tenant does *not* purchase its own store but buys the store next door. With this approach, each owner becomes the landlord of an adjoining store and remains a tenant in the present location.

Under this system, the income tax benefits are expanded considerably for the tenant–store purchaser. In becoming an owner, a tenant actually loses the opportunity to deduct rent as a business expense. Depreciation on the building only, not on the land, becomes an allowable deduction. By remaining a tenant in the original building and purchasing the structure next door, the tenant continues to enjoy rent as a fully deductible expense while simultaneously sheltering the income from the adjoining investment with depreciation.

Case 10.2: **Neighborhood Shopping Center.** The ten-year-old center in this case contains numerous shops, medical suites and office spaces arranged around a centrally landscaped mall. It is connected to the residential area it serves by major arterial streets with traffic lights that control ingress and egress. The tenant mix is intended to provide the surrounding residential neighborhood with basic everyday needs. Its anchor tenants are a national chain food market and a drugstore. The complete tenant mix of the center is listed in the tabulation.

CASE 10.2 Neighborhood Shopping Center Tenant Mix—100,000 Square Feet

Food market	25,000 square feet	Interior decorator	2,500 square feet
Drugstore	13,500	Bank	2,500
Sporting goods store	5,000	Sewing center	2,500
Motorcycle dealer	5,000	Savings association	1,500
Hardware store	5,000	Dry cleaner	1,500
Medical offices	4,500	Carpet store	1,500
Insurance broker	4,250	Real estate broker	1,500
Shoe store	3,600	Florist shop	1,200
Liquor store	3,600	Women's wear shop	1,200
Restaurant	3,600	Gift shop	1,200
Men's shop	3,000	Small shops (10)	6,850

The total value of the center is $3,650,000, including $650,000 for the ten-acre site, $500,000 for site improvements and $2.5 million for construction. There is a $3 million mortgage payable at 9 percent interest-only. The improvements were booked at cost and depreciated over 31½ years at a straight-line rate. Total minimum rent is $500,000, with the tenants required to contribute to common-area maintenance and promotional activities. These contributions result in a total net operating expense of 30 percent of the minimum gross rents collected. A one-year financial analysis follows:

Neighborhood Shopping Center
First-Year Profitability Analysis

$500,000	Minium gross annual income
−150,000	30% operating expense ratio
350,000	Net operating income
−270,000	Interest expense
80,000	Taxable income before depreciation (12.3% return on $650,000 investment)
− 95,000	Depreciation (31½ years straight-line on $3 million, rounded)
($15,000)	Excess loss carryover

Note that this analysis is based on a *minimum* rental income. Assuming that the center's management has percentage leases with the tenants, a higher return is probable. The actual bottom-line return would need to await the sale of the property (see the analysis in Case 9.1).

Neighborhood shopping centers, especially those anchored by a supermarket or drugstore, were hit exceptionally hard during the recent recession . The business failure of many of the tenants in these centers raised vacancy rates and eliminated investors' interest. Currently, the REITs are being attracted to these shopping centers because of low cash investment requirements and the expectations of a turnaround in the market. Of particular interest are the so-called "power centers"—those that are anchored by a number of tenants that dominate its retail class. The best known are Kmart and Wal-Mart, both of which appeal to today's discount-oriented shoppers.

Strip centers are still in enormous oversupply, and vacancy rates have not declined noticeably. Purchasing through REITs have pulled this market out of its deep rut, but real economic improvement is needed for a broader recovery. In addition, it is uncertain how much of an impact the growing trend toward mail orders and TV shopping will have on these retail properties.

COMMUNITY SHOPPING CENTERS

In addition to the convenience goods and personal services offered by the neighborhood center, a **community shopping center** provides an even wider range of facilities for the sale of large appliances, furniture, apparel and related services.

Designed around a major department and/or variety store as the **anchor tenants** plus a supermarket and other retail and service stores, a community shopping center has a gross leasable area ranging from 100,000 to 300,000 square feet, needs 10 to 30 acres or more and serves a trade-area population of 40,000 to 150,000 people.

Tenant Mix

A community shopping center devotes approximately 20 percent of its space to a supermarket, 30 percent to a major general merchandise tenant, 25 percent to other clothing and shoe retailers and the balance to other kinds of merchandisers and service businesses.

This type of center is midway between the neighborhood and the regional shopping center and incorporates a little of both in its design. Some community shopping centers include a major national department store plus a locally prominent department store, positioning them at either end of a group of stores occupied by smaller tenants. The two magnets create foot traffic that is attracted into the connecting stores by window displays, signs and other promotional devices.

Community shopping centers are usually designed with the stores lining a central **mall** area. In warm-weather states the mall is generally uncovered, but in most inclement-weather areas the mall is either covered or enclosed completely and the temperature is controlled for customer comfort. Whereas the neighborhood center's format encourages a quick shopping trip, the community shopping center's design entices the customer into spending more time wandering from shop to shop and making purchases in the process.

Because these centers are larger than neighborhood centers, many overlapping types of businesses are represented. This situation offers a customer the opportunity to compare prices and quality on similar articles in a number of competing stores. The intent is to convince shoppers that the center can serve most of their needs—all they have to do is seek out the appropriate vendor to achieve satisfaction.

Community shopping centers do not grant tenants the same exclusivity for their lines as do neighborhood centers. Thus, there may be a number of men's clothing establishments, dress shops and shoe stores in one community shopping center. However, to prevent unusual shifts in lines of merchandise, it is necessary to include in each lease the general types of products or services the store will be allowed to carry. Each store is thus limited in the type of business to be conducted, and the landlord can maintain an appropriate tenant mix.

In this regard, management is always concerned that tenants generate the type of traffic flow that will provide all of the businesses in the center with customers on a continuous basis. The owners of a successful center enjoy the opportunity of carefully choosing tenants from a list of those waiting for openings to occur, thus ensuring the symbiosis that a successful center requires.

On the other hand, the managers of centers with high turnovers and a number of vacancies are often reduced to accepting tenants who do not generate traffic just to fill their spaces. These tenants include those that rent space for warehousing their merchandise, those that need office space, recruiting centers and other nonretail vendors.

During the recent recession, many retailers closed their shops at various centers, with some companies going bankrupt. Those that closed because it was less expensive to pay rent on the closed store than to continue to operate created a special problem for the center's management. If the lease contained a clause specifying that the tenant had to remain open and continue its business on 100 percent of its premises, the landlord had the right to obtain specific performance of this provision. This covenant of continuous operation is designed to create the ambiance of a successful center and to ensure that the needs of the shoppers are met, regardless of retailer difficulties.

Management Requirements

The management of a community shopping center usually involves the services of a professional who has had experience in dealing with national tenants as well as with more prominent local retailers. Besides the normal leasing duties of the manager, daily responsibilities include the supervision of maintenance personnel and security guards. These duties require an on-premises supervisor, although many community as well as neighborhood shopping centers are managed by companies with offices located away from the centers. The efficiency of these centralized activities expands a management company's ability to handle a number of shopping centers, plus other income properties, from a single main office.

Lease terms for major tenants usually range from 15 to 20 years, whereas local tenants' leases may range from only five to ten years. Renewal options are often based on a right of first refusal. The leases of untried tenants invariably include a landlord's cancellation clause that can be exercised if the gross volume of business does not meet expectations.

To pay for the costs of maintaining the parking area and joint walkways, community shopping center tenants are usually charged a **common-area fee** in addition to their rent. These fees are also used to offset the charges incurred for advertising, flyers, bulk mailings and parking area promotional activities. Common-area charges are usually based on the ratio of the tenant's floor area to the center's total floor area. Sometimes they are imposed as a flat charge.

Management often plays a more prominent role in the activities of community shopping centers than it does in those of neighborhood centers. Special promotions are continually designed to attract shoppers to the center. These activities may directly involve the tenants, as do sidewalk sales, or they might involve such outside attractions as carnivals or art fairs.

Community shopping center tenants often find it expedient to join together in an association whose elected leaders represent them in disputes with the management. The association often accepts responsibility for supervising activities designed to promote the center.

REGIONAL AND SUPER-REGIONAL SHOPPING CENTERS

The largest of the shopping center designs is the **regional center,** which provides general merchandise, apparel, furniture and home furnishings in full depth and variety. At least one national, full-line department store is the major drawing power; most regionals have two, and some even three such tenants to establish the magnetic nodes for the foot traffic between shops. Regionals range in scope from 300,000 to 1,000,000 square feet of gross leasable area on at least 30 acres of ground and serve a trade area of 150,000 to 400,000 or more people. This trade area may extend upwards of 15 miles, depending on the accessibility of highways. Regionals are, in effect, a wide assortment of downtown stores, all collected under one roof with controlled free parking, offering the suburban customer convenient, full-line shopping facilities.

Some regional shopping centers, also known as **megacenters** or **super-regional centers**, are part of a larger, overall land plan that includes a buffer of office towers and apartment buildings and that creates a self-contained consumer market. However, the size of the center itself, is limited by a shopper's ability to walk a certain distance, especially with packages in hand. Consequently, regionals are relatively compact in design and generally offer a basement and second floor as an alternative to lateral expansion. This requires vertical transportation facilities in the common areas. Elevators and escalators are sometimes located within the stores themselves and act as subtle enticements to shoppers to do some impulse buying.

Tenant Mix

Unlike the other centers, the regional usually has no food market, although various packaged grocery items are found in its many stores. Rather, fully 50 percent of the center is occupied by general merchandise stores, 15 percent by clothing and shoe retailers, 10 percent by other dry goods shops and 25 percent by services and related businesses. Most regionals include an auditorium that is available for special community meetings as well as for promotional efforts. Movie theaters are also available, as are numerous eating establishments and entertainment facilities.

Building Design

To achieve the greatest interplay among the stores, a regional center is usually designed around a mall area, with the major national tenants located at either end. The inclusion of a third major tenant would require a central location opening on the mall, while a fourth major would be positioned directly across and facing the central area.

When the key tenants have been assembled, the other tenants, large and small, are strategically located where they will be most appealing to the pedestrian traffic flow in the mall, while attractive kiosk displays liven the mallways. Some types of businesses have special locational requirements. For instance, a drugstore and a dry cleaner need to be immediately accessible from the parking area. Furniture stores require many square feet of display area, which can be expensive if on the main floor. Thus, a typical furniture store layout includes a main-floor entry, an attractive display room in a basement and a second-floor area or a dogleg wrapped around the rears of adjacent smaller stores.

Specialty shops and those that feature high-quality, high-priced lines are normally grouped near the department store featuring the same type of merchandise, while the popularly priced stores are grouped in immediate proximity to their complementary department store. Stores that specialize in convenience goods are located as close as possible to the parking area. Supplementary stores—such as those that offer hardware, electrical repair and home furnishings—are usually located close together. Complementary stores—for instance, those selling men's or women's clothing and accessories—are also grouped together. Gasoline stations, repair shops, auto supply stores, garden nurseries, outdoor furniture stores and other stores of this nature are usually located at the exterior of the center or even in separate buildings.

Some regionals are designed around an open mall, but most have enclosed malls to provide a comfortable shopping environment that is heated in the winter and cooled in the summer. Sculptural displays or fountains usually highlight important mall areas, while many benches for resting are conveniently located along the preplanned pedestrian routes.

MANAGEMENT REQUIREMENTS

Regional centers require at least one full-time manager to be on the premises and available during shopping hours. Management is responsible for securing new tenants, renewing existing leases, supervising daily operations and dealing with shoppers' complaints. A full crew of maintenance engineers is available at all times, as is a corps of security guards charged with maintaining decorum and handling emergency situations. Because fully 60 percent of the shopping in this country occurs at night, lighting and security are important management responsibilities.

All regional centers include an active merchants' association to which, according to their leases, all tenants must belong. Together with the center's management, this association is responsible for the varied promotional activities so essential to this form of shopping enterprise. Ranging from antique shows and artists' displays to programs of entertainment and enlightenment, regional promotional activities are making retail centers entertainment magnets.

There are numerous shopping centers that combine many of the individual attributes of the three major types described. They are known as *hybrid* shopping centers, and they fall somewhere between the neighborhood, community and regional classifications.

FACTORY OUTLET MALLS

Although few enclosed regional shopping malls have been constructed in recent years, the emergence of factory outlets—both individual stores and entire malls—has been the major success story of commercial property development over the past ten years. Even during the recent recession, this form of real estate development has continued unabated. According to manufacturers, shopping center developers and other industry executives, this form of investment is expected to continue to expand at a faster rate.

Since 1992, 65 factory outlet shopping centers have been opened, with many more scheduled to open in 1994. More than 500 manufacturers now operate some 9,000 stores, with a new manufacturer entering the industry every six days. Outlets now open much closer to regional malls: the accepted distance has shrunk to 20 miles or less. Some open right next to the regionals. Locations near tourist attractions are becoming the most desirable for factory outlet centers. Department store chains are also opening clearance centers in outlet projects.

Marketing for outlets is expected to become more sophisticated and creative. Stores and centers will be better designed and more appealing. More amenities will be introduced, and outlets will become more like other regional malls.

A variation on this discount outlet theme is the development of the large, warehouse-type stores and clubs such as Tandy's "Incredible Universe," Home Depot, Sam's, Price Club, Big Box, Category Killers and other such behemoths found in suburban centers.

SUMMARY

This chapter examined the opportunities for investing in commercial property. In most American cities and towns, small store buildings line both sides of the community's busiest streets. Housing all forms of retail businesses and services, the strip store building offers a small real estate investor a viable alternative for investment dollars. The flexibility of the store module allows a property owner to create new uses at a relatively "low" cost to meet the demands of an ever-changing market. Thus, a store that houses a pizza vendor for one period may be easily converted into a real estate office for the next.

Although strip stores generally have a higher tenant turnover than do larger shopping centers, the tenancies of successful entrepreneurs may continue indefinitely. In addition, commercial tenants usually accept the responsibility for maintaining the structure, which, when coupled with long-term occupancy, appeals to a great many real estate investors.

Strip store rents are invariably based on a fixed amount for a set period of time, with the inclusion of escalation clauses for longer leases. Percentage clauses are usually included for those strip stores that occupy a unique or monopolistic site, such as a corner gas station. In most strip store leases the tenant is able to secure an option to renew, which tends to place control in the tenant's hands.

Neighborhood, community and regional shopping centers appeal to investors with financial capacities for larger projects. Neighborhood shopping centers are designed to cater to the everyday needs of residents in the center's immediate vicinity. With a food market and a drugstore as basic tenants, the neighborhood center also provides shopping facilities for other necessary goods and personal services.

The community center expands the number of tenants to include department and variety stores, as well as the convenience goods tenants found in the neighborhood arrangement. This enlarged tenant mix allows the community center to serve a market area of up to 150,000 people.

The regional center provides the greatest variety of comparison shopping by housing a number of purveyors of the same type of product. Regionals are generally composed of at least two nationally prominent department store tenants that anchor each end of a mall area. With dozens of smaller tenants lining this mall, the shopper is able to choose goods and services from competing shops.

In terms of management responsibilities and lease arrangements, the three types of shopping centers have much in common. Most tenants are required to pay a basic minimum rent plus or against a specified percentage of gross business. Thus, a landlord participates in the success of the tenants and capitalizes on the monopolistic quality of the center. In exchange, the management provides the maintenance and security required in such large projects.

Most centers require their tenants to join an association that assumes the responsibility for generating and supervising advertising and promotional activities designed to attract shoppers. In addition, the associations' directors usually represent the tenants in their negotiations with management regarding store hours, participation in promotion and determination of assessments for common-area maintenance.

Factory outlet malls and warehouse-type retailers provide additional opportunities for commercial investment.

EXERCISE 10   (Answers may be checked against the Answer Key.)

1.   All of the following tenants generate traffic in a shopping center *except* a/an

    a.   supermarket.
    b.   discount store.
    c.   auto repair shop.
    d.   furniture warehouse.

2.   All of the following statements are correct *except*

   a.   strip stores provide neighborhood shopping services.
   b.   neighborhood shopping centers provide their customers with necessary goods and services.
   c.   community shopping centers service a trade-area population of over 400,000 persons.
   d.   regional shopping centers are constructed on parcels of land containing at least 30 acres.

3.   Most strip store leases are drawn for

   a.   one year.
   b.   three to five years.
   c.   five to ten years.
   d.   longer than ten years.

4.   Which one of the following types of shopping center does not usually include competitive stores selling the same merchandise?

   a.   Strip stores
   b.   Neighborhood centers
   c.   Community centers
   d.   Regional centers

5.   The small investor is attracted to strip store buildings for all of the following reasons *except*

   a.   affordability.
   b.   ease of financing.
   c.   off-street parking conveniences.
   d.   convertibility to other uses.

6.   When a commercial tenant has the right to extend the lease at a price and terms established at the time of the lease inception, the lease provides for a/an

   a.   option to renew.
   b.   right of first refusal.
   c.   right of subordination.
   d.   right of redemption.

7.   When a tenant does $5,000, $6,000 and $7,000 gross business in each of three successive months, all of the following relationships are correct *except*

   a. $500, $600 and $700 = $500 monthly minimum against 10 percent of the gross.
   b.   equal rentals of $500 per month for each of the three months = $6,000 as fixed annual rental.
   c.   monthly rents of $500, $600 and $700 = $6,000 per year as a graduated monthly rental.
   d.   monthly rents of $1,000, $1,100 and $1,200 = a $500 monthly minimum plus 10 percent of the gross.

8.   The figure at the right represents a

   a.   neighborhood shopping center.
   b.   set of strip stores.
   c.   community shopping center.
   d.   regional shopping center.

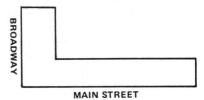

9.   Shopping center common-area fees are utilized to pay all of the following costs *except*

   a.   promotional advertising.
   b.   parking-area maintenance.
   c.   common-area utilities.
   d.   common-area property taxes.

10.   The type of shopping center that would generally include office towers and apartment buildings in its design is a

   a.   regional center.
   b.   community center.
   c.   super-regional center.
   d.   strip store grouping.

DISCUSSION

1.   Investigate what rent-up requirements the permanent lenders in your area demand before they will issue a standby loan commitment on a new community or regional shopping center. Include in your analysis the various leasehold insurance plans available from private companies to be used to meet a lender's requirements.

2.   Choose a neighborhood shopping center in your area and compose a feasibility study on its conversion to condominium ownership. Compare the value of the center as a single investment entity to its total value as a condominium.

EXHIBIT   Lease Agreement for Shopping Center Property

LEASE AGREEMENT

THIS INDENTURE OF LEASE, made on the _____ day of _____, 19__, by _____, an _____ corporation, _____ herein called "Owner", and _____ herein called "Tenant".

WITNESSETH:

ARTICLE I
GRANT AND TERM

SECTION 1.01. Leased Premises. In consideration of the rents, covenants and agreements hereinafter reserved and contained on the part of Tenant to be observed and performed, the Owner demises and leases to the Tenant, and Tenant rents from Owner, those certain premises, now or hereafter to be erected in the Shopping Center, (herein called the "Shopping Center") in _____ store, (herein called the "leased premises"), in _____ which premises consists of a store outlined in red on the site plan of the Shopping Center, which is marked Exhibit "A" attached hereto and made a part hereof. The use and occupation by the Tenant of the leased premises shall include the use in common with others entitled thereto of the common areas, employee and customer car parking areas, service roads, loading facilities, sidewalks and customer car parking areas, and other facilities as may be designated from time to time by the Owner, subject however to the terms and conditions of this agreement and to reasonable rules and regulations for the use thereof as prescribed from time to time by the Owner.

SECTION 1.02. Commencement and Ending Date of Term. The term of this lease and Tenant's obligation to pay rent hereunder shall commence upon: (a) the date thirty (30) days after the day Owner, or Owner's supervising architect, notifies Tenant in writing that the leased premises are ready for occupancy; or (b) the date on which Tenant shall open the leased premises for business to the public, whichever of said dates shall first occur. The term of this lease shall end on the last day of the _____ (____) consecutive full lease year as said term "lease year" is hereinafter defined.

The term "lease year" as used herein shall mean a period of twelve (12) consecutive full calendar months. The first lease year shall begin on the date of commencement of the term hereof if the date of commencement of the term hereof shall occur on the first day of a calendar month; if not, then the first lease year shall commence upon the first day of the calendar month next following the date of commencement of the term hereof. Each succeeding lease year shall commence upon the anniversary date of the first lease year.

SECTION 1.03. Failure of Tenant to be Open. In the event that the Owner notifies the Tenant that the leased premises are ready for occupancy as herein defined and the Tenant fails to take possession and to open the leased premises for business fully fixtured, stocked and staffed within the time herein provided, or in the event the leased premises open for business unless prevented from so doing by causes beyond Tenant's control, at any time during the entire term of this lease, then the Owner shall have in addition to any and all remedies herein provided the right at its option to collect not only the minimum rent herein

ARTICLE II
RENT

SECTION 2.01. Minimum Rent. The Tenant agrees to pay to Owner at the office of Owner, or at such other place designated by Owner, without any prior demand therefor and without any deduction or set-off whatsoever, and as fixed minimum rent

(a) The sum of $ _____ in advance upon the first day of each calendar month of (each lease year) (the first through the _____ lease year) inclusive;

(b) The sum of $ _____ in advance upon the first day of each calendar month of the _____ lease year through the _____ lease year inclusive; and

(c) The sum of $ _____ in advance upon the first day of each calendar month of the _____ lease year through the _____ lease year inclusive.

If the term shall commence upon a day other than the first day of a calendar month, then the Tenant shall pay, upon the commencement date of the term, a pro rata portion of the fixed monthly rent described in the foregoing clause (a) prorated on a per diem basis with respect to the fractional calendar month preceding the commencement of the first lease year hereof.

SECTION 2.02. Percentage Rent. (a) In addition to the fixed minimum rent aforesaid, Tenant agrees to pay to Owner, in the manner and at the times hereinafter set forth during each lease year, and as per-

---

centage rent hereunder, a sum equivalent to the amount, if any, by which _____ per cent (____%) of the gross receipts, as hereinafter defined, exceeds the fixed minimum rent payable during a lease year. Said percentage rent shall be payable as hereinafter provided at the office of Owner or at such other place as Owner may designate without any prior demand therefor and, except as provided in clause (b) of this section, without any set-off or deduction whatsoever.

(b) Said percentage rent shall be paid quarter-annually. The first payment of percentage rent shall be paid on or before the fifteenth (15th) day after the last day of the first three (3) calendar months of the first lease year of the term hereof, and another payment of percentage rent shall be paid on or before the fifteenth (15th) day after the end of each successive 3-month-calendar-period thereafter. The amount of each payment of percentage rent shall be equal to the amount, if any, by which the percentage (described in the foregoing clause (a) of this section) of the gross receipts for the immediately preceding three (3) calendar months exceeds one-fourth (¼) of the fixed minimum rent for a lease year. If, at the end of any lease year, the total amount of rent paid by Tenant exceeds the total amount of fixed and percentage rent required to be paid by Tenant during such lease year, Tenant shall receive a credit equivalent to such excess which may be deducted by Tenant from the next payment of percentage rent due under the foregoing provisions hereof.

(c) For the purpose of computing the percentage rent payable hereunder with respect to the first lease year of the term hereof, the gross receipts received during the first fractional calendar month, if any, shall be added to the gross receipts for the first 3-month period of the first lease year of the term hereof.

SECTION 2.03. Gross Receipts Defined. The term "gross receipts" as used herein is hereby defined to mean receipts from gross sales of Tenant and of all licensees, concessionaires and tenants of Tenant, from all business conducted upon or from the leased premises by Tenant and others, and whether such sales be evidenced by check, credit, charge account, cash or otherwise, and shall include, but not be limited to, the amounts received from the sale of goods, wares and merchandise and for services performed on or at the leased premises, together with the amount of all orders taken or received at the leased premises, whether such orders be filled from the leased premises or elsewhere, and whether such sales be made by means of merchandise or other vending devices in the leased premises. If any one or more departments or other divisions of Tenant's business shall be sublet by Tenant or conducted by any person, firm or corporation other than Tenant, then there shall be included in gross receipts for the purpose of fixing the percentage rent payable hereunder all the gross sales of such departments or divisions, whether such sales be made at the leased premises or elsewhere, in the same manner and with the same effect as if the business or sales of such departments and divisions of Tenant's business had been conducted by Tenant itself. Gross sales shall not include sales of merchandise for which cash has been refunded, or allowances made on merchandise claimed to be defective or unsatisfactory, provided they shall have been included in gross sales; and there shall be deducted from gross sales the sales price of merchandise returned by customers for exchange, provided that the sales price of merchandise delivered to the customer in exchange shall be included in gross sales. Gross receipts shall not include the amount of any sales, use or gross receipts tax imposed by any federal, state, municipal or governmental authority directly on sales and collected from customers, provided that the amount thereof is added to the selling price or absorbed therein, and paid by the Tenant to such governmental authority. No franchise or capital stock tax and no income or similar tax based upon income or profits as such shall be deducted from gross receipts in any event whatever. Each charge or sale upon installment or credit shall be treated as a sale for the full price in the month during which such charge or sale shall be made, irrespective of the time when Tenant shall receive payment (whether full or partial) therefor.

SECTION 2.04. Increased Taxes. Owner will pay in the first instance all real property taxes which may be levied or assessed by any lawful authority against the land and improvements in the Shopping Center. If the amount of the real property taxes levied or assessed against the land and building of which the leased premises form a part at the time of commencement of the term hereof shall exceed in any lease year the amount of such taxes for the first full tax year, Tenant shall pay that portion of such excess equal to the product obtained by multiplying said excess by a fraction, the numerator of which shall be the square-foot area of the leased premises, and the denominator of which shall be the square-foot area of the Shopping Center, exclusive of common areas. The term "first full tax year" shall mean the lease year in which the building (of which the leased premises form a part shall have been first assessed as a completed building to such lease year. The additional rent provided for in this Section 2.04 shall be deemed to correspond to such lease year. The additional rent provided for in this Section 2.04 shall be paid within twenty (20) days after demand therefor by Owner. A tax bill submitted by Owner to Tenant shall be sufficient evidence of the amount of taxes assessed or levied against the parcel or real property to which such bill relates.

SECTION 2.05. Additional Rent. The Tenant shall pay as additional rent any money or other charges required to be paid by Tenant under this lease, whether or not the same be designated "additional rent." If such amounts or charges are not paid at the time provided in this lease, they shall nevertheless, if not paid when due, be collectible as additional rent with the next installment of rent thereafter falling due hereunder, but nothing herein contained shall be deemed to suspend or delay the payment of any money or charge at the time the same becomes due and payable hereunder, or limit any other remedy of the Owner.

SECTION 2.06. Past Due Rent and Additional Rent. If Tenant shall fail to pay, when the same is due and payable, any rent or any additional rent, or amounts or charges of the character described in Section 2.05 hereof, such unpaid amounts shall bear interest from the due date thereof to the date of payment at the rate of Six Per Cent (6%) per annum.

ARTICLE III
RECORDS AND BOOKS OF ACCOUNT

SECTION 3.01. Tenant's Records. For the purpose of ascertaining the amount payable as rent, Tenant agrees to prepare and keep on the leased premises for a period of not less than two (2) years following the end of each lease year adequate records which shall show inventories and receipts of merchandise at the leased premises, and daily receipts from all sales and other transactions on or from the leased premises by Tenant and any other persons conducting any business upon or from said premises. Tenant further agrees to keep on the leased premises for at least two (2) years following the end of each lease year the gross income, sales

EXHIBT (continued)

and occupation tax returns with respect to said lease years and all pertinent original sales records. Pertinent original sales records shall include: (a) cash register tapes, including tapes from temporary registers; (b) serially numbered sales slips; (c) the originals of all mail orders at and to the leased premises; (d) the original records of all telephone orders at and to the leased premises; (e) settlement report sheets of transactions with sub-tenants, concessionaires and licensees; (f) the original records showing that merchandise returned by customers was purchased at the leased premises by such customers; (g) memorandum receipts or other records of merchandise taken out on approval; (h) copies of all sales, gross receipts and use tax reports and such other sales records, if any, which would normally be examined by an independent accountant pursuant to accepted auditing standards in performing an audit of Tenant's sales; and (i) the records specified in (a) to (h) above of sub-tenants, assignees, concessionaires, or licensees. Owner's authorized representative shall have the right to examine Tenant's records aforesaid during regular business hours.

SECTION 3.02. Reports By Tenant.
Tenant shall submit to Owner on or before the 15th day following each three (3) month period during the term hereof (including the 15th day of the month following the end of the term) at the place then fixed for the payment of rent, together with the remittance of quarterly percentage rent, a written statement signed by Tenant, and certified by it to be true and correct showing in reasonably accurate detail, the amount of gross receipts for each month during the preceding three months and fractional month, if any, prior to the commencement of the first lease year. Tenant shall submit to the Owner on or before the 60th day following the end of each lease year at the place then fixed for the payment of rent a written statement signed by Tenant, and certified to be true and correct showing in reasonably accurate detail the amount of gross receipts during the preceding lease year, and duly certified by independent certified public accountants of recognized standing. The statements referred to herein shall be in such form and style and contain such details and breakdown as the Owner may reasonably determine.

ARTICLE IV
AUDIT

SECTION 4.01. Right to Examine Books.
The acceptance by the Owner of payments of percentage rent shall be without prejudice to the Owner's right to an examination of the Tenant's books and records of its gross receipts and inventories of merchandise at the leased premises in order to verify the amount of annual gross receipts received by the Tenant in and from the leased premises.

SECTION 4.02. Audit.
At its option, Owner may cause, at any reasonable time upon forty-eight (48) hours prior written notice to Tenant, a complete audit to be made of Tenant's entire business affairs and records relating to the leased premises for the period covered by any statement issued by the Tenant as above set forth. If such audit shall disclose a liability for rent to the extent of Five Per Cent (5%) or more in excess of the rentals theretofore computed and paid by Tenant for such period, Tenant shall promptly pay to Owner the cost of said audit in addition to the deficiency, which deficiency shall be payable in any event, and, in addition, Owner, at Owner's option, may terminate this lease upon five (5) days notice to Tenant of Owner's election so to do. Any information obtained by the Owner as a result of such audit shall be held in strict confidence by Owner.

ARTICLE V
CONSTRUCTION, ALTERATION AND RELOCATION OF IMPROVEMENTS AND ADDITIONS THERETO

SECTION 5.01. Owner's Obligation.
Owner shall at its cost and expense construct the leased premises for Tenant's use and occupancy in accordance with plans and specifications prepared by Owner or Owner's architect, incorporating in such construction all items of work described in Exhibit "B" attached hereto and made a part hereof. Any work in addition to any of the items specifically enumerated in said Exhibit "B" shall be performed by the Tenant at its own cost and expense. Any equipment or work other than those items specifically enumerated in said Exhibit "B" which the Owner installs or constructs in the leased premises on the Tenant's behalf shall be paid for by the Tenant within fifteen days after receipt of a bill therefor at cost, plus Twenty Per Cent (20%) for overhead and supervision.

SECTION 5.02. Relocation and Additional Construction.
The Owner shall construct and maintain the parking areas substantially as shown on Exhibit "A". The purpose of the site plan attached hereto as Exhibit "A" is to show the approximate location of the buildings, parking and other common areas; the Owner reserves the right at any time to relocate any building, parking area or common area shown on said site plan. The Owner also reserves the right to construct other buildings or improvements in the Shopping Center from time to time and to make alterations thereof or additions thereto and to build additional stories on any building in the Shopping Center and to build adjoining same and to construct double-deck or elevated parking facilities, provided the ratio of the area for parking to the leased area in the Shopping Center shall not be reduced to less than three to one.

ARTICLE VI
CONDUCT OF BUSINESS BY TENANT

SECTION 6.01. Use of Premises.
Tenant shall use the leased premises solely for the purpose of conducting the business of:

Tenant shall occupy the leased premises within thirty (30) days after the date of the notice provided for in Section 1.02 hereof, and shall conduct continuously in the leased premises the business above stated. Tenant will not use or permit, or suffer the use of, the leased premises for any other business or purpose. Tenant shall not conduct catalogue sales in or from the leased premises except of merchandise which Tenant is permitted to sell "over the counter" in or at the leased premises pursuant to the provisions of this Section 6.01.

SECTION 6.02. Operation of Business.
Tenant shall operate all of the leased premises during the entire term of this lease with due diligence and efficiency so as to produce all of the gross sales which may be produced by such manner of operation, unless prevented from doing so by causes beyond Tenant's control. Subject to inability by reason of strikes or labor disputes, Tenant shall carry at all times in said premises a stock of merchandise of such size, character and quality as shall be reasonably designed to produce the maximum return to Owner and Tenant. Tenant shall conduct its business in the leased premises during the regular customary days and hours for such type of business in the city or trade area in which the Shopping Center is located, and will keep the leased premises open for business during the same days, nights and hours agreed upon by a majority of the voting power of the Merchants Association provided for in Section 16.03 hereof. Tenant shall install and maintain at all times displays of merchandise in the display windows (if any) of the leased premises. Tenant shall keep the display windows and signs, if any, in the leased premises well lighted during the hours from sundown to 11:00 o'clock P.M., unless prevented by causes beyond the control of Tenant.

SECTION 6.03. Competition.
During the term of this lease Tenant shall not directly or indirectly engage in any similar or competing business within a radius of one mile from the outside boundary of the Shopping Center. Tenant shall not perform any acts or carry on any practices which may injure the building or be a nuisance or menace to other tenants in the Shopping Center.

SECTION 6.04. Storage, Office Space.
Tenant shall warehouse, store or stock in the leased premises only such goods, wares and merchandise as Tenant intends to offer for sale at retail at, in, from or upon the leased premises. This shall not preclude occasional emergency transfers of merchandise to the other stores of Tenant, if any, not located in the Shopping Center. Tenant shall use for office, clerical or other non-selling purposes only such space in the leased premises as is from time to time reasonably required for Tenant's business in the leased premises. No auction, fire or bankruptcy sales may be conducted in the leased premises without the previous written consent of Owner.

ARTICLE VII
OPERATION OF CONCESSIONS

SECTION 7.01. Consent of Owner.
Tenant shall not permit any business to be operated in or from the leased premises by any concessionaire or licensee without the prior written consent of Owner.

ARTICLE VIII
PARKING AND COMMON USE AREAS AND FACILITIES

SECTION 8.01. Control of Common Areas by Owner.
All automobile parking areas, driveways, entrances and exits thereto, and other facilities furnished by Owner in or near the Shopping Center, including employee parking areas, the truck way or ways, loading docks, package pick-up stations, pedestrian sidewalks and ramps, landscaped areas, exterior stairways, first-aid stations, comfort stations and other areas and improvements provided by Owner for the general use, in common, of tenants, their officers, agents, employees and customers, shall at all times be subject to the exclusive control and management of Owner, and Owner shall have the right from time to time to establish, modify and enforce reasonable rules and regulations with respect to all facilities and areas mentioned in this Article. Owner shall have the right to construct, maintain and operate lighting facilities on all said areas and improvements; to police the same; from time to time to change the area, level, location and arrangement of parking areas and other facilities hereinabove referred to; to restrict parking by tenants, their officers, agents and employees to employee parking areas; to enforce parking charges (by operation of meters or otherwise), with appropriate provisions for free parking ticket validating by tenants; to close all or any portion of said areas or facilities to such extent as may, in the opinion of Owner's counsel, be legally sufficient to prevent a dedication thereof or the accrual of any rights to any person or the public therein; to close temporarily all or any portion of the parking areas or facilities; to discourage non-customer parking; and to do and perform such other acts in and to said areas and improvements as, in the use of good business judgment, the Owner shall determine to be advisable with a view to the improvement of the convenience and use thereof by tenants, their officers, agents, employees and customers. Owner will operate and maintain the common facilities referred to above in such manner as Owner, in its sole discretion, shall determine from time to time. Without limiting the scope of such discretion, Owner shall have the full right and authority to employ all personnel and to make all rules and regulations pertaining to and necessary for the proper operation and maintenance of the common areas and facilities.

ARTICLE IX
COST OF MAINTENANCE OF COMMON AREAS

SECTION 9.01. Tenant to Bear Pro Rata Share of Expense.
The Tenant agrees to reimburse the Owner for Tenant's share of the actual cost incurred by Owner in lighting the common areas, in keeping same clean and cleared of snow and ice, and in maintaining the common areas in good repair and in heating and cooling all enclosed malls, excluding, however, the cost of any capitalizable heating and cooling equipment, improvements or additions to the common areas. Tenant shall so reimburse Owner after receipt of satisfactory evidence of said costs and the amount due from Tenant, but not more often than once each month. Tenant's share shall be a fraction of said costs, the numerator of which fraction shall be the area of the leased premises and the denominator of which shall be the total leased area in the Shopping Center, including the leased premises.

ARTICLE X
SIGNS, AWNINGS, CANOPIES, FIXTURES, ALTERATIONS

SECTION 10.01. Installation by Tenant.
All fixtures installed by Tenant shall be new or completely reconditioned. Tenant shall not make or cause to be made any alterations, additions or improvements or install or cause to be installed any trade fixture, exterior signs, floor covering, interior or exterior lighting, plumbing fixtures, shades or awnings or make any changes to the store front without first obtaining Owner's written approval and consent. Tenant shall present to the Owner plans and specifications for such work at the time approval is sought.

SECTION 10.02. Removal and Restoration by Tenant.
All alterations, decorations, additions and improvements made by the Tenant, or made by the Owner on the Tenant's behalf by agreement under this lease, shall remain the property of the Tenant for the term of the lease, or any extension or renewal thereof. Such alterations, decorations, additions and improvements shall not be removed from the premises prior to the end of the term hereof without prior consent in writing from the Owner. Upon expiration of this lease, or any renewal term thereof, the Tenant shall remove all such alterations, decorations, additions and improvements, and restore the leased

EXHIBIT (continued)

premises as provided in Section 11.03 hereof. If the Tenant fails to remove such alterations, decorations, additions and improvements and restore the leased premises, then upon the expiration of this lease, or any renewal thereof, and upon the Tenant's removal from the premises, all such alterations, decorations, additions and improvements shall become the property of the Owner.

SECTION 10.03. Tenant Shall Discharge All Liens.

Tenant shall promptly pay all contractors and materialmen, so as to minimize the possibility of a lien attaching to the leased premises, and should any such lien be made or filed, Tenant shall bond against or discharge the same within ten (10) days after written request by Owner.

SECTION 10.04. Signs, Awnings and Canopies.

Tenant will not place or suffer to be placed or maintained on any exterior door, wall or window of the leased premises any sign, awning or canopy, or advertising matter or other thing of any kind, and will not place or maintain any decoration, lettering or advertising matter on the glass of any window or door of the leased premises without first obtaining Owner's written approval and consent. Tenant further agrees to maintain such sign, awning, canopy, decoration, lettering, advertising matter or other thing as may be approved in good condition and repair at all times.

ARTICLE XI
MAINTENANCE OF LEASED PREMISES

SECTION 11.01. Maintenance by Tenant.

Tenant shall at all times keep the leased premises (including maintenance of exterior entrances, all glass and show window mouldings) and all partitions, doors, fixtures, equipment and appurtenances thereof (including lighting, heating and plumbing fixtures, escalators, elevators, and any air conditioning system) in good order, condition and repair (including reasonably periodic painting as determined by Owner), damage by unavoidable casualty excepted, except for structural portions of the premises, which shall be maintained by Owner, but if Owner is required to make repairs to structural portions by reason of Tenant's negligent acts or omission to act, Owner may add the cost of such repairs to the rent which shall thereafter become due.

SECTION 11.02. Maintenance by Owner.

If Tenant refuses or neglects to repair property as required hereunder and to the reasonable satisfaction of Owner as soon as reasonably possible after written demand, Owner may make such repairs without liability to Tenant for any loss or damage that may accrue to Tenant's merchandise, fixtures, or other property or to Tenant's business by reason thereof, and upon completion thereof, Tenant shall pay Owner's costs for making such repairs plus Twenty Per Cent (20%) for overhead, upon presentation of bill therefor, as additional rent.

SECTION 11.03. Surrender of Premises.

At the expiration of the tenancy hereby created. Tenant shall surrender the leased premises in the same condition as the leased premises were in upon delivery of possession thereto under this lease, reasonable wear and tear excepted, and damage by unavoidable casualty excepted, and shall surrender all keys for the leased premises to Owner at the place then fixed for the payment of rent and shall inform Owner of all combinations on locks, safes and vaults, if any, in the leased premises. Tenant shall remove all its trade fixtures, and any alterations or improvements as provided in Section 10.02 hereof, before surrendering the premises as aforesaid and shall repair any damage to the leased premises caused thereby. Tenant's obligation to observe or perform this covenant shall survive the expiration or other termination of the term of this lease.

SECTION 11.04. Rules and Regulations.

Owner reserves the right to adopt and promulgate rules and regulations applicable to leased premises and the Shopping Center and from time to time to amend or supplement said rules and regulations. Notice of such rules and regulations, and amendments and supplements, shall be given to Tenant and Tenant agrees to comply with and observe such rules and regulations and amendments thereto and supplements thereof; provided, the same shall apply uniformly to all tenants of the Shopping Center.

SECTION 11.05. Miscellaneous.

All loading and unloading of merchandise shall be done only at such times, in the areas, and through the entrances, designated for such purposes by the Owner. No radio or television or other similar device shall be installed without first obtaining in each instance Owner's consent in writing. No aerial shall be erected on the roof or exterior walls of the premises, or on the grounds, without in each instance, the written consent of Owner. Any aerial so installed without such written consent shall be subject to removal without notice at any time. No loud speakers, televisions, phonographs, radios or other devices, shall be used in a manner so as to be heard or seen outside of the premises without the prior written consent of Owner. Tenant shall keep the leased premises at a temperature sufficiently high to prevent freezing of water in pipes and fixtures. The outside areas immediately adjoining the leased premises shall be kept clean and free from snow, ice, dirt and rubbish by Tenant, and Tenant shall not place or permit any obstructions or merchandise in such areas. Tenant and Tenant's employees shall park their cars only in those portions of the parking area designated for that purpose by Owner. Tenant shall furnish Owner with State automobile license numbers assigned to Tenant's car or cars, and cars of Tenant's employees. In the event that Tenant or its employees fail to park their cars in designated parking areas as aforesaid, then Owner at its option shall charge Tenant Ten ($10.00) Dollars per day per car parked in any area other than those designated, as and for liquidated damage. The plumbing facilities shall not be used for any other purpose than that for which they are constructed, and no foreign substance of any kind shall be thrown therein, and the expense of any breakage, stoppage, or damage resulting from a violation of this provision shall be borne by Tenant, who shall, or whose employees, agents or invitees shall have caused it. Tenant shall, at Tenant's expense, have the leased premises serviced by a pest exterminator at such intervals as the Owner may reasonably require. Tenant shall store all trash, garbage and rubbish within the leased premises and Tenant shall provide for the prompt and regular removal thereof for disposal outside the area of the Shopping Center, and Tenant shall not burn any trash, garbage or rubbish of any kind in or about the Shopping Center area.

ARTICLE XII
INSURANCE AND INDEMNITY

SECTION 12.01. Liability Insurance.

Tenant shall, during the entire term hereof, keep in full force and effect a policy of public liability and property damage insurance with respect to the leased premises, and the business operated by Tenant and any sub-tenants of Tenant in the leased premises in which the limits of public liability shall be not less than $200,000 per person and $500,000 per accident and in which the property damage liability shall be not less than $50,000. The policy shall name Owner, any person, firms or corporations designated by Owner, and Tenant as insured, and shall contain a clause that the insurer will not cancel or change the insurance without first giving the Owner ten days prior written notice. The insurance shall be in an insurance company approved by Owner and a copy of the policy or a certificate of insurance shall be delivered to Owner.

SECTION 12.02. Increase in Fire Insurance Premium.

Tenant agrees that it will not keep, use, sell or offer for sale in or upon the leased premises any article which may be prohibited by the standard form of fire insurance policy. Tenant agrees to pay any increase in premiums for fire and extended coverage insurance that may be charged during the term of this lease on the amount of such insurance which may be carried by Owner on said premises or the building of which they are a part, resulting from the type of merchandise sold by Tenant in the leased premises, whether or not Owner has consented to the same. In determining whether increased premiums are the result of Tenant's use of the leased premises, a schedule, issued by the organization making the insurance rate on the leased premises, showing the various components of such rate, shall be conclusive evidence of the several items and charges which make up the fire insurance rate on the leased premises.

In the event Tenant's occupancy causes any increase of premium for the fire, boiler or casualty rates on the leased premises or any part thereof above the rate for the least hazardous type of occupancy legally permitted in the leased premises, the Tenant shall pay the additional premium on the fire, boiler or casualty insurance policies by reason thereof. The Tenant also shall pay in such event, any additional premium on the rent insurance policy that may be carried by the Owner for its protection against rent loss through fire. Bills for such additional premiums shall be rendered by Owner to Tenant at such times as Owner may elect, and shall be due from, and payable by Tenant when rendered, and the amount thereof shall be deemed to be, and be paid as, additional rent.

SECTION 12.03. Indemnification of Owner.

Tenant will indemnify Owner and save it harmless from and against any and all claims, actions, damages, liability and expense in connection with loss of life, personal injury or damage to property arising from or out of any occurrence in, upon or at the leased premises, or the occupancy or use by Tenant of the leased premises or any part thereof, or occasioned wholly or in part by any act or omission of Tenant, its agents, contractors, employees, servants, lessees or concessionaires. In case Owner shall, without fault on its part, be made a party to any litigation commenced by or against Tenant, then Tenant shall protect and hold Owner harmless and shall pay all costs, expenses and reasonable attorney's fees incurred or paid by Owner in connection with such litigation. Tenant shall also pay all costs, expenses and reasonable attorney's fees that may be incurred or paid by Owner in enforcing the covenants and agreements in this lease.

SECTION 12.04. Plate Glass.

Owner shall replace, at the expense of Tenant, any and all plate and other glass damaged or broken from any cause whatsoever in and about the leased premises. Owner may insure, and keep insured, at Tenant's expense, all plate and other glass in the leased premises for and in the name of Owner. Bills for the premiums therefor shall be rendered by Owner to Tenant at such times as Owner may elect, and shall be due from, and payable by, Tenant when rendered, and the amount thereof shall be deemed to be, and be paid as, additional rent.

SECTION 12.05. Boiler Insurance.

The Tenant hereby authorizes the Owner to obtain boiler broad form insurance, if any is applicable, in the amount of $50,000 in the name of the Tenant and for and in the name of the Owner. Bills for the premiums therefor shall be rendered by Owner to Tenant at such times as Owner may elect, and shall be due from, and payable by, Tenant when rendered, and the amount thereof shall be deemed to be, and be paid as, additional rent.

ARTICLE XIII
UTILITIES

SECTION 13.01. Utility Charges.

Tenant shall be solely responsible for and promptly pay all charges for heat, water, gas, electricity or any other utility used or consumed in the leased premises. Should Owner elect to supply the water, gas, heat, electricity or any other utility used or consumed in the leased premises, Tenant agrees to purchase and pay for the same as additional rent at the applicable rates filed by the Owner with the proper regulatory authority. In no event shall Owner be liable for an interruption or failure in the supply of any such utilities to the leased premises.

ARTICLE XIV
ASSIGNMENT AND SUBLETTING

SECTION 14.01. Consent Required.

Tenant will not assign this lease in whole or in part, nor sublet all or any part of the leased premises, without the prior written consent of Owner in each instance. The consent by Owner to any assignment or subletting shall not constitute a waiver of the necessity for such consent to any subsequent assignment or subletting. This prohibition against assigning or subletting shall be construed to include a prohibition against any assignment or subletting by operation of law. If this lease be assigned, or if the leased premises or any part thereof be underlet or occupied by anybody other than Tenant, Owner may collect rent from the assignee, under-tenant or occupant, and apply the net amount collected to the rent herein reserved, but no such assignment, underletting, occupancy or collection shall be deemed a waiver of this covenant, or the acceptance of the assignee, under-tenant or occupant as tenant, or a release of Tenant from the further performance by Tenant of covenants on the part of Tenant herein contained. Notwithstanding any assignment or sublease, Tenant shall remain fully liable on this lease and shall not be released from performing any of the terms, covenants and conditions of this lease.

ARTICLE XV
WASTE, GOVERNMENTAL REGULATIONS

SECTION 15.01. Waste or Nuisance.

Tenant shall not commit or suffer to be committed any waste upon the leased premises or any nuisance or other act or thing which may disturb the quiet enjoyment of any other tenant in the building in which the leased premises may be located, or in the Shopping Center, or which may disturb the quiet enjoyment of any person within five hundred feet of the boundaries of the Shopping Center.

EXHIBIT (continued)

SECTION 15.02. Governmental Regulations.
Tenant shall, at Tenant's sole cost and expense, comply with all of the requirements of all county, municipal, state, federal and other applicable governmental authorities, now in force, or which may hereafter be in force, pertaining to the said premises, and shall faithfully observe in the use of the premises all municipal and county ordinances and state and federal statutes now in force or which may hereafter be in force.

ARTICLE XVI
ADVERTISING, MERCHANTS ASSOCIATION

SECTION 16.01. Change of Name.
Tenant agrees not to change the advertised name of the business operated in the leased premises without the written permission of Owner.

SECTION 16.02. Solicitation of Business.
Tenant and Tenant's employees and agents shall not solicit business in the parking or other common areas, nor shall Tenant distribute any handbills or other advertising matter in automobiles parked in the parking area or in other common areas.

SECTION 16.03. Merchants' Association.
Tenant agrees to become a member of and abide by the bylaws and regulations of the Windamere Merchants' Association. The purpose of such Association is to assist the business of the tenants by center-wide advertising and sales promotions. Tenant agrees to pay such reasonable dues as may be adopted by the Association, not exceeding an amount equal to fifteen cents (15c) per annum for each square foot of the building on the leased premises. Owner shall pay to the Association an amount equal to one-fourth (¼) of the aggregate monthly dues payable by all other members of the Association. Each member of the Association shall have voting rights in the Association in the same proportion as that member's contribution bears to the total contributions.

ARTICLE XVII
DESTRUCTION OF LEASED PREMISES

SECTION 17.01. Total or Partial Destruction.
If the leased premises shall be damaged by fire. the elements, unavoidable accident or other casualty, but are not thereby rendered untenantable in whole or in part, Owner shall at its own expense cause such damage to be repaired, and the rent shall not be abated. If by reason of such occurrence, the premises shall be rendered untenantable only in part, Owner shall at its own expense cause the damage to be repaired, and the fixed minimum rent meanwhile shall be abated proportionately as to the portion of the premises rendered untenantable. If the premises shall be rendered wholly untenantable by reason of such occurrence the Owner shall at its own expense cause such damage to be repaired, and the fixed minimum rent meanwhile shall abate until the leased premises have been restored and rendered tenantable, or Owner may at its election, terminate this lease and the tenancy hereby created by giving to Tenant within the sixty (60) days following the date of said occurrence, written notice of Owner's election so to do and in event of such termination rent shall be adjusted as of such date. Nothing in this Section shall be construed to permit the abatement in whole or in part of the percentage rent, but for the purpose of Section 2.02 hereof the computation of percentage rent shall be based upon the revised minimum rent as the same may be abated pursuant to this Section 17.01.

SECTION 17.02. Partial Destruction of Shopping Center.
In the event that Fifty Per Cent (50%) or more of the rentable area of the Shopping Center shall be damaged or destroyed by fire or other cause, notwithstanding that the leased premises may be unaffected by such fire or other cause, Owner may terminate this lease and the tenancy hereby created by giving to Tenant five (5) days prior written notice of Owner's election so to do which notice shall be given, if at all, within the sixty (60) days following the date of said occurrence. Rent shall be adjusted as of the date of such termination.

ARTICLE XVIII
EMINENT DOMAIN

SECTION 18.01. Total Condemnation of Leased Premises.
If the whole of the leased premises shall be acquired or condemned by eminent domain for any public or quasi-public use or purpose, then the term of this lease shall cease and terminate as of the date of title vesting in such proceeding and all rentals shall be paid up to that date and Tenant shall have no claim against Owner nor the condemning authority for the value of any unexpired term of this lease.

SECTION 18.02. Partial Condemnation.
If any part of the leased premises shall be acquired or condemned as aforesaid, and in the event that such partial taking or condemnation shall render the leased premises unsuitable for the business of the Tenant, then the term of this lease shall cease and terminate as of the date of title vesting in such proceeding. Tenant shall have no claim against Owner nor the condemning authority for the value of any unexpired term of this lease and rent shall be adjusted to the date of such termination. In the event of a partial taking or condemnation which is not extensive enough to render the premises unsuitable for the business of the Tenant, then Owner shall promptly restore the leased premises to a condition comparable to its condition at the time of such condemnation less the portion lost in the taking, and this lease shall continue in full force and effect without any reduction or abatement of rent.

SECTION 18.03. Total Condemnation of Parking Area.
If the whole of the common parking areas in the Shopping Center shall be acquired or condemned as aforesaid, then the term of this lease shall cease and terminate as of the date of title vesting in such proceeding unless Owner shall take immediate steps to provide other parking facilities substantially equal to the previously existing ratio between the common parking areas and the leased premises, and such substantially equal parking facilities shall be provided by Owner at its own expense within ninety (90) days from the date of acquisition. In the event that Owner shall provide such other substantially equal parking facilities, then this lease shall continue in full force and effect without any reduction or abatement of rent.

SECTION 18.04. Partial Condemnation of Parking Area.
If any part of the parking area in the Shopping Center shall be acquired or condemned as aforesaid, and if, as the result thereof the ratio of square feet of parking field to square feet of the sales area of the entire Shopping Center buildings is reduced to a ratio below three to one, then the term of this lease shall cease and terminate upon the vesting of title in such proceeding, unless the Owner shall take immediate steps toward increasing the parking ratio to a ratio in excess of three to one, in which event this lease shall be unaffected and remain in full force and effect without any reduction or abatement of rent. In event of termination of this lease as aforesaid, Tenant shall have no claim against Owner nor the condemning authority for the value of any unexpired term of this lease and rent shall be adjusted to the date of said termination.

SECTION 18.05. Owner's Damages.
In the event of any condemnation or taking as aforesaid, whether whole or partial, the Tenant shall not be entitled to any part of the award paid for such condemnation and Owner is to receive the full amount of such award, the Tenant hereby expressly waiving any right or claim to any part thereof.

SECTION 18.06. Tenant's Damages.
Although all damages in the event of any condemnation are to belong to the Owner whether such damages are awarded as compensation for diminution in value of the leasehold or to the fee of the leased premises, Tenant shall have the right to claim and recover from the condemning authority, but not from Owner, such compensation as may be separately awarded or recoverable by Tenant in Tenant's own right on account of any and all damage to Tenant's business by reason of the condemnation and for or on account of any cost or loss to which Tenant might be put in removing Tenant's merchandise, furniture, fixtures, leasehold improvements and equipment.

ARTICLE XIX
DEFAULT OF THE TENANT

SECTION 19.01. Right to Re-enter.
In the event of any failure of Tenant to pay any rental due hereunder within ten (10) days after the same shall be due, or any failure to perform any other of the terms, conditions or covenants of this lease to be observed or performed by Tenant for more than thirty (30) days after written notice of such default shall have been given to Tenant, or if Tenant or an agent of Tenant shall falsify any report required to be furnished to Owner pursuant to terms of this lease, or if Tenant or any guarantor of this Lease shall become bankrupt or insolvent, or file any debtor proceedings or take or have taken against Tenant or any guarantor of this Lease in any court pursuant to any statute either of the United States or of any State a petition in bankruptcy or insolvency or for reorganization or for the appointment of a receiver or trustee of all or a portion of Tenant's or any such guarantor's property, or if Tenant or any such guarantor makes an assignment for the benefit of creditors, or petitions for or enters into an arrangement, or if Tenant shall abandon said premises, or suffer this lease to be taken under any writ of execution, then Owner besides other rights or remedies it may have, shall have the immediate right of re-entry and may remove all persons and property from the leased premises and such property may be removed and stored in a public warehouse or elsewhere at the cost of, and for the account of Tenant, all without service of notice or resort to legal process and without being deemed guilty of trespass, or becoming liable for any loss or damage which may be occasioned thereby.

SECTION 19.02. Right to Relet.
Should Owner elect to re-enter, as herein provided, or should it take possession pursuant to legal proceedings or pursuant to any notice provided for by law, it may either terminate this lease or it may from time to time without terminating this lease, make such alterations and repairs as may be necessary in order to relet the premises, and relet said premises or any part thereof for such term or terms (which may be for a term extending beyond the term of this lease) and at such rental or rentals and upon such other terms and conditions as Owner in its sole discretion may deem advisable; upon each such reletting all rentals received by the Owner from such reletting shall be applied, first, to the payment of any indebtedness other than rent due hereunder from Tenant to Owner; second, to the payment of any costs and expenses of such reletting, including brokerage fees and attorney's fees and of costs of such alterations and repairs; third, to the payment of rent due and unpaid hereunder, and the residue, if any, shall be held by Owner and applied in payment of future rent as the same may become due and payable hereunder. If such rentals received from such reletting during any month be less than that to be paid during that month by Tenant hereunder, Tenant shall pay any such deficiency to Owner. Such deficiency shall be calculated and paid monthly. No such re-entry or taking possession of said premises by Owner shall be construed as an election on its part to terminate this lease unless a written notice of such intention be given to Tenant or unless the termination thereof be decreed by a court of competent jurisdiction. Notwithstanding any such reletting without termination, Owner may at any time thereafter elect to terminate this lease for such previous breach. Should Owner at any time terminate this lease for any breach, in addition to any other remedies it may have, it may recover from Tenant all damages it may incur by reason of such breach, including the cost of recovering the leased premises, reasonable attorney's fees, and including the worth at the time of such termination of the excess, if any, of the amount of rent and charges equivalent to rent reserved in this lease for the remainder of the stated term over the then reasonable rental value of the leased premises for the remainder of the stated term, all of which amounts shall be immediately due and payable from Tenant to Owner. In determining the rent which would be payable by Tenant hereunder, subsequent to default, the annual rent for each year of the unexpired term shall be equal to the average annual minimum and percentage rents paid by Tenant from the commencement of the term to the time of default, or during the preceding three full calendar years, whichever period is shorter.

SECTION 19.03. Legal Expenses.
In case suit shall be brought for recovery of possession of the leased premises, for the recovery of rent or any other amount due under the provisions of this lease, or because of the breach of any other covenant herein contained on the part of Tenant to be kept or performed, and a breach shall be established, Tenant shall pay to Owner all expenses incurred therefor, including a reasonable attorney's fee.

ARTICLE XX
ACCESS BY OWNER

SECTION 20.01. Right of Entry.
Owner or Owner's agents shall have the right to enter the leased premises at reasonable times to examine the same, and to show them to prospective purchasers or lessees of the building, and to make such repairs, alterations, improvements or additions as Owner may deem desirable, and Owner shall be allowed to take all material into and upon said premises that may be required therefor without the same constituting an eviction of Tenant in whole or in part and the rent reserved shall in no wise abate while said repairs, alterations, improvements, or additions are being made, by reason of loss or interruption of business of Tenant, or otherwise. During the six months prior to the expiration of the term of this lease or any renewal term, Owner may exhibit the premises to prospective tenants or purchasers,

EXHIBT (continued)

and place upon the premises the usual notices "To Let" or "For Sale" which notices Tenant shall permit to remain thereon without molestation. Nothing herein contained, however, shall be deemed or construed to impose upon Owner any obligation, responsibility or liability whatsoever, for the care, maintenance or repair of the building or any part thereof, except as otherwise herein specifically provided.

ARTICLE XXI
TENANT'S PROPERTY

SECTION 21.01. Taxes on Leasehold.
Tenant shall be responsible for and shall pay before delinquency all municipal, county or state taxes assessed during the term of this lease against any leasehold interest or personal property of any kind, owned by or placed in, upon or about the leased premises by the Tenant.

SECTION 21.02. Loss and Damage.
Owner shall not be liable for any damage to property of Tenant or of others located on the leased premises, nor for the loss of or damage to any property of Tenant or of others by theft or otherwise. Owner shall not be liable for any injury or damage to persons or property resulting from fire, explosion, falling plaster, steam, gas, electricity, water, rain or snow or leaks from any part of the leased premises or from the pipes, appliances or plumbing works or from the roof, street or sub-surface or from any other place or by dampness or by any other cause of whatsoever nature. Owner shall not be liable for any such damage caused by other tenants or persons in the leased premises, occupants of adjacent property, of the Shopping Center, or the public, or caused by operations in construction of any private, public or quasi-public work. Owner shall not be liable for any latent defect in the leased premises or in the building of which they form a part except for a period of one (1) year from the date Tenant takes possession of the leased premises. All property of Tenant kept or stored on the leased premises shall be so kept or stored at the risk of the Tenant only and Tenant shall hold Owner harmless from any claims arising out of damage to the same, including subrogation claims by Tenant's insurance carrier, unless such damage shall be caused by the willful act or gross neglect of Owner.

SECTION 21.03. Notice by Tenant.
Tenant shall give immediate notice to Owner in case of fire or accidents in the leased premises or in the building of which the premises are a part of defects therein or in any fixtures or equipment.

ARTICLE XXII
HOLDING OVER, SUCCESSORS

SECTION 22.01. Holding Over.
Any holding over after the expiration of the term hereof, with the consent of the Owner, shall be construed to be a tenancy from month to month at the rents herein specified (prorated on a monthly basis) and shall otherwise be on the terms and conditions herein specified, so far as applicable.

SECTION 22.02. Successors.
All rights and liabilities herein given to, or imposed upon, the respective parties hereto shall extend to and bind the several respective heirs, executors, administrators, successors, and assigns of the said parties; and if there shall be more than one tenant, they shall be bound jointly and severally by the terms, covenants and agreements herein. No rights, however, shall inure to the benefit of any assignee of Tenant unless the assignment to such assignee has been approved by Owner in writing as provided in Section 14.01 hereof.

ARTICLE XXIII
QUIET ENJOYMENT

SECTION 23.01. Owner's Covenant.
Upon payment by the Tenant of the rents herein provided, and upon the observance and performance of all the covenants, terms and conditions on Tenant's part to be observed and performed, Tenant shall peaceably and quietly hold and enjoy the leased premises for the term hereby demised without hindrance or interruption by Owner or any other person or persons lawfully or equitably claiming by, through or under the Owner, subject, nevertheless, to the terms and conditions of this lease.

ARTICLE XXIV
MISCELLANEOUS

SECTION 24.01. Waiver.
The waiver by Owner of any breach of any term, covenant or condition herein contained shall not be deemed to be a waiver of such term, covenant or condition or any subsequent breach of the same or any other term, covenant or condition herein contained. The subsequent acceptance of rent hereunder by Owner shall not be deemed to be a waiver of any preceding breach by Tenant of any term, covenant or condition of this lease, other than the failure of Tenant to pay the particular rental so accepted, regardless of Owner's knowledge of such preceding breach at the time of acceptance of such rent. No covenant, term or conditions of this lease shall be deemed to have been waived by Owner, unless such waiver be in writing by Owner.

SECTION 24.02. Accord and Satisfaction.
No payment by Tenant or receipt by Owner of a lesser amount than the monthly rent herein stipulated shall be deemed to be other than on account of the earliest stipulated rent, nor shall any endorsement or statement on any check or any letter accompanying any check or payment as rent be deemed an accord and satisfaction, and Owner may accept such check or payment without prejudice to Owner's right to recover the balance of such rent or pursue any other remedy in this lease provided.

SECTION 24.03. Entire Agreement. Rider.
This lease and the Exhibits annexed hereto and forming a part hereof, set forth all the covenants, promises, agreements, conditions and understandings between Owner and Tenant concerning the leased premises and there are no covenants, promises, agreements, conditions or understandings, either oral or written, between them other than are herein set forth. Except as herein otherwise provided, no subsequent alteration, amendment, change or addition to this lease shall be binding upon Owner or Tenant unless reduced to writing and signed by them.

SECTION 24.04. No Partnership.
Owner does not, in any way or for any purpose, become a partner of Tenant in the conduct of its business, or otherwise, or joint adventurer or a member of a joint enterprise with Tenant. The provisions of this lease relating to the percentage rent payable hereunder are included solely for the purpose of providing a method whereby the rent is to be measured and ascertained.

SECTION 24.05. Force Majeure.
In the event that either party hereto shall be delayed or hindered in or prevented from the performance of any act required hereunder by reason of strikes, lock-outs, labor troubles, inability to procure materials, failure of power, restrictive governmental laws or regulations, riots, insurrection, war or other reason of a like nature not the fault of the party delayed in performing work or doing acts required under the terms of this lease, then performance of such act shall be excused for the period of the delay and the period for the performance of any such act shall be extended for a period equivalent to the period of such delay. The provisions of this Section 24.05 shall not operate to excuse Tenant from prompt payment of rent, percentage rent, additional rent or any other payments required by the terms of this lease.

SECTION 24.06. Notices.
Any notice, demand, request or other instrument which may be or are required to be given under this lease shall be delivered in person or sent by United States certified mail postage prepaid and shall be addressed (a) if to Owner at the address first hereinabove given or at such other address as Owner may designate by written notice and (b) if to Tenant at the leased premises or at such other address as Tenant shall designate by written notice.

SECTION 24.07. Tenant Defined, Use of Pronoun.
The word "Tenant" shall be deemed and taken to mean each and every person or party mentioned as a tenant herein, be the same one or more, and if there shall be more than one tenant, any notice required or permitted by the terms of this lease may be given by or to any one thereof, and shall have the same force and effect as if given by or to all thereof. The use of the neuter singular pronoun to refer to Owner or Tenant shall be deemed a proper reference even though Owner or Tenant may be an individual, a partnership, a corporation, or a group of two or more individuals or corporations. The necessary grammatical changes required to make the provisions of this lease apply in the plural sense where there is more than one Owner or Tenant and to either corporations, associations, partnerships, or individuals, males or females, shall in all instances be assumed as though in each case fully expressed.

SECTION 24.08. Partial Invalidity.
If any term, covenant or condition of this lease or the application thereof to any person or circumstance shall, to any extent, be invalid or unenforceable, the remainder of this lease, or the application of such term, covenant or condition to persons or circumstances other than those as to which it is held invalid or unenforceable, shall not be affected thereby and each term, covenant or condition of this lease shall be valid and be enforced to the fullest extent permitted by law.

SECTION 24.09. Recording.
Tenant shall not record this lease without the written consent of Owner, however, upon the request of either party hereto the other party shall join in the execution of a memorandum of this lease for the purposes of recordation. Said memorandum of this lease shall describe the parties, the leased premises and the term of this lease and shall incorporate this lease by reference.

SECTION 24.10. Rider.
A rider consisting of _____ pages, with sections numbered consecutively _____ through _____ is attached hereto and made a part hereof.

IN WITNESS WHEREOF, Owner and Tenant have signed and sealed this lease as of the day and year first above written.

        —Owner

By _____
    Authorized Officer

        —Tenant

By _____
    Authorized Officer or Agent

11
Investing in Industrial Properties

Key Terms

business park
functional obsolescence
general obligation bonds
incremental taxes
incubator industrial building
industrial development bonds
industrial park
infant industry

labor-intensive
loft buildings
miniwarehouse
net lease
railroad spur
revenue bonds
warehouse buildings

The technical and legal expertise required to develop industrial property makes it one of the more complicated types of real estate investment. The developer must not only help provide the industrialist with labor pools, utilities and transportation facilities but also satisfy the rigorous regulations of governmental agencies concerned with zoning, licensing and environmental controls. It is no longer possible simply to convince a prospective industrialist to move to a new community, purchase a parcel of land near a freeway, railroad or airport, and quickly construct a building. Now an industrial developer must be concerned with the adequacy of the available utilities and waste disposal provisions, as well as with the various impacts the project will have on the environment, both local and regional.

For these reasons, investment in industrial properties often becomes the province of insurance companies, trust divisions of commercial banks and others who view the stability and longevity of the industrial tenant as a complement to their investment portfolios. By combining properly designed leases with financially creditable tenants, industrial investments develop profitable yields with a minimum of management responsibility.

This chapter reviews the characteristics of industrial property and examines the opportunities for investing in this form of real estate.

THE INDUSTRIAL REAL ESTATE MARKET

Paralleling the post–World War II shifts in other sectors of the real estate market, the industrial segment has largely overcome the inertia caused by the high costs of relocation and is moving from its traditional northern and eastern bastions to the southern and western parts of this country. Accompanying this general southwestern shift is the tendency for new establishments or branch facilities to be located in the suburban and rural areas surrounding a community.

The move to the suburbs has received impetus from the continual development of better roads and highways connecting the various areas within cities as well as connecting cities across the nation. The improved network of freeways allows workers to drive more easily to and from factories, even over relatively long distances, and complements the emergence of the freight-trucking industry. Many industrial firms are no longer forced to locate near rail facilities and are now free to leave the congested central metropolitan areas.

Land Use Patterns

Most industrial developments have in common the basic locational dilemma of isolation from the residential areas of a community. A concern for the health of citizens has led community regulatory agencies to require that industrial activities that create noise, smoke and waste be isolated in designated areas, preferably as far away from homes as possible. As a result, transportation facilities must be available to provide workers with easy access and to allow for ease in receiving raw materials and shipping finished goods. Isolation also creates the problem of securing the utility services needed for manufacturing, including facilities for electricity, natural gas, water and waste disposal.

Some businesses, such as electronic-component-part assembly plants and research and development corporations, enjoy the distinction of being considered "clean" industries. These companies are usually located in industrial parks and are generally sought after by expanding communities.

Attracting New Industry

Despite the no-growth attitudes of political leaders in some cities throughout this country, many others actively seek to attract industry. Because they recognize the numerous economic benefits that stem from new employment opportunities, many expanding communities offer special incentives to induce manufacturers and other employers to relocate to their cities.

Subsidized Plant Locations.   One technique uses the community's taxing power to float **industrial development bonds** and then uses the proceeds to purchase land and build the plants required by new firms moving to the community. The payments on these bonds are made by the city from taxes collected for this purpose (**general obligation bonds**) or from the rents collected from the industrial tenants (**revenue bonds**). In either case, a community can adjust the charges to prospective employers and thereby provide economic incentives for locating in that particular area.

Tax Waivers.   In addition to low rents, city leaders may offer a new industry certain tax waivers. Property taxes may be waived for long periods of time if a company agrees to purchase a plant instead of leasing it. Inventory taxes may be waived for the term of the lease or longer, depending on circumstances. Local income taxes, as well as state income taxes in certain cases, may be waived for prescribed time periods to allow an **infant industry** an opportunity to mature.

Theoretically, these tax waivers—as well as the plant subsidies—will cost a community little, if any, money because of the **incremental taxes** that will be generated. These extra taxes will emanate from the incomes of the newly employed and the properties they will require for housing and peripheral services.

Economic Feasibility

In addition to industrial developments sponsored directly by community leaders, usually under the direction of an industrial development board, individuals and corporations also invest in industrial properties. The objective of an industrial developer is to match a particular property to a specific firm. This process requires a detailed study of the local market conditions as well as of the tenant's needs.

Locational Preferences.   When selecting plant sites, industrial firms look to minimize transportation costs in the acquisition of raw materials and the distribution of finished goods. In addition, production costs are analyzed in terms of wages, rents, taxes and other necessary expenses. In a highly competitive market, the site offering the lowest costs will be chosen.

The special characteristics of a firm determine to a large extent where it will locate. Companies that are *market-oriented* and rely on a large consumer population will locate close to these customers. A bottler of soft drinks is an example of this type of industry. A firm that depends on heavy or bulky *raw materials* will elect to locate near these resources to minimize transportation costs; for instance, a steel mill should be located near supplies of iron ore or coal deposits. A *labor-oriented* firm requires a location that will attract the types of workers required for its activities. Thus, a research company would seek a site near a university, but a manufacturing plant might prefer a location closer to a large market of semiskilled laborers.

Local Market Conditions.   An industrial firm that anticipates a move into a new area requires precise data concerning the economic base of the community and its demography. First, the firm will accumulate data describing the available labor force—its skills, educational levels and turnover ratios. In addition, an industrialist will require first-hand knowledge of the political attitudes of the community leaders and the degree to which they will cooperate in establishing a new plant. Sources of income and property taxes, tax rates, assessment policies, municipal services and zoning ordinances are all vital inclusions in the evaluation of a community.

Much of this information can be obtained from public sources, such as the Census Bureau, property-tax rolls and local employment agencies. Other data can be gathered from development groups, municipal agencies, utility companies and research bureaus maintained by universities and local banks.

CHARACTERISTICS OF INDUSTRIAL REAL ESTATE

The term *industry* includes all activities involved in the production, storage and distribution of tangible goods. Industrial property includes the plants, lofts and warehouses located throughout this country, and the construction of these facilities requires vast amounts of investment capital. Many manufacturers feel that their own funds are more productive when used in the operation of their industry. Consequently, industrial real estate is generally investor-owned, with the manufacturer assuming a tenant's role. Frequently, a sale-leaseback-buyback ownership agreement, described in chapter 3, is used.

Building Characteristics

Industrial buildings are classified as general-purpose, special-purpose or single purpose, depending on their adaptability. *General-purpose buildings* have a wide range of alternative uses. These properties can be adapted for light manufacturing or assembly plants or simply used as warehouses. *Special-purpose buildings* have certain physical characteristics that limit the scope of their use. For instance, only a few industrial enterprises require heavily insulated cold-storage facilities. *Single-purpose buildings* are suitable for only one use, such as a steel mill. These single-purpose properties are difficult, if not impossible, to convert to other uses. Institutional buildings such as theaters, churches, and government structures should not be considered special-purpose property since they are not used for industrial purposes.

Because of the specific purpose of some buildings and the unusual size of others, industrial property is considered a slow turnover commodity in the real estate market. This poor liquidity increases an investor's risk and requires that an industrial property owner seek out an experienced and knowledgeable tenant. The value of this type of property is closely intertwined with the profitability of the firm that occupies the premises. If the tenant is unsuccessful, the building will be vacated and difficult to rent.

More so than in any other form of real estate investment, an industrial tenant's installation of heavy equipment and machinery will ensure the longevity of the tenancy. In fact, the cost of installing expensive and bulky equipment often forms the basis for the inertia of large manufacturing firms that remain in one location for several generations. Although this longevity is favorable to an investor's yield, **functional obsolescence** can sometimes place the operating firm at an economic disadvantage in competing with companies that have located in modern, more efficient plant facilities.

When industrial firms locate in outlying areas, they tend to prefer single-story buildings because of the efficiency of manufacturing operations made possible by this design. A single-level plant lends itself to greater flexibility in the use of open areas and promotes the efficient flow of goods through the building. The expediency of a horizontal floor plan, which allows for greater ease in the handling of materials as well as for an assembly-line arrangement for the use of machinery, gives the one-story industrial tenant a competitive edge in the marketplace.

Land Characteristics

Industrial property development requires land that is properly zoned, includes a sufficient amount of square footage for buildings and off-street parking and has access to major transportation arteries and utility facilities adequate to serve the prospective enterprise.

Utilities.   One of the important variables for an industrial developer to consider is the availability of electricity, gas and sewers. In the future, developers may only be allowed to improve lands that can be serviced with these utilities for industrial use. Where these utilities are available, their costs must be included in the feasibility analysis of a major project. Utility charges are becoming an important part of an operations statement because their increasing costs can seriously erode the profits from an otherwise potentially successful investment.

Waste disposal facilities must be provided. The treatment of solid and liquid wastes is now an essential concern of every industrial developer. Proof must exist to the satisfaction of all concerned parties—both public and private—that appropriate provisions are being made for the disposal of wastes without disturbing the natural environment. The recent emphasis on control of polluters has placed new industrial developments under the careful scrutiny of zoners, planners, air and water quality-control agencies and environmentalists of every order.

Compounding the problem of sewage disposal is the isolation required for activities that create the greatest amount of waste. Whereas clean industry can locate in towns and on existing sewer lines, heavy industry is relegated to more distant areas where no sewage disposal facilities exist. Faced with this problem, industrial developers of outlying properties must often provide their own disposal systems, which usually have high installation costs. Septic tanks and leaching fields are generally not adequate to service a manufacturing plant, so a treatment pond must be constructed, along with sewer lines to transport the waste over a substantial distance. And just imagine the clamor of owners of property that adjoins such a malodorous pond!

Railroad Spurs.   Generally, industries produce products in large volume and require facilities for the receipt of bulk raw materials as well as for the shipment of finished goods. Although companies dealing in relatively small, expensive items may be able to justify the costs of air freight, many manufacturing operations require a plant location adjoining a **railroad spur**. The railroad cars can then be available at dockside for efficient loading and unloading.

Most railroad companies will cooperate in constructing a spur line to a new plant to serve a potential shipper. Allocations for the costs of such installations are based on the anticipated volume of business—that is, the higher the volume, the more likely the possibility that the railroad company will absorb the costs. Often, a developer will have to pay for the installation of a spur line; but in the case of an **industrial park**, railroad service may well provide the marketing attraction necessary for a successful sales effort.

Highway Access.   Easy access to a major highway is considered an essential factor in most decisions concerning an industry's location. An ideal site is one situated *between* a railroad and a major highway. Highway access must also be considered for employee commuters. In addition to railroads, almost all industries rely on trucks to transport goods into and out of their plants. Every industrial plant design includes provisions for loading docks to serve truck traffic. Smaller companies, lacking access to an adjoining railroad spur, often deliver their products by truck to a railroad siding, where the merchandise is transferred to a railroad car for shipment to the customer. The reverse process is used when goods are received.

Harbor Facilities.   Containerized cargos have revolutionized the way we ship goods and commodities; smaller units are placed into boxcar-like containers for more efficient handling. These containers are then transported by truck or rail to their destinations or to marshalling yards at major ports for transshipment overseas.

Despite the efficiency with which the railroad and trucking systems provide shipping facilities for manufacturing activities in this country, most of our major metropolitan cities have well-developed seaports. The only large metroplex in the nation without a seaport is Dallas–Fort Worth. The good harbor facilities found in the various river, gulf, Great Lake and ocean port cities are a reflection of the vast quantities of goods being transferred by water in national and international trade.

In keeping with the North American Free Trade Agreement (NAFTA) and the General Agreement on Taxes and Tariffs (GATT), trade with Mexico, Canada and the Pacific Rim countries is exploding. Port cities such as Tacoma and Seattle in Washington and Port Brownsville in Texas, to name a few, have been receiving increased attention because of their potential for growth due to this expanding base of world trade.

Water routes are used primarily by shippers of heavy and/or bulky items from materials-oriented industries. Internal waterways provide an inexpensive means for transporting sand, gravel, coal, ore and other cargo of this nature. Towed by tugs, fully laden barges of these raw materials are delivered to their users up and down the navigable rivers of this country. Storage areas are often constructed at strategic points on the periphery of a community, where the materials can be dumped from barges and held in anticipation of shipment inland by truck or rail.

Labor Supply

A feasibility study of an industrial development should include a careful analysis of both the quantity and the quality of the available labor supply. Whether an industry requires the extensive use of machines or an intensive use of workers, an available pool of potential employees, trained or trainable, is essential to its success.

In addition to the personnel needed for a **labor-intensive** industry, the strength of their unions is an important consideration in industrial location decisions. A brief glance at the burgeoning industrial South and the diminished industrial North is adequate to illustrate the movement of industrialists away from powerful labor unions. Of course, there is no way to escape the impact of unionization because workers tend to join together for mutual benefits, and unions continue to emerge in each new geographic location.

An interesting pattern of commuting habits evolves when the labor supply is analyzed in terms of white-collar and blue-collar workers. Many labor-intensive manufacturing enterprises are restricted to the outlying areas of a community. This situation requires blue-collar workers to travel from their homes, usually in the central city areas, out to the plants. At the same time, central city areas have evolved into financial, government and office centers that require the services of white-collar workers, who must travel from their suburban homes into the center of the city. This, of course, results in horrendous rush-hour traffic jams. A logical solution to this daily dilemma would be to revitalize the downtown areas with industrial parks and the outlying areas with office parks.

Lease Characteristics

An industrial lease usually takes one of two forms—gross or net. Both forms contain many of the provisions already discussed in residential, office and commercial property leases, including a description of the premises, lease term, rent, security deposit, use of premises and legal responsibilities and remedies of the parties. However, the conditions of an industrial lease involving taxes, insurance, maintenance responsibilities and other legal factors are highly individualized, and each lease must be negotiated specifically between the individual owners and tenants.

Mainly because of the high costs involved in establishing a manufacturing operation, most industrial leases are designed to run for long periods of time. As a result, these long-term leases are established on a fully net basis. Unlike a gross lease, in which the landlord pays the property taxes, insurance premiums and maintenance costs, the fully **net lease** requires the *tenant* to pay these expenses *in addition to* the basic rent. Thus, an owner of an industrial property is guaranteed an agreed-on return on the investment over the lease period.

Of course, there are innumerable variations on the basic gross and net leases. For example, a tenant may be required to pay only incremental property taxes and insurance premiums, with the landlord obligated to pay the costs for these items as they existed when the lease originated. A tenant may be required to contribute a specified sum to offset any increase in maintenance cost or be obligated to pay an escalating base rental amount as a result of the fluctuations of the consumer price index—one measurement of inflation over the lease period. Other variations can be designed to reflect the special relationships that exist between specific parties to an industrial lease.

As with most decisions to invest in real estate, competent legal advice should be sought in the preparation of the documents required in each industrial property transaction. Some thought should be given to the recording of leases with major tenants.

TYPES OF INDUSTRIAL INVESTMENTS

Industrial activities range from upholstering living room chairs to manufacturing air cargo planes and include the entire spectrum in between. The upholsterer can work in a room behind a retail furniture store; the plane manufacturer requires acres of space. Thus, large or small, industrial activities are usually housed in some form of improved real estate.

Industrial Parks

Currently, the most popular form of industrial property development is the *industrial park,* which offers many advantages to both industry and the community.

Industry benefits by having a choice of readily available sites at relatively reasonable costs. Operating economies, such as a common sewerage facility, can be realized, and amenities can be offered that will give the park a prestigious atmosphere. With properly designed subdivision restrictions, tenants and owners alike may enjoy protective covenants that enable them to control their environment and provide opportunities for them to interrelate.

An industrial park benefits a community because of its ability to attract new industries. As a result, the community can expand its economic and tax base, provide more efficient utilization of municipal services and exercise control over isolated industrial operations.

One form of industrial park is designed as a land-banking operation and is usually developed either by a railroad on land earmarked for large shippers or by a community-sponsored organization empowered to expand the industrial base. Raw acreage is subdivided into lots, improved with street and utility installations and offered for sale or lease. Often, an active campaign is mounted to entice manufacturers to move into the area from another community.

Another form of industrial park is developed by an individual owner-investor who offers a complete package of land and building to prospective buyers or tenants. The user can specify the design of the construction, usually a form tailored to specific needs, and the industrial park owner thus acts as a land banker, holding lots until they are needed.

In either case, an industrial park is a preplanned subdivision designed to satisfy the needs of industrial users and to provide the lot sizes, utilities, road installations and restrictions essential for an efficient and prestigious operation.

One basic rule for all industrial park developments is to provide as much flexibility as possible in the layout plan. This can be accomplished by effective block planning and stage development. Block designs should include parcels of differing dimensions that can be used separately or combined to satisfy special requirements. Stage development specifications restrict activities to one area at a time, preclude checkerboarding of the entire park by haphazard locational decisions and allow for flexibility in future development.

Restrictive covenants prepared by the developer are established to ensure compatibility among occupants and between the park and the community in which it is located. Again, flexibility is required to avoid any unreasonable impositions that might be unacceptable to potential occupants. Most restrictions prohibit any uses that might prove offensive, such as those generating excessive odors, smoke or noise. Some restrictions establish minimum site sizes, site coverage, building setbacks, designated parking and loading areas, outdoor storage limitations, landscaping responsibilities, construction design, sign control and other provisions peculiar to a specific park.

Besides planning homogeneous landscaping, the developer should weigh the value of providing restaurants and other amenities conducive to attracting tenants to larger parks. Some industrial developments include a clubhouse with sleeping facilities, as well as showers, saunas, swimming pool, gymnasium, exercise equipment and meeting rooms.

Tenants usually execute long-term net leases or purchase their own properties. In the latter case, the owners usually form an association similar to that of a condominium group to solve mutual problems. In a tenancy situation, as discussed previously, the terms of the net industrial lease usually require the tenants to assume responsibility for paying property taxes and insurance and for maintaining their individual properties.

Manufacturing Buildings

In addition to industrial parks, there are numerous free-standing industrial buildings housing all forms of manufacturing activity and located on individual plots of land in various areas of a community. A typical investment for the small limited partnership is an **incubator industrial building** of 5,000 to 25,000 square feet. Designed to house new companies during their start-up periods, these buildings are located on numerous available lots throughout a community. A variation on this theme is the **business park**, increasingly popular in the Southwest. These parks are patterned after the industrial park but include retail, office, manufacturing and storage facilities in one cohesive unit.

Historically, most manufacturing operations were located in the central area of a community, with housing developing along major streets in a radial pattern from these job nuclei. Many of these older manufacturing establishments, called **loft**

buildings, are currently obsolete, made so by technological improvements and the need for greater operating efficiency. A tall building housing a single manu- facturer and designed so that various operations are carried out on different floors causes vertical transportation problems that most manufacturers prefer to avoid. Currently, a one-story building that permits horizontal traffic flow is pre- ferred for most manufacturing operations.

The operational dictates of manufacturing therefore require large industrial plants to move to the periphery of communities where ample land is available at reasonable costs. This movement often results in the abandonment of many older buildings in central city areas. Depending on their physical condition, these buildings may be converted to other uses or destroyed in urban renewal projects.

Despite the general movement to the suburbs, some loft buildings continue to house the activities of manufacturers for whom moving would be unprofitable or who can still operate with relative efficiency in the old vertical manner. An example is the garment manufacturing industry, which continues its production in the old loft buildings of New York City. For the most part, however, the loft is becoming obsolete, and virtually no new buildings have been constructed in this style within the past two decades. The vacant spaces in many loft buildings have been filled by tenants who require inexpensive storage areas or unusually large office spaces at rents much lower than those available in competing office build- ings.

Warehouse Buildings

Throughout the country, there is a proliferation of **warehouse buildings** designed to provide enclosed storage facilities for goods and merchandise of all types and descriptions. Individuals and businesses alike use these warehouses to store goods for extended periods of time, as well as to facilitate the shipment of smaller lots of merchandise from a larger initial bulk quantity.

In addition to privately owned industrial warehouse buildings, the large ware- houses of major furniture-moving companies, such as Bekins and Mayflower, can be found in most American communities. These storage facilities are offered for rent to the general public, and customers may pick up and deliver their own goods or hire the transfer company for these services. The managers of these warehouses charge a fee for every entry to either add or remove goods held in storage.

The wide-span, open-bay design of these warehouse buildings allows most items to be placed into standard-sized containers, which are then stacked efficiently by forklift trucks, and the high ceilings allow maximum use of the interior ware- house space. Thus, rents are based on the number of cubic feet occupied by the goods and are imposed as a monthly charge.

Miniwarehouses.   A different system of short-term storage is the **miniware- house**, in which separate bins are rented by individuals who retain complete control during the term of tenancy. By affixing a lock to the storage bin door, the tenant of a miniwarehouse space may add or remove belongings as often as desired without incurring extra charges. The rent for these spaces is a fixed monthly rate, with the tenant responsible for pickup and delivery of the stored goods. The miniwarehouse management supervises the project during regular operating hours and provides 24-hour security in the form of custodians or guard dogs.

In some areas, these ministorage facilities are constructed as an interim use of the land until it can be developed more intensely.

Grain Elevators.   Generally located at convenient collection points along a railroad line, grain elevators cater to the needs of local farmers, who bring their harvested crops for storage. These elevators are usually designed to hold one type of grain at a time; because the produce is completely homogeneous, farmers receive warehouse receipts for the quantity of grain deposited. They are unable to identify their particular grain but are entitled to draw out a like amount whenever they choose.

The grain is stored in elevators to protect it from the elements and to accumulate an economically practical shipping load at acceptable prices. The elevator operator charges a fee for handling services as well as for storage costs, much like the industrial warehouser. Sometimes a number of investors, usually farmers, will join together in a cooperative to own their own grain elevator(s).

In some areas of the country, "county elevators" are constructed near the farmers, facilitating short hauls. The grain is then moved to larger, "terminal elevators," located at transportation centers on major rail lines or seaports. Here, the grain is tested, treated against pests, aerated and dried (when necessary) in order to maintain its quality. These larger elevators often contain more than one type of grain. There are a few elevators available for storage of products other than grain—for instance, sugar.

Conversions of Lofts and Warehouses

Old lofts and warehouses are currently regaining popularity with real estate investors. From abandoned lofts in downtown areas to older warehouses in the suburbs, innovative and economically successful conversions to other profitable uses are taking place. Not only is loft space being converted into low-cost offices, but downtown buildings are also being transformed into interesting and desirable apartments. High ceilings and huge rooms are effective marketing attractions for rentals and have led to remarkable success for this type of enterprise.

Depending on market demands, upper floors can be utilized for offices or apartments while the ground-floor space is converted into specialty restaurants and retail stores. The unfinished look of exposed bricks and pipes is blended into a counterculture decor that appeals to customers' sense of adventure. Some cities have had entire areas redeveloped into new and unusual uses that attract throngs of visitors. The Quay in Kansas City, Haymarket Square in downtown

Boston, Old Town in Omaha and much of downtown Cleveland are just a few of these rejuvenated areas.

At the same time, individual large old warehouse buildings are becoming community focal points after their conversion to other uses. Such remodeled structures may house spaghetti or steak houses, such as Denver's Larimer Square Spaghetti House, the Spaghetti Factory in downtown San Diego or the Spaghetti Warehouse restaurants throughout Texas. An old chocolate factory is the cornerstone of the famous Ghirardelli Square on the San Francisco Embarcadero, which houses numerous small shops and boutiques catering to the tastes of thousands of daily visitors. Other examples of successful conversions are the Trolley Square Shopping Center in Salt Lake City (once the stables and trolley barn for the old street transportation company) and the Jackson Brewery in New Orleans. Creative investment opportunities are available everywhere for the developer who remains alert.

Case 11.1:   **Industrial Park Development.**   A 40-acre parcel of land on the periphery of a community was purchased for use as an industrial park. The ground is flat, has good drainage, faces a paved county highway that leads to a freeway interchange within three miles and has access to a nearby railroad trunk line. The property is serviced by city water and sewage facilities, and natural gas and electric utilities are available.

The development plans include subdivision of the land into 40 light industrial sites, each with road and rail access, according to the illustration below.

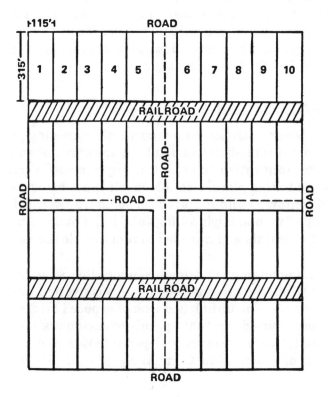

In addition to providing for the organization of a property owners' association, the developers have established a set of restrictions and regulations detailing setback requirements and controls on parking and property uses. The intent of the protective covenants is to:

- ensure that the park will be maintained as an attractive setting with landscaping, open areas and well-developed structures;
- protect the owners, lessees and subtenants against improper and undesirable use of the surrounding property;
- protect against the property's depreciation in value; and
- prevent haphazard and unharmonious improvements in the park.

The protective covenants require that all plans and specifications for new structures and other improvements be approved in writing by a committee of the owners' association. In addition, no building can be constructed closer than 30 feet to any lot line or road, and the association may require a ten-foot easement on all sides of each lot for the purpose of planting and maintaining trees, shrubs and bushes. Minimum standards must be observed regarding fences, building elevations, compatibility of accessory buildings, shielding of roof-mounted equipment and signs. The owners are also required to contribute to a fund for the maintenance of the roadways and landscaping. Finally, the restrictions provide for the developer to repurchase any tract at the same price paid for the property if, after two years, the buyer has not begun construction. This clause effectively prohibits parcels from being left idle or used for speculative purposes.

Financial Analysis. The 40-acre parcel was purchased for $20,000 per acre and the developer spent an additional $5,000 per acre for roads, railroad spurs, utility services and landscaping. A market study reveals that the 40 sites can probably be sold over a five-year period at an average price of $54,000 per lot. Sales costs are projected to include 10 percent for commissions and $104,000 for other costs, including interest, title searches and service fees. The developer anticipates a 25 percent average annual return on the total investment. The buyer made a $200,000 cash down payment and agreed to make $150,000 annual payments on the balance.

Analysis A: Annual Cash-on-Cash ROI

Item	Year 1	Year 2	Year 3	Year 4	Year 5
Cash payment	$200,000	$150,000	$150,000	$150,000	$ 150,000
Improvements	200,000				
Negative		32,000			
Total cash	400,000	582,000	732,000	882,000	1,032,000
Income	432,000	432,000	432,000	432,000	432,000
Expenses	64,000	64,000	64,000	64,000	64,000
Net income	368,000	368,000	368,000	368,000	368,000
Yields	(32,000)	218,000	218,000	218,000	218,000
+ Cash	400,000	582,000	732,000	882,000	1,032,000
C/C ROI	(8%)	37.46%	29.78%	24.72%	21.12%

Analysis B: IRR using HP-12C

1. Clear financial register, press ⬚ f   ⬚ REG

2. Keystroke 400000

3. Change sign, press ⬚ CHS

4. Enter into register, press ⬚ g   ⬚ CFo

5. Keystroke 218000, press ⬚ g   ⬚ CFj

6. Keystroke 4, press ⬚ g   ⬚ Nj

7. Keystroke 368000, press ⬚ g   ⬚ CFj

8. Press ⬚ f   for IRR = 49.64%

SUMMARY

This chapter examined the unique qualities and characteristics of industrial property as a form of real estate investment. The technical and legal expertise required to develop industrial property makes it one of the more complicated types of investment. In addition to satisfying the plant design and locational requirements of a potential tenant, the industrial property developer must also meet increasingly stringent environmental controls and other regulations of local government agencies

Despite the number of communities committed to no-growth policies, many cities are still actively seeking to attract new industry. These expanding communities establish industrial property development agencies, which are empowered to offer new employers subsidized plant locations and tax waivers to entice them to their cities.

Basically, the possibility of more economical operation is what attracts a firm to a new site. Suburban and rural locations provide inexpensive land for one-story construction but also present problems in securing utility connections and waste disposal services. Adequate transportation facilities and the quantity and quality of the labor supply also affect locational decisions. Finally, a knowledgeable potential tenant will analyze the community's tax base, zoning ordinances and political attitudes toward industry before making a move.

Many industrial buildings are designed as general-purpose structures with a wide range of alternative uses. These buildings provide an investor with flexibility for reuse if a tenant leaves, thus reducing risk. Special-purpose or single-purpose industrial structures designed for a specific firm require long-term leases from highly creditable tenants to offset an investor's risk. Generally, industrial real estate is considered nonliquid because of the many unique physical requirements for development.

In addition to the zoning, utilities and labor factors essential to develop industrial property, adequate transportation facilities must be readily accessible. Railroad spurs and sidings, as well as major highways, are usually prerequisites for a successful industrial investment. Often a railroad company will pay for the installation of a spur track to a new industrial tenant in anticipation of new shipping business. Just as often, an industrial park developer will have to pay for construction of a spur track into the subdivision to attract new tenants.

Most industrial leases are drawn for long time periods and are designed on the basis of net rents. A net lease requires that a tenant pay property taxes, insurance and maintenance costs in addition to a base rent. Thus, because the cost of these items is absorbed by the tenant over the term of the lease, the landlord's yield is preserved. Often an escalation clause is included in a long-term net industrial lease to offset the effects of inflation.

Industrial investments include industrial parks, manufacturing buildings, warehouse buildings and the conversion of old lofts and warehouses into new and profitable uses. Industrial parks are preplanned subdivisions that house all forms of commercial activities, including manufacturing, storage, distribution, sales, service, and research and development. One kind of park is designed only for the sale or lease of lots, whereas another may include a lot and a building in a package deal. In either case, the park generally is designed around a set of restrictive covenants that specify the types of uses allowed as well as the architecture of the buildings. Industrial park management is active at its inception and usually becomes passive once the park is established.

Old loft buildings are generally obsolete but are still being used to house the activities of businesses for whom moving would be unprofitable or for tenants who desire inexpensive bulk storage or office space. Warehouse buildings are designed to provide enclosed storage facilities for goods and merchandise for extended periods of time. Tenants pay for the use of space in these buildings by the cubic foot and must also pay a fee each time the goods are moved. Miniwarehouses, on the other hand, provide enclosed storage in the form of individual bins that remain under the complete control of the tenant during the term of occupancy.

Conversions of old lofts and warehouses into new uses such as restaurants, offices, apartments, low-income housing and shopping centers are a promising source of real estate investment opportunities.

EXERCISE 11   (Answers may be checked against the Answer Key.)

1. Modern industrial buildings are generally constructed as all of the following types *except*

    a. custom-designed, specialized facilities.
    b. multistoried, highrise structures.
    c. single-floor complexes in parklike environments.
    d. plants adjoining a railroad line and/or highway.

2. The demand for industrial space depends to a large degree on all of the following circumstances *except*

    a. the condition of the business cycle in the overall national economy.
    b. the supply of available and proposed industrial space.
    c. the number of new housing starts.
    d. local and regional economic conditions.

3. The growing popularity of industrial parks depends to a large extent on all of the following conditions *except*

    a. the trend toward one-story buildings on large sites.
    b. downtown traffic congestion and parking limitations.
    c. expansion and improvement of interstate highways.
    d. the economic difficulties of the nation's railroads.

4. An incubator industry is one that

    a. is being approached to come to a community.
    b. has been in one location for many years.
    c. is just beginning to be successful.
    d. has expanded to branches in other states.

5. From an industry's point of view, locating an industrial park include all of the following benefits *except*

    a. immediate site readiness.
    b. symbiosis with other firms in the park.
    c. operating economies.
    d. unrestricted site uses.

6. From a community's point of view, encouraging the development of an industrial park would include all of the following benefits *except*

    a. economic-base expansion.
    b. tax-base expansion.
    c. limiting urban sprawl.
    d. efficient use of municipal services.

7. A "beggar-thy-neighbor" policy would be exemplified by

    a. an upstream community dumping raw sewage into a river.
    b. one community setting less stringent air pollution standards than its neighbors'.
    c. two adjoining communities constructing a mutually beneficial urban renewal project.
    d. a community engaging in an active campaign to entice manufacturers from other communities to move into its area.

8. Industrial park restrictive covenants usually include all of the following items *except*

    a. specified lot sizes.
    b. prohibitions against incompatible lot uses.
    b. building setback requirements.
    d. construction design controls.

9. Revenue bonds issued to develop industrial properties are repaid from

    a. taxes imposed on local property owners.
    b. incremental taxes earned from increased values.
    c. rents charged new industrial tenants.
    d. inventory taxes charged to new tenants.

10. Functional obsolescence is most clearly defined as the

    a. costs of removing hazardous wastes.
    b. outmoded condition of a building.
    c. obsolete design of a building.
    d. equipment deterioration.

DISCUSSION

1. Determine what, if anything, is being done in your community to entice new industry to locate there.

2. Research the economic results of the multiplier effect of a new industry coming to your town. Estimate how it would affect your community if the new enterprise hires 500 people.

12
Special Real Estate Investments

Key Terms

air rights
congregant living centers
discount
face value
Federal Home Loan Mortgage
    Corporation (FHLMC)
Federal National Mortgage
    Association (FNMA)
franchising
Government National Mortgage
    Association (GNMA)
junior loan

life care
mineral rights
modular homes
property tax liens
Real Estate Mortgage Investment
    Conduits (REMICs)
repossessions
royalty income
secondary market
strips
tranches

In addition to the more traditional forms of real estate investment—land, houses, apartments, offices, commercial properties and industrial developments—there are numerous opportunities to participate in profitable ventures in specialized real estate. This category includes mobile-home parks, motels, amusement parks and golf courses. Other alternate forms of real estate investment are franchises, minerals, air rights and real estate securities. This chapter examines these and other diverse opportunities.

MOBILE-HOME PARKS

An important category in real estate investment is the development of land for mobile-home parks, both for rental and for sale. Renting a space in a park is similar to renting an apartment, whereas purchasing a condominium mobile-home lot is like purchasing a residential lot in a subdivision.

The successful development of mobile-home parks, both as rentals and as condominiums, is attracting investors to this form of realty venture. Their growing interest is based on three interrelated phenomena—a dramatic increase in the costs of constructing more traditional housing, our population's increasing longevity and the effective vesting of numerous pension and retirement programs. Mobile homes appeal to people who cannot afford the costs of more traditional housing, as well as to a large segment of retired people attracted by the amenities that the various parks provide. In many cases, the receipt of both pension and social security benefits allows retirees to move to warm-weather states, where mobile-home parks are found in abundance.

Also known as "manufactured homes," mobiles were first regarded as minimal-quality housing. Since 1976, this type of housing has been regulated by the Department of Housing and Urban Development under the Manufactured Home Construction and Safety Code. The standards in the code are similar to those established for site-built housing and, as a result, manufactured homes have become not only more durable and safer but also more attractive. Modern manufactured housing is often entirely compatible with site-built housing and may well be the most affordable type of housing on the market today.

In some cases, the establishment of a mobile-home park is a strategic use of land while the owner waits for development to move into the area. It may also be an answer to a shortage of affordable homes, providing a viable alternative for low-income and moderate-income occupants. The cost of housing in a mobile-home park is frequently 20 to 30 percent less than the cost of conventional housing elsewhere in a community.

The word *mobile,* when applied to this type of housing, is misleading. Aside from travel trailers, most factory-built homes are far from mobile. In fact, units may be single-wide (12' by 60'), double-wide (24' by 60') or even triple-wide (36' by 60') and require the services of professional movers to transport and place them on a lot. When affixed to their concrete pads, these homes become permanent and are considered real estate and not personal property.

Location and Design

The land for mobile-home parks is invariably located in relatively isolated areas of a community because this form of real estate development has not generally been accepted by either land planners or owners of more traditional housing. In many communities, mobile-home parks are considered to be undesirable developments, a stigma traceable to the growth of a myriad of "trailer parks" after World War II. These trailer parks were jammed with up to 20 units per acre, and they became havens for transients. They developed into slum-like environments detrimental to the values of surrounding properties. With the advent of the modern, well-landscaped, preplanned mobile-home park, featuring only seven to ten units per acre, this negativism is largely being overcome in a growing number of communities.

Because many parks are located on outlying parcels of land, the initial outlay of funds required for site acquisition may be relatively small. However, improving this property with roads, utilities, concrete pads and amenities is a costly investment, much of which can be financed through local banks or savings institutions.

The FHA also provides special mortgage insurance for mobile-home park financing.

The design of a mobile-home park can follow a horizontal grid pattern, a herringbone layout or a series of concentric circles or half circles around a centrally located clubhouse, as shown in the illustration. The grid pattern places the units in a horizontal position, with each pad parallel to all others. A more efficient design is the placement of units at an angle to the street, herringbone style, which allows the homes to be more easily maneuvered in and out of position.

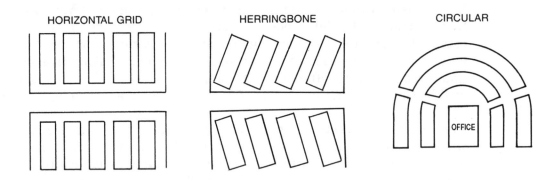

HORIZONTAL GRID   HERRINGBONE   CIRCULAR

Adapted from Steve Shenitzer Development Co., Tucson, Ariz.

Most new parks provide occupants with special amenities, including swimming pools, clubhouses, tennis and shuffleboard courts, laundry rooms and storage facilities. Many modern parks also include a separate parking area for travel trailers and other recreational vehicles. Apparently, mobile-home owners have a tendency to acquire additional, truly mobile units.

Spaces for Rent

The rent for spaces in mobile-home parks can run from $75 to $400 per month, depending on the size of the unit and the amenities included in the project. Some parks require leases for specific terms; others operate on a month-to-month basis. The tenant is usually responsible for moving the unit into place and setting it up. Most quality parks insist that the unit be skirted to hide the wheels and undercarriage and that a front patio and cabana be installed as a condition of the lease. These improvements are attractive in themselves and are required to create an atmosphere of unity and permanence in the park.

The financial success of a rental park is largely a function of the managerial skills of the owner or manager. The availability of well-planned social activities and the constant maintenance and cleanliness of a park often determine whether it suffers chronic vacancies or enjoys full occupancy. Some parks are so popular that they maintain a list of potential tenants waiting to move in as soon as a vacancy occurs.

The profitability of a rental park is based on the same variables that exist in other improved-property investments. However, the deductions for depreciation are limited to the improvements made to the land: utility installations, concrete pads, the clubhouse, laundry rooms and storage buildings. When compared for tax purposes to other improved income property, the lack of depreciation shelter, plus the high degree of personal involvement required in management, inhibits investment in this form of real estate. In effect, a rental park is a business venture, in addition to being a real estate investment.

When rental spaces are in short supply in a particular community, local mobile-home dealers sometimes develop new parks to provide unit spaces for customers. Occasionally, dealers enter into joint ventures with landowners for such purposes.

Sometimes rental-park owners have the opportunity to acquire ownership of mobile units from tenants who wish to dispose of their holdings or from executors of the estates of deceased owners. These units can be rented by the park owner, and the income can be sheltered by allowable depreciation deductions.

Spaces for Sale

Another approach to mobile-home park development is the sale of individual lots to mobile-home owners. This is an increasingly popular application of the condominium concept, in which a buyer secures a deed to a lot plus an undivided interest in the common areas. The lot is described in legal terms and is an identifiable portion of land lying within the park area. The common property includes the roadways, clubhouse and amenities.

After acquiring a suitable site, a developer subdivides the land into a prescribed number of lots according to an officially approved plan. These lots—fully improved with concrete pads, sewer and water connections, and other utilities—are then sold to individual owners. The development includes a set of bylaws that call for the establishment of an association of lot owners to manage the common areas and to enforce the covenants, conditions and restrictions of the park.

Mobile-home dealers engage in condominium park developments and sell package deals that include both lot and unit for one price under a single financial arrangement. A report titled "Mobile Home Park Development and Operations" is available from the Real Estate Center, Texas A & M University, College Station, TX 77843-2115.

Modular Homes

The pattern of developments for **modular homes**, also known as prefabs or manufactured homes, resembles that of the mobile-home parks. Developments for this type of housing are currently under construction in the states of Washington and Oregon. These subdivisions are designed much like those for stick-built or brick-built homes, but move-in-and-assemble premanufactured homes generally require smaller lots.

DIVERSE REALTY INVESTMENTS

As in the case of ownership of a mobile-home rental park, it is often difficult to distinguish between real estate as an investment and real estate as a business venture. A clear delineation exists when one person owns the real estate and another operates a business on the property. Here, the real estate is clearly its owner's investment, and the business owner pays rent. However, there are diverse investments that involve real estate as a part of the business itself—for example, motels, amusement parks and golf courses.

Motels

The hospitality industry has many categories of development, including luxury vacation properties such as Club Med, convention hotels, interstate motels, airport-oriented properties, economy motels, micro motels, suite hotels and specialty resorts, among others.

The motel industry has emerged as a result of our mobile society's demands for convenient temporary housing along the nation's major highways. Development of land for motel construction is considered a real estate investment, and the operation of the motel itself is a business venture. When the operator of a motel also owns the real estate, the charges for mortgage interest, property taxes, insurance premiums, maintenance costs and depreciation become deductible expenses on the operating statements of the business, and the income from the operations is considered active.

There are three general types of motels: city, highway and recreational resort.

The City Motel.   Constructed as highrise towers in the centers of major communities, city motels provide many of the services of a hotel, in addition to on-site parking. The success and popularity of motels, as compared to hotels, is generally attributable to privacy of access, ease of parking and informality of atmosphere. In addition, most newer city motels offer relatively luxurious accommodations at costs below those charged at comparable hotels. The city motel primarily caters to businesspeople dealing with centrally located clients and to travelers visiting for more than one night.

The Highway Motel.   Highway motels are located close to travel routes and offer drivers both comfortable and convenient accommodations at reasonable rates. Easy roadway accessibility and clear visibility to travelers are basic requirements for this type of investment. Motels located near airports are included in this category. Both highway and airport motels generally serve the traveler who is remaining in the area for just one or two days.

The Recreational Resort Motel.   The distinctive quality of a resort motel is the design of its accommodations. Customers in these establishments generally stay for longer periods of time than do customers of city or highway motels. Guests at resort motels generally occupy their rooms from three days to three weeks or longer. Therefore, these motels often provide kitchen facilities as well as suites of rooms to create an apartment atmosphere.

Resort motels range from the small *Ma and Pa* enterprises located along the eastern and western seaboards and on inland lakes to the luxury chalets and highrise complexes of the ski and island resort areas. Regardless of size, each resort motel manager seeks tenants for protracted visits, and many provide entertainment and amenities to attract them.

An inherent hazard in resort motel investment is the cyclical nature of the market. Most resorts enjoy peak seasonal occupancies followed by high-vacancy off-season periods. Rental rates fluctuate accordingly, and the owner of a resort motel must be prepared for these dramatic changes in cash flows. A variation of the resort motel is the "bed and breakfast" inns found in many resort areas.

A fourth category of motels, found in increasing numbers in metropolitan areas, is the combination city motel-convention center. An example of this concept is the Town and Country Motel-Hotel in San Diego, California, designed to attract conventioneers and house them on the premises.

Amusement Parks

The amusement park is also enjoying popularity as a real estate investment throughout the country. Based on the continuing successes of Disneyland and Knotts Berry Farm in the Los Angeles area, theme amusement parks have emerged in all parts of the nation. Just a few examples of these enterprises are Disney World and EPCOT Center in Florida; the three Sea Worlds; Silver Dollar City; Worlds of Fun; the Marine Worlds; Six Flags over Texas; Astroworld; Cedar Point in Ohio.

An amusement park development requires a high level of technical expertise, beginning with the choice of its theme and continuing through the design and construction of its various attractions. Many larger parks incorporate peripheral complementary real estate developments into their overall designs. Often hotels, motels, shopping centers, restaurants and, occasionally, houses and apartments are made part of the park development.

Golf Courses

Although golf courses as business enterprises are sometimes located in isolated areas, they are more often developed as an integral part of a centrally located municipal park or new subdivision. A number of golf courses are designed as private clubs, with membership and greens fees providing the cash flows necessary for financial success.

The construction of a golf course is a complicated, highly technical undertaking. The success of such a project is largely a function of its location, site suitability and challenging layout. Most large courses are designed by professional golfers, who act as consultants to the developers.

The acreage needed for a golf course is determined to a great extent by what type of course is planned. Normally, 120 to 180 acres of gently rolling land are considered adequate for a regulation 18-hole course, while approximately 70 acres are needed for a nine-hole course. Par-3 courses can be constructed on 30 to 45 acres if the fairways are designed in parallel.

Although the costs of constructing a golf course vary greatly, they are generally estimated at an average of $50,000 to $75,000 per hole, depending on the terrain and natural setting. This cost includes the price of the land, its preparation, the installation of fairways, greens and sprinkler systems and the acquisition of necessary equipment. Course maintenance costs have been rising dramatically in the past few years and are estimated to approach $5,000 per hole per year, including capital expenses and costs of watering.

Housing for the Elderly

A special form of new community is designed to cater to the growing retirement market. These real estate developments stress recreation, shopping convenience, comfort, minimum maintenance and a high degree of security. Private investors usually organize as limited partners to manage the diversified types of developments involved in these villages. Blended into a well-planned unity, retirement developments include single-family dwellings, condominiums, garden apartments, town houses, shopping centers and recreational areas. Some larger projects include golf courses, swimming pools, clubhouses, hobby shops, congregate care centers, medical clinics, convalescent centers and nursing homes.

The most successful of these specialized communities include the Sun City projects of the Del Webb Corporation and the Leisure World developments of the Rossmoor Corporation. Sun Cities are located near Phoenix and Tucson, Arizona; Bakersfield, California; and Tampa, Florida. Leisure Worlds are located near Seal Beach and Laguna Hills in southern California; Walnut Creek near San Francisco; Olney, Maryland; and Princeton, New Jersey. Special mention should be made of the Rio Grande Valley Retirement Community in Texas, a leader in this category.

A special form of housing for the elderly is emerging as an important investment alternative. Although "old-age" or "rest" homes have been developed in the past, the current vogue is to construct an apartment-hotel complex with a health care center nearby but separate. Patterned after "life care" centers, where tenants made a large single payment and were promised continual care for the rest of their lives, these new retirement **congregant living centers** provide all of the required services but on a monthly charge basis.

Because of the increase in the life spans of those who entered the one-payment life care facilities, many projects went bankrupt, unable to continue to care for residents. Now, rental rates have been made adjustable to meet current costs, and residents who need the more intensive care of a nursing home are required to pay their own way. New projects designed to serve the increasing numbers of elderly persons are being developed at a fast pace throughout the country.

Medical Buildings

Specialization has long been the custom within the medical profession, but specialization of facilities for doctors' offices has not kept pace with the need. Private investors may now participate in providing real estate facilities for medical practitioners under FHA Title XI (mortgage insurance for constructing or rehabilitating group-medical-practice buildings) and Title XV (mortgage insurance for new or rehabilitated hospitals owned by nonprofit organizations). Doctors generally prefer locations close to major medical facilities in buildings that can provide complementary, as well as peripheral, medical services.

Successful medical developments require proper consideration of doctors' unique needs. Proper planning includes constant consultation with architects and the doctors themselves on how best to design the complex. Large, multidoctor facilities produce maximum tenant interest and better utilization of the land. The larger projects offer a greater potential patient-referral system, based on a proper mix of tenants as well as on such auxiliary facilities as a pharmacy and a clinical pathology lab.

Repossessions and Property Tax Liens

There are numerous opportunities for real estate investments through the acquisition of property from **repossessions**, which occur most frequently as a result of default on mortgage payments and less frequently from the nonpayment of property taxes, income tax liens and other obligations.

In seeking out leads to these opportunities, investors usually contact the various local banks and savings and loan associations, as well as community lawyers. Perusal of the local newspapers can also alert readers to foreclosures and tax delinquencies.

The market for repossessions took a dramatic turn in the late 1980s and early 1990s. It grew from a relatively small portion of the real estate market, including the occasional foreclosed property, to the many thousands of properties offered for sale by the Resolution Trust Corporation (RTC) in its efforts to dispose of the defaulted assets of defunct savings associations. Activities in the repossession market became the main game in many towns of in the United States for a few years. Now the RTC's portfolio of property has diminished substantially, and with an improved economy, it probably will be phased out over the next few years.

The RTC was created in 1989 to help the government dispose of the assets of the bankrupt thrift institutions. Its national office is located at 801 Seventeenth Street NW, Washington, DC 20429. Four regional offices in Atlanta, Kansas City (Missouri), Dallas and Denver have been opened, in addition to various local offices.

Careful consideration should be given to the legal ramifications of acquiring good title to these properties. The services of a knowledgeable real estate attorney and/or title company are strongly recommended.

There are thousands of owners who, for one reason or another, do not pay their property taxes on time. After a year, these unpaid taxes become liens of the highest priority against the property itself. These **property tax liens** come before any existing loans or other liens, even IRS liens.

In most county jurisdictions, property tax liens are auctioned to investors, who buy them for the interest they pay. For example, in Pima County, Arizona, tax liens incur a penalty interest rate of 16 percent after one year's delinquency. They are then auctioned to the bidder who will bid the *least* amount of interest under 16 percent. If a successful bidder offers 10 percent, which is the lowest amount bid, the county continues to charge 16 percent, but pays the bidder the 10 percent when the taxes are redeemed, keeping the difference for the county. Most bids are made at the full 16 percent.

The property owner has three years to redeem the property, after which the successful bidder can perfect ownership in the property by filing a foreclosure. This rarely occurs, because most owners do not want to lose their property. Property tax liens, which may be handled differently in other parts of the country, offer another investment opportunity.

ALTERNATE INVESTMENT OPPORTUNITIES

A number of investments that are not classified as real estate per se are definitely real estate–oriented. These alternate investment opportunities include franchises, mineral and air rights and dealing in real estate securities.

Franchises

Franchising has become such an integral part of our economy that it is difficult to recall a time when this type of cooperative business arrangement did not exist.

Real estate investors often negotiate with franchise owners when arranging leases. A franchise is created when a franchisor grants to a franchisee an exclusive right to engage in the distribution of services or goods under a prescribed marketing plan or system. The operation of the business then follows this plan, using the franchisor's trademark and designated operating format to provide uniformity among all franchise members. Among the many nationally known franchises are McDonald's, Kentucky Fried Chicken, U-Haul, Midas mufflers and Orkin.

Although some franchise operators prefer to purchase land and develop their own buildings, others prefer to be tenants. A lease for property designed to house a franchise operation is usually a three-party agreement among the landlord, the franchisee and the franchisor. The building frequently has an easily recognized architectural design and is built from plans provided by the franchisor. Many of these buildings are designed for a single purpose; therefore, to offset the risks involved, a developer usually requests a lease that generates enough rental cash flow not only to yield a required return on the investment but also to return the developer's entire cash outlay during the initial lease period. Any renewals can be negotiated at rents appropriate to the market, depending on specific circumstances.

Mineral Rights

In this country, an owner of real property is legally entitled to control the minerals, natural gas, oil and water that lie below the surface of the land. Once minerals are removed from the ground, they assume the quality of personal property and can be sold separately from the real estate itself. Because minerals, natural gas and oil have value, whenever the existence of a substantial quantity of any of these commodities is discovered in a specific location, a market develops for their exploitation. Dealers in **mineral rights** are very active in some areas of the country, such as Arizona, California, New Mexico, Montana, Oklahoma, Texas and Wyoming, where some land is purchased and sold primarily on the basis of its mineral content.

Often, owners of mineral-bearing lands retain the rights to these minerals when they dispose of the real estate. This allows them to sell or lease their mineral rights to others engaged in the mining business. Generally, the retention (also known as the *reservation*) of mineral rights is accompanied by some specified surface access for their removal. Without the opportunity to enter the surface of a property for direct vertical excavation or drilling, the owner or lessee of the mineral rights may be forced to arrange for vertical descent on an adjoining property and then make a lateral underground approach to the minerals.

Owners of mineral rights receive income in one of three ways—by selling or leasing their rights or by selling the minerals themselves. Selling the rights yields a one-time payment, whereas leasing the mineral rights provides **royalty income**, which may continue for the term of the lease. For example, the owner of oil rights might receive a royalty per barrel of oil extracted, and the owner of copper rights might receive a royalty per pound of refined ore over the duration of the excavator's lease.

Investors are attracted to mineral exploration for the tax shelter it offers. Operating expenses for mining activities, as well as generous depletion allowances, have been preserved under TRA '86.

Air Rights

Although dealing in **air rights** has hitherto been unheard of in many parts of this country, as the cost of urban land continues to rise, the air is becoming a new arena for real estate investments. The sale or lease of air rights offers an investor a vastly expanded opportunity for constructing highrise buildings on strategically located sites in central city areas.

The use of the airspace over a specific property often implies the presence of an existing building or other improvements, such as roadways or railroad tracks. Thus, any contract involving the construction of a new building into the air requires an agreement with the base-property owner concerning the surface area to which the edifice will be affixed.

Some developments are anchored by huge columns that straddle the existing building and support a platform on which the new construction is erected. Other buildings are constructed on a platform supported by a central core, much like a golf tee. This core is constructed in the center of the existing building with access to the street through a hallway. The core contains the utilities and elevators that serve the offices or apartments built in the airspace above.

Other uses of airspace include the construction of buildings over roadways, in which the streets actually become tunnels through these structures. Properties developed over Riverside Drive in New York City illustrate this technique. The Merchandise Mart in Chicago is an example of a building constructed over railroad tracks.

Airspace can sometimes be a vital part of a real estate investment that depends for its success on an ongoing, uninterrupted view of a lake or ocean, because the rents are a function of this view. Owners of such properties might be well-advised to ensure this view by either purchasing or leasing the airspace over adjoining properties that might be utilized for other buildings. A case in point is the Lake Point Tower in Chicago, which was constructed near, but not quite at, the very end of a strip of land extending into Lake Michigan. Developers purchased the tip of the land and erected a high-rise building that effectively blocked the view from the existing structure.

Real Estate Securities

Although not technically real estate investors in the truest sense of the word, dealers in real estate securities involving senior and junior (second and third) mortgages are actively participating in the market by providing the funds necessary to complete most realty transactions. Lenders who originate most of the senior mortgage loans often sell these securities in the **secondary market** through the services of the **Federal National Mortgage Association (FNMA), Government National Mortgage Association (GNMA)** and **Federal Home Loan Mortgage Corporation (FHLMC).**

Dealing in real estate securities offers an investor a viable alternative to the responsibilities that accompany the more active management role associated with traditional real estate investments. A lender assumes a passive role in the operations of a realty venture but still participates as a sort of partner, collecting a portion of the profits in the form of interest. Even more attractive to those who enter this field, the payments do not stop until the loan is repaid, despite the fluctuations of the marketplace. Thus, a lender can anticipate receiving a steady income stream in the future, an income that develops a return on the investment commensurate with the risk involved. And if the borrower does not fulfill the contractual obligations, the property that is the collateral for the loan reverts to the lender.

Junior Securities.   In addition to the activities of the secondary mortgage market in dealing with the purchase and sale of senior mortgages, there is a growing demand to use money for trading in junior real estate securities. Because of the rising cost of land and the expenses connected with its preparation, as well as increasing construction costs and the climbing prices for used properties, a second or third mortgage or a land contract is often the only way a property can be financed. Generally, the seller ends up carrying back a **junior loan** to facilitate the sale of the property.

By its very nature, junior finance is a relatively high-risk investment. *Junior* means second in priority behind an existing first mortgage lien; thus, there is a greater risk of loss in the event of a default. In a foreclosure, the senior mortgagee is paid first, and then the junior lienholders receive their payments from any excess funds secured at the property's auction.

However, junior financing instruments can be made more secure. Junior lenders often insist on the inclusion of a "cross defaulting" clause in their contracts, whereby the senior lender will inform the junior lenders of an impending foreclosure and allow them to pick up the payments. Wraparound contracts can be established, with payments routed through a collection agency or a trustee to ensure the loan's close supervision. Property subject to a contract for deed can be placed into a trust, eliminating all of the inherent risks.

Generally, returns required for junior loans are secured by contracted interest rates, substantial placement fees or discounting.

Discounting.   Discounting raises the yield of a receivable for its buyer without affecting the terms of the loan contract. When a real estate loan, senior or junior, is originated at 9 percent nominal (contracted) interest and is sold to a securities dealer for its **face value**, the purchaser earns a true 9 percent return on the investment. If, however, the current market interest rate is lower than 9 percent, the contract will be sold at a *premium*—an amount higher than its face value—which has the effect of reducing the yield to more closely reflect the current market conditions.

More commonly, however, a mortgage is sold at a **discount**—an amount less than its face value— to *raise* the yield for its purchaser. The amount of the discount is a function of the mortgage buyer's yield requirements, the contract's interest rate and the term of the loan.

EXAMPLE: Examine a mortgage for $10,000 with interest-only payments at the rate of 9 percent per year, due in full in five years. A securities purchaser who requires a 12 percent return on the investment will pay exactly $8,918.57 for this contract.

$ 900.00	Annual Interest-Only Payment
× 3.604776	Factor for PWA @ 12%, 5 Years
$3,244.29	Present Worth of Annuity
$10,000.00	Reversion at End of 5 Years
× 0.567427	Factor for PW of $1 @ 12%, 5 years
5,674.27	Present Worth of Reversion
+ 3,244.29	Present Worth of Annuity
$ 8,918.57	Present Worth of Contract (rounded)

This answer can also be derived with the use of an HP-12C:

USING THE HP-12C

1. Clear financial register, press   [f]   [FIN]

2. Keystroke 10000, press   [FV]

3. Keystroke 900, press   [PMT]

4. Keystroke 5, press   [n]

5. Keystroke 12, press   [i]

6. Press   [PV] = −$8,918.57

Note: The negative answer indicates an outlay of $8,918.57 now to receive $900 per year for five years and a balloon payment of $10,000 at the end of the fifth year to earn 12 percent annual ROI.

Real Estate Mortgage Investment Conduits (REMICs)

Created by TRA '86, **Real Estate Mortgage Investment Conduits (REMICs)** are an ownership entity that can hold mortgages and issue multiple classes of ownership interests in the form of pass-through certificates, bonds or other securities. The overall goal of this entity was to simplify the structure of the secondary mortgage market. Even more important, however, the *income* from a REMIC is considered passive rather than portfolio. Thus, it may be used to offset passive *losses*.

Under a REMIC, mortgages are pooled in various categories called **tranches** and sold to investors requiring specific yields for specific risks. For example, one tranche may include only fixed-rate loans; another only variable-rate loans. One may pool only long-term loans and another only short-term loans.

All of the tranches offer pass-through services, in which interest-only, principal-only or a combination of both is passed through to the holder of the securities. Various arrangements can be made with receipts as well. For instance, payments can be passed through as they are received, or they can be paid on a guaranteed basis, whether the REMIC receives them or not. The prices of the tranches reflect the risks and yields expected.

The most recent innovations in this program are interest-only and principal-only (IO/PO) **strips**. Strips can be either highly speculative or act as a hedging vehicle, depending on when the loans in the pool are paid in full. IO strips *decrease* in value when interest rates fall and refinancing induces accelerated prepayments of existing loans. Thus, the holders will receive less interest. However, PO strips will *increase* in value under these same circumstances, because their holders will receive principal payments at a faster rate. In the event of rising interest rates, the reverse is true.

SUMMARY

This final chapter examined the opportunities for private investment in mobile-home parks and such diverse realty projects as motels, amusement parks and golf courses, as well as alternate ventures into franchises, minerals, air rights and mortgage securities. All of these investments are somewhat removed from the more standard real estate opportunities and, as a result, require special skills and knowledge to ensure success.

The successful development of mobile-home parks, both as rentals and as condominiums, is attracting investors to this form of realty venture. Mobile homes and other factory-built housing appeal to a growing segment of the American population because of increased costs in more standard housing, increased life expectancies and the effective vesting of many pension and retirement funds. Despite its increasing importance, many community planners frown on this form of property development because of the notion that a trailer park is detrimental to property values and places undue strain on city services. As a result, many new mobile-home parks are relegated to less than choice locations.

Despite this handicap, most modern mobile-home parks are designed to provide a comfortable and secure residential environment, and some parks offer relatively luxurious accommodations at reasonable rates. These parks include such amenities as swimming pools, clubhouses, meeting rooms, organized social activities and other provisions for tenant comfort and entertainment. Tenants in these modern parks are often required to install skirts around their mobile homes and to erect patios and cabanas to meet the terms of their leases.

Another approach to a profitable land-development program is to construct a modern mobile-home park and sell the spaces to individual owners in a condominium format. The mobile-home owners join in an association for their mutual benefit, much as they do in condominium apartment developments.

Motels, theme amusement parks and golf courses may be considered businesses as well as realty investments. As a result, the land involved is very much a part of the business activity. City, highway and recreational resort motels serve travelers' needs for short-term housing accommodations. The investment opportunities in this form of real estate run the entire gamut, from small Ma and Pa operations to luxurious resorts. Amusement parks are specialized investments that require high levels of technical and managerial skill to ensure success. These same requirements are essential to any golf course investment if it is to succeed.

Many real estate investors deal with franchises when leasing property for the operation of their special businesses. Franchises are designed to direct the operation of a business so that it follows a prescribed marketing plan under a recognized trade name and property design.

Trading in mineral rights often results in substantial royalties on precious minerals, natural gas and oil removed from under the land. Some investors deal only in buying and selling the rights to minerals and never actually become involved in the excavation or drilling process themselves.

A relatively new market in air rights is emerging in this country as a result of the increasing costs of urban land. As a result, the sale or lease of air rights offers an investor expanded opportunities. Dealers in air rights must make arrangements to control a portion of the surface if they anticipate constructing a building.

Dealing in mortgage securities offers an investor a viable alternative to the responsibilities that accompany the ownership of real estate. In effect, a mortgagee is, to a limited extent, a partner with the owner of the property and collects a portion of the profits in the form of interest on the loan, despite the fluctuations of the marketplace.

Real estate mortgages are created by both large and small lenders and the securities they originate are often sold in the market. Senior loans are traded in the secondary market through the FNMA, GNMA and FHLMC. Junior loans are sold to securities buyers, who normally require discounts to enhance their yields. Thus, a mortgage is sold for some amount less than its face value to raise its buyer's effective return on the investment.

EXERCISE 12   (Answers may be checked against the Answer Key.)

1. When you own your own space in a mobile-home park, you are in a/an

    a. cooperative.
    b. condominium.
    c. rental park.
    d. RV park.

2. Depreciation deductions in a mobile-home park that leases vacant spaces can be taken on all of the following items *except*

    a. concrete pads.
    b. tenants' mobile homes.
    c. the recreation center.
    d. blacktop roads.

3. Which relationship is *not* described accurately?

    a. City motel—highrise with hotel services
    b. Airport motel—highrise, entertainment, long stays
    c. Recreational resort motel—apartment atmosphere, long stays
    d. Highway motel—easy freeway access, short stays

4. Knotts Berry Farm, Silver Dollar City and Six Flags are

    a. new communities.
    b. theme amusement parks.
    c. recreational condominiums.
    d. urban renewal projects.

5. The retention of mineral rights in a parcel of land is known as a/an

    a. agglomeration.
    b. amalgamation.
    c. reservation.
    d. restriction.

Answer the next two questions using the table below:

Annual Compound Interest @ 12 Percent		
Period	PW$1	PWA $1
1	.8928	.8928
2	.7972	1.6900
3	.7118	2.4018
4	.6355	3.0373
5	.5674	3.6048

6. What will a 12 percent investor pay for a new, 8 percent, four-year, $5,000 interest-only second mortgage? (Answers are rounded.)

    a. $4,200
    b. $4,392
    c. $4,460
    d. $5,000

7. What will a 12 percent investor pay for a two-year-old, 8 percent, five-year, $5,000 interest-only second mortgage? (Answers are rounded.)

    a. $4,375
    b. $4,519
    c. $4,400
    d. $5,000

8. All of the following types of housing are designed specifically for the elderly *except* a/an

    a. congregate care center.
    b. assisted living project.
    c. life care center.
    d. low-cost rental.

9. Investors in property tax liens mainly earn profits from the

    a. interest charged on the liens.
    b. rents from the properties.
    c. sale of the properties after foreclosure.
    d. sale of the liens at discounts.

10. Strips and tranches are part of which of the following alternatives to real estate investment?

    a. FSLIC
    b. Mineral rights
    c. REMICs
    d. Repossessions

DISCUSSION

1. Discuss the desirability and location of new mobile-home rental and sales parks with the planning and zoning officials in your area. Did you discern any prejudice in their remarks and, if so, do you think the prejudice is valid?

2. Examine the deed to your property (or any property). Are your mineral rights reserved by the government or by a private individual?

Glossary

absolute fee simple title (fee simple) A title that is unqualified; the best title one can obtain; conveys the highest bundle of rights.

abstract of title A condensed history of the title to a property, consisting of a summary of the original grant and all subsequent conveyances and encumbrances relating to the particular parcel of real estate.

accelerated depreciation A method for calculating depreciation that allows larger deductions to be made in the early years of the economic life of an improvement, with a decrease in deductions in later years. Not available for real estate purchased after January 1, 1987.

acceleration clause The clause in a mortgage or trust deed that stipulates that the entire debt is due immediately if the borrower defaults under the terms of the contract.

active income Income acquired in the pursuit of a taxpayer's main occupation.

add-on interest A method of computing interest whereby interest is charged on the entire principal amount for the specified term, regardless of any periodic repayments of principal that are made.

agglomeration Gathering in one ownership properties that belong to a number of owners.

agreement of sale *See* contract for deed.

air rights The right to use the open space above a property. Generally the surface is used for another purpose.

alienation clause *See* due-on-sale clause.

all-inclusive income Another name for a wraparound loan.

all-inclusive trust deed *See* wraparound encumbrance.

allodial system Land ownership free and clear of any rent or service due the government; the basis of real property law in the United States.

alternative minimum tax Required if its application to the taxpayer's special preference items exceeds the regular tax amount.

amortization The systematic repayment of a loan by periodic installments of principal and interest over the entire term of the loan agreement.

anchoring tenant The major department store in a shopping center.

ancillary probate Process of settling an estate when property is located in a state other than the deceased's main residence.

annual percentage rate (APR) The effective or actual interest rate, which may be higher or lower than the nominal or contract interest rate because it includes loan closing costs.

annuity A series of regular income payments or receipts over a period of years.

anticipation, principle of An appraisal principle that states that the selling price of property is affected by the expectation of its future higher or lower value.

appraisal An estimate of the quantity, quality or value of something. An appraisal of real property value is based on a comparison of real estate prices as well as the current market for real estate.

assessment The imposition of a tax, charge or levy, usually according to established rates.

assets All things of value owned by a person, corporation and so forth, whether encumbered or not.

assignment The transfer of the right, title and interest in the property of one person, known as the assignor, to another, known as the assignee. There are assignments of, among other things, mortgages, bonds, leases and sales contracts.

assumption The financing of a real estate purchase by taking over, or assuming, full responsibility for the existing mortgage.

balance, principle of The oversupply or undersupply of one type of real estate that affects the values of all of these properties in the market.

balloon note Requires the payment of a specified portion or all of the principal owed at a designated time. (*See* term loan.)

beneficiary In a trust agreement, the entity in whom the property will vest at the completion of the trust term.

betterments Improvements to property made by tenants.

blanket mortgage A mortgage secured by pledging more than one property as collateral.

blue-sky Refers to the laws drawn to control puffing by land promoters.

BOMA The Building Owners and Managers Association, International.

bonds Securities issued by a corporation or a governing body to raise funds. Bonds are backed by a promise to pay a certain sum of money on a specific date, plus interest payable in installments during the term of the bonds.

book value The acquisition costs of an asset less any accrued depreciation.

boot Money or property given to make up any difference in value or equity between two properties in an exchange.

break-even point That point at which gross income equals fixed costs plus variable costs.

build-to-suit A building to be constructed to serve the special needs of a specific tenant.

bundle of rights Describes the owner's limits of control over property.

business park A preplanned conglomeration of buildings in one area designed to house activities of a business nature.

buyer's market When the supply of a commodity exceeds the demand.

call clause A provision in a mortgage or trust deed that gives the mortgagee or beneficiary the right to accelerate payment of the mortgage debt in full on a certain date or under specified conditions. (*See also* acceleration clause.)

capital Money or goods used to acquire other money or goods.

capital gain The taxable profit derived from the sale of a capital asset.

capital loss A loss derived from the sale of a capital asset.

capitalization A method of estimating a property's value by considering net annual income as a percentage of a required rate of return on an investment.

$$\frac{\text{Income}}{\text{Rate}} = \text{Value}$$

cash flow The net spendable income from an investment, determined by deducting all operating and interest expenses from the gross income. If expenses exceed income, a negative cash flow is the result.

cash-on-cash return Derived by dividing net income before depreciation by the owner's cash investment.

central business district (CBD) An agglomeration of businesses and services in the center of a city; "downtown."

collapsible corporation A corporation designed to exist only during the course of constructing a large project. After completion, it is dissolved.

collateral Property, real or personal, pledged as security to back up a promise to repay a debt.

commercial leasehold insurance Insurance available to developers that guarantees the payment of rent in the event of a rent default.

Commercial Leasehold Insurance Corporation (CLIC) Owned by Mortgage Guarantee Insurance Corporation (MGIC), this company provides leasehold insurance for commercial and industrial properties, lease payments and leasehold improvement loans.

common-area fees In condominiums, the charge for taxes, insurance, maintenance and so forth, apportioned to each owner, and, in shopping centers, to each tenant.

common elements Parts of a property that are in common use by all of the residents of a cooperative or a condominium. All condominium owners have an undivided ownership interest in the common elements.

community property A system of property ownership based on the theory that each spouse has an equal interest in property acquired by the efforts of either spouse during marriage. This system stemmed from Germanic tribes and, through Spain, came to the Spanish colonies of North and South America. The system was unknown under English common law. Only eight states recognize community property.

community shopping center A type of center that is larger than a neighborhood center, smaller than a regional center.

completion bond A surety bond posted by a landowner or developer to guarantee that a proposed development will be completed according to specifications, free and clear of all mechanics' liens.

component depreciation A tax-saving method of depreciating the components of a building separately. Eliminated by TRA '86.

compound interest   Interest paid on interest earned.

condominium   The fee simple ownership of an apartment or a unit, generally in a multiunit building, plus an undivided interest in the common elements.

conformity, principle of   An appraisal principle that states that building appraisals should be based on other buildings in the neighborhood that are similar in design, construction and age.

congregant living   A form of housing, usually for the elderly, in which tenants have access to a central dining area, physical and social amenities and, often, a health care center.

construction loan   An open-end mortgage loan, usually for a short term, obtained to finance the actual construction of buildings on a property.

contract for deed   A contract under which the purchase price is paid in installments over a period of time during which the purchaser has possession of the property but the seller retains title until the contract terms are completed; usually drawn between individuals. Also called land contract, installment contract or agreement of sale.

contribution, principle of   An appraisal principle that states that any improvement to a property, whether to vacant land or a building, is worth only what it adds to the property's market value, regardless of the improvement's intrinsic cost.

conventional mortgage   A mortgage loan made without any additional guarantees for repayment, such as FHA insurance, a VA guarantee or private loan insurance; usually given at an 80 percent loan-to-value ratio.

conversion   1. To change to another use, as changing rental apartments to condominiums or lofts to apartments. 2. The appropriation of property that belongs to another.

cooperative   A residential multiunit building whose title is held by a trust or corporation, owned by and operated for the benefit of persons living in the building. The residents are beneficial owners of the trust or shareholders of the corporation, each possessing a proprietary lease and having joint liability for the mortgage on the property.

Cooperative Farm Credit System   A national banking network composed of several types of specialty banks, each owned by its members and created to aid farm and ranch owners, operators and investors in financing their activities.

corporation   An entity or organization created by operation of law whose rights of doing business are essentially the same as those of an individual. The entity has continuous existence until dissolved according to legal procedures.

cost approach   The process of appraising the value of a property by adding to the estimated value of the land the appraiser's calculations of the replacement cost of the building, less depreciation.

credit union   A cooperative organization in which members place money in savings accounts, usually at higher interest rates than are paid by other savings institutions. Members may borrow money from a credit union, usually at lower interest rates than those charged by other lending institutions.

curtesy   The rights of a widower in the estate of his deceased wife.

cycles   Events that repeat themselves on a predictable basis, may be a business cycle, an economic cycle or a real estate cycle.

declining-balance method   A method of computing depreciation whereby the undepreciated cost of a building is multiplied by a fixed percentage rate. Its application is limited under TRA '86.

deed-of-trust   *See* trust deed.

default   Nonperformance of a duty; failure to meet an obligation when due.

deferred exchange   A time-delayed trading of like properties.

demand   The desire to acquire properties or services.

Department of Housing and Urban Development (HUD)   A federal cabinet department that regulates FHA and GNMA.

Department of Veteran Affairs (VA)   A federal agency that, since 1944, has guaranteed the top portion of eligible veterans' loans. Now has cabinet status.

depreciation   Loss of values due to all causes, but usually considered to include physical deterioration, functional obsolescence and economic obsolescence.

discount   A payment of less than the face amount of a security as a consequence of the contract interest rate being lower than the market rate.

discounted cash flows   The present worth of a series of receipts over time.

discretionary funds   Money available for investment, in excess of that needed for necessities.

discretionary trust   A trust that may be changed at the will of its owners.

disintegration   A condition of declining value in the life cycle of a property.

dower   The rights of a wife in the estate of her deceased husband.

draws   A system of payments made by a lender to a contractor as designated stages of a building's construction are completed.

due-on-sale clause   A clause in a mortgage or trust deed that stipulates that a borrower cannot sell or transfer the property without prior written consent of the borrower. Also called an alienation clause.

duplex   A two-family dwelling with the units placed either side by side or one above the other.

easy money   When interest rates are low and funds for loans are plentiful.

economic life   The total number of years of useful life that may be expected from a building.

effective demand   A situation in which buyers not only have the desire to buy but also have the financial means to complete their purchase.

effective rate   *See* annual percentage rate.

Environmental Protection Agency (EPA)   A federal agency that sets standards, determines how much pollution is tolerable, establishes time-tables to bring polluters into line with its standards and enforces environmental law.

equilibrium   A condition of stable property values.

equitable interest   Under a land contract (contract for a deed), the buyers' (vendees') interest in the property.

equity   The interest or value that an owner has in real estate over and above any mortgage against it.

escalator clause   A clause in a loan instrument that provides for increases in payments or interest based on predetermined schedules or on a specified economic index, such as the cost-of-living index.

escrow   A process by which a third-party agent receives, holds and/or disburses certain funds or documents on the performance of certain conditions; also the third-party agent who conducts the escrow.

eviction   The legal dispossession of an errant borrower or tenant.

exchange   To trade like properties, thus avoiding income tax liability.

exculpatory clause   1. A clause sometimes inserted in a mortgage note in which the lender waives the right to a deficiency judgment. 2. As used in a lease, a clause that intends to relieve the landlord from liability for tenants' personal injuries and property damage.

face value   The actual amount contracted for.

factoring   Securities sold or pledged as collateral to generate cash flow.

Fair Housing Law   A federal law that prohibits discrimination in the sale, rental, financing or appraisal of most types of housing.

Fannie Mae   *See* Federal National Mortgage Association.

Farmers Home Administration (FmHA)   A federal agency that lends funds to farmers who are unable to obtain financial assistance from other sources.

feasibility study   An analysis of a proposed subject or property with emphasis on the attainable income, probable expenses and most advantageous use and design.

Federal Deposit Insurance Corporation (FDIC)   A federal agency that provides insurance of $100,000 per depositor account and supervises the operations of banks that qualify for membership in the insurance program.

Federal Home Loan Mortgage Corporation (FHLMC, Freddie Mac)   This organization operates much like the FNMA to provide a secondary market for mortgages issued by the members of the FHLB system.

Federal Housing Administration (FHA)   A federal agency that insures loans made by approved lenders to qualified borrowers in accordance with its regulations.

Federal National Mortgage Association (FNMA, Fannie Mae)   A privately owned corporation, originally created as a federal agency, that provides a major secondary mortgage market.

Federal Reserve System   The nation's economic manager.

Federal Savings and Loan Insurance Corporation (FSLIC)   Was a federal agency that provided insurance of $100,000 per depositor account and supervised operations of its member savings and loan associations. Now defunct and replaced by FDIC.

fee simple   *See* absolute fee simple title.

FHA   *See* Federal Housing Administration.

fiduciary   A relationship that implies a position of trust or confidence wherein one person is usually entrusted to hold or manage property or money for another. Also a person who represents another in a position of trust or confidence; an agent.

financial intermediary   Financial fiduciary institution that acts as an intermediary between savers and borrowers.

first mortgage   A mortgage that has priority as a lien over all other mortgages.

fixed expenses   Costs that are more or less permanent and vary little from year to year, such as real estate taxes and insurance for fire, theft and hazards.

fixity   Real estate that is permanently attached to the ground.

foreclosure   Court action initiated by the mortgagee or a lienor for the purpose of having the debtor's real estate sold to pay the mortgage or other lien.

franchise   A private contractual agreement to run a business using a designated trade name and operating procedures.

Freddie Mac   *See* Federal Home Loan Mortgage Corporation.

functional obsolescence   Defects in a building or structure that detract from its value or marketability; usually the result of layout, design or other features that are less desirable than features designed for the same functions in newer property.

general obligation bonds   System of financing in which the community is held responsible for making payments for capital improvements, usually included in property taxes.

general partner   The manager of a limited partnership.

Ginnie Mae   *See* Government National Mortgage Association.

Government National Mortgage Association (GNMA, Ginnie Mae)   A federal agency created in 1968 to take over special assistance and liquidation functions of FNMA. GNMA participates in the secondary market through its mortgage-backed securities pool.

graduated lease   A contract specifying rental increases in regular increments.

graduated payment loan   A loan for which payments increase regularly over time.

gross income   The total income from a property before any expenses are deducted.

gross lease   A lease of property under the terms of which the landlord pays all property charges regularly incurred through ownership, including repairs, taxes, insurance and operating expenses.

ground lease   A contract for the use of the land only.

growth management   Policies that control growth of a community.

highest and best use   That possible use of property that will produce its greatest net income and thereby develop its highest value.

hobby tax rules   Rules that limit allowable deductions on enterprises that do not clearly show a profit motive.

homogeneous tenants   Business tenants that offer similar or complementary goods or services.

horizontal regime   A legal term for a high-rise condominium.

HUD   *See* Department of Housing and Urban Development.

hypothecation   The act of pledging real estate as security without surrendering possession of the property.

improvement   1. Improvement on land—any structure, usually privately owned, erected on a site to enhance the value of the property; for example, buildings, fences and driveways. 2. Improvement to land—usually a publicly owned structure, such as a curb, sidewalk, street or sewer.

income approach   A process of estimating the value of an income-producing property by capitalization of its net annual income.

incremental taxes   Additional taxes generated as a result of new industry moving into an area.

incubator industrial building   A structure designed to encourage growth of a new company.

industrial development bonds   Securities issued to pay for the development of a new industry, usually in the form of general obligation bonds.

industrial park   A controlled parklike development designed to accommodate specific types of industry, provides public utilities, streets, railroad sidings, water, sewage facilities and so forth.

infant industries   Newly formed businesses.

inheritability   Under our allodial system, the ability to leave property to heirs.

inheritance tax   A tax imposed on the estates of deceased persons by the federal government and most states. The federal estate tax exemption is currently at the level of $600,000 net value per person plus an additional $750,000 per farm owner.

installment contract   *See* contract for deed.

installment factor   Gain divided by equity and applied to annual portions of principal received as payments on an installment contract to determine taxable amount.

installment sale   A method of reporting income received from the sale of real estate when the sales price is paid over time. If the sale meets certain requirements, a taxpayer can postpone reporting such income to future years.

interest   Rent charged for the use of borrowed money.

interest factor (IF)   The proportion that determines the time value of money.

interim financing   *See* construction loan.

interim loan   A construction loan.

internal rate of return (IRR)   The rate at which the present worth of an annuity plus reversion exactly equals the investment price.

Interstate Land Sales Full Disclosure Act   A federal law that regulates interstate land sales by requiring registration of real property with HUD's Office of Interstate Land Sales Registration. The act requires disclosure of full and accurate information regarding the property to prospective buyers before they decide to buy.

inter vivos trust   *See* living trust.

investment   Money directed toward the purchase, improvement and development of an asset in expectation of income or profits.

investment trust   A trust designed to act as an investment conduit for small investors that enables them to pool their resources.

irrevocable trust   A permanent arrangement that cannot to be changed until the goals of the trust have been met.

joint tenancy   Ownership of real estate by two or more parties where the deceased's interest passes automatically to the surviving joint tenant(s).

joint venture   The joining of two or more people in a specific business enterprise. A common joint venture is a type of equity participation arrangement in which a lender puts up funds, a developer contributes expertise and the two become partners in the project.

junior mortgage   A second mortgage, third mortgage and so forth; a lien that is subordinate to a first mortgage.

key lot   A lot located two or three lots from an important commercial corner.

labor-intensive   A business depending more on labor than on machines.

land   The earth's surface extending downward to the center of the earth and upward infinitely into space.

land bank   Land purchased and held for future development.

land contract of sale   *See* contract for deed.

land lease   *See* ground lease.

lease   A written or an oral contract between a landlord (the lessor) and a tenant (the lessee), transferring the right to exclusive possession and use of the landlord's real property to the lessee for a specified period of time and for a stated consideration (rent). Leases for more than one year must be in writing to be enforceable.

leasehold interest   The tenant's legal interest in a property.

leasehold mortgage   A mortgage loan secured by a tenant's leasehold interest in a property.

lessee   *See* lease.

lessor   *See* lease.

leverage   The use of borrowed money to finance the bulk of an investment.

liabilities   Debts incurred.

lien   A legal claim that one party has against the property of another as security for a debt.

life care   A form of congregant living for the elderly that includes total care for the balance of a resident's life.

limited partnership   A legal entity that includes a general partner, who actively manages the investment, and limited partners, whose only personal liability is their investments and income

taxes at each individual partner's level of taxation.

liquidity   State in which something can be disposed of promptly.

living trust   An arrangement whereby legal title to property is transferred by the owner (trustor) to a third person (trustee) to be held and managed by the trustee for the trustor's benefit and under the trustor's control for a certain period of time until specific goals have been attained. Also known as an inter vivos trust. Established to facilitate the management of properties during the grantors' lives. Usually resolves into a testamentary trust on their deaths.

location/situs   An indispensable component for an evaluation analysis.

lock-in clause   A clause incorporated into a loan agreement that prevents the borrower from repaying the loan prior to a specified date.

loft building   A large, warehouse-type building usually located in a central city area.

mall   The common walking areas of large shopping centers.

market data approach   Process of appraising the value of a property through examination and comparison of actual sales of comparable properties.

market value   The highest price for which a property would sell, assuming a reasonable time for the sale and a knowledgeable buyer and seller acting without duress.

megacenter   Center that includes highrise apartments and offices in its design, as well as shops and many department stores.

MGIC   *See* Mortgage Guarantee Insurance Corporation.

mineral rights   Ownership rights to all minerals located on or under land and to the profits realized from the sale of these minerals.

miniwarehouse   Neighborhood storage facilities usually designed as individual cubicles; accessible daily.

mobile-home mortgage   A mortgage loan on a large mobile home considered to be real property; usually drawn for a shorter period than a conventional real estate mortgage.

modular homes   Factory-built houses.

moratorium   A temporary suspension of payments due under a financing agreement to help a distressed borrower recover and avoid a default and foreclosure.

mortgage   A conditional transfer or pledge of real property as security for the payment of a debt. Also, the document used to create a mortgage lien.

mortgage banker   A semifiduciary financial intermediary who originates new mortgage loans, collects payments, inspects the collateral and forecloses, if necessary.

mortgage broker   A semifiduciary who acts as an intermediary between borrower and lender for a real estate loan, thereby earning a placement fee.

Mortgage Guarantee Insurance Corporation (MGIC)   An independent insurance corporation that provides insurance for the top 5 to 25 percent of mortgage loans made by approved lenders to qualified borrowers.

mortgage insurance premium   A fee paid to assure lenders that in the event a borrower does not make the required mortgage payments, the insurance company will.

necessary goods   Food, clothing, drugs and so forth.

negative amortization   Less than interest-only loan payments, which cause the balance of a loan to increase by the amount of the deficient interest.

neighborhood   A residential or commercial area with many similar types of properties; defined by natural boundaries, such as highways or rivers, land use, average value or age of homes and income level of residents.

neighborhood shopping center   The smallest kind of planned center.

net lease   A lease requiring the tenant to pay rent as well as all the costs of maintaining the building, including taxes, insurance, repairs and other expenses of ownership.

nominal interest rate   The rate of interest defined in the contract.

note   A signed instrument acknowledging a debt and promising repayment.

occupancy rate   A percentage of the total amount of space occupied. *See also* vacancy rate.

office park   *See* business park.

off-street parking   Parking spaces on private land, as in shopping centers.

open market operations   The Fed's activities in buying and selling securities to control the money supply.

operating expenses   Periodic and necessary expenses essential to the continuous operation and maintenance of an income property.

OPM   Other People's Money; a way to describe leverage.

opportunity cost   The amount of money that could be earned through alternative investments.

option   An agreement to keep open an offer to sell or purchase property for a set period.

ordinary income   Income earned from regular employment or business ownership, as distinguished from capital gains. Now called active income.

partnership   An association of two or more individuals who carry on a continuing business for profit as co-owners. *See* limited partnership.

passive income   Income from real estate investments, as defined under TRA '86.

percentage lease   A contract under which a tenant pays a fixed percent of the gross income against a stipulated minimum rental.

permanence   *See* fixity.

personal property   Movable property that does not fit the definition of realty.

planned unit development   A system of land use that eliminates side yard setbacks.

plottage value   The subsequent increase in value of a group of adjacent properties when they are acquired by the same owner and combined into one property.

portfolio income   Income from interest, dividends and royalties, as defined in TRA '86.

power of attorney   A written instrument authorizing one person to act as the agent of another to the extent indicated in the instrument.

premium   1. In discounting, a payment of more than face value for a security. 2. In insurance, the fee paid for coverage.

prepayment clause   A clause in a mortgage or trust deed that provides for a penalty to be levied against a borrower who repays a loan before the specified due date.

present worth   Discounting money to be received in the future to determine its value today.

private mortgage insurance   Mortgage insurance issued by companies not associated with the federal government. *See* mortgage insurance premium.

proprietary lease   In a corporation cooperative, the lease issued to an individual shareholder occupant.

pyramiding   A method of acquiring additional properties through refinancing existing mortgages.

quitclaim deed   A conveyance by which a grantor transfers whatever interest he or she has in a property without warranties or obligations.

railroad spur   A branch line constructed to an industrial project for dockside loading and unloading.

real estate   A portion of the earth's surface, extending downward to the center of the earth and upward into space, including all things permanently attached thereto by nature or people, and all legal rights therein.

Real Estate Mortgage Investment Conduit (REMIC)   A pool of mortgages in which investors may purchase proportionate interests.

Real Estate Investment Trust (REIT)   An unincorporated trust set up to invest in real estate that must have at least 100 investors, with management, control and title to the property in the hands of trustees.

Real Estate Mortgage Trust (REMT)   A business trust, similar to a REIT, that invests in mortgage securities, rather than in real estate.

real property   The rights of real estate ownership; often called the "bundle of legal rights." *See also* real estate.

realized gain   Profit from the sale of an investment that is not taxable until it becomes a recognized gain. Postponement can be achieved through an IRS Section 1031 exchange or by a sale on an installment basis.

realty   *See* real estate.

recapture rate   The percentage of a property's original cost that is returned to the owner as income during the property's remaining economic life.

recognition clause   A clause included in a blanket contract for deed used to purchase a tract of land for subdivision and development; provides for the protection of the rights of buyers of small parcels in case of default by the developer/promoter.

recognized gain   Profit from the sale of an investment that is taxable in the current year.

redemption rights   The rights of an errant borrower to preserve ownership after default but prior to final foreclosure proceedings.

regional center   A large agglomeration of shops and stores in one location. Includes more than one department store.

Regulation Z   The truth-in-lending portion of the Consumer Credit Protection Act of 1968. It requires complete disclosure of the total costs involved in most credit activities.

relative scarcity   A situation in which the consumer perceives a shortage and bids up the value of the commodity accordingly.

release clause   A clause included in a blanket mortgage that provides that on payment of a specific sum of money, the lien on a particular parcel or portion of the collateral will be released.

rent control   The exercise of police power by local governments to establish equitable rental rates.

rent schedule   Preestablished amounts for rent under a property lease. *See also* graduated lease.

rental concessions   Perquisites offered to entice new tenants, such as free rent for a few months or build-outs in the form of partitions or paint.

repossession   The act of placing property into the hands of the holder of the security after foreclosure.

reserves   A portion of business earnings or bank assets set aside to cover possible losses or withdrawals.

restrictive covenant   A private agreement, usually contained in a deed, that restricts the use and occupancy of real property.

return on investment (ROI)   An annual percentage derived from dividing cash invested into net after-tax income.

revenue bonds   Bonds to be repaid by the fees charged for the use of the funded project.

rezoning   The process of changing from one land use to another, usually more intensive and for the purpose of raising the land value.

right of first refusal   The right of a person to have the first opportunity to either purchase or lease a specific parcel of real property.

royalties   Profits secured from mineral rights, oil wells and publications. *See* also portfolio income.

sale-leaseback   A financing arrangement under which an investor purchases real estate owned and used by a business corporation, then leases the property back to the business; may include a buy-back option.

secondary market   A marketplace in which mortgages and trust deeds are traded. *See also* FNMA, FHLMC and GNMA.

security   Something given, deposited or pledged to make secure the fulfillment of an obligation, usually the repayment of a debt. Generically, mortgages, trust deeds and other financing instruments backed by collateral pledges are termed securities for investment purposes.

sellers' market   When demand exceeds supply.

separate property   Individual ownership by a married person.

setback requirement   Local zoning and building code specifications stipulating the amount of open areas to be preserved in the front, rear and side yards.

several tenancy   *See* tenancy in severalty.

severalty   *See* tenancy in severalty.

sinking fund   A compound interest savings account designed to accumulate funds in anticipation of a balloon payment.

sole ownership   *See* separate property.

sole tenancy   *See* tenancy in severalty.

speculator   One who acquires properties with the expectation that prices will greatly increase.

split fee   A type of equity participation in which a lender purchases the land, leases it to a developer and finances the leasehold improvements in return for a basic rental plus a percentage of the profits.

spot zoning   A single property with a permitted use not in conformity with the surrounding properties.

straight-line depreciation   A method for computing depreciation that assumes a constant wearing out or recapture process over a specified period.

strips Part of a REMIC's assets; interest-only (IO) or principal-only (PO) portions of their inventory can be sold separately.

strip stores Store buildings found along a community's arterial roads.

subchapter S corporation A corporation which, for tax purposes, has elected to be treated as a partnership. Also called a tax-option corporation.

subject to In real estate sales, a designation of the various existing conditions, covenants and restrictions on a property. In financing, the grantee's nonacceptance of personal liability in the assumption of an existing loan.

"subject to" existing loan Becoming responsible, but not assuming personal liability, for an existing loan.

subleasing The right of a primary tenant to rent a property to another tenant. Usually requires the continued liability of the primary tenant.

subordination The act on the part of a mortgagee, or a landowner in the case of a leasehold mortgage, acknowledging by written recorded instrument that his or her mortgage or interest can be placed in an inferior position to a mortgage given to another mortgagee and secured by the same collateral.

substitution, principle of Basic appraisal premise that the market value of real estate is influenced by the cost of acquiring a substitute or comparable property.

super-regional center A regional shopping center that includes apartment and office buildings.

supply Products and services available for consumption.

survivorship, rights of *See* joint tenancy.

syndication A group of two or more people united for the purpose of making and operating an investment. A syndicate may operate as a corporation, general partnership or limited partnership.

tax clause In a lease, a clause passing to the tenant any increase in property taxes over the base year's amount.

tax credit A credit applicable directly against taxes due; a 100 percent deduction.

Tax Reform Act of 1986 (TRA '86) A sweeping revision of the income tax code.

tax preference items Items specified for special tax treatment; items such as excess accelerated depreciation over the straight-line rate. *See* also alternative minimum tax.

tax shelter A phrase often used to describe some of the tax advantages of real estate investment, such as deductions for depreciation, interest, taxes and so forth.

tax waivers A community's technique to entice new industry.

taxable income The net income, after allowable deductions and adjustments, on which the tax rate is applied.

tax-option corporation *See* subchapter S corporation.

tenancy by the entirety The joint ownership, recognized in most states, of property acquired by husband and wife during marriage. On the death of one spouse, the survivor automatically becomes the owner of the property.

tenancy in common A form of inheritable co-ownership under which each owner holds an undivided interest in real property.

tenancy in severalty Ownership of property vested in one person alone. Also called several tenancy or sole tenancy.

tenant mix A description of occupants by the types of businesses in which they are engaged.

term loan A loan to be paid in full at a specified time; not an amortizing loan.

testamentary trust A trust that commences on the demise of the trustor.

tight money When interest rates are high and funds for loans are scarce.

time value of money The present worth of future income.

timesharing A modern approach to communal ownership and use of real estate that permits multiple purchasers to buy undivided interests in real property (usually in a resort condominium or hotel) with a right to use the facility for a fixed or variable time period.

title insurance A policy insuring the owner or mortgagee against loss by reason of defects in the title to a parcel of real estate other than those encumbrances, defects and other matters that are specifically excluded by the policy.

topography The surface characteristics of land.

tranches Part of a REMIC's assets; tradable homogeneous pools of securities, (e.g., variable-interest-rate loans or fixed-interest-rate loans.)

triplex A building composed of three dwelling units.

trust An agreement appointing a third-party trustee to hold property for a beneficiary, under specified terms and conditions.

trust deed A financing instrument in which the borrower/trustor conveys title into the hands of a third-party trustee to be held for the beneficiary/lender. When the loan is repaid, title is reconveyed to the trustor. If default occurs, the trustee exercises the power of sale on behalf of the lender/beneficiary. Also known as a deed of trust.

trustee   The appointed third-party operator of a trust.

trustor   The originator of a trust.

underwriting   The process of evaluating borrower credit, collateral value and the risks involved in making a loan.

Uniform Partnership Act   An act that controls real estate partnerships and syndicates. Requires full revelation of risks to potential investors.

usable space   The area actually used upon which the rental rate is applied (e.g., 1,000 square feet @ $7.20 per square foot per year equals a rental of $600 per month).

VA   *See* Department of Veterans Affairs.

vacancy rate   The percentage of the total space that is unoccupied. *See* also occupancy rate.

value   The power of an item to command other goods in exchange; the present worth of future rights to income and benefits arising from ownership.

value in use   A specific use that defines a property's value.

variable cost ratio   The operating expenses, including taxes, insurance, maintenance, management and utilities, when specified as a percentage of the gross revenue.

variable interest rate   An approach to financing in which the lender is permitted to alter the interest rate, with a certain period of advance notice, based on a specific base index. Monthly loan payments can then be increased or decreased and/or maturity can be extended, depending on how the base index fluctuates.

Veterans Administration Mortgage Loan Guarantee Program   The vehicle under which eligible veterans and their dependents can secure federal guarantees for their home loans.

warehouse   A building used for storage.

waste management   In industrial leases, care in the disposal of solid, liquid and airborne wastes.

wraparound encumbrance   A method of refinancing in which the new mortgage is placed in a secondary, or subordinate, position. In essence, it is an additional mortgage in which another lender refinances a borrower by lending an amount over the existing first-mortgage amount without disturbing the existence of the first mortgage. Also known as an all-inclusive trust deed.

yield   Income or profit earned on an investment.

Answer Key

CHAPTER QUIZ ANSWERS

Detailed mathematics for answers with an asterisk are shown below. Page reference follows answer.

Questions

Exercise 1

1. c 3	3. c 11	5. d 4	7. d 6	9. b 3
2. a 6	4. d 2	6. c 5	8. b 11	10. a 7

Exercise 2

1. c 19	3. c 19	5. a 22	7. c 20	9. b 32
2. d 25	4. d 27	6. c 28	8. c 37	10. c 29

Exercise 3

1. d 47*	3. b 57	5. b 47	7. c 63*	9. c 60
2. b 53	4. d 62	6. c 54	8. d 59	10. c 59*

Exercise 4

1. c 80	3. b 80	5. d 82	7. a 76	9. d 81*
2. c 80	4. b 75	6. c 73	8. c 80	10. b 84*

Exercise 5

1. c 97	3. b 101	5. d 105	7. b 100*	9. c 92
2. d 101	4. c 94	6. d 106	8. a 101	10. d 102

Exercise 6

1. b 126*	3. c 126*	5. b 139	7. d 141	9. b 112
2. c 126*	4. b 120	6. d 140	8. b 122	10. b 112

Exercise 7

1. c 145*	3. b 138	5. b 139	7. d 141	9. c 144
2. a 138	4. a 140	6. d 140	8. c 143	10. d 148

Exercise 8

1. c 159	3. b 164	5. c 164	7. b 163	9. c 173
2. c 159	4. b 160	6. a 177	8. d 163	10. a 165

Exercise 9

1. d 188	3. b 195	5. c 192	7. d 194	9. c 189
2. c 194	4. c 196	6. d 195	8. a 192	10. b 191

Exercise 10

1. d 208	3. b 207	5. c 206	7. c 209	9. d 213
2. c 211	4. b 208	6. a 207	8. b 206	10. c 214

Exercise 11

1. b 228	3. d 232	5. d 232	7. d 227	9. c 226
2. c 226	4. c 233	6. c 232	8. a 233	10. c 228

Exercise 12

1. b 245	3. b 246	5. c 251	7. c 253*	9. a 249
2. b 244	4. b 247	6. b 253*	8. d 248	10. c 254

Mathematics

3.1   d   Loans are from depositors' monies, thus infinite yield.

3.7   c $100,000 \times .075 = 7,500/12 = 625$; $700 - 625 = 75$;

100,000 − 75 = 99,925 × .075 = 7,494.37 ÷ 12 = 624.53125;

700.00 − 624.53125 = 75.46875 or 75.47 rounded.

4.9   d   100,000 − 20,000 = 80,000 × .031746 = 2,539 × 10 = 25,390;

80,000 − 25,390 = 54,610 + 20,000 = 74,610.

4.10 b   Gain/Equity = 40,000 ÷ 60,000 = 66 2/3.

5.7   b   220 − 20 = 200; 385 − 35 = 350 × 200 = 700,000 ÷ 3,500 = 20.

6.1   b   50,000 − 15,000 = 35,000 − 25,000 = 10,000 ÷ 100,00 = 10%.

6.2   c   300,000 × .036 = 10,800; 10,000 − 10,800 = (800).

6.3   c   300,00 − 54,000 + 50,000 = 296,000 adjusted book basis;

385,000 − 296,000 = 89,000 gain − 4,000 loss carryover =

85,000 × .28 = 23,800 taxes; 85,000 − 23,800 = 61,200;

61,200 ÷ 5 yrs = 12,240 + 10,000 = 22,240 ÷ 100,000 = 22.24%.

6.4 b $100,000 \div 17.001 = 5,882.$

6.5 a $100,000 \div 133.3339 = 749.99.$

6.6 c $100,000 \div 7.8431 = 12,750.$

6.7 b $10,000 \times 6.8109 = 68,109; 150,000 \times .1827 = 27,405;$

$68,109 + 27,405 = 95,514.$

6.8 b $5.6502 - 3.6048 = 2.0454$ 2cd 5yr IF; $6.8109 - 5.6502 =$

1.1607 3rd 5yr IF; $5,000 \times 3.6048 = 18,024; 10,000 \times$

$2.0454 = 20,454; 15,000 \times 1.1607 = 17,410; 87,500 \times$

$.1827 = 15,986 + 17,410 + 20,454 + 18,024 = 71,874.$

7.1 c $6,000 \times 10 = 60,000 - 30,000 = 30,000/.10 = 300,000.$

12.6 b $5,000 \times .08 = 400 \times 3.0373 = 1,214.92; 5,000 \times .6355 =$

$3,177.50 + 1,214.92 = 4,392.42.$

12.7 c $5,000 \times .08 = 400 \times 2.4018 = 960.72; 5,000 \times .7118 =$

$3,559.00 + 960.72 = 4,519.72.$

Index